Interpreting Rurality

The British countryside is a national institution; most Britons aspire to live there, many use it for leisure and recreation, and we can all watch rural life played out on our television screen, read about it in novels or consume its imagery in art and cinematography. The aim of this book is to explore the way that these aspirations and perceptions influence the way that the term 'rural' is interpreted across different academic disciplines. Definitions of 'rural' are not exact, leaving room for these interpretations to have a significant impact on the meanings conveyed in different areas of research and across different economic, social and spatial contexts.

In this book contributors present research across a range of subjects allowing critical reflections upon their personal and disciplinary interpretations of 'rural'. This resulting volume is a collection of diverse chapters that gives an emergent sense of how the notion of 'rural' changes and blurs as the disciplinary lens is adjusted. In drawing together these strands, it becomes clear that human relations with rural space morph materiality into highly complex representations, wherein both disadvantage and social exclusion persist within a rurality that is also commodified, consumed and cherished.

Gary Bosworth is a Reader in Enterprise and Rural Economies at the University of Lincoln. He has published widely on issues affecting the rural economy including counterurbanisation, structural and cyclical economic changes, home-working, neo-endogenous development approaches, and the growth of rural tourism.

Peter Somerville is Professor of Social Policy and Head of the Policy Studies Research Centre at the University of Lincoln. He has published widely on housing, community (including rural community, community enterprise, and community policing), cooperatives, equalities, homelessness, participation and social theory.

Interpreting Rurality
Multidisciplinary approaches

Edited by
Gary Bosworth and
Peter Somerville

Routledge
Taylor & Francis Group
LONDON AND NEW YORK

First published 2014
by Routledge
2 Park Square, Milton Park, Abingdon, Oxfordshire OX14 4RN

and by Routledge
711 Third Avenue, New York, NY 10017

First issued in paperback 2016

Routledge is an imprint of the Taylor & Francis Group, an informa business

British Library Cataloguing in Publication Data
A catalogue record for this book is available from the British Library

Library of Congress Cataloging-in-Publication Data
Interpreting rurality: multidisciplinary approaches/edited by Peter Somerville and Gary Bosworth.
pages cm
1. Sociology, Rural. 2. Rural geography. 3. Economic geography.
I. Somerville, Peter, editor of compilation. II. Bosworth, Gary.
HT421.I58 2013
307.72 – dc23
2013018117

ISBN 13: 978-1-138-68715-8 (pbk)
ISBN 13: 978-0-415-69672-2 (hbk)

Typeset in Times New Roman by
Florence Production Ltd, Stoodleigh, Devon, UK

Contents

Illustrations

Figures

Tables

Contributors

Sue Bestwick is a Senior Lecturer in History at the University of Lincoln. Her main teaching and research interests are within the discipline of environmental history. She has successfully developed the subject area at Lincoln with a specific interest in the perceived rural/urban divide on countryside issues, from attitudes to wildlife, modern farming methods, country 'sports' and the 'rural idyll'.

Gary Bosworth is a Reader in Enterprise and Rural Economies at the University of Lincoln. He has published widely on issues affecting the rural economy including counterurbanisation, structural and cyclical economic changes, home-working, neo-endogenous development approaches, and the growth of rural tourism.

Ignazio Cabras is a Lecturer in Economics, Business and Management at The York Management School, University of York. His research interests are focused on economics and the environment, with particular emphasis on regional growth and development, urban–rural dynamics, community cohesion and social capital. He has written more than 30 published works comprising journal articles, books and book chapters, and research reports.

Sue Frith Grau has been a Senior Lecturer at the University of Lincoln for twelve years, teaching across the multifaceted disciplines of the humanities. She has maintained an enthusiasm for cultural studies throughout, and this is evident in her research into the cultural history of brass bands. A lifelong brass bander, Sue has played for many of the Lincolnshire bands at one time or another and currently enjoys a position in the horn section of Foss Dyke Band.

David Gray is a Principal Lecturer in Economics at the University of Lincoln. He has published on regional unemployment, house prices and the ripple effect, exchange rates and spillover, and Adam Smith and business ethics.

Margaret Greenfields is Research Reader and Director of the Institute of Diversity Research, Inclusivity, Communities and Society at Buckinghamshire New University. She specialises in devising participatory action research programmes in partnership with service users, especially UK Gypsy and Traveller communities (and more latterly Roma migrants), with a particular interest in their health, economic inclusion, accommodation needs and family support.

Stephen J. G. Hall is Emeritus Professor of Animal Sciences at the University of Lincoln. His research has been in ecology, genetics and behaviour, and most recently he has been working on the cultural history and conservation of Britain's native livestock breeds.

Dr Keith Halfacree is a Reader in Human Geography at Swansea University. He is a culturally inclined geographer who has published widely on theories and representations of rurality, counterurban migration and rural counter-cultures.

Claire Haven-Tang is a Reader in Tourism and Management in the Welsh Centre for Tourism Research in the Cardiff School of Management at Cardiff Metropolitan University. She has published on issues relating to destination development, tourism SMEs, sense of place, rural tourism leadership, business and event tourism best practice, and tourism industry training provision.

Rebecca Herron is a Reader in O R and Systems at the University of Lincoln. Her research interests relate to community organisation and self-organisation, including supporting, learning and problem structuring in rural communities. She has published on community operational research, problem-structuring, community-based learning and modelling complex systems.

Rupert Hildyard is Principal Lecturer in English at the University of Lincoln. His doctoral research was on modernism and the short story, and he has published on early twentieth-century cultural history and the fiction and journalism of John Lanchester. His most recent work has been to edit (with Sian Adiseshiah) and contribute to a collection of essays on twenty-first-century fiction, and he is currently writing on the work of the ecological historian Oliver Rackham. He is an executive committee member of the Association for the Study of Literature and Environment (UKI). He comes from a farming family and has a small farm with a beef suckler herd of British White cattle.

Jennifer Jackson is a Research Fellow in Community Research at the University of Lincoln. Her research interests within rural community issues have included community health profiles and improving health lifestyles, the role of Lincolnshire's horticulture industry and the development of community capacity within Lincolnshire's villages.

Karen Johnson has a Master's degree in Rural Resources and Countryside Management from the University of Newcastle. She has lived in a Lincolnshire village for over ten years. She is very active in village life, being the secretary of the parish plan committee, volunteering on the village magazine and bell ringing for church services. She is currently employed as a community development officer with a rural district council.

Eleri Jones is Associate Dean (Research) in the Cardiff School of Management at Cardiff Metropolitan University. She has published widely on issues relating to innovation, information technology and human resource management in a tourism context, sustainable tourism development, sense of place, community-based tourism, and destination development.

Wesley Key is a Lecturer in Social Policy at the University of Lincoln. His research is centred on the impact of poverty and social exclusion upon older people, particularly those who are living in rural areas.

Claire Markham is a Ph.D. candidate at the University of Lincoln, and is researching public houses in rural communities. Her research interests are rural studies, micro-breweries, public house development and symbolic culture literature.

Alison Moore is an academic who researches and writes on the uses of animals in culture. Her past papers have addressed the farm as performance, the representation of farm animals in media and culture, and the literary animal at sea. Her research currently centres on the laboratory animal, focusing particularly on the lab animal in the media and its use in humour-based popular cultural forms.

Angus Nurse is a Senior Lecturer in Criminology in the School of Law at Middlesex University and is a Senior Researcher in Middlesex's Centre for Crime and Conflict Research. He has published widely on the topic of wildlife and environmental crime, miscarriages of justice, environmental law enforcement and alternative dispute resolution. *Animal Harm*, his book on the causes of animal abuse and wildlife crime, was published by Ashgate in 2013.

Catherine Parry is a Ph.D. candidate and Visiting Lecturer at the University of Lincoln, and is researching the human–animal divide in recent fiction. Her research interests are literary animal studies, ecocriticism, posthumanism and postmodernist literature.

Juliana Siwale is a Senior Lecturer in Economics and International Business at the University of Lincoln. Her research interests are in microfinance in developing countries, the political economy of development and small business enterprise growth. She has published on issues affecting development finance, failure of microfinance institutions and accountability in non-governmental organisations in developing countries. Recent publications have been in the *International Small Business Journal* and the *International Journal of Critical Accounting*.

Peter Somerville is Professor of Social Policy and Head of the Policy Studies Research Centre at the University of Lincoln. He has published widely on housing, community (including rural community, community enterprise and community policing), cooperatives, equalities, homelessness, participation and social theory. His most recent book was *Understanding Community: Politics, Policy and Practice* (Routledge, 2011).

Andrew Walker is Vice Principal at Rose Bruford College of Theatre and Performance. Before his current appointment, he taught history at the University of Lincoln. His research interests include the social and cultural history of rural England and the articulation of local and regional identities. His published work examines aspects of Lincolnshire's urban and rural history, nineteenth-century Yorkshire dialect literature, and the development of several nineteenth-century South Yorkshire coalmining and steelmaking communities.

Preface

The British countryside is a national institution; most Britons aspire to live there, many use it for leisure and recreation, and we can all watch rural life played out on our television screen, read about it in novels or consume its imagery in art and cinematography. An increasingly asked question, however, is: 'Why is the countryside important?' People from all over the world, not just in Britain, have attachments to British notions of rurality – the Campaign to Protect Rural England, for example, has been chaired by Bill Bryson, an American.

In this volume we hope to shed some light on why 'rural' evokes idyllic imagery, strong feelings and lifelong commitments. We have brought together a wide variety of researchers, from many different disciplines – history, economics, literary criticism, sociology, operational research, cultural studies, criminology, housing studies, social gerontology, tourism studies, geography and social policy – in order to explore the diversity of interpretations of the rural, and to try and make sense of this extraordinary variety. Above all, we aim to give the reader a glimpse of the vitality of research in this area and to open up new questions concerning the meaning of rurality today and the implications of this for us all.

Gary Bosworth and Peter Somerville
4 July 2013

1 Introduction

Gary Bosworth and Peter Somerville

The countryside is different from the city. It looks different, it functions differently, it attracts different people to live and work there, and attitudes towards rural places originate from many different starting points. Academics across a range of disciplines distinguish between urban and rural in aspects of their research, and this collection will highlight the ways that 'rural' is used to confer certain meanings that go far beyond generalised statistical measurement. Hodge and Monk (2004: 271) called for 'new characterisations of rural change and disadvantage that get beyond the stylised fallacies of popular debate', and, throughout this volume, we aim to challenge common-sense assumptions about the rural in order to inform and educate public understanding. In particular we look to place interpretations of 'rural' at the heart of our analysis rather than seeing it as a pre-defined category within which our research is inescapably fixed.

Since Philo (1992) originally described a scene of 'neglected rural geographies', rural studies have been enriched by illuminating volumes such as *Country Visions* (Cloke, 2003), *Rural Geography* (Woods, 2005), *Handbook of Rural Studies* (Cloke *et al.*, 2006) and *Rural* (Woods, 2011). Such increased attention to rural research has been justified on the grounds of an accelerating pace of rural change, which has resulted in the countryside 'being challenged as never before by issues of agricultural restructuring, declining service provision, depopulation and counterurbanisation, communication and infrastructural deficits and the degradation of the natural environment' (McAreavey and McDonagh, 2010: 175). However, while the growing academic interest in the rural may relate to perceived threats and challenges, public perceptions of the countryside seem to be considerably more positive. In the UK, the BBC has aired a television programme, 'Welly Telly' (BBC, 2011), that charts the rise in popularity of rural themed programmes, rural tourism has grown (Woodward, 2009) and counterurbanising trends continue to see large numbers of people expressing a preference for rural lifestyles (Bosworth, 2010).

One indicator of the status conferred upon rurality is the emotive language that is often used by authors. For example, the farming journalist, Graham Harvey, used the title 'The Killing of the Countryside' (1997) when charting the damaging outcomes of productivist and increasingly Europeanised agricultural policies, while environmentalist and former Council for the Protection of Rural England (CPRE) campaigner, Marion Shoard (1980), described the 'Theft of the Countryside'. These perspectives on the rural infiltrate policy too. Planning Policy Statement 4 in the UK includes guidance stipulating that

> Local planning authorities should ensure that the countryside is protected for the sake of its intrinsic character and beauty, the diversity of its landscapes, heritage and wildlife, the wealth of its natural resources and to ensure it may be enjoyed by all.
>
> (Policy EC6.1)

This raises the significant questions of what is this 'intrinsic character' and who defines it – questions that are addressed in many ways throughout this volume.

Mormont considers 'rural' to be a 'category of thought' (1990: 40), confirming the elusiveness of any typology that could be said to truly encompass all aspects of rurality. Furthermore, Carolan (2008) has observed that the embodiment of rural goes beyond social constructions, noting how the tractor enables a farmer to feel the land, while a cyclist or walker (see, for example, Wylie, 2003) also experience the contours, smells and sounds of rurality in a physical, sensory manner. Some of these experiences are increasingly remote in an urbanised society yet, through travel, recreational pursuits and even images of rurality, everyone develops their own personal views of rurality. The inevitable incommensurability, and even contradictoriness, of experiences, clearly makes them difficult to measure. Bill Bryson, for example, comments on his walk of the 2,200 mile Appalachian Trail:

> I had come to realise that I didn't have any feelings towards the AT [Appalachian Trail] that weren't thoroughly contradictory. I was weary of the trail, but captivated by it; found the endless slog increasingly exhausting but ever invigorating; grew tired of the boundless woods but admired their boundlessness; enjoyed the escape from civilisation and ached for its comforts. All of this together, all at once, every moment, on the trail and off.
>
> (1997: 318)

Aims and approaches

The aim of this volume is to provide a variety of chapters, each of which contributes new research and/or ideas to its own particular discipline while simultaneously taking a self-reflective approach towards the application or interpretation of the concept of 'rural'. The task of the editors has then been to identify common themes among the chapters as well as relationships linking interpretations of rurality that occur, for example, within public perceptions, policy processes and research practices.

The editors' task has been both challenging and highly rewarding. The opportunity to contrast the implications of portrayals of rurality in the children's novel *Stig of the Dump* (Parry) with questions of regional economic theory (Gray) is possibly unique, and hopefully the reader will find value in such analyses. Effectively, we have sought to relate cultural foundations of rurality with changing economic, demographic and political issues in order to challenge assumptions and to improve our understanding of processes that have produced the rurality that is experienced today. To this end, we have included a wide variety of academic disciplines and theoretical approaches across the arts, humanities, social sciences and natural sciences.

These approaches to understanding rurality highlight that its spatial, cultural and environmental significance may involve different interpretations. For some, rural is a mental construct while for others it is an abstract concept 'where rural places are distinct "entities" from other (urban) places' (Hoggart *et al.*, 1995: 24). Throughout this volume, the reader must consider the meaning of the terms 'location', 'space' and 'place'. While a location is very precise topographically, space is considered to be constituted by relations that involve numerous kinds of entities and performances. Space is not static but is continually recreated by human and non-human actions (Jones and Cloke, 2002). In further contrast, a place is defined as somewhere with an identity and boundaries. The identity may be impermanent, and the boundaries may be permeable and blurred, but the term 'place' is nevertheless significant as an indicator of socio-cultural and environmental values that can be assigned to that place.

Statistical approaches to defining rurality

Although much of this volume is about perceptions and the implications of the way that people understand 'rural', it seems important to set out briefly the ways in which governments and other national and international organisations categorise rural space. This will further illustrate not only the diversity of existing approaches but also the factors that dictate how different approaches are designed and chosen in specific geographical and political contexts. We are aware that governmental categories have been widely criticised in academic literature, but in this book we aim to understand all the main current interpretations of rurality (Bell, 2007).

Beginning at the international level, the United Nations (UN) states that

> because of national differences in the characteristics that distinguish urban from rural areas, the distinction between the urban and the rural population is not yet amenable to a single definition that would be applicable to all countries or, for the most part, even to the countries within a region.
>
> (UN, 2011)

Instead, it is easier to identify what is urban and assume that the remainder is rural. Defining urban is seen to be critical because policies need to reflect the reality of where people live and work (OECD, 2012), although this perception seems to imply that rural areas either require less differentiation or simply merit less attention.

From a European perspective, the fact that rural areas 'are immediately understood by everybody, in that they evoke a physical, social and cultural concept, which is the counterpart of "urban"' (Boscacci and Arcaini, 1999: 6) makes categorisation no easier. The European Union (EU) therefore relies on OECD data, where categorisation is effectively determined by a combination of population density at the settlement scale and the proportion of the population living in rural communities at the regional scale. This is then adjusted for the presence of larger urban centres. In its rural development reporting, however, it accepts that the typology has imperfections (EU, 2009). The outcome can be 'a predominantly rural region', 'an intermediate region' or 'a predominantly urban region' (ibid.: 3).

A similar approach is used in England and Wales by the Department for Environment, Food and Rural Affairs (Defra), where the rural definition was determined according to two measurement criteria. First, hectare grid squares were each assigned a settlement form as dispersed dwellings or hamlet, village, small town or urban fringe, and urban (greater than 10,000 population); and, second, sparsity was assessed according to the number of households in surrounding hectare squares up to a distance of 30 km (Defra, 2011). Taken together, this gives an eightfold Urban/Rural Classification ranging from 'less sparse urban' through to 'sparse dispersed dwelling or hamlet'. The classification of hectare grid squares can then be aggregated and applied to different scales of geography to allow other statistical data to be examined in relation to degrees of rurality. In contrast, in Scotland, a rural settlement is defined as one with a population of *less than 3,000*. A further distinction is made between accessible, remote and very remote rural areas, where *accessible* rural settlements are within 30 minutes drive from a settlement with a population of 10,000 or more and very remote rural areas are 60 minutes drive from such a settlement (The Scottish Government, 2012).

In the USA, distinctions are made not only between urban and rural but also between metropolitan and non-metropolitan. In the census, urban and rural are differentiated according to population size and density thresholds. Defining rural as somewhere with no settlement above 2,500 persons and no population core of 1,000 or more persons per square mile, 21 per cent of the US population was rural in the 2000 Census (Bell, 2007). In contrast to this approach, the US Office of Management and Budget uses a combination of demographic and economic criteria to identify specifically metropolitan regions. This has advantages for governmental administration but places arbitrary cut-off points between urban and rural, which sit awkwardly in the minds of the reflective scholar or planner (ibid.: 405). As we write, the United States Department of Agriculture is reviewing its current definition (USDA, 2011) to include more, larger towns. This raises fears that the wider scope will disadvantage the smallest and most needy rural communities with less capacity to lobby on rural policy issues (Botts, 2013).

Whether defined as rural or non-metropolitan, these more remote and more sparsely populated areas are treated as residuals, being defined by what they are not, rather than what they are (Champion and Brown, 2012). Researching statistical definitions has shown that this approach predominates throughout OECD countries, with the consequence that policies are developed that do not take account of the distinctive and substantive needs and intricacies of rural areas. The UK government's policy of 'rural proofing' in the early 2000s provides a good example of such policy failure (Atterton, 2008).

In New Zealand, the classification of rural areas is divided into three categories to reflect those with 'high', 'medium' or 'low urban influence' (Statistics New Zealand, 2013), recognising that understanding the level of connectivity to other centres is of great importance for rural policy design. In Australia, however, major urban areas are defined as those with a population of 100,000 or greater, and other urban areas include all population clusters from 1,000 to 99,999 people (Australian Bureau of Statistics, 2011). The rural population is then divided into two groups to reflect small 'localities' with clusters of at least 200 residents and then the 'rural balance', which represents the remainder of a state or territory with little more than scattered dwellings (ibid.). Once again, the rural is defined according to what it is not rather than what it is, leading to concerns that the smaller rural population in Australia is subjected to urban-centred policies (Charters *et al.*, 2011).

These examples highlight that each nation sets its own boundaries between urban and rural, depending upon both its urban and rural demographics, but they also confirm the basic presumption that, from a policy perspective, the most important metrics are population size or density and remoteness from urban centres. Such metrics are important because they enable policy approaches to be targeted towards different 'rural' territories. It needs to be remembered, however, that they are little more than statistical tools, and the driving forces behind their construction are statistical reliability, the availability of data at local levels and widespread applicability. Indeed, analysis in England highlights that although rural areas generally do better on measures of well-being and less well on measures of productivity than their urban counterparts, a city region model based on urban-centric commuting patterns shows greater urban–rural differences compared to the Defra model outlined earlier (Curry and Webber, 2012). Ultimately, the limitations of statistical approaches stem from their function as part of a wider governmentality (Foucault, 1991), which is designed to control and regulate populations. In this book, however, we are mainly interested in approaches that attempt to understand the meaning of rurality as it is experienced, imagined and performed.

The volume therefore goes beyond statistical approaches to present a range of historical, social, economic, spatial, perceptory, literary, imaginary and cultural aspects in order to display as fully as possible the many and varied interpretations of rurality.

Organisation of the volume

The book contains a range of case studies and research into niche changes that are impacting on the composition of rural areas. Most of these studies are set in the context of wider macro-economic and societal changes, and we claim that the nature of the issues raised, the degree of attention afforded to them and the approaches to researching them, all add significantly to the understanding of rurality in the twenty-first century.

Influenced by Halfacree's work on the rural triad (Halfacree, 2006, 2007) we have grouped the chapters according to the aspects of rurality on which they focus. We begin with 'Material Rurality', where chapters focus on rurality as territory and practice within that territory. The second part, entitled 'Represented Rurality', includes a range of case studies that highlight different representations of rurality in different subject areas. The third part, 'Contested Rurality', contains studies of rural conflict, largely related to incompatibilities between material and represented ruralities. The final part then looks at 'Consumed Rurality', focusing on particular icons or 'selling points' for those who live in, visit, move to, or otherwise consume rural areas. Building on Slee (2005) and Garrod *et al.* (2006), these chapters examine how and why rurality, despite its contestation and material disadvantages, is viewed as desirable by a range of consumers. In bringing all these themes together in the conclusion, we assert that any attempt to understand or develop policy for rural areas must take cognisance of the contrasting perspectives involved.

Under 'Material Rurality' four chapters are included that adopt economic, historical and community perspectives. The first of these (Siwale) offers a contrast to the developed-world and largely British focus of the book. In Zambia, most rural places have no running water, no electricity, no public or private transport and few other services, providing a sobering reminder that the 'disadvantages' of a rural location are all relative. In economic terms, they truly are the periphery, with minimal access to finance and high rates of out-migration, especially among younger people. Interestingly, though, despite their undesirability, there appear to be some occasions where nostalgia towards rural places continues to show through.

The second economic chapter (Gray) develops the notion of peripherality to indicate that, in developed economies, the 'remote' or 'non-commutable' rural can be distinguished as peripheral to core regions wherein dominant cities and beneficial economies of scale attract labour and other resources. As populations gain greater mobility, these urban economies stretch out into their more 'accessible rural' hinterlands, particularly in terms of housing and labour markets. Beyond these hinterlands, we see rural areas that continue to rely on primary industries and tourism, lacking the infrastructure or critical mass of people to overcome their comparative disadvantage. Gray's chapter suggests that there are serious problems for policy makers to address in deciding how best to develop the economies of more remote rural areas.

One possible way of solving these problems, which is emerging in some rural communities, is through cooperative movements where communities are coming together to provide the businesses and services that they consider essential to sustain their quality of life. In Chapter 4, Cabras describes the emergence of cooperative enterprises in rural areas but also recognises that their diversity raises further questions about the extent to which community-focused enterprise models can sustain those areas. The role of community is then explored further in Chapter 5, where the concept of the parish as a unit of community organisation is unpacked to explore why this historical administrative delineation continues to resonate so strongly as a feature of rurality.

Each of these chapters in the first section tells its own story about material components of rural space. Representations of rurality, however, can be just as important as its materiality. Chapter 6 (Walker), for example, presents case studies of the historical cattle markets and horse fairs that used to take place in Lincoln, in which the material rurality of these unsophisticated, often uncontrollable, activities is contrasted with the represented rurality of the anti-urban, romantic pastoralism that existed at that time.

This 'Represented Rurality' is explored through four further contributions. The first of these (Parry) draws on three books of children's fiction, each of which provokes an emotional response and a reflexive imaginative engagement both with the literary rural idyll and with an alternative to it. Parry's eco-critical analysis challenges the reader to see beyond the 'timeless paradise' portrayed in *Wind in the Willows* to consider alternative images from *Wind in the Pylons* and of cement works in *Stig of the Dump*, and a very impersonal impression of rurality conveyed by the narrator in *Never Let Me Go*. Chapter 8 (Hall) presents the case that livestock forms a rich component of our visions of rurality. Both the appearance and dispersal of breeds have been shaped by farming practices over many centuries, and mapping these breeds gives an alternative picture of rurality delineated by the interactions of farming and landscape in the production of the recognisable, and often locally cherished, livestock breeds that we see today. Further contrasting portrayals of rurality are presented through the interpretation of two 'farm texts' in Chapter 9 (Hildyard), where the farmers' perceptions of rurality in each case were shaped by their personal backgrounds. Rather than being viewed romantically as in earlier fiction, the farm in these texts is presented as a heterotopia, in Foucault's terminology, its meaning being simultaneously represented, contested and inverted. Rural representations are further challenged by Grau (Chapter 10), whose historical investigation of brass bands, which have traditionally been associated with urban, or at least industrial, landscapes in Britain, yields new evidence of their existence and cultural significance in rural areas.

With each of the aforementioned chapters already illustrating aspects of contestation, it may seem strange to have a section focused specifically on 'Contested Rurality'. However, in Chapters 11–15, particular issues are addressed concerning agricultural intensification (Moore), attitudes towards wildlife (Bestwick), class and affordability in rural housing (Somerville), rural crime and policing (Nurse), and ethnicity and Gypsies and Travellers

(Greenfields). Through studies of particular discords, the importance of rurality is highlighted. It is not so much the rural characteristics themselves, but the ways in which different groups can acquire and communicate their own interpretations of these characteristics, which determine outcomes. For example, in Moore's chapter, we see the struggle between those seeking to 'modernise' agriculture, presenting the case for a more efficient, technological approach to dairy farming, and opponents seeking to protect a less intensively farmed rurality, in keeping with popular imagery.

Bestwick identifies class tensions through differing attitudes towards wildlife between urban and rural, and Somerville also draws on class issues with regard to rural housing. In each case, being part of the rural is seen to confer particular rights on those who are continuing traditions of hunting animals or seeking to 'protect' rural areas from 'undesirable' new developments. The issue of attitudes towards wildlife is also picked up by Nurse who notes that 'rural people' such as gamekeepers may have a contrasting view to 'urbanites' about what constitutes animal crime, with the assumption that rural lore must carry greater weight than popular opinion. In a second strand to his chapter, Nurse notes very different definitions of the rural between the police force, who need practical delineation of territories based on intensity of activity, and others who seek to claim 'rural crime' as being important for a range of reasons that are less about location or intensity but more about types of activities. In Chapter 15, Greenfields adds to debates on the question of racial 'mono-cultures', which are often perceived to exist in rural space. Attitudes towards minority groups, especially in-migrants (de Lima *et al.*, 2012), are attracting significant attention as both international and urban–rural boundaries become increasingly porous. Here, however, we see evidence from a minority group with historic attachments to rural areas, who have existed at the margins for generations.

The final section considers how, once certain representations of rurality can be claimed by groups in society, there is potential for added value to be generated. In the case of rural pubs, rural tourism, and rural residential locations generally, the epithet 'rural' is used to add a meaning that transcends location. In Chapter 16 (Haven-Tang and Jones), it is claimed that micro-enterprises in the tourism industry in a rural part of Wales could benefit from coordinated activity around their shared, albeit not necessarily consistent, rural identity. From a touristic perspective, rurality can be both an attractor and an impediment for development, and Key, in Chapter 17, notes a similar ambiguity for individuals. Rural areas can be attractive to people nearing retirement age, yet the same features that attract them in their 'third age' can cause them to be socially isolated and excluded in their 'fourth age'.

In Chapter 18 (Markham) the case of the rural public house presents an affinity that village communities have with a building that connotes both a meeting place and an emblem of their rural identity. Economically and numerically speaking, rural pubs are declining in the UK but Markham's findings indicate that the role of rural public houses as social and cultural hubs remains strong. Business owners and campaigners are emphasising these features in order to press for greater support, and are using perceptions of rural communities and visions of rural settings to draw on the cultural capital that is attached to rurality in such scenarios.

In order to elicit a common understanding of rurality from this collection of chapters, the final chapter searches for different kinds of structured coherences that might exist. What emerges is the identification of a variety of types of possible rural structured coherence, some of which might only exist for certain time periods and others might only apply in particular geographies. All structured coherences, however, involve exclusion as well as inclusion, and rural coherences are no exception. The chapter also argues that structured coherence can never be complete or permanent but is always in a process of being undermined by both internal contradictions and external social forces.

From the statistical approaches included in this chapter through the multi-disciplinary studies presented ahead, this book not only challenges preconceptions about rurality but also questions whether a single coherent rurality can even exist, given the nature of capitalist society. In reading the chapters to follow, we urge readers to reflect on how rurality is being interpreted and how multiple interpretations can meaningfully co-exist.

References

Atterton (2008) *Rural Proofing in England: A Formal Commitment in Need of Review*. Centre for Rural Economy Discussion Paper Series, No. 20, accessed 28 March 2013 at: www.ncl.ac.uk/cre/publish/discussionpapers/pdfs/dp20.pdf.

Australian Bureau of Statistics (2011) *Australian Statistical Geography Standard (ASGS): Volume 4 – Significant Urban Areas, Urban Centres and Localities*, accessed 3 April 2013 at: www.abs.gov.au/ausstats/abs@.nsf/mf/1270.0.55.004.

BBC Television (2011) *Welly Telly: The Countryside on Television*. Broadcast 29 May 2011, directed by John Moulson.

Bell, M. M. (2007) The two-ness of rural life and the ends of rural scholarship. *Journal of Rural Studies*, 23: 402–15.

Boscacci, F. and Arcaini, E. (1999) *Strategic Study: Towards A New Urban Rural Partnership in Europe*, accessed 6 June 2011 at: www.nordregio.se/filer/spespn/Files/2.3.ruralareas.pdf.

Bosworth, G. (2010) Commercial counterurbanisation: An emerging force in rural economic development. *Environment and Planning A*, 42(4): 966–81

Botts, A. (2013) Speak your piece: Plan could hurt rural. *Daily Yonder*, Centre for Rural Strategies, US, accessed 28 March 2013 at: www.dailyyonder.com/rural-definition-would-hurt-small-towns/2013/02/28/5683.

Bryson, B. (1997) *A Walk in the Woods*. London: Doubleday.

Carolan, M. (2008) More-than-representational knowledge(s) of the countryside: How we think as bodies. *Sociologia Ruralis*, 48(4): 408–22.

Champion and Brown (2012) 'Annex', in *Rural Transformations and Rural Policies in the UK and US*, edited by J. Vergunst, M. Shucksmith, D. Brown, S. Shortall and M. Warner. New York and Abingdon, UK: Routledge: 304–6.

Charters, K., Vitartas, P. and Waterman, P. (2011) Identifying and communicating current issues for regional Australia. *Journal of Economic and Social Policy*, 14(3), article 2.

Cloke, P. (2003) *Country Visions*. Harlow, UK: Pearson.

Cloke, P., Marsden, T. and Mooney, P. (2006) *Handbook of Rural Studies*. London: Sage.

Curry, N. and Webber, D. (2012) Economic performance in rural England, *Regional Studies*, 46(3): 279–92

DEFRA (2011) *Statistical Digest of Rural England*, accessed 6 June 2011 at: www.defra.gov.uk/publications/files/rural-digest-2011.pdf.

EU (European Union) (2009) *Rural Development in the European Union; Statistical and Economic Information*. Report by the Directorate-General for Agriculture and Rural Development, accessed 6 June 2011 at: http://ec.europa.eu/agriculture/agrista/rurdev2009/RD_Report_2009.pdf.

Foucault, M. (1991) 'Governmentality', tr. R. Braidotti, revised by C. Gordon, in G. Burchell, C. Gordon and P. Miller (eds), *The Foucault Effect: Studies in Governmentality*. Chicago, IL: University of Chicago Press: 87–104.

Garrod, B. Wornell, R. and Youell, R. (2006) Reconceptualising rural resources as countryside capital: The case of rural tourism. *Journal of Rural Studies*, 22(1): 117–28.

Halfacree, K. (2006) 'Rural space: Constructing a three-fold architecture', in P. Cloke, T. Marsden, P. Mooney (eds), *Handbook of Rural Studies*. London: Sage: 44–62.

Halfacree, K. (2007) Trial by space for a 'radical rural': Introducing alternative localities, representations and lives. *Journal of Rural Studies*, 23: 125–41.

Harvey, G. (1997) *The Killing of the Countryside*. London: Jonathan Cape.

Hodge, I. and Monk, S. (2004) The economic diversity of rural England: Stylised fallacies and uncertain evidence. *Journal of Rural Studies*, 20: 263–72.

Hoggart, K., Buller, H. and Black, R. (1995) *Rural Europe: Identity and Change*. London: Arnold.

Jones, O. and Cloke, P. (2002) *Tree Cultures: The Place of Trees and Trees in their Place*. Oxford: Berg.

de Lima, P., Parra, P. A. and Pfeffer, M. J. (2012) 'Conceptualizing contemporary immigrant integration in the rural United States and United Kingdom', in M. Shucksmith, D. L. Brown, S. Shortall, J. Vergunst and M. E. Warner (eds), *Rural Transformations and Rural Polices in the UK and US*. London: Routledge: 77–99.

McAreavey, R. and McDonagh, J. (2010) Sustainable rural tourism: Lessons for rural development. *Sociologia Ruralis*, 51(2): 175–94.

Mormont, M, (1990) 'Who is rural? Or how to be rural: Towards a sociology of the rural', in T. Marsden, P. Lowe and S. Whatmore (eds), *Rural Restructuring: Global Processes and Their Responses*. London: David Fulton, 21–44.

OECD (2012) *Redefining 'Urban': A new way to measure metropolitan areas*. OECD Publishing, accessed 1 July 2013 at: www.oecd.org/gov/regional/measuringurban.

Philo, C. (1992) Neglected rural geographies: A review. *Journal of Rural Studies*, 8: 193–207

The Scottish Government (2012) *2001–2012 Urban Rural Classification*, accessed 26 April 2012 at: www.scotland.gov.uk/Resource/0039/00399487.pdf.

Shoard, M. (1980) *Theft of the Countryside*. London: Temple Smith

Slee, R. W. (2005) From countrysides of production to countrysides of consumption? *Journal of Agricultural Science*, 143: 255–65

Statistics New Zealand (2013) *Defining Urban and Rural New Zealand*, accessed 13 March 2013 at: www.stats.govt.nz/browse_for_stats/people_and_communities/geographic-areas/urban-rural-profile/defining-urban-rural-nz.aspx.

UN (United Nations) (2011) *Population Density and Urbanization*, accessed 6 June 2011 at: http://unstats.un.org/unsd/demographic/sconcerns/densurb/densurbmethods.htm.

USDA (United States Department of Agriculture) (2011) *Report on the Definition of 'Rural'*. Washington DC: Office of the Secretary of the United States Department of Agriculture.

Woods, M. (2005) *Rural Geography; Processes, Responses and Experiences in Rural Restructuring*. London: Sage.

Woods, M. (2011) *Rural*. Abingdon: Routledge

Woodward, A. (2009) *Today's Opportunities in Farm Tourism*, accessed 28 September 2011 at: www.insights.org.uk/articleitem.aspx?title=Today%E2%80%99s%20Opportunities%20in%20Farm%20Tourism#Case%20studies.

Wylie, J. (2003) 'Landscape, performance and dwelling: A Glastonbury case study', in P. Cloke (ed.), *Country Visions*. Harlow: Pearson: 136–57.

Part I

Material rurality

2 Challenging Western perceptions

A case study of rural Zambia

Juliana Siwale

Introduction

This chapter concerns the international perspective of understanding the 'rural', and the challenges of living in an African countryside compared to that of the Western countryside. In so doing, I acknowledge that there are large differences between the experiences of rural life in Africa compared to that of the more developed world, making the two rurals almost incomparable. Further, this chapter is not a representation of Africa as a whole, but focuses on sub-Saharan Africa, with specific reference to Zambia as a case study to demonstrate that, from a development point of view, rural areas are neglected and their inhabitants remain poorer, invisible, and voiceless, and excluded from decision-making processes. The chapter, drawing upon a historical and political-economy perspective, seeks to highlight the factors that have (re)shaped perceptions and development of the rural over time and the implications that this can have for the rural together with its inhabitants. It will also compare and contrast the rural idyllic representations of the West with those of Africa.

Defining the rural

Defining 'rural' has always been a challenging task as attested by several scholars. There are many definitions of the term rural, but no consensus on a specific definition. As a result, an analyst's choice of 'rural' definition matters. Different definitions generate a different populations of 'rural' people and degrees of classification.[1] According to Woods (2010), the rural is a messy and slippery idea that eludes easy definition and demarcation. Nevertheless, most literature emphasises the role of agriculture as an activity essential to the vitality of rural areas (Cloke, 2003; Shubin, 2006; Madu, 2010; Woods, 2010), while Ellis (2000) queries the tendency to equate the rural with agriculture, noting the increasing diversification of rural economies. Other scholars take open landscape and a sparse settlement structure as generic characteristics of rurality. The use of the term, however, varies from country to country, and rurality can be of diverse types such as rural urban fringe or peri-urban, accessible rural or remote rural. In Zambia, for instance, the national statistics office classifies rural by population and activity. Thus, while the term 'rural' in many countries invokes images of farms, villages, small towns and open spaces, in Zambia it is synonymous with low population densities, an abundance of land, poverty and an environment in which barter and self-sufficiency from peasant farming is common. The discussion here, however, does not aim to enter into definitional debates, as these have received adequate coverage elsewhere in this book. Notwithstanding these differences, several contributions have proposed conceiving of 'rurality' as subjective and socially constructed (Halfacree, 1993; Cloke, 1997, 2003). Borrowing from this understanding, stark realities emerge in presenting rurality from an African perspective.

Brief historical background

Colonial rural

An understanding of rurality in the southern African context requires consideration of the colonial experience and the consequent problematic history of development itself (Cohen, 2004; Freidberg and Goldstein, 2011). Before political independence, local people (especially men) were uprooted, forced or attracted to leave their homes to proffer cheap labour while their families remained behind. The mining industry in southern Africa created a domestic migratory system that fostered urbanisation and concentrated economic activity and wealth within urban areas. Consequently, rural regions in the global South were first imagined by colonial powers as spaces of exploitation and extraction (Johnson, 2004; Woods, 2010). Development concentrated on the core commercial activities and the infrastructure required to support them (Stren and Halfani, 2001). As noted by Potts (2005), this developmental approach served the interests of colonial masters well while the rural populations were paid little regard. These patterns of commerce and trade, in turn, led to new patterns of migration as Africans sought work in mines, plantations, or newly developing urban areas (Cohen, 2004). Nelson Mandela in his book paints a vivid picture of colonial government's perceptions thus: 'The [colonial] government, in order to keep Africans in the countryside or working on the mines, maintained that Africans were by nature a rural people, ill suited to city life' (1994: 2).

Colonial policies aimed at deterring black people from becoming mobile. As such, Lynch (2005) notes that colonial powers placed very strict controls on urban migration by indigenous people to prevent the cities developing too rapidly. According to Stren and Halfani, the urban space was then 'partitioned into highly uneven zones: a "European" space that enjoyed a high level of urban infrastructure and services, and an "indigenous" space that was marginally serviced' (2001: 468). To be in cities, Africans were required to carry a pass giving them permission to be in a certain location – and usually without their family. Colonialism therefore devised a system where migrant labourers were in towns or cities solely for employment, while keeping their permanent home in the village or rural areas. Slater's (1975) study of Tanzania, for example, showed that rural areas supplied labour to support industrialisation and resource exploitation of the core, but derived very little benefit from the activities of the core (such as mining in Zambia, Zimbabwe and South Africa). Rural areas, therefore, served as labour pools for mining urban areas. This encouraged labour migration into cities and changed the relationship between towns and rural areas, as males migrated leaving wives and children behind, with unintended consequences on gender relations and agricultural output. Families left behind in the village survived on subsistence agriculture (managed by women) and remittances sent home. Lifting of the restrictions on migration to the towns came soon after political independence in most African states, resulting in rapid rural to urban migration. For instance, Lynch (2005) notes that, after the democratic elections in South Africa in 1994 and the abolition of the Pass Laws, some 20,000 people were moving into urban areas (especially Gauteng Province) every month, but Bird *et al.* (2002) note that even after the colonial era had ended the vast majority of the population of developing countries was still resident in rural areas.

Post-colonial rural

To understand why most of the rural areas in southern African countries have experienced impoverishment, one has to reflect on the urban-biased policies implemented following their political independence. During the early period of independence, many of these countries concentrated on developing the capital city and other urban areas, resulting in what Lynch (2005) calls 'urban primacy' – a situation where the main city dominates a society. Lipton's (1977) 'urban bias' thesis argued that living conditions improved faster in urban than in rural areas, since urban dwellers exert a considerable influence on government because they are politically aware, more vocal and better organised. Newly independent governments under massive political pressure to appease the electorate subsequently implemented economic policies that favoured their industrial and urban sectors (Potts, 2005). Influenced by the classical economic theory which suggested a potential for a 'trickle-down effect' from urban to rural, post-independence governments often supposed that development would trickle out to rural areas, but instead rural areas remained in stagnation, neglected, poorly organised and beyond the reach of social safety nets (if any were even distantly available) and poverty programmes, as government policies in general tended to favour urban over rural areas (IFAD, 2007). In Nigeria, for example, Bryceson (2002) notes that the oil boom of the mid-1970s led to neglect of rural areas and a massive exodus to urban centres resulting in severe disorientation of rural agricultural production. In response to this apparent bias, donor agencies then promoted a multi-sectoral (infrastructure, agriculture, health, education and sometimes institution building) investment approach in Zambia and other sub-Saharan countries (Bird *et al.*, 2002) through 'integrated rural development projects' (IRDPs). However, this multi-pronged approach to rural neglect and poverty yielded varied country experiences and soon became displaced by laissez-faire structural adjustment. The belief that reduced state activity and ensuing economic liberalisation would allow rural areas to prosper as they built on their comparative advantage in food production did not materialise, as many rural small scale farmers could no longer benefit from hitherto state funded agricultural extension services and agricultural marketing boards.

From the mid-1980s to mid-1990s the World Bank through its neo-liberal policies imposed structural adjustment programmes (SAPs) and market liberalisation with drastic impact on rural agriculture, in particular through the removal of subsidies on inputs such as fertilizers, seeds and pesticides as well as through dismantling marketing boards (Bryceson, 2002). Rural farmers in Zambia, for instance, have since faced a more uncertain market environment with input prices skyrocketing and most rural areas turning from surplus producers to become deficit food baskets or stuck with mountains of unsold grain going to waste. The trade liberalisation, removal of subsidies and growth of export oriented agriculture that followed resulted in the marginalisation of many small farmers who then migrated to urban areas or turned to non-agricultural activities (Bryceson, 2000; Tacoli, 1998). The consequence of this policy was that rural areas and agriculture were being deprived of labour, with families fragmented and livelihoods put under pressure. Despite many years of political independence and rapid growth of towns and social change, the vast majority of Africa's population remains rural (Bird *et al.*, 2002), and agriculture is still the backbone of Africa's economy. UNECA (2007) estimates that about 70 per cent of Africans and roughly 80 per cent of the continent's poor live in rural areas and depend mainly on agriculture for their livelihood. As Table 2.1 shows, all sub-Saharan countries except South Africa and Botswana are predominantly rural, in the sense defined by the World Bank (2011a), namely that 60 per cent of their population lives in rural areas.

This brief historical account seems to indicate that rural areas have been subjected to both 'market failure' leading to exploitation of resources without much benefit to the rural poor and 'state failure' where infrastructure development, basic services and social protection are inadequately provided or non-existent.

Context of rural living in southern Africa: the case of Zambia

Zambia, as Table 2.1 indicates, still has a significant percentage of its population classified as rural. Its population is estimated at 13.2 million (UN 2010) with a GDP per capita of US$985 (World Bank, 2011a). Approximately 68 per cent of the population is living in poverty (FinScope Zambia, 2009), with the rural taking the brunt as their levels of poverty are exceptionally high compared to urban poverty as indicated in Figure 2.1. The majority

Table 2.1 Percentage of rural population in some countries of sub-Saharan Africa

Country	*Rural population (%)*
Burundi	89
Uganda	86.86
Malawi	80.70
Kenya	78.10
Tanzania	74.04
Congo DR	65.42
Zambia	64.40[a]
Mozambique	62.30
Zimbabwe	62.10
Senegal	57
Nigeria	51
Ghana	49
Angola	42
Botswana	39.7
South Africa	38.78

Note:
a The 2010 Census of population and Housing from the Central Statistical Office reports a figure of 61 per cent as rural (Zambia Central Statistical Office, 2011).
Source: Table re-created using data from World Bank (2011b).

(64.4 per cent) of the adult population live in rural areas, while 50 per cent of rural and 27 per cent of urban adults do not have a regular monthly income (FinScope Zambia, 2009). Over half (55 per cent) of formal employment in rural areas is provided by government and less than 3 per cent of rural adults earn a salary or wages from a company or business (FinMark Trust, 2011). Across much of Zambia, rural life depends on subsistence farming. Despite several years of steady economic growth (averaging 5–6 per cent per year) poverty remains high in rural areas and formal employment continues to shrink (World Bank, 2011a).

Rural people do have aspirations but feel that they have been socially, politically and economically marginalised, with little government intervention, and only a few non-governmental interventions, for example, by faith-based non-governmental organisations (NGOs) and donor supported developmental programmes helping with provision of access to education, health and water. Most rural areas in Zambia still lack the basic socio-economic infrastructure that might encourage in-migration. And in contrast to developed countries, rich people live in urban areas while the poor are in rural and the rural–urban fringe areas or shanties around cities. While land and housing can be very expensive in rural England, there is no premium on land in most rural areas of Zambia.[2] Village/local chiefs preside over its allocation to their subjects or in-migrants and in some cases to outside investors as well. Homelessness does not arise either, due to extended family relations, while males take the customary responsibility for providing housing. A minority, including those in receipt of remittances from relatives in urban areas, retirees and

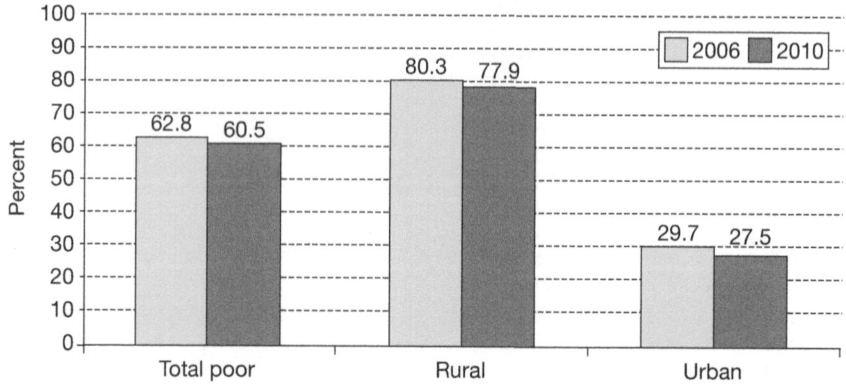

Figure 2.1 Changes in poverty levels by residence, 2006 and 2010
Source: Zambia Central Statistical Office (2011).

economically active young people, can afford to have houses with iron roofing sheets and burnt bricks. A survey by FinScope Zambia (2009) found that 87 per cent of adults in rural areas did not have title deeds to their land and houses, a phenomenon that characterises most rural areas in developing countries. Land has no commercial exchange value hence the lack of housing development. Agriculture, though the main source of livelihood, is still at a subsistence level.

Rural areas in Zambia usually invoke images of despair, with their inhabitants portrayed as homogeneous and trapped in dangerous conservative beliefs and practices (Ferguson, 1999). They are places without urban features (e.g. streetlights) or infrastructures (e.g. banks, post offices, public transportation, educational facilities and leisure services). Limited access to amenities, such as retail stores or services, is also characteristic of rural communities. These are areas where there are either no roads or only gravel roads, and so travel is very difficult, especially after heavy rains. Access to services (see Figure 2.2) such as banks, post offices, hospitals, health centres, schools and convenient stores is a pipe dream many long to be fulfilled. Electricity supply in outlying areas (and also in cities) is unreliable and in some areas non-existent. The telecommunications system is poorly developed, making it difficult to communicate. Health centres, where available, are either inaccessible, have little or no basic drugs or equipment, or have no trained personnel to manage them. A number of school buildings are in a deplorable state and lack basic furniture, though in recent years the government has embarked on projects to build or repair schools in selected rural areas. Libraries are non-existent, and in many places children learn sitting on hard floors or mud bricks. Porter (2011) makes similar observations in her study of rural Ghana and Malawi where mobility is a huge problem. People walk long distances to access services and, where roads are accessible, public transport can be irregular and fares out of reach for many. Unlike Western rural areas where public transport subsidised by the county might be available, there is no public subsidised transport in rural (or urban) Zambia, for instance, and neither do the over sixties get any concessions. Figure 2.2 illustrates the Zambian rural/urban divide in access to facilities and infrastructure, which goes to demonstrate the real struggles of rural life, especially for children, women and older people. What the chart does not reflect, yet is very important, is the lack of physical access to schools and health centres and the impact this has on young children's life chances.

Zambian rural areas are therefore neither idyllic nor healthy because people have no access to clean running water, suffer from water-borne diseases, and in extreme cases drink contaminated water from stagnant wells. Access to treated water is a luxury for most rural households compared to those in urban areas. Figure 2.3 shows that, while 78.4 per cent of Zambian adults in urban areas have access to either personal or public tap water, only 6.4 per cent in rural areas are so fortunate, leaving 92.9 per cent of the rural population to drink water from (protected and unprotected) natural sources. Women and girls, in particular, are disproportionately affected as they take the burden of fetching water for the family and in some cases walk long distances in search of relatively clean drinking water. While this might be an 'accepted' chore for females, school-going girls tend to be disadvantaged compared to boys because they are expected to prioritise this chore before school, in addition to other chores like cooking and house cleaning.

Other countries in the region have similar difficulties and challenges. For instance, the indicators of socio-economic status in rural Kenya also highlight the problem of access to clean water and sanitation. In the case of Kenya, 25 per cent of rural compared to 11 per cent of urban population sourced water from the river or stream, while 96 per cent of the rural population had no access to proper sanitation compared to 62 per cent in urban areas (AudienceScapes National Survey of Kenya, 2009).

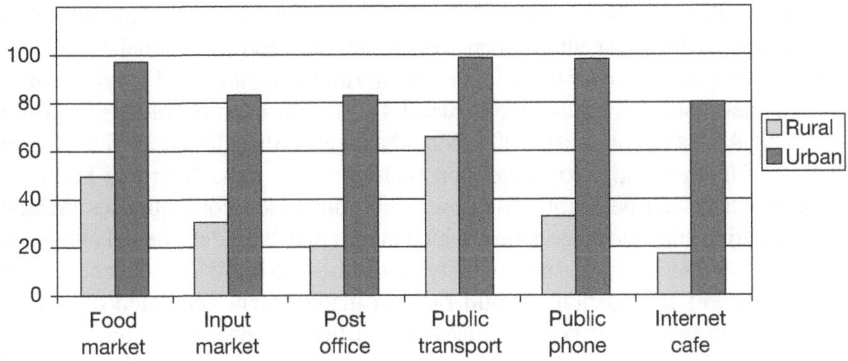

Figure 2.2 Percentages of households with access to facilities within 5 km

Source: Zambia Central Statistical Office (2011).

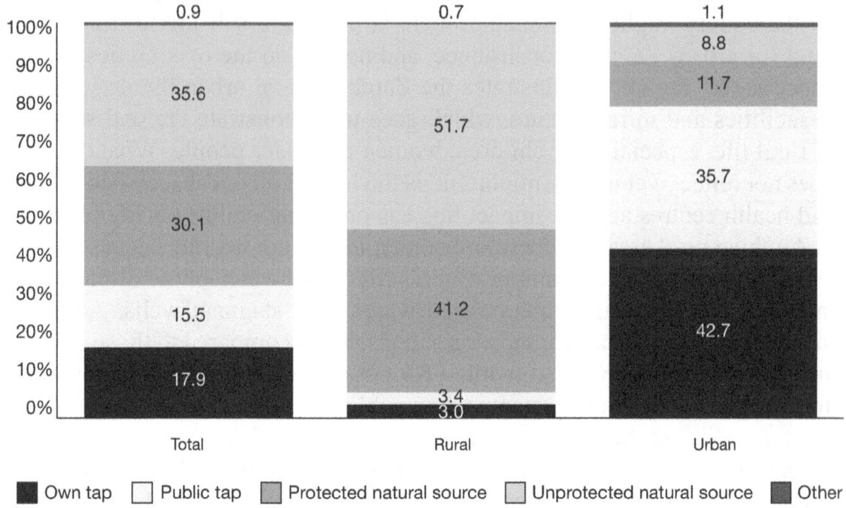

Figure 2.3 Access to drinking water: percentage of Zambian adults
Source: FinScope Zambia, 2009.

The above figures not only highlight a lack of basic necessities of clean water and access to sanitary facilities but also underline how the lack of water and sanitation can interact with other rural challenges such as health, education and gender empowerment and economic wellbeing of rural people. Rural infrastructure shortfalls also include electricity. Few rural residents can claim to own durable goods such as televisions and refrigerators that are so basic in the Western world. As shown in Figure 2.4, rural households in Zambia are less likely than urban ones to have electricity of any kind.

Webb (2012) reports that 80 per cent of energy use in sub-Saharan Africa is firewood and charcoal, and that the picture is worse in rural areas. A study by FinScope Zambia (2009) found that more than 90 per cent of adults living in rural areas and 61 per cent in urban areas relied on wood or charcoal as cooking fuel. On the other hand, only 3.9 per cent in rural compared to 38.6 per cent in urban areas used electricity (see Figure 2.4). This problem pervades most rural areas in Africa (Economist, 2007; Madubansi and Shackleton, 2007), leaving many of them relying extensively on fuel-wood, candles, dung and kerosene lamps, which can be highly polluting. The unintended consequences include deforestation and land degradation, which in turn may have detrimental outcomes for livelihood security and sustainability. There are also health consequences from the inefficient combustion of solid fuels in inadequately ventilated buildings, as well as the economic consequences of insufficient power for income generation and other basic services like health care and education. This limited accessibility to electricity impacts negatively on rural businesses with only 6 per cent of small and medium enterprises (SMEs) in the rural areas connected to the public electricity grid, compared to 24 per cent of urban SMEs (Zambia Business Survey, 2010). Like most other sub-Saharan countries, Zambia suffers from a lack of basic infrastructure in rural communities, and, as far as the need for good quality of life goes, rural people in some ways feel hard done by.

Having an extended family structure in place means that most urban Zambian families tend to have their clan roots in the countryside, yet it rarely features as a preferred option for most working families or urban retirees because it is generally seen as a place of hopelessness and deprivation. While rurality in the West is associated with good quality of life (McLaughlin, 1986), most urban Zambians and the educated perceive it as where you go when you have failed in life. Others have claimed that the long held general belief that, to be successful in the village, one has to have some 'protective charms' for the family and their business, including a good crop harvest, has served to scare away in-migrants. Whether this claim is true or not, sadly, in most rural areas of Zambia, successful people are not just envied but can be tormented or eliminated through witchcraft or attract an 'evil eye' (Elyachar, 2005) because they appear to make rapid economic gains in the midst of widespread poverty. Such beliefs have created some commercial gain for those with the 'know-how' of the protective charms and witchcraft, but have a downside as they tend to act as social barriers to individual initiative towards fighting poverty and to 'outsiders' – a 'hostile' place in which to live. Consequently, most young people migrate out, and a great number of retirees tend to settle on the outskirts of urban areas, thereby putting more pressure on the already stretched urban services, where available.

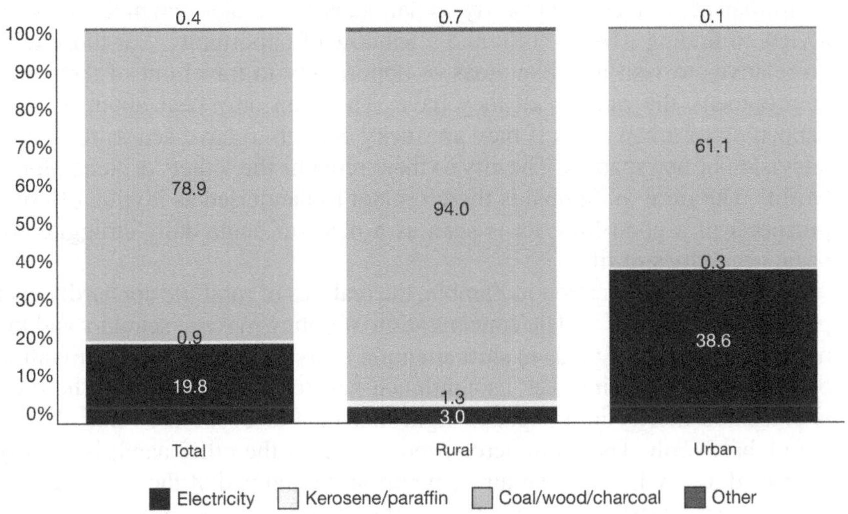

Figure 2.4 Energy sources used for cooking: percentage of Zambian adults

Source: FinScope Zambia, 2009.

Contrasting images of rurality: Western versus African rurality

In Britain, as in many other industrialised countries, the media has played a major role in constructing idyllic pictures of the countryside or rural in contrast to those in Africa. Rural areas in Western countries are often perceived to be places where people can walk, ride, and cycle, sightsee, or simply escape urban strains in search of a slice of tranquillity (Pugh, 2003). They are valued for their picturesque landscapes, their natural environments and dense social structures (Woods, 2010). For instance, Cloke (2003) and Cloke and Milbourne (1992) describe rural areas as offering opportunities for living a lifestyle that is socially cohesive, happy and healthy, and presenting a pace and quality of life that differs from that in the city. This presents the rural as an idyll, a place of peace and solitude, representing an escape from modernity (Rye, 2006; Scott *et al.*, 2007) and a place that is attractive for raising children (Villa, 1999b) as it radiates the impression of innocence.

In Africa, representations of the rural are generally negative rather than positive. The rural is often seen as a place that is lifeless, rigid in expectations of attitudes and behaviour, and unchanging, while cities embody and instil new cultural values (Iliffe, 1987). Its inhabitants are seen as socially isolated, trapped in old-fashioned assumptions, dangerous beliefs and practices (such as witchcraft), and unwilling to adapt to the fast-moving life of cities and modernisation. Rural areas or villages are often equated with ignorance of political, social and economic transformations and cut off from active participation and knowledge that is crucial for their advancement. Rural people themselves are viewed as not active but passive citizens. Consequently, those rural people who can do so (especially the young) move to urban or peri-urban areas to escape poverty, isolation, and lack of social mobility, with a view to finding a better 'life' and a window of opportunity. For those with no relatives to visit in urban areas or opportunity to travel out of their own environment, the rural is all they have. They can only hear about what is happening in urban areas if they are lucky enough to have access to radios, television or newspapers. The city to them remains the 'other' or 'unexplored world'. The rural in Zambia is therefore not romanticised as idyllic, offering prospects of a good life, but is seen as a place of acute daily struggles for basic necessities of life.

For the urban population in Zambia, the realities of rural life are hardly ever played out on local TV. The concentration of policy makers, scholars and the media in urban areas tends to shift attention away from economic deprivation of rural areas and reinforces its continued neglect. When captured, the rural is presented mostly in a negative light that fails to evoke the rural idyll of the global North. The 'commercialised rural', on the other hand, is usually portrayed as idyllic, with an air of luxuriousness aimed at the very wealthy and foreign tourists that can afford safari holidays and enjoy the natural beauty of national parks. However, the once beautiful forests and landscapes in some areas have come under threat of deforestation as people practise shifting cultivation and cut trees for fuel, which then disturbs the ecosystem on which most depend for their livelihood (Madubansi and Shackleton, 2007). Comparatively, therefore, there is little idyll to be imagined. Consequently, most Zambians do not aspire to live there,[3] and rarely view the countryside as a place for leisure and recreation. From a lived experience, there is only the prospect of drudgery, in contrast to Western countries' idealisation of the countryside as a paradise. Overall, life moves at a slow pace and the community is more interdependent, which encourages neighbourly interest, but is perceived by some (especially the young) as intrusive.

Rural North and South: are they worlds apart?

For some readers the stark differences outlined so far could be hard to believe or just unimaginable. However, it might be helpful to note that some differences are a matter of scale and that in terms of rural dynamics there are some shared characteristics between rural England (North) and southern Africa (South). One point of connection is found in the predominant activity. Rural areas in the North as well as in the South have agriculture as their key activity but one is more intensive and more capitalised while the other is labour intensive and with lower productivity. Another commonality can be found in young people's view of the rural, irrespective of their spatial differences. The young in Norway, for instance, were found to have a more negative perception of rurality (Rye, 2006). They resented the 'everyone knows everyone' notion and found it intrusive and controlling. From their point of view, the rural was simply 'primitive'. Elsewhere, Waara (2000) shows that young people perceive the countryside as 'traditional', 'under-developed', 'backward' and 'old-fashioned'. In a phone conversation with two young people in urban Zambia for instance, they summed up the rural as a 'dark world'.

Out-migration of people also characterises the rural areas of the North and South but to varying levels. Lynch (2005) notes that in the global South, rural-to-urban migration is fuelled by push factors (such as poverty) as well as pull factors represented by prospects of better employment opportunities, healthcare and education. This out-migration is particularly acute among young people because the rural economy is low key, resulting in the drain of the most economically active residents. Several researchers (Stockdale, 2004; Bosworth, 2009; Woods, 2010) have noted a net out-migration of young people from rural communities in England. This is primarily due to a lack of local employment and housing opportunities – see Champion (2007) and Somerville, this volume. Others point to the desire of young people to escape the perceived dullness of rural life (Rye, 2006; Bye, 2009). For the migrating young in Zambia, though, their daily struggles take on another dimension as they find themselves in slums as an alternative, but convinced they are moving away from the grind and uncertainty of their rural livelihood. Effectively, their rural gets transferred into the urban but with different characteristics and challenges. For them, anything is better than being in a rural area.

There is also a lack of infrastructure and high transport cost in rural relative to urban areas, but to varying degrees. While there have been reports of rural services in England getting consistently worse as post offices close and historic bus routes end (Defra 2011), there are hardly any such services in rural Zambia, where walking and cycling are the most common modes of travel, with very limited government support to facilitate easy mobility, resulting in even young school children, on average, walking long distances to school.

What are the implications for the economy of the rural South?

The countryside in Africa is characterised by low financial intermediation (Basu *et al.* 2004; Aterido *et al.*, 2011; Gardeva and Rhyne, 2011). As such the rural population has limited access to financial services, an important input into business enterprise development. A FinScope Zambia report (2009) found very high levels of financial exclusion for rural populations. My own field research, into how microfinance can improve financial access for the low income and small businesses both in the rural and the informal sector of the urban (Siwale, 2006; Siwale and Ritchie, 2012), found very limited levels of economic activity and an absence of formal (lending) financial institutions. The rural economy primarily operates in cash or in kind. In this research, most rural women with micro-businesses (mainly selling farm produce from their fields, sales of prepared snacks and petty retailing) complained about lack of markets, lack of electricity, limited business opportunities and unreliable transport networks, which then affected their ability to sustain their businesses, let alone to contemplate income diversification. For those with surplus produce, much of the harvest rots before it gets to the market because of the time it takes to move food into towns. Most of the trading tended to cluster around some basic institutions such as schools, health centres, and local government offices or bus stations. The implications here are that, for most of the countryside, far away from the business 'centre nodes', the economy is largely based on the bartering of goods and generally sluggish, and the rural continues to be an unattractive place in which to live and do business, which in turn limits economic diversification and employment creation.

Despite such financial exclusion, the picture is mixed. In many parts of Zambia, rural populations are increasingly dependent on non-agricultural income generating activities, though some agriculture-based rural enterprises and subsistence farmers, in particular, women, tend to survive because many urban enterprises – especially in the informal sector – rely on rural produce. It is common to find various types of agricultural crops grown in the rural but consumed in the urban areas, where the informal sector thrives. There is, however, growing activity in non-farm activities (such as transport, restaurants, retail/grocers and hammer-mills) promoted by young people who have failed to make it into college and urban life. Mustapha (1999), in Nigeria, noted a tendency for youth to be engaged in activities outside agriculture, while in

Tanzania, Madulu (1998) observed a remarkable rush into trade by rural youth and unmarried adults. Equally, the high cost of farm inputs, lack of organised markets and low returns from farming have served to increase the importance of non-farm income and employment (Ellis, 2000). These activities are attractive to young people because of the opportunity they provide to move in and out of the rural and their ability to generate cash most of the year as compared with the seasonal-based income from agriculture. However, it is interesting to note that rural communities are not detached and sheltered from urban influences either. Increased mobility and transport has meant that rural space is being increasingly penetrated by urban influences and interests. For instance, while visiting my home village in the northern part of Zambia, in September 2007, I observed a growing appetite among rural youth to 'import' some of the urban lifestyles (such as the dress style of close-fitting clothes for girls and improvising entertainment places for cinema) into their 'dull' surroundings, much to the displeasure of the older, traditional population.

Despite this rise in rural economy diversification, one of the sticking points of village/rural-based trade activities is the lack of basic infrastructure in telecommunications and transport networks, high operation costs, and limited access to markets and financial institutions, coupled with unreliable electricity supplies where available. Also, however, as Bryceson (2002) has observed, the lack of *in situ* purchasing power means that, over time, the majority of businesses remain stagnant or fail. Whereas cash transactions dominate the urban, barter is still common in rural areas, making it difficult for rural enterprises to survive and create the needed employment. Therefore, while neo-liberal perspectives might favour support for entrepreneurship and market-led solutions to rural poverty, constraints on enterprise may not make this a viable approach unless infrastructure and access to finance can be made easier for the rural population.

Conclusion

The discussion here, though not a representation of all southern African countries, has in a limited way attempted to add an international perspective on understanding rurality, and to identify the challenges of living in an African countryside compared to a Western countryside. As in other southern African countries, the Zambian countryside commands very negative representations, making the rural idyll more of a Western construct. While rurality is embedded in the social fabric of both rural and urban populations, in practice government planning and development policies eschew this vital link to addressing the apparent unattractiveness of rural areas. As with many other areas of the economy, it is usually those with an organised voice that get governments' attention and resource commitment, suggesting that the rural poor in southern Africa are not only confronted with marginalisation over public policy, but also have limited bargaining power in the market place. From the policy perspective, most governments' complacency about rural deprivation needs confronting, together with the barriers that limit the exploitation of the huge economic opportunities to transform rural livelihoods. A transformative change is needed to facilitate rural people running their farms as businesses and marketing their surpluses to cities. In addition, the rural non-farm economy requires support if it is to create new economic opportunities that rural people, particularly the young, can grasp. Therefore, provisioning village water supply, road access and electrification are first steps to bringing the town to the countryside, which could encourage in-migration for diversity of skills and rural business development. Rural populations generally want to make a difference to their well-being but are let down by lack of basic infrastructure and access to financial services. Extending microfinance services to rural areas through mobile banking, as demonstrated in Kenya and Malawi, and promoting community owned cooperatives, is a vision that needs embracing in order to work towards reducing rural poverty. Changing long-held perceptions of rurality, as discussed in this chapter, requires governments within the region to recognise these challenges and to have an explicit rural dimension to virtually everything they do, in order to address the continued disengagement between rural people and government and work towards one of the United Nations' Millennium Development Goals of alleviating extreme poverty and hunger by 2015 (UN, n.d.).

Notes

1 Chomitz *et al.* (2005) proposed an operational definition of rurality based on population density and distance to large cities. According to this report, the rural is presented as a place where population densities are low, markets of all kinds are thin, and the unit cost of delivering most social services and many types of infrastructure is high.
2 The land tenure system in Zambia is dual and the majority of land is held under customary land arrangements with limited transfer possibilities.
3 Those in urban areas with family roots in the countryside make short visits to their rural 'home' to see their parents and/or grandparents, while others, passionate about preserving their cultural heritage for future generations, organise and attend annual traditional ceremonies aimed at promoting cultural identities that are under increasing threat from Western cultural influences due to globalisation.

References

Aterido, R., Beck, T. and Iacovone, L. (2011) Gender and finance in sub-Saharan Africa: Are women disadvantaged? The World Bank, Policy Research Working Paper No. 5571. Available at: www.wds.worldbank.org/servlet/WDSContentServer/WDSP/IB/2011/02/23/000158349_20110223113408/Rendered/PDF/WPS5571.pdf (accessed 5 March 2012).

AudienceScapes National Survey of Kenya (July, 2009) Available at: www.audiencescapes.org/country-profiles/kenya/demographic-profiles/urban-rural-divide/urban-rural-divide-319 (accessed 12 April 2012).

Basu, A., Blavy, R. and Yulek, M. (2004) Microfinance in Africa: Experience and lessons from selected African countries. IMF Working Paper. African Department, WP/04/174.

Bird, K., Hulme, D., Moore, K. and Shepherd, A. (2002) Chronic poverty and remote rural areas. CPRC Working Paper No. 13, Institute for Development Policy and Management. University of Manchester. Available at: www.chronicpoverty.org/uploads/publication_files/WP13_Bird_et_al.pdf (accessed 5 March 2012).

Bosworth, G. (2009) Education, mobility and rural business development. *Journal of Small Business and Enterprise Development*, 16(4): 660–77.

Bryceson, D. F. (2000) Rural Africa at crossroads: Livelihood practices and policies. *Natural Resources Perspectives*, No. 52, April 2000, London: Overseas Development Institute.

Bryceson, D. F. (2002) The scramble in Africa: Reorienting rural livelihoods. *World Development*, 30(5): 725–39.

Bye, Marie Linda. (2009) 'How to be rural man': Young men's performances and negotiations of rural masculinities. *Journal of Rural Studies*, 25(3): 278–88.

Champion, A. G. (2007) Reviewing Rural Futures: Population projections and migration across the urban–rural system. Rural Evidence Research Centre, Birkbeck, University of London. Available at: www.rerc.ac.uk/findings/documents_demography/Proj_Ests_ReportsA_F.pdf (accessed 30 October 2012).

Chomitz, K. M., Buys, P. and Thomas, S. T. (2005) Quantifying the rural–urban gradient in Latin America and the Caribbean. World Bank Policy Research Working Paper No. 3634. Available at: https://openknowledge.worldbank.org/bitstream/handle/10986/8317/wps3634.pdf?sequence=1 (accessed 15 November 2012).

Cloke, P. (1997) Country backwater to virtual village? Rural studies and 'The cultural turn'. *Journal of Rural Studies*, 13(4): 367–75.

Cloke, P. (2003) *Country Visions*. Harlow, UK: Pearson Prentice Hall.

Cloke, P. and Milbourne, P. (1992) Deprivation and lifestyles in rural Wales: Rurality and the cultural dimension. *Journal of Rural Studies*, 8(4): 359–71.

Cohen, B. (2004) Urban growth in developing countries: A review of current trends and a caution regarding existing forecasts. *World Development*, 32(1): 23–51.

Defra (2011) Statistical Digest of Rural England 2011. Available from: www.defra.gov.uk/publications/files/rural-digest-2011.pdf (accessed 28 February 2012).

The Economist (2007) The dark continent, 384(8542): 39.

Elyachar, J. (2005) *Markets of Dispossession: NGOs, Economic Development, and the State in Cairo*. Durham, NC, and London: Duke University Press.

Ellis, F. (2000) *Rural Livelihoods and Diversity in Developing Countries*. Oxford: Oxford University Press.

Ferguson, J. (1999) *Expectations of Modernity: Myths and Meanings of Urban Life on the Zambian Copperbelt*. Berkeley and Los Angeles, CA: University of California Press.

FinMark Trust (2011) Financial Education in Zambia: What does FinScope tell us? Nov. 2011, No. 6. Available at: www.finmark.org.za/wp-content/uploads/2011%20FAM6_Zambia_Final.pdf (accessed 6 March 2011).

FinScope Zambia (2009) Top Line Findings. Available at: www.boz.zm/FSDP/Zambia_report_Final.pdf (accessed 6 March 2011).

Freidberg, S. and Goldstein, L. (2011) Alternative food in the global south: Reflections on a direct marketing initiative in Kenya. *Journal of Rural Studies*, 27(1): 24–34.

Gardeva, A and Rhyne, E. (2011) Opportunities and Obstacles to Financial Inclusion Survey Report. Centre For Financial Inclusion Publication 12, July, ACCION International.

Halfacree, K. (1993) Locality and social presentation: Space, discourse and the alternative definitions of the rural. *Journal of Rural Studies*, 9: 23–37.

IFAD (International Fund for Agricultural Development) (2007) Rural Poverty in Africa. Available at: www.ruralpovertyportal.org/web/guest/region/home/tags/africa (accessed 5 August 2011).

Iliffe, J. (1987) *The African Poor: A History*. Cambridge: Cambridge University Press.

Johnson, H. (2004) Subsistence and control: The persistence of the peasantry in developing world. *Undercurrent*, 1(1): 55–65

Lipton, M. (1977) *Why Poor People Stay Poor: A Study of Urban Bias in World Development*. London: Temple Smith.

Lynch, K. (2005) *Rural–Urban Interaction in Developing World*. London: Routledge.

McLaughlin, B. P. (1986) The rhetoric and the reality of rural deprivation. *Journal of Rural Studies*, 2(4): 291–307.

Madu, I. A. (2010) The structure and pattern of rurality in Nigeria. *GeoJournal*, 75(2): 175–84.

Madubansi, M. and Shackleton, C. M. (2007) Changes in fuelwood use and selection following electrification in the Bushbuckridge lowveld, South Africa. *Journal of Environmental Management*, 83: 416–26.

Madulu, N. F. (1998) Changing lifestyles in farming societies of Sukumaland: Kwimba District, Tanzania. African Studies Centre, Leiden. Working Paper, vol. 27. Available at: https://openaccess.leidenuniv.nl/handle/1887/424 (accessed 21 December 2011).

Mandela, N. (1994) *Long Walk to Freedom*. London: Little, Brown & Co.

Mustapha, A. R. (1999) Cocoa farming and income diversification in South-western Nigeria. Working Paper, vol. 42, Kano: Center for Documentation and Research and Leiden: African Studies Center. Available at: https://openaccess.leidenuniv.nl/handle/1887/413 (accessed 4 January 2012).

Porter, G. (2011) 'I think a woman who travels a lot is befriending other men and that's why she travels': Mobility constraints and their implications for rural women and girls in sub-Saharan Africa. *Gender, Place and Culture*, 18(1): 65–81.

Potts, D. (2005) Counter-urbanisation on the Zambian Copperbelt? Interpretations and Implications. *Urban Studies*, 42(4): 583–609.

Pugh, R. (2003) Considering the countryside: Is there a case for rural social work? *British Journal of Social Work*, 33(1): 67–85.

Rye, J. F. (2006) 'Rural youths': Images of the rural. *Journal of Rural Studies*, 22(4): 409–21.

Scott, A., Gilbert, A. and Gelan, A. (2007) The Urban–Rural Divide: Myth or reality? SERG Policy Brief, No. 2. Aberdeen: The Macaulay Institute.

Shubin, S. (2006) The changing nature of rurality and rural studies in Russia. *Journal of Rural Studies*, 22: 422–40.

Slater, D. (1975) Underdevelopment and spatial inequality: Approaches to the problem of regional planning in the Third World. *Progress in Planning*, 4(2): 97–167.

Siwale, J. (2006) The role of loan officers and clients in the diffusion of microfinance: A study of PRIDE Zambia and CETZAM in Zambia. University of Durham. Unpublished Ph.D. thesis.

Siwale, J. and Ritchie, J. (2012) Disclosing the loan officer's role in microfinance development. *International Small Business Journal*, 30(4): 432–50.

Stren, R. and Halfani, M. (2001) The cities of sub-Saharan Africa: From dependency to marginality. In R. Paddison (ed.), *Handbook of Urban Studies*. London: Sage: 466–85.

Stockdale, A. (2004) Rural out-migration: Community consequences and individual migrant experiences. *Sociologia Ruralis*, 44(2): 149–76.

Tacoli, C. (1998) Rural–urban interactions: A guide to the literature. *Environment and Urbanization*, 10(1): 147–66.

UNECA (United Nations Economic Commission for Africa) (2007) Accelerating Africa's Development through Diversification. Available at: www.uneca.org/sites/default/files/publications/era2007full.pdf (accessed 13 June 2013).

UN (United Nations) (2010) Country Profile: Zambia. Available at: http://data.un.org/CountryProfile.aspx?crName=ZAMBIA (accessed 10 February 2012).

UN (United Nations) (n.d.) United Nations Millennium Goals: We can end poverty 2015. Available at: www.un.org/millenniumgoals/ (accessed 1 July 2013).

Villa, M. (1999b) Rural life courses in Norway: Living within the rural–urban complementary. *History of the Family*, 5: 473–90.

Waara, P. (2000) Rural Young People in Norrbotten and Västerbotten in the north of Sweden, in Helve, Helena (ed.) *Rural Young People in Changing Europe: Comparative Study of Living Conditions and Participation of Rural Young People in Estonia, Finland, Germany, Italy and Sweden*. Helsinki: Finnish Youth Research Society: 134–40.

Webb T. (2012) Greener energy trumps dirty diesel power: Private sector investment is being tapped to put power plants on the grid. *The Times*, London, 19 March 2012, p. 14.

Woods, M. (2010) *Rural*. London: Routledge.

World Bank (2011a) More Jobs and Prosperity in Zambia: What would it take? Based on the jobs and prosperity: Building Zambia's competitiveness program. Report No. 62376-ZM. Available at: www-wds.worldbank.org/external/default/main.

World Bank (2011b) Africa Development Indicators 2011. Available at: https://openknowledge.worldbank.org/handle/10986/2770 (accessed 4 June 2012).

Zambia Business Survey (2010) The Profile and Productivity of Zambian Businesses. FinMark Trust, June 2010. Available at: www.finmark.org.za/wp-content/uploads/ZBS_summaryreport.pdf.

Zambia Central Statistical Office (2010) Census of Population and Housing. Available at: http://unstats.un.org/unsd/demographic/sources/census/2010_phc/Zambia/PreliminaryReport.pdf (accessed 26 June 2013).

Zambia Central Statistical Office (2011) Living Conditions Monitoring Survey Report 2006 and 2010. Available at: http://images.mofcom.gov.cn/zm2/accessory/201111/1320414853386.pdf (accessed 13 June 2013).

3 Economic approaches to the rural

David Gray

Introduction

This chapter approaches the rural through the lens of regional economic analysis. A range of spatial economic models are examined to consider how the rural is treated, or possibly not considered as an entity of interest. These include: neo-classical growth theory; cumulative causation and growth pole theory; export base and Dixon–Thirlwall–Kaldor models; the New International Division of Labour; the evolution of industrial structure, path dependency and long wave theories; and social and network concepts including the nexus of untraded dependencies. Some models, such as a neo-classical growth model, treat the rural as a spatial unit with specific trade and growth characteristics. Others, such as cumulative causation, envisage a system where the rural periphery is somehow linked to, and constrained by, the urban core. However, housing literature would point to one part of the rural within commuting distance of a concentration of employment as being distinct from another, namely the more remote rural. To some extent, the distinction between urban and rural labour markets is blurred (Ali *et al.* 2011), leaving the policy maker with the conundrum: should the commutable rural be seen as part of the urban or the rural?

The rural is one of those areas that, while being difficult to define, one can describe. The mode of delineation depends on the means and the purpose of the classification. The rural is a territorial unit of analysis below the level of the nation. If all territories were fractals or perfect miniature replicas of the nation, they would be homogeneous, negating the rationale for a sub-national economic consideration; sub-economies would behave identically and produce the same products. At the other extreme, if all territories were unique, no general statement could be formulated about any set, and the whole would be a weighted average of its sub-sets. Thus, from a top-down approach, sub-dividing a larger unit, like a nation, into regions, would require homogeneity internally but heterogeneity inter-regionally. From the bottom up, a region would be a collection of sub-regional units with commonalities among the differences.

The criteria or models that one deploys to combine territories are likely to proffer competing patterns of sub-national groups. For government policy making, it is common to use measures of employment, wealth-generation or wages. But one could argue that these are proxies for utility. Moreover, from the perspective of a productive system, the collections of territories should reflect the economic forces that determine the fluctuation of utility or well-being of those collections. Just because an indicator, such as the unemployment rate, suggests a territory is distinct from its neighbours, it does not follow that its economic fortunes are dissimilar also. A static indicator may point to one collection whereas a dynamic one could highlight another.

The region is bifurcated into rural and urban territories. Urban economics can trace much of its heritage to microeconomics. Marginal analysis of land-use and rents, location and transport costs are featured (Vickerman, 1984). By contrast, rural economics tends to be a residual or bound up in agricultural analyses. Regional economics is squeezed in between macro and micro-economics and draws on industrial and international economic insights. In microeconomics, the focus of attention is on the behaviour of the representative individual, firm or sector. Macroeconomics focuses on the spaceless world of aggregate measures of activity. Thus, there is no rural economics to draw on.

One characteristic above others that delineates urban from rural is the concentration of economic activity (Bogart, 1998). Population densities in the regions of Yorkshire and Humberside and the East Midlands of England are highlighted in Figure 3.1. These two regions contain some of the more sparsely populated areas in the UK. Using four quantiles one can see that there is a decline in the density of population as one moves away from cities such as Leeds-Bradford (which are highlighted in dark grey) towards more rural areas. The second highest density surrounds that. The third quantile is displayed in medium grey with horizontal stripes. This reveals many market towns. The least dense areas displayed in light grey with vertical stripes account for the vast majority of the regional space.

Giuliano and Small's (1991) method for delineating an employment (sub)centre entails defining clusters of contiguous tracts of land where gross employment density is at least ten employees per acre, and contains at least 10,000 employees. Thus, the rural area is distinguishable from the urban when it has low densities of people, firms and employment.

Used by the Office for National Statistics (ONS), Birkbeck College's Rural Evidence Research Centre's 'Technical Methodology Paper for Rural–Urban Definition' (RERC, 2004) defines six types of settlement in England and Wales. Based on boundaries and land use, areas forming settlements with populations of over 10,000 are classified as Urban (Less Sparse), colour coded as black. To illustrate the ONS classification and how it relates to population density, the map in Figure 3.2 is again of Yorkshire and Humberside and the East Midlands of England. Town and Fringe (Less Sparse) are coloured medium grey; and Village, Hamlet and Isolated Dwellings (Less Sparse) are light grey with vertical stripes. Other rural settlement types are Urban (Sparse) (medium grey with vertical stripes); Town and Fringe (Sparse) (medium grey with horizontal stripes); and Village, Hamlet and Isolated Dwellings (Sparse)

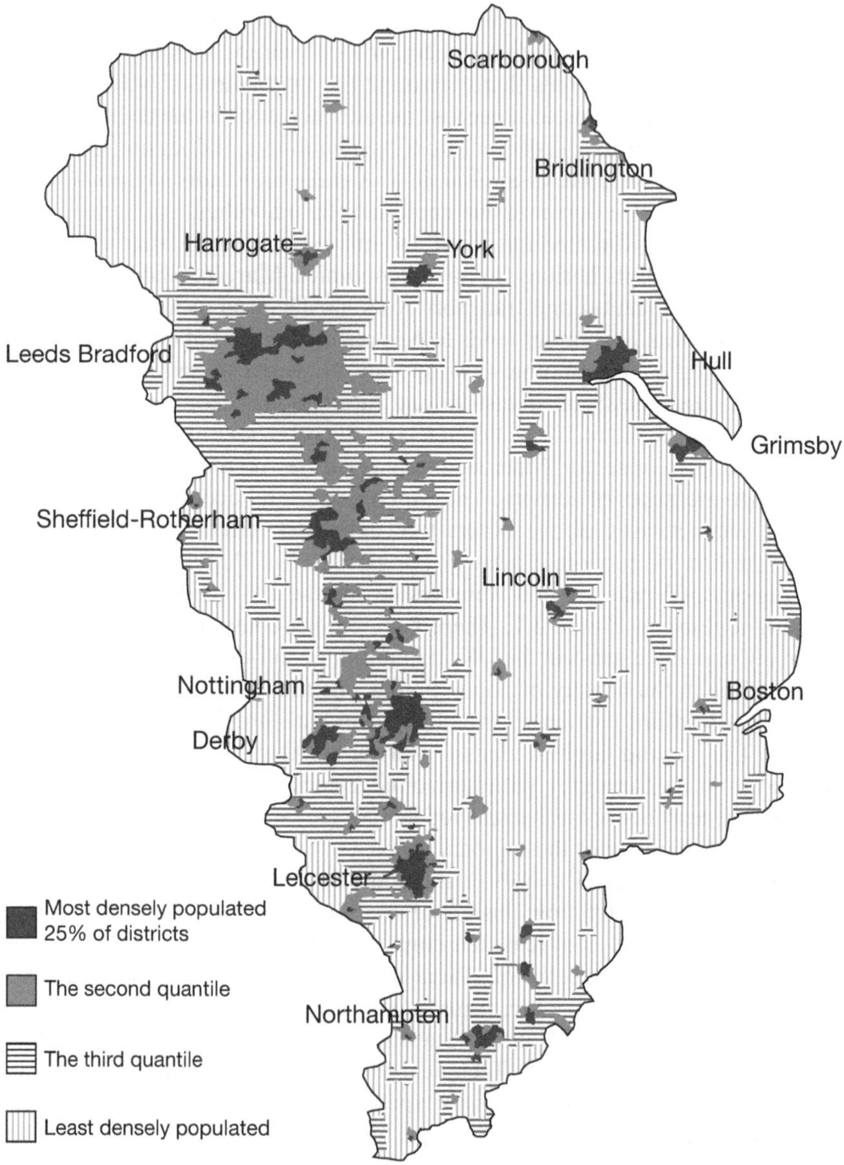

Figure 3.1 Population densities in Yorkshire and Humberside and the East Midlands of England

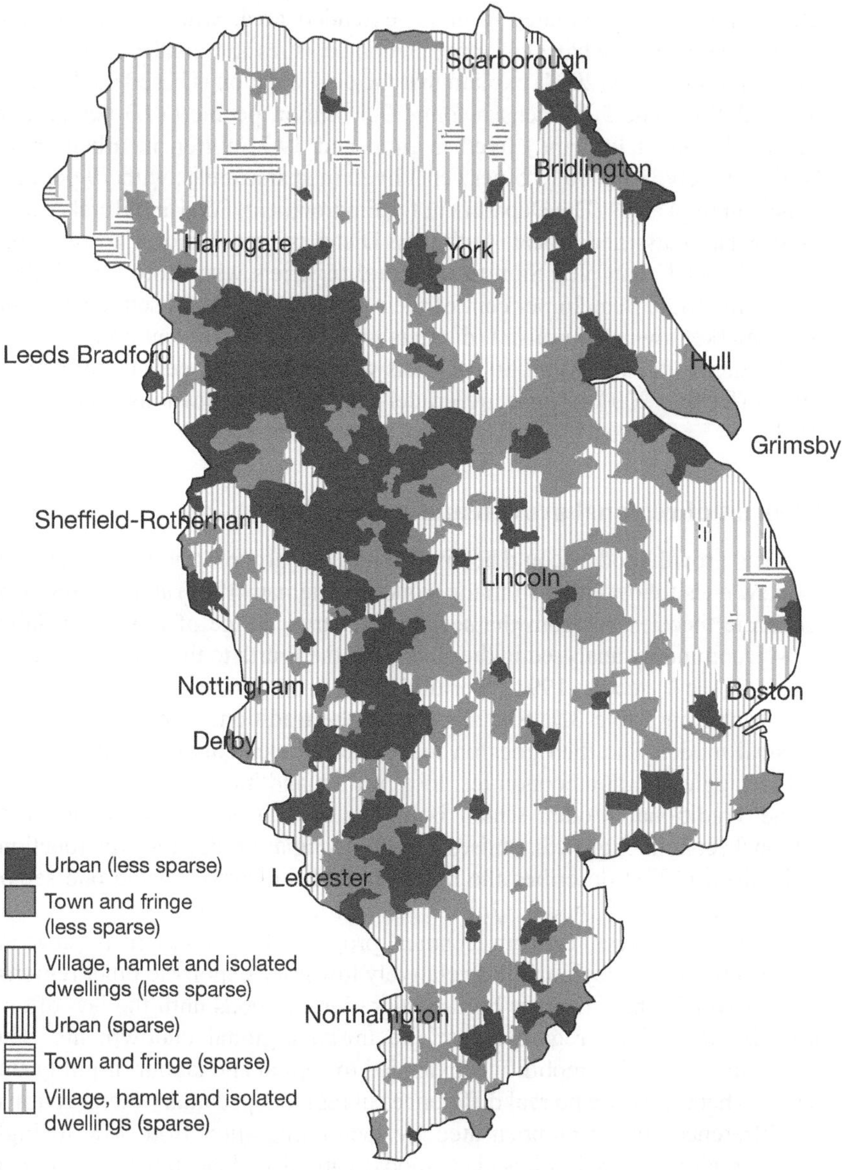

Figure 3.2 Urban and rural delineations in Yorkshire and Humberside and the East Midlands of England

(light grey, wide vertical stripes). Rural town and fringe areas tend to be relatively densely populated over an extended area, whereas village and hamlet areas generally have lower population densities and smaller settled areas. Bibby and Shepherd (2004) explain that the classification is based on densities of population. The 2001 census found 9.5 million people (19.3 per cent of the population of England) lived in rural and 39.7 million in urban areas. Approximately, 760,000 (1.5 per cent) lived in sparse areas, with 79 per cent of them in rural areas. The Department for Environment, Food and Rural Affairs (Defra) has classified Local Authority Districts into Major Urban, Large Urban, Other Urban plus Significant Rural (districts with more than 37,000 people *and* more than 26 per cent of their population in rural settlements and larger market towns), Rural-50 (districts with 50 to 80 per cent population in rural settlements) and Rural-80 (districts with over 80 per cent larger market towns) (RERC, 2004). These are cruder than the classifications used by the ONS.

Theories of regional growth and interaction

Regional growth models could be divided into two groups: traditional and new. The new ones follow either from the work of Krugman (1991) and new regional economic theories, or from the second industrial divide of Piore and Sabel (1984), commonly analysed in the shift from the fourth to the fifth long waves or styles (see Tylecote, 1991). Terluin's (2003) summary of growth theories is presented in Table 3.1. She starts with the traditional single sector neo-classical model. She then goes on to extend the elements in the function to include agglomeration economies, local milieu and innovation.

The Traditional Model, which is a (one sector) neo-classical model of (national economic) growth, utilises a Cobb–Douglas production type function. Richardson (1978) describes the macro-spatial dimension of the one sector neo-classical growth model. Growth in income comes from more factors of production (resources) or from technical progress. Given regions produce an identical product, a region with a relatively low price exports to other regions. In other words, there is cross border migration of goods until the law of one price is adhered to, regardless of the initial regional endowments. The assumption of perfect mobility is extended to capital and labour. Equilibrium occurs where there are no real differences in regional pecuniary factor returns, the differences being compensated by factor migration from low to high reward regions. This implies that goods, capital and people move until a common rate of return on capital, a common real-wage, and a common price exist across the regions. This assumes that factors are homogeneous, perfectly mobile, traded in perfectly competitive markets, and only respond to differences in potential factor returns; each region has the same production function and wages are measured in real terms. Workers would relocate if they believed that their pecuniary rewards would be enhanced by taking a job elsewhere. There is no reward to labour or capital relocation if the real returns are the

Table 3.1 Regional growth models

Types	*Growth model*	*Examples*
Traditional model	Growth is determined by combinations of labour and capital plus technical progress	Neo-classical growth theory Keynesian
Pure agglomeration	Growth is determined by combinations of labour and capital which are enhanced by traditional nations of agglomeration economies	Cumulative causation Growth pole New Economic Geography theories
Local milieu	Growth is determined by combinations of labour and capital which are enhanced by new notions of agglomeration economies and growth paths	Endogenous growth models Reorganisation of labour ideas
Territorial innovation models	Growth is determined by combinations of labour and capital which are enhanced by new notions of agglomeration economies and fostering innovation	Nexus of untraded dependencies Porter's Diamond Innovative milieu

Source: Adapted from Terluin (2003).

same in all areas. Firms would employ a combination of labour and capital so as to ensure that the ratio of returns from employing the last unit of each factor equalled the ratio of their prices. This would mean that the capital–labour ratio, and, hence, income per head, would be the same in each region. In this perspective, everywhere has the same potential for output, given the same technology.

A Two-Sector Traditional Regional Model draws on the standard Heckscher–Ohlin factor proportions trade theorem (see Krugman and Obstfeld, 2006, for a general explanation). The two-sector model perhaps better reflects the agricultural specialisation of the rural trading with the urban. The rural is land abundant and so should specialise in producing land intensive goods. An extension, the Heckscher–Ohlin–Samuelson Factor Price Equalisation Theorem, predicts that factor mobility is not necessary to accomplish equality of factor returns across space, as the movement of goods will serve the same purpose. Although Krugman (1991) is a keen advocate of the idea, the factor price equalisation theorem is built on some very restrictive assumptions, such as common production functions, which could leave the policy maker with unrealistic goals, given the production limitations in the local.

Although policy makers use the predictions of the neoclassical models, pushing for cuts in costs to enhance competitiveness, the assumptions can be very restrictive. In both approaches rural areas would have the same production function as urban ones, and so would have the same income per head potential, and what is produced and how they are generated is immaterial. Moreover, in the absence of agglomeration economies, there is no urban, so in a sense there is no rural. Land will be set aside for agriculture because that resource utilisation generates the highest return, not because there is legislation protecting it from the bulldozer and the builder.

Agglomeration economies

Of key importance to understanding urban and rural relative performances is the agglomeration economy. Agglomeration economies arise when spatial proximity between firms and other economic agents produces benefits that are not available outside these locations (Rosenthal and Strange, 2003). Richardson (1978) identifies three categories of agglomeration economies:

1 Social agglomeration economies are concerned with social infrastructure and services. If a large number of people are living in close proximity, certain public services become economically viable, such as a bus service or a hospital. These amenities become an attribute for the area, adding to its attractiveness.
2 Household agglomeration economies are the benefits of living in an urban environment. As with social agglomeration economies, certain activities are more likely to be financially viable. For example, a larger market could provide sufficient demand, and so revenue streams, to cover the high initial costs and other overheads of, say, banks and post offices, as well as providing scope for specialist shops and offering the householder greater choice. Again, a non-pecuniary reward from living in a large city can be the amenity factor. In a Christallerian spatial system, larger agglomerations (higher order nodes) would offer a wider range of services serving not only the centre itself, but also lower order nodes within its system (McCann, 2001).
3 Business agglomeration economies are the advantages that businesses derive from locating together. Krugman (1991) describes [Marshall's 1920] three traditional explanations for industrial districts. The first concerns a larger pool from which to draw labour, which may be offset for those firms in the same industry experiencing greater competitive pressure from close proximity to rivals. Second, there is the fostering of specialised suppliers of inputs and services, dependent to some extent on a minimum efficient scale of production and, by implication, market. Certain types of business become viable with a greater market size, such as financial, legal and consultancy work. The third is where industrialists facing broadly the same technological constraints, information flows and technological spillovers, reinforce and build on each other's knowledge and innovativeness.

The notion of a node or concentration of activity that has growth-enhancing effects can be seen in many old and new regional theories. For example, knowledge spillovers in traditional agglomeration ideas can be seen in innovative milieu and untraded dependencies. Localised knowledge spillovers are well documented in R&D (Jaffe *et al.*, 1994). Knowledge spillovers are a function of interaction, which is itself a function of a density of business. In the social networking analysis, 'buzz' or knowledge exchange, reducing transaction costs, and trust building are now another advantage of agglomeration (Storper and Venables, 2004).

Export base models

Drawing on international economics, regions are sometimes modelled as small, open economies that trade with the outside world. Richardson (1973) describes export base models as being too feeble to provide a theory of regional growth. However, they provide a useful vehicle for growth theories (Dixon–Thirlwall–Kaldor 1975, cumulative causation model), explaining regional disparities (Fothergill and Gudgin's 1982 analysis of regional problems) and delineations of territories (North, 1955).

The export base hypothesis is based on a bifurcation of industrial sectors into a regional dependent and a regional exporting sector. The exporting sector derives wealth from the rest of the world, on which the non-exporting sector feeds. The dependent sector comprises professional service firms such as lawyers and accountants, as well as broader personal and retail services. The presumption is that services are not [as] exportable. North (1955) suggested that a region does not develop from a subsistence region into an exporting one. Instead, a region grows from, and with, the exporting sector. Such dependency would lead to an exaggeration of the fortunes of the exporting sector.

Historically, an urban area could not develop without the sustaining supply of food from its local farmers. Where the food supplies were abundant, the surplus could be traded. Indeed, in many areas, their exports were and remain primary goods, such as minerals or food. The rural is almost certainly more specialised than any urban counterpart. Indeed, the rural economy is likely to be so specialised that it must trade with other areas for products and services. This means its growth and development are dependent on the fortunes of spaces elsewhere.

The regional Keynesian income multiplier and the Verdoorn effects exacerbate imbalances. If there were an increase in investment expenditure in the region, a multiplier effect is expected to increase aggregate income within the region. The Verdoorn effects concern the rate of increase of productivity, which was found to have a direct relationship with increases in the rate of growth of output. If output increases, so does productivity; and if productivity increases, output and income growth should follow, leading to further multiplier and productivity effects. If this investment attracts mobile capital and labour from elsewhere, it would lead to a further multiplier effect. In those regions donating investment and labour, the Keynesian multiplier would work in reverse, causing a fall in aggregate income beyond that due to the initial out-migration. The relative economic prosperity of the two regions would diverge with any net flow in one direction. Thus, the tendency to move to an area of greater reward could exacerbate, not mitigate, regional economic disadvantages. Clearly, this is at odds with the atomistic neo-classical models where trade improves well-being.

Thirlwall (1982, 1992) and Fothergill and Gudgin (1982) have postulated that manufacturing has certain desirable qualities that agriculture and the service sector would be hard-pressed to replicate. Thirlwall (1980) suggested that manufacturing has growth inducing characteristics, summarised by the Verdoorn and balance of payments effects, which make a strong engineering base essential for a vibrant economy. The Dixon–Thirlwall–Kaldor model, and Thirlwall's Balance of Payments Constraint hypothesis suggest that regional growth disparities are a function of relative income [and price] elasticities for the goods and services the region trades. Indeed, in the long-run, a peripheral region's growth is constrained to be no faster than that permitted by its balance of payments.

With any income growth, those regions that produce high-income elasticity goods should benefit the most. Again, the industrial structure theme is evident. McCombie (1988) points out that the staple industries of the UK, which produce goods with relatively low-income elasticities, are concentrated in the north and west. Thus, regional problems are balance of payments problems. Taking this one stage further, food, particularly unprocessed food and mineral commodities, have low-income elasticities, which could limit the growth of the rural region to be slower than urban areas. Thus, Thirlwall's model predicts that the rural area dependent on low-income elastic goods will grow slowly and exhibit the same growth constraints as poor, declining regions. Worse, the rural attached to a declining urban area is doubly fated. Moreover, if a region faces large leakages in the form of net imports, government transfers to the region could be altered under the general heading of regional policy. In the absence of such fiscal transfers, local demand would be curtailed, revealing [greater] excess capacity, some of which may be scrapped, reducing aggregate demand still further. In a dynamic sense, the drop in demand could lead to a dampening of investment leading to a decline in the rate of output growth and technological progress. This, in turn, should undermine the slow process of improving of the income elasticity characteristics of exports and hence their desirability, so worsening the region's long-run net leakage problem and setting a vicious circle in motion. Lower wages and out-migration would result. If this out-flow is slower than the natural growth of the working population, adverse labour market characteristics become persistent.

Krugman (1981, 1991) described a cumulative process that is based on external economies and leads to a core and a periphery. A telling part of Krugman's (1991) discussions is that a two-region model predicts an agricultural region that becomes the periphery and the other, the manufacturing one, the core region. Through agglomerative economies, the relative price of manufactured goods falls compared with those of the other region, profits are positive, capital stocks grow and further growth ensues. Krugman points out that this process can continue until one region is the sole producer of manufactured goods.

Industrial structure and its evolution

The performance of the region, its trade cycle and its ability to disperse an asymmetric shock are associated with its industrial structure. Here, industrial economics provides useful insights. In a sense, the production function, which is not specific about the industrial mix or spatial unit, sidesteps key local wealth-generating advantages or limitations. How this mix and its subtle variations evolve are, in part, associated, with the changing role of mobile capital (Massey, 1979) but also with networks of economic agents (Storper, 1997). The urban environment implies a relatively densely populated area with a set of production activities that are distinguished from rural ones. The rural economy is associated with land intensive production activities and a less dense population than the urban.

Not dissimilar to export base models, the industrial mix of a territory strongly affects a territory's economic fortunes. This mix, although not static, is possibly locked-in to a process of industrial evolution that is relatively persistent. Massey (1979) develops a historical perspective to explain the change of relative territorial competitive advantages, based on a spatial division of labour. This term refers to the specialisation of certain areas in particular skills or functions.

Massey shows how a round of new investment in factories, labour skills, processes, and products made by an industry at a given period of time, builds on the consequences of previous rounds. Take for example, a round of investment in the car industry. This investment would be concentrated in certain areas reflecting the uneven distribution of the spatial attributes required for car production. The impact of this investment would change the skills and relative cost advantages of the host territories and thus alter the attractiveness of those districts for the next round of new investment. This could enhance an already advantaged area. Coventry, in the heart of England, inherited an industrial and skills structure associated with watchmaking in the nineteenth century. This industry became the foundation for bicycle fabrication, and through it the motor industry flourished (Hobsbawm, 1968). Car fabrication skills are transferable to the aircraft industry. This would entice aircraft manufacturing to be situated in close proximity to car fabrication. This example illustrates how each round forms a layer of economic sediment that becomes the basis of the next round of investment. This process would apply to all industries and all districts. The decline of a particular industry would affect those areas that specialised in it. The more specialised the area, the greater the local economic disruption when one of the staple industries declines.

Local growth prospects are based on the exploitation of previous innovations, given an earlier technological opportunity set. Industries survive by producing products or services in demand. They flourish by improving production techniques, reinventing divisions of labour and reinvesting capital for further expansion. Spatial competitive advantage is created through investment, but this advantage may come at a price. Not only is the current investment-induced spatial advantage relatively inflexible, it also automatically narrows the range of product, process and potential developments available to a territory. The current industrial structure will preclude investments in a range of future opportunities. Changes in tastes and technological opportunity will alter competitive advantages. The scope of industries to respond to these changes in tastes and technological opportunities will be limited by the inherited characteristics of the local environment. Hence, the future growth trajectory of a region is strongly influenced by the investment decisions of the past. Although this does not preclude the rural economy from high value-added production, it lacks the concentration of resources that might encourage investment from a new round to locate there.

In keeping with Massey, Storper (1995) stresses the point that development is *path dependent*, where the outcome of spatial competition is, to a great extent, influenced by historical accidents. Storper (1992) defines lock-in as relatively resistant to change. If an economy is locked-in to a certain development path, then the long-term rate of growth of income in that territory is unlikely to be affected by short-run activity. As such, lock-in could be viewed in reverse. The possibility for local entrepreneurs to pursue certain opportunities and, hence, the economy to follow a potentially fertile development path can be made uneconomic because the necessary structures have not been laid down in previous investment rounds in sufficient quantity or quality. If this is so, policy directed at permanently increasing the rate of growth of an area could be rendered ineffective.

For some schools of regional thought there are phases in capitalism associated with long waves, technologies or styles. These are water, steam transport, steel and electricity, the Fordist style, and microelectronics and biotechnology. Tylecote (1991) argues that these styles present new factors of production that are clearly cheap by existing standards. These foster further innovations. One can see Massey's rounds of investment and path dependency in this long wave context. Marshall (1987) characterises each regional employment growth pattern for Great Britain in the context of long or carrier-waves. The fortunes of a region are linked to the industries that it hosts. Some British regions have benefited more than others by certain long waves. The north-east of England flourished in the eras of steam transport and steel but has been passed by by later rounds of investment.

The role of the region – or the city

In many newer (e.g. Porter, 1990; Storper and Walker, 1989), and traditional theories (e.g. Perroux, 1950), there is an emphasis on long-run regional competitiveness emerging from innovation that becomes associated with the clustering of firms in an agglomeration. *De facto*, regional growth models feature firms that are closely associated industrially and physically – regional growth is modelled on urban competitiveness.

The agglomeration economy is picked up in much of regional economics. One of the major contributions, due to Perroux (1950), concerns the growth pole. A propulsive economic unit, probably a large monopolist or oligopolist that had developed a 'Schumpeterian' innovation, would encourage growth in other businesses around it, such as happened in the Coventry car industry. These firms would complement one another's activities while the propulsive unit would enhance their growth. The propulsive unit would exploit internal economies of scale and engage in more innovation, enhancing its cost advantages. Hence, the propulsive unit and its associated firms form what is known as a growth pole; that is, a centre of closely related firms or industries that, both through scale economies and through forward and backward links, achieves co-locational advantages with other businesses in a Marshallian sense. As profits and wages would be higher, this growth pole would attract better quality factors from non-growth pole areas. This has a dual effect: it enhances the competitive position of the growth pole and undermines the non-growth pole areas (polarisation). However, through the wealth generated, some of this growth may spread to other areas via driving up land prices and wages or increasing the size of the local market for other goods and services. Myrdal (1957), writing at about the same time as Perroux and working from the same observation, produces a similar analysis. He uses the term 'cumulative causation' to explain differences in regional growth. Given the concentration on a central innovation, the growth pole conceptualisation is consistent with Massey's work and path dependency.

New International Division of Labour

Massey's spatial division of labour model explained how industrial structures evolve. Agglomeration economies focused industry in cities, with the distribution of industry that emerged in the nineteenth century marking urban areas as specialising in certain products that utilised certain skills. However, with the rise of the highly vertically integrated oligopoly and the shift towards 'monopoly capitalism' the exploitation of opportunity changed. The conceptualisation of a division of labour within global systems of production, expressed as the New International Division of Labour (NIDL), emerged in the 1960s reporting on a period of late Fordism. Massey (1979), in her key work, 'In what sense a regional problem?', outlined how regional differences were exploited. The global systems version of this, due to Wallerstein, suggests that there is spatial specialisation for the headquarters, R&D functions and routine production but also that the multi-plant, multinational was using space in a different way to the one predicted by a traditional spatial division of labour from trade theory. Rather than utilising specialist knowledge or skill, the firm was using the location as part of a global production strategy.

The substitution of the biotech fifth wave for the late variety of the Fordist style became a key focus of analysis. The mass produced product increasingly served a homogenised international market. What was once the domain of the skilled or semi-skilled worker could be replaced by sophisticated machinery, relieving the firm of the need to be based near those pools of labour, which, in the 1960s, were becoming more militant and expensive to manage. The improvement in technology, vertical integration and large pools of cheap labour meant that the branch plant became footloose and this led to a reconsideration of the reshaping of economic terrain. The first wave of production relocations concerned the move away from the urban area. The disagglomerative effects of rising urban congestion and rising land and labour costs led to the move to more rural (so called urban–rural shift), but well connected areas. The labour was cheaper, less skilled, less unionised and fresh. The firm could hire more flexible workers on limited-term contracts. Fothergill and Gudgin identified large cities as a major disadvantage to a region. Further shifts included production moving to designated high-unemployment areas to benefit from the regional grants available in those blighted territories. The shifts became international and then global with the shift to cheap labour countries, such as Spain and the industrialising world. The branch plant of one company could sit next to another from a different industry, not because they were drawing from the same pool of labour or sharing information, but because both were looking for cheap, flexible workers available locally. The skill element, the one that gave the region its flavour, was not such a strong locational driver.

The NIDL envisages the rural attracting growth-enhancing investment, but only to exploit the cheap land and labour on offer. Like developing countries, there can be a desire in the rural to break the cycle of low-income growth and dependence on primary produce. Direct (foreign) investment (DFI) might offer a way to change the situation, implied by the rounds of investment-path dependence perceptions of development. Accepting some form of exploitation now with the possibility of development in the future is a route to change. Indeed, other DFI may follow. Alternatively, as with Thirlwall's models, the rural may be stuck in a similar cycle to the declining region, where the DFI does not change the competitive disadvantage of the area, but reinforces it.

The social side of capital

In a sense, the NIDL weakens agglomerational benefits. The branch plants are so feebly interlinked into the local economy that they have been described as cathedrals in the desert (Amin and Malmberg, 1992). There has been a reaction to this with the re-emergence of interest in the region as a distinct entity and the engine of growth in a post-Fordist era, the age of flexible specialisation, or networks, or alliance capitalism. Many models envisaged the collapse of the late-Fordist model upon which the NIDL is based. However, recent activity in the developing world, such as in manufacturing in China (e.g., Foxconn), or in the service sector in the developed world (e.g., call centres), suggest that the 'cathedrals' are still being filled with less skilled, low-paid workers.

Piore and Sabel (1984) engendered interest in regions anew with the notion of Flexible Specialisation. They propose that mass production superseded craft by 1900 as the major mode of production. This mass production was itself superseded in the 1970s by flexible specialisation. This form entails a wide range of products for highly differentiated markets. These are constantly amended in response to fluid market tastes/conditions. Competition encourages innovation. Cooperation is achieved through social learning and more formal business rules/institutions, which create/sustain a local business community. The production system is flexible either through changing suppliers or outputs. Networks of small, highly specialised firms share knowledge, mutually sub-contract, and develop new, high-income elastic goods/improved processes.

Firms employ flexible technologies and general-purpose machines. Production innovation is not so constrained by expensive capital investment. Workers are flexible and multi-skilled and products are conceived and developed by related groups. These are often highly agglomerated, creating a new form of Marshall's industrial district. This approach, which is institutionally oriented, revolves around decentralised large firms/groups or industrial districts of small- and medium-sized firms. The former behaves like an industrial district whereas the latter is one. Both feature the utilisation of common services of the type that feature in external economies of scale. New industrial districts have characteristics that go beyond those envisaged by Marshall. These include supportive social and cultural attributes and a network of public and private institutions that help bond the small- and medium-sized firms into a cluster. Amin (1999) describes this as 'institutional thickness'. There is a high trust environment. Trust is a central concept in many new regional models involving networks. How it emerges is contested, but all views require contact, most often face-to-face interaction, for it to reduce transaction costs. For example, it could be fostered by long-term association and through unwritten rules that govern relationships between individuals and networks of civic engagement. The economic actors benefit from high social capital. For example, based on a number of successful clusters of SMEs collectively called the 'Third Italy' (Emilia-Romagna, Veneto, Trentino and Toscana), small craft and artisanal firms produce furniture, luxury apparel, machine tools and ceramics.

The social side of agglomerations spawned a series of variations on the new industrial district. The Milieu is a socio-economic environment of a region, engendered by the interactions of firms, institutions and workers, which, through collective and institutional learning, reduce uncertainties during changes in technological paradigms (after Sternberg, 1996). Learning is fostered by supplier–buyer relations, especially face-to-face, and other contacts with firms/employees. As such, proximity is a key element. An Innovative Milieu has information technology at its heart. Since protagonist firms incorporate advanced technologies drawn from the application of scientific and technological expertise, high-technology firms are not found just in manufacturing. Existing firm R&D networks, government or university establishments could provide this. A sufficiently large pool of mobile technical employees needs to be available, plus entrepreneurs interested in investing in new technology. Again, there is a concentration. High-technology industries show a clear tendency to form spatial clusters, such as Silicon Valley, Cambridge, Grenoble and Sophia Antipolis.

Storper (1997), who coined the phrase 'untraded dependencies', suggests that a distinctive feature of places in which globalisation is consistent with the localisation of economic activity is the strength of their 'relational assets', which draw on the social properties of networks in which economic agents are implicated. They include tacit knowledge based on face-to-face interaction, embedded routines, habits and norms, local conventions of communication and interaction, and reciprocity, which promote a high-trust environment. The 'learning region' benefits from the knowledge accumulation properties of local, industry-specialist business networks. These networks of reciprocated trust, shared know-how, spillover expertise and strong enterprise support systems are sources of learning. Again, operating within a supportive, high-trust environment, the more valuable informal knowledge for competitive advantage is best generated and transferred through face-to-face contact. Indeed, this has been described as 'buzz' (Storper and Venables, 2004).

Through the trust engendered by the network of input–output relations due to inter-firm trading, Scott's (1998) version highlights the reduction of transactions costs. Thus, flexible industrialisation formed the basis for the new industrial district that emerged in the 1980s. Where the trading involves complex issues, tacit knowledge, or trust, these transaction costs that need to be accommodated, vary with distance. Again, the localisation of production and exchange promotes higher added-value. Network and milieu concepts differ in that networks involve formal input–output relations, while milieu links are less formal or persistent.

Porter's (1990) 'competitive advantage of nations' is, in fact, a regional model where the clustering of related businesses enhances the drive for innovativeness and, hence, provides the competitive edge of the firms concerned to compete in international markets. The degree of competitiveness of the localised supporting industries underpins the competitive advantage of the firms producing the final products.

Compensation in wages and housing

In addition to growth models and the emphasis on exchange, another body of work relevant to the rural economy concerns the role of compensation and locational choice. Here, an implicit value is placed on non-pecuniary aspects of living, such as quality of life. Curry and Webber (2012), in their work on rural England and economic performance, highlight the shift of policy emphasis from productivity goals to those concerning lifestyle choices and quality of life. Rural, particularly remote rural, areas are not expected to 'keep up' with productivity growth elsewhere.

One would expect that working in an attractive environment is preferable to an unattractive one and will be taken into account by an individual when selecting from employment opportunities. Proponents of equilibrium migration models view labour migration as driven primarily by changes in the demand for and supply of consumption amenities. Equilibrium occurs when utility is equal across space. The 'compensation', in this case, is for differences in amenities. This can be extended to housing. Proximity to both job opportunities and amenities form part of locational decision for workers. As a non-pecuniary reward from living and working, a local amenity should drive wages down and house prices up. If the rural environment is deemed an amenity, its housing would be less affordable than elsewhere *ceteris paribus*.

DiPasquale and Wheaton (1996) assert that a local housing market area is derived from workers being able to substitute residences without changing jobs, or switching jobs without moving home. Thus, it is difficult to distinguish housing market delineation from labour market definitions. From McCann's analysis of housing markets, one can explore the role of commuting and amenities/disamenities using trade-off or compensation analysis. Assuming that higher income families value amenities and space but seek to limit their exposure to commuting and disamenities personified by an unpleasant urban employment centre, utility may increase with distance from it. In Figure 3.3 there is an analysis of three income groups associated with a common employment centre. The low-income group has little recourse to alternative transport and so is limited to the bus service within the urban area. It is presumed that middle and higher income groups are better able to move away from the unattractive environment. The medium income group follows the pattern of high-income family group but is outbid for space beyond *d2*. It is likely that the high rich group, valuing space, will live in the rural but commute to the urban. The wealth generated in the urban is spread to the 'commutable rural'. Ali *et al.* (2011) show the blurring of urban and rural labour and, hence, housing markets. This presents the disadvantaged rural periphery in a very different light. The commutable rural is wealthier than would warrant the peripheral epithet. Based on a representative life cycle, a high-income family winning the space beyond *d2* is likely to be mature, of a relatively high social-economic group, and climbing a housing ladder, of which the dwelling in the rural village could be a significant rung. It is the non-commutable rural where the term 'peripheral' is more appropriate: the commutable and the non-commutable rural have distinct characteristics that put them in separate territorial groupings.

The issue of housing and commuting makes it clear that the city-region or the functional urban region provides a better unit of analysis than the rural or urban as separate entities. These are cities (concentrations of employment or core areas) supplemented by all spatial units from which more workers commute to the core areas in question than to some others (Cheshire and

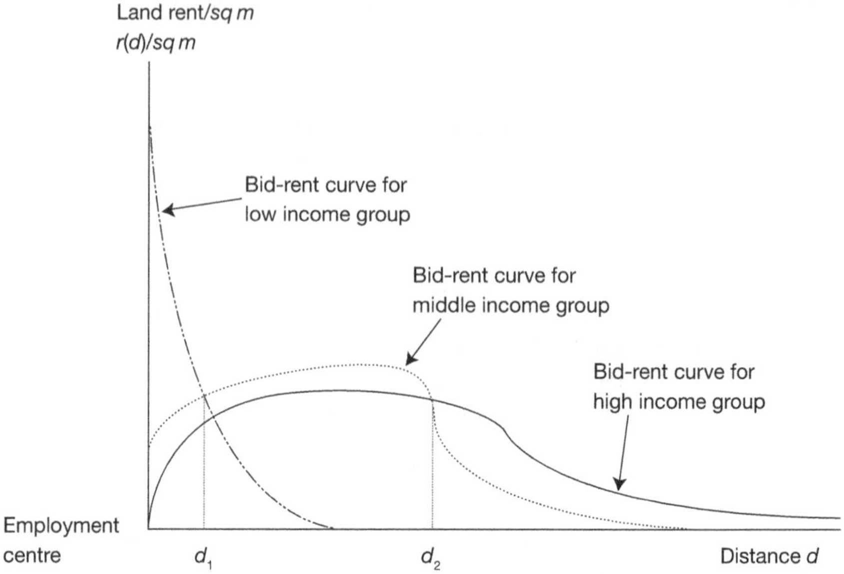

Figure 3.3 Bid-rent analysis of a house renting market with an unattractive city centre

Carbonaro, 1996). If there is no major employment centre and the population is dispersed, the existence of an amenity in an area, such as the Lake District in Cumbria in the north-west of England, is likely to be characterised by expensive housing but low wages. Employment would be dominated by hotels and catering with some low-reward farming. The economic performance would be characterised by weak productivity growth but an attractive quality of life. In this context, the policy maker's measure of success is likely to favour the latter (Curry and Webber, 2012).

One can see a commuting effect operating in the East Midlands of England. Output for Leicester and Nottingham suggest that they are major centres of industry. The gross values added (GVA) per capita in 2007 were £21,311 and £26,106 respectively; both above the East Midlands' average of £17,614. The gross disposable household income (GDHI) picture offers a different story. Both Leicester (£10,760) and Nottingham (£10,081) were below the East Midlands benchmark (£13,178). In 2008, they were in the bottom five of the NUTS2 regions in the UK. The wealth generated in the cities is 'commuted' or spread to the more rural areas. Poorer people tend to live in inner cities, pushing down the estimate of average income. As posited above, some richer people live outside, in more rural territories, pushing up house prices. Thus, there is a patchwork of rich and poor in both the urban and the commutable rural.

Final thoughts

Terluin (2003) finds hope for the rural in the ideas of new economic geography. These do not explicitly exclude the rural but emphasise a concentration of businesses. Terluin does concede that not all rural areas can benefit and the emphasis is on non-agricultural growth. These new ideas have an implicit predisposition towards manufacturing and services, where innovations in product and process are possible and income elasticity is relatively high. There is also a bias towards tradeable output.

The rural must be defined carefully for policy purposes. Partridge *et al.* (2010) assert that the key to a strategic approach to rural development policy is an understanding of rural–urban integration through commuting affecting the decision over local job creation vs. integrated rural–urban labour market initiatives. Where the rural benefits from the spread effects of commuting to the local city, it can be seen as part of an urban system. Thus, the focus of growth for policy makers, the city-region, would include part of the non-urban space within its spatial policy boundary. From Figure 3.1 it is evident that cities are surrounded by less densely populated areas that are close enough to commute from. This boundary could be drawn up by, say, Local Enterprise Partnerships. In Figure 3.4, using population densities and setting a limit of influence to around 20 km, the distance that the average rural commuters travel to work (Littlefield and Nash, 2008), one could draw up a market town (medium grey), an urban (dark grey), a commutable rural (medium-dark grey, vertical stripes), and remote rural (light grey, vertical stripes) delineation. The Lincolnshire and North Yorkshire areas stand apart from the central urbanised belt as having few population centres and low concentrations of population, employment and jobs.

Segregating the rural into commuting and non-commuting would offer policy makers a less heterogeneous rural space so that initiatives better focus on the drivers of growth for the local area. The more remote rural would face poor and declining infrastructure and social services, loss of population, local monopoly suppliers and insufficient local market demand. This countryside would have more in common with a remote rural area in another county than with the nearest city.

More traditional views of regional economics would not recognise this segregation into urban, commutable rural and remote rural. With all spaces having a common production function, a slow growing rural is a market failure. Recognising that the remote rural cannot 'keep up' with productivity growth elsewhere is, in part, an acknowledgment of the limitations of the traditional growth models. Indeed, it also suggests that the disadvantages that the remote rural faces cannot be overcome by the (by-)products of greater trust and social interaction. The models that rely on social capital and trust commonly emphasise geographical proximity and the high added value of development, but not necessarily high-tech products. There is no reason to presume that the strength of rural 'relational assets' would be not be as high as elsewhere,

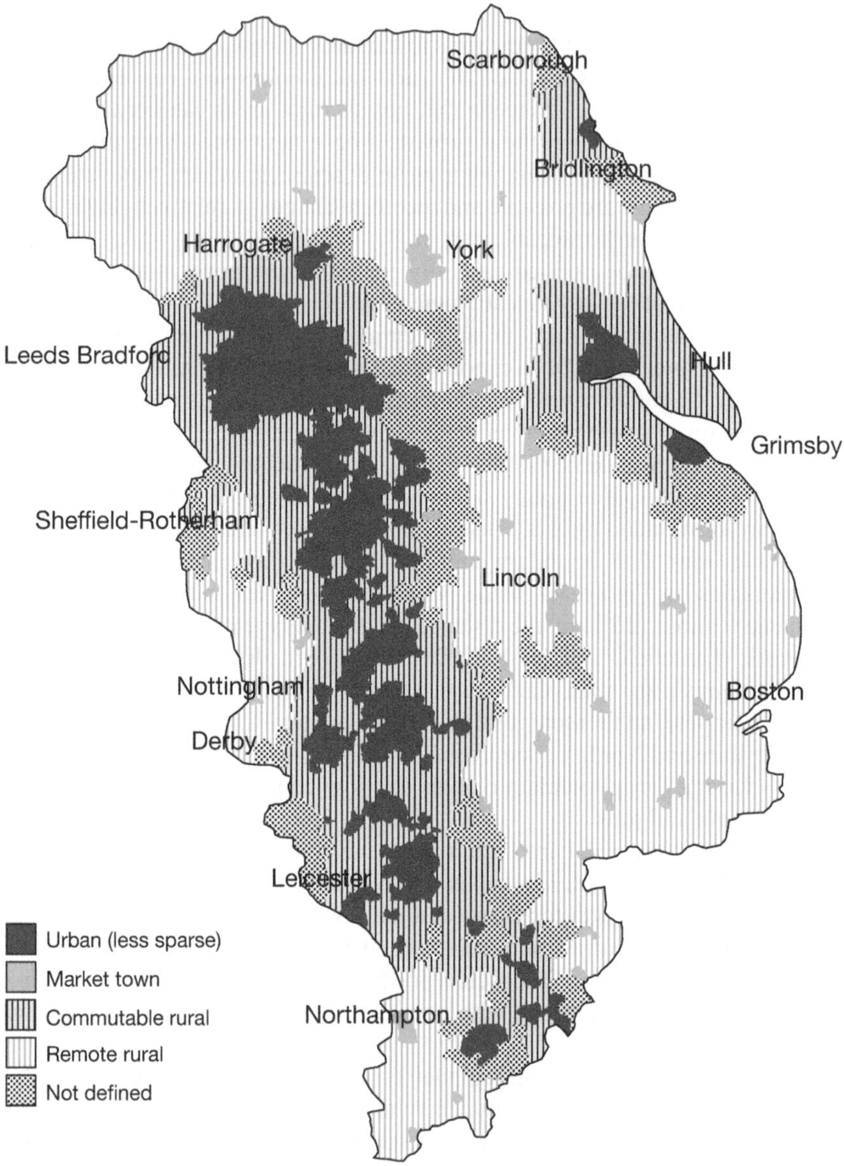

Figure 3.4 Cities and their commutable zones in Yorkshire and Humberside and the East Midlands of England

particularly if they must emerge over decades. However, if the entrepreneurial population needs to be reinvigorated with new blood, and trust comes from interaction, the remote rural is at a disadvantage. The commutable rural should benefit from the regular influxes of high income, bright, cash-rich, skilled urban, perhaps middle-aged commuters, who could live in enclaves, building up trust, not because of the commercial, but because of their social links. It is the rural beyond the reach of these urban agglomerative effects that is more likely to be subject to the classic rural disadvantages.

As a final technical point, the distinction between urban and rural depends on the extent of the concentration of economic activity. As indicated, agglomerations have distinct growth advantages. It is unlikely that a rural area can grow beyond a certain limit without becoming an urban centre, implying the rural is characterised by low densities of population, jobs and firms. It is posited that parts of the rural offer a higher quality of life than the urban. In a remote rural world, preserving and promoting the environment as a local amenity emphasising well-being, rather than productivity, is something policy could target successfully. To compensate for the disadvantages of remoteness, a successful rural territory would need to control expansion. Unsympathetic expansion could undermine those features that make the area attractive to certain incomers, such as a certain pace of life or an 'unspoilt' built environment. The gentrification that is implied by such a policy could, if too rapid, alter the social character of the locale threatening its appeal.

References

Ali, K., Olfert, M. and Partridge, M. (2011) Urban footprints in rural Canada: Employment spillovers by city size, *Regional Studies*, 45(2): 239–60.

Amin, A. (1999) An institutionalist perspective on regional economic development, *International Journal of Urban and Regional Research*, 23: 365–78.

Amin, A. and Malmberg, A. (1992) Competing structural and institutional influences on the geography of production in Europe, *Environment and Planning* A, 24: 401–16.

Bibby, P. and Shepherd, J. (2004) Developing a New Classification of Urban and Rural Areas for Policy Purposes – The Methodology. Office for National Statistics. Available at: www.statistics.gov.uk/geography/downloads/Methodology_Report.pdf (accessed 20 October 12).

Bogart, W. (1998) *The Economics of Cities and Suburbs*. Upper Saddle River, NJ: Prentice Hall.

Cheshire, P. and Carbonaro, G. (1996) Urban economic growth in Europe: Testing theory and policy prescriptions, *Urban Studies*, 33(7): 1111–28.

Curry, N. and Webber, D. (2012) Economic performance of rural England, *Regional Studies*, 46(3): 279–91.

DiPasquale, D. and Wheaton, W. (1996) *Urban Economics and Real Estate Markets*. Englewood Cliffs, NJ: Prentice Hall.

Dixon, R. and Thirlwall, A. (1975) A model of regional growth rate differentials along Kaldorian lines, *Oxford Economic Papers*, 27: 201–14.

Fothergill, S. and Gudgin, G. (1982) *Unequal Growth*. Guildford, UK: Heinemann.

Giuliano, G. and Small, K. (1991) Subcenters in the Los Angeles region, *Journal of Regional Science and Urban Economics*, 21: 163–82.

Hobsbawm, E. (1968) *Industry and Empire*. London: Wiedenfeld & Nicolson.

Jaffe, A., Trajtenberg, M. and Henderson, R. (1994) Geographic localization of knowledge spillovers as evidenced by patent citation, *Quarterly Journal of Economics*, 109: 577–98.

Krugman, P. (1981) Trade, accumulation, and uneven development, *Journal of Development Economics*, 8: 149–61.

Krugman, P. (1991) *Geography and Trade*. Cambridge, MA: MIT Press.

Krugman, P. and Obstfeld, M. (2006) *International Economics: Theory and Practice*, 7th edition. New York: Pearson.

Littlefield, M. and Nash, A. (2008) Commuting Patterns as at the 2001 Census, and their Relationship with Modes of Transport and Types of Occupation. ONS. Available at: www.neighbourhood.statistics.gov.uk/HTMLDocs/images/Commuting%20by%20Occupation%20and%20Transport%20-%20Final%20for%20pdf_tcm97–70153.pdf (accessed 20 October 2012).

Marshall, A. (1920) *Principles of Economics*. London: Macmillan.

Marshall, M. (1987) *Long Waves of Regional Development*. London: Macmillan.

Massey, D. (1979) In what sense a regional problem? *Regional Studies*, 13: 233–43.

McCann, P. (2001) *Urban and Regional Economics*. Oxford: Oxford University Press.

McCombie, J. (1988) A synoptic view of regional growth and unemployment: II the post-Keynesian theory, *Urban Studies*, 25: 399–417.

Myrdal, G. (1957) *Economic Theory and Underdeveloped Regions*. London: Duckworth.

North, D. (1955) Location theory and regional economic growth, *Journal of Political Economy*, 63: 243–58.

Partridge, M., Ali, K. and Olfert, M. (2010) Rural-to-urban commuting: Three degrees of integration, *Growth and Change*, 41(2): 303–35.

Perroux, F. (1950) Economic space, theory and applications, *Quarterly Journal of Economics*, 64: 89–104.

Piore, M. and Sabel, C. (1984) *The Second Industrial Divide*. New York: Basic Books.

Porter, M. (1990) *The Competitive Advantage of Nations*. New York: Free Press.

RERC (Rural Evidence Research Centre) (2004) Technical Methodology Paper for Rural–Urban Definition, DEFRA. Available at: www.defra.gov.uk/statistics/rural/what-is-rural/rural-urban-definition (accessed 20 October 2012).

Richardson, H. (1973) *Regional Growth Theory*. London: Macmillan.

Richardson, H. (1978) *Regional and Urban Economics*. London: Penguin.

Rosenthal, S. and Strange, W. (2003) Geography, industrial organization, and agglomeration, *The Review of Economics and Statistics*, 85(2): 377–93.

Scott, A. (1998) *Regions and the World Economy*. Oxford: Oxford University Press.

Statistical Digest of Rural England (2012) Available at: www.defra.gov.uk/publications/files/201209-rural-stats-digest.pdf (accessed 1 December 2012).

Sternberg, F. (1996) Regional growth theories and high-tech regions, *International Journal of Urban and Regional Research*, 20: 518–38.

Storper, M. (1992) The limits to globalization: Technology districts and international trade, *Economic Geography*, 68: 60–93.

Storper, M. (1995) The resurgence of regional economies, ten years later: The region as a nexus of untraded interdependencies, *European Urban and Regional Studies*, 2: 191–222.

Storper, M. (1997) *The Regional World*. London: Guilford Press.
Storper, M. and Venables, A. (2004) Buzz: Face-to-face contact and the urban economy, *Journal of Economic Geography*, 4(4): 351–70.
Storper, M. and Walker, R. (1989) *The Capitalist Imperative: Territory, Technology, and Industrial Growth*. Oxford: Blackwell.
Terluin, I. (2003) Differences in economic development in rural regions of advanced countries: An overview and critical analysis of theories, *Journal of Rural Studies*, 19: 327–44.
Thirlwall, A. (1980) Regional problems are balance of payments problems, *Regional Studies*, 14: 419–25.
Thirlwall, A. (1982) Deindustrialization in the United Kingdom, *Lloyds Bank Review*, 144: 22–37.
Thirlwall, A. (1992) The balance of payments and economic performance, *National Westminster Bank Quarterly Review*, May: 2–11.
Tylecote, A. (1991) *The Long Wave in the World Economy*. London: Routledge.
Vickerman, R. (1984) *Urban Economics*. Salisbury, UK: Philip Allen.

4 The potential for rural cooperatives in the UK

Ignazio Cabras

Introduction

The aim of this paper is to set out and discuss cooperative organisations in rural areas in the UK. In particular, the author explores the potential offered by cooperatives in generating business opportunities as well as enhancing cohesion among individuals living in rural communities and villages. The different forms of cooperative and mutual initiatives are analysed with regard to fostering or discouraging growth and development in rural areas. In particular, cooperatives are investigated in relation to a number of issues faced by many rural communities in Britain, such as the disappearance of essential services and the achievement of sustainable development.

The structure of the paper comprises seven sections, including the introduction. The second section defines and distinguishes between communal ownership and cooperative and mutual ownership. The third section explores the structures and types of cooperatives in detail. The fourth section examines cooperative and mutual ownership, discussing the main causes of success. The fifth section focuses on rural cooperatives in Britain, analysing the case of cooperative-owned public houses. The sixth section discusses forms of support available for rural cooperatives in Britain. The seventh section concludes.

Communal ownership and cooperatives

Very frequently, communal ownership is assumed to be almost interchangeable with cooperative and mutual ownership. This misleading opinion is probably related to the historical development of the concept of ownership. Since Roman times, individual ownership and its related rights have always been addressed and clearly identified by rules and laws. These codes regulated and defined boundaries within which owners could exercise their rights. The same level of clarity did not apply to common land and goods, sometimes leaving the definition of communal ownership vague.

Communal ownership can be defined as an arrangement in which people who, for example, live in the same place or come from the same ethnic background, use an asset (typically land, using the fruits of the land) without excluding any others from using that asset. Land that is so communally owned is usually known as common land. Communal ownership played an important role in Britain, probably from before Roman times. Manorial and feudal structures established after the Norman Conquest, however, extended private ownership, with the result that communal ownership became a residual category (Woodin *et al.*, 2010). Nevertheless, communal ownership continued to be an important feature of British society until the eighteenth century, when much of the common land was enclosed by powerful landlords. Later attempts to redistribute land in the form of allotments failed to compensate for the loss of common land (Mingay, 1997). Since the end of the nineteenth century, however, there has been a renewed interest in communal ownership, starting with organisations such as the Land Nationalisation Society in 1892. Today, there are about 2,300 square miles of common land in England and Wales, with approximately 5,000 green spaces in towns and villages. These figures clearly indicate the continuing importance of communal ownership in Britain.

The development of communal ownership over time provided the terrain for the formation of other models of ownership, such as cooperative ownership (Woodin *et al.*, 2010). Cooperative and mutual organisations can be defined as voluntary, democratic and autonomous enterprises owned and run by and for their members, whether they are customers, employees or residents (Cooperatives UK, 2010). Forms of cooperative can be traced back to Roman times, and have been developed throughout different ages. Medieval guilds, for instance, can be assumed to be proto cooperative organisations. Similarly, forms of communal ownership can be found in different historical times, from prehistoric tribal systems up to early Christian sects. However, many authors (Hechter, 1986; Fairbairn, 1994; Birchall, 1997; Hind, 1997) identify the origin of the modern cooperative movement with the Rochdale Equitable Pioneers Society. This society was founded in 1844 by workers in the cotton industry who decided to unite their resources and work together in order to open a grocery shop and trade unadulterated food. Its main objective was to increase the possibility for members to buy basic goods at a lower price, giving customers a say in the business by conferring automatic membership on them (Fairbairn, 1994).

Today, cooperatives play an important role in British society. According to figures taken from the most recent report provided by Cooperatives UK (2012), their number in UK passed from 4,820 in 2008 to 5,933 in 2012, generating a turnover of £35.6 billion. The number of members in the UK has also been constantly increasing since the late 2000s, reaching 13.5 million in 2012. In this context, an overlap between communal ownership and cooperative/mutual ownership is not rare to find, especially in situations when these organisations operate in small communities.

Community benefit societies operating at sub-regional and local levels may present examples of this overlap. These societies are run primarily for the benefit of the community, implying that the interest of members and shareholders is secondary (Parliament, 2010). Community benefit societies have the power to pay interest on members' share capital, but they cannot distribute surpluses to members in the form of a dividend. Members of a community benefit society only have a right to the return of their capital, with no rights related to a share of the underlying assets (or equity). These rules normally make alternative provisions for the application of any surplus on a solvent termination (Parliament, 2010).

One form of cooperative is the mutual guarantee society (MGS), significantly present in Western Europe. This is a self-help initiative designed particularly for small companies in the area of financial services, usually set up by entrepreneurs in a region or sector with the assistance of public sector bodies or local economic associations, for example chambers of commerce, industry federations or banks specialising in credits to small and medium enterprises (SMEs) (European Commission, 2004). In a MGS, the capital is provided directly by the SMEs that apply for a loan guarantee in the form of cooperative or mutual shares. MGSs operate as an external guarantor who can increase the bank's lending readiness towards their SME members (European Commission, 2004).

There are also forms of cooperative/mutual ownership among social enterprises, a category of businesses that comprises a number of groups, societies and enterprises operating in sectors such as environment protection and social support. Only a few countries have a legal definition of what constitutes a social enterprise. Within the UK, social enterprises are defined as 'organisations with primarily social objectives, whose surpluses are principally reinvested for that purpose in the business or community, rather than being driven by the need to maximise profit for shareholders and owners' (DTI, 2002: 7). This definition focuses on two main aspects of social enterprise: their social objectives and the sustainability of the business (Defourny and Nyssens, 2006), leaving room for a variety of ownership cases which may include volunteering and charitable as well as domestic and private spheres (Woodin *et al.*, 2010).

This legal form for social enterprises, namely, community interest companies (CICs), was introduced into Britain in 2005 by the Companies Act approved the year before (Parliament, 2004). This Act allows for social enterprises that intend to utilise their profits and assets for the public good to take the form of a company but also provides some special features to ensure they are working for the benefit of the community. CICs are businesses with primarily social objectives; any profit or surplus generated by the company is principally reinvested within the company itself (to pursue its objectives) or in the community (Spear, 2005). CICs tackle a wide range of social and environmental issues and operate in all parts of the economy. CICs can be community enterprises and social firms as well as mutual organisations such as cooperatives, in which the type of control (e.g., decisions made by a small group of leaders or by all members together) and the nature of activities (e.g., paid or unpaid work) may change from case to case. In addition, the size of CICs can vary considerably in terms of employment and annual turnover, as these companies can operate locally, regionally, nationally or internationally (Regulator of CICs, 2012).

Peredo and Chrisman (2010) describe community benefit societies, social enterprises and forms of mutual ownership in relatively small communities as 'community-based enterprises' (CBEs). These originate entirely within the community, where residents join forces by creating a collective business venture, for example, a cooperative, which generates both economic and social development for the local area. Peredo and Chrisman (2010) refer to CBEs as a special kind of enterprise that resembles and embodies the social structure of the community from which and within which it operates. According to Somerville and McElwee, the existence of CBEs appears to be possible only in very specific communities with 'significant collectively owned cultural, social and ethnic endowments, high levels of solidarity among community members and receptivity to collective action, and exceptional ability to marshal and exploit social capital' (2011: 320). Finding these conditions concentrated in any community is a very challenging task. However, forms of enterprise displaying many of the characteristics of a CBE may exist in very small hamlets and villages located in spatially remote areas, where interactions and personal relationships among local residents may be facilitated and even strengthened by the context in which they live. Nevertheless, a relatively isolated context should not be assumed as the only factor that may create the right conditions for CBEs to exist. Frictions and disagreements among individuals are not rare to find, even within small communities located in rural and remote areas, and their presence has an impact on the making of any communal initiative, including enterprise initiatives (Van der Horst, 2008).

In principle and historically, therefore, it is possible to distinguish between communal ownership and cooperative ownership, but in contemporary practice it has to be recognised that the two can overlap to a significant extent.

Structure of cooperatives: definition and types

While cooperatives have evolved with regard to structure and functions significantly over time, the principles that underpinned the Rochdale Equitable Pioneers Society are still largely accepted today as the main foundation on which all cooperatives worldwide are based. However, cooperatives have developed and proliferated in a plethora of forms since then, entering into contact with other forms of businesses different in nature (e.g. social enterprises or charitable organisations) and breaking, in some cases, the link between membership and mutuality that characterises cooperative businesses. In addition, the expansion of the cooperative movement in the past century generated diverse situations that today characterise cooperative businesses located and operating in different areas of the world. While these businesses subscribe to the same basic cooperative principles, there are some attributes that are unique to cooperatives in Britain, Europe and North America.

In the 1990s, a new type of cooperative, namely New Generation Cooperatives (NGCs), attracted a lot of interest among researchers (Zeuli and Cropp, 2004). NGCs distinguish themselves from traditional cooperatives by self-imposed limitations on the number of members, the strict association between membership shares and delivery rights, and the possibility for members to sell their shares to other patrons. Shares in NGCs have a market value and their transferability to other members can influence the level of equity among members over time (Zeuli and Cropp, 2004). Alongside NGCs, Patron-Investment Cooperatives (PICs) appeared in the late 1990s. These types of cooperative allow non-member individuals to become investors, investing them with all the rights associated with membership. Zeuli and Radel (2005) point to the case of the Canadian multiple stakeholder model, which comprises three categories of members: users, workers and 'sustainers' – any person or organisation that invested in the cooperative (Girard and De Bortoli, 2004).

NGCs may introduce some interesting features into cooperative business, but these features can deeply modify the nature of the cooperative form. By allowing external investments of any kind, members are liable to lose control over the enterprise. Further, with the opening to non-members with basically the same rights as members, a cooperative organisation ceases *de facto* to be a cooperative as defined by Cooperatives UK (2010). The introduction of categories of stakeholders may also undermine the cooperative status of the organisation, unless there are strict rules in place concerning the roles of those categories and the valuation of their shares in the cooperative.

In the UK, cooperatives operating as community benefit societies present some interesting attributes and features. Their members can pull out of the organisation without particular restrictions and without incurring any loss specifically associated with their withdrawal. The maximum amount an individual shareholder can hold is £20,000 in share value, although there is no limitation with regard to the number of shares a society decides to issue. The interest paid to shareholders is limited to 'what is necessary to obtain and retain enough capital to run the business' (Brown, 2008). Cooperatives operating as community benefit societies can also install an asset lock, which prevents the society being sold and the proceeds distributed among shareholders. This aspect makes these societies extremely valuable, particularly when it comes to raising investment capital, as asset locks provide tangible guarantees for the investment made by members (Cabras, 2011). Finally, this form of cooperative organisation is treated differently from other types of companies when raising share capital from the public. For instance, they do not need to obtain authorisation from the Financial Services Authority (FSA) in the case of share capital withdrawal, while other companies would need to. Share capital withdrawn is also not subject to the Money Laundering Regulation (Financial Services 2007). Moreover, these cooperatives benefit from other exemptions regarding the approval of financial promotions.

The structure of a cooperative may vary also in relation to the type of asset owned and managed by the organisation. This statement assumes even more importance with regard to cooperatives operating as community benefit societies. In this case, Aiken *et al.* (2011) identify three categories: 'stewards', 'community developers' and 'entrepreneurs'. 'Stewards' are mainly small groups who control a long-standing asset (e.g. a building or a dedicated space) and use it for initiatives or events held within the community. Stewards' level of income is generally very small, and they operate mainly with the support of volunteers on an informal basis. 'Community developers' are medium-sized organisations which own and manage a number of assets located in proximity to the community they serve. Their structure is more complex and diverse, with employed paid staff and a mix of sources in relation to generated income. Finally, 'entrepreneurs' are larger organisations, comprising a mix of assets, mainly capital intensive, used to pursue social and commercial purposes. Aiken *et al.* (2011) indicate that community developers and entrepreneurs are more concentrated in urban areas with the majority of stewards located in suburban peripheries and rural areas.

Cooperatives and rurality

One of the most important advantages of cooperatives is probably associated with their ability to raise investment capital, a vital function of any enterprise. While investor-owned businesses invite the purchase of share capital as a speculation where control of the capital is in proportion to the amount invested, members in a cooperative contribute with capital in equal manner, eliminating speculation and unlocking resources by spreading control and risk among members (Robb *et al.*, 2010). Nilsson *et al.* describe the financial capital of a cooperative as a sort of conversion of the social capital embedded among its members, often generated 'because they have voluntarily abstained from some patronage funds' (2012: 189). This function assumes even more importance for small and medium businesses located in areas where finding sufficient capital for funding entrepreneurial initiatives is more difficult. This could help to explain why the vast majority of cooperatives, mainly in the form of community benefit societies, are located in villages and rural areas (Brown, 2008).

The success of cooperatives depends on a number of factors. Their structure, for instance, guarantees an equal say to each member with regard to decisions affecting their society and avoids the possibility of any member winning a majority vote by purchasing or accumulating shares. The level of loyalty and commitment of members towards a cooperative and the level of trust among members are two fundamental factors on which cooperatives base their success. Van Vugt and Hart (2004) state that members' loyalty within cooperatives depends highly on the level of 'social identity', defined as 'the reduced differentiation between one's own and others' outcomes associated with in-group formation' (Brewer, 1979). In cooperatives, particularly in small ones, membership is lived as a group experience, rather than experienced as a business initiative. This situation implies that members are ready to make personal sacrifices in order to help the group's welfare. According to Van Vugt and Hart, 'once people start to identify with their group, their welfare becomes intertwined with the welfare of the group' (2004: 586).

Individuals' identification with the cooperative's mission works as an incentive for members to engage and join in the cooperative's initiatives and reduces the risk of members' withdrawal (Nilsson *et al.*, 2012). In addition, it reduces the number of 'sleeping memberships', i.e. members who do not take an active part in the group life. Apparently, sleeping membership becomes more common when cooperatives become larger. On the other hand, participation in the life of a cooperative may depend on more specific characteristics proper to each member. Craig (1980) classifies members into four groups: customers, enthusiasts, disillusioned and organisational people. When organisational people outnumber the other three groups over time, cooperative organisations stop focusing on their initial member-centred goals (e.g. provision of good quality services) in favour of more corporate-oriented objectives, such as profitability and financial stability. This statement partially supports findings from studies conducted by Zeuli *et al.* (2004) on US cooperatives, indicating that members' identification tends to decrease in large national cooperatives, but stays high in small and rural cooperatives.

The rural dimension appears to be an ideal incubator for cooperative initiatives. In rural areas, joining a local cooperative may reinforce the sense of members belonging to a specific group. Bhunyan (2007) indicates that active membership in small cooperatives enhances social relationships inside the cooperative and increases members' interest and satisfaction, creating a sort of a 'circle of trust' that strengthens their sense of proprietorship (Zeuli *et al.*, 2004). The process is also facilitated by the socio-economic context in which these individuals live, which presents a reduced diversity in terms of employment and variety of lifestyles compared to major urban centres, bringing a higher level of uniformity when it comes to evaluate and decide about communal needs and priorities (Ray, 1998). Cooperatives 'provide vital local places where people have the chance to interact [and] can be very inclusive, involving many different stakeholder groups within a community' (Zeuli *et al.*, 2004: 21). In particular, cooperatives in small rural villages are likely to have the majority of villagers among their shareholders. This situation produces positive effects for the community itself in terms of social networking and engagement (Cabras, 2011). If a high proportion of a rural community are active in local networks, then this may benefit any cooperative initiative in that community, particularly with regard to members' loyalty and trust.

The presence of cooperatives in rural areas brings a number of benefits with regard to community development. Higher levels of community cohesion (defined as the amount of positive interactions and interrelations in the community) and social engagement within rural communities are often at the basis of communal initiatives undertaken by groups of individuals at a local level. This is a significant factor in the functioning of cooperatives located in rural areas. A number of studies (Borzaga and Spear, 2004; Zeuli and Radel, 2005; Bhunyan, 2007; Cabras, 2011) indicate that the pursuit of profits for members in rural cooperatives is often associated with the achievement of social objectives for their communities. Zeuli and Radel state that cooperatives are important vehicles for 'community development because they mobilize local resources into a critical mass and their structure allows them to be more community-oriented' (2008: 43). This particular aspect perhaps differentiates rural cooperatives from larger regional and national cooperatives: benefits secured by cooperative initiatives may be perceived by local communities almost immediately. Resources may be easier to localise and made available readily to local communities, avoiding some dispersion which characterises larger cooperative organisations (Nilsson *et al.*, 2012).

Members of rural cooperatives are usually local residents who tend to be the promoters as well as the primary buyers/users of the cooperatives' products and services. This situation increases the retention of local resources and enlarges business profits for local communities compared to those obtainable from investor-owned firms whose investors are scattered across the country (Zeuli and Radel, 2005). Cooperatives can also unlock and improve individuals' potential through the provision of skills and training. Members can improve their skills in a number of areas, such as business management, leadership, organisation and problem solving (Borzaga and Spear, 2004). In rural areas, these skills increase the provision of social capital at a local level, providing a basin also for other organisations, with a lower risk of geographic dispersion or delocalisation associated with spatial remoteness (Zeuli *et al.*, 2004; Zeuli and Radel, 2005).

Furthermore, cooperatives can tie communities together, especially in situations in which they represent the last resort to solve issues concerning community well-being. Several studies demonstrate how cooperative enterprises have been successfully formed in order to provide basic as well as specific services for communities when no other alternatives were available (Moseley *et al.*, 2004; Zeuli *et al.*, 2008; Mayo and Ross, 2009; Cabras, 2011). Cooperative enterprises may then represent a valuable alternative (if not the only feasible one) for those communities where both public and private sectors fail or struggle to deliver.

Rural cooperatives in Britain: the case of cooperative owned village pubs

According to Brown (2008: 7), there are approximately 8,200 cooperatives, with over 10 million members, in the UK. However, most recently the Plunkett Foundation (2011), referring to England, where the majority of these businesses are located, identified only 489 businesses as rural cooperatives, generating £2.98 billion annual turnover, which represents about 11 per cent of the total turnover of cooperatives in England. Many rural cooperatives (241) operate within the agricultural sector, although their number is expanding rapidly within sectors such as energy, housing and retailing. Members number at least 90,000 with £260 million held in members' reserves. These figures show that the presence of rural cooperatives may appear not very significant in terms of the number of businesses, but they are extremely important with regard to the impact on the rural economy.

Research shows that rural cooperatives in Britain prove to be an important instrument when it comes to preventing the closure of essential services and providing facilities for local communities (Borzaga and Spear, 2004; Mayo and Ross, 2009; Plunkett Foundation, 2011). Services such as shops and small retailers may struggle to function properly in rural areas due to a low density of population, an infrastructure deficit and spatial remoteness. These factors affect the level of custom and may be a major cause of decline, particularly for small and medium businesses. Local communities can opt for cooperative ownership in response to the withdrawal of services by either public or private sector organisations, and make these businesses sustainable. In some cases, rural cooperatives can locate many diverse services (e.g., post office, internet cafe, or doctor's surgery) at a single site to reduce costs and maximise efficiency (Moseley *et al.*, 2004).

There are a number of examples of successful rural cooperatives. Cooperatives set up to save village pubs in recent years represent an interesting case. Village pubs embody both assets and services, which are highly visible and perceivable to local communities, and their disappearance creates a physical 'black hole' in villages. The rise of cooperatively owned and managed pubs, registered since the early 2000s especially in Northern England and Wales, brings villagers together in the effort to preserve essential, vital places for their community (Cabras and Reggiani, 2010).

Cabras (2011) documents a number of successful cases of rural cooperatives created to rescue pubs as well as other local businesses from closure. The case of Hesket Newmarket, a village of about 250 residents located at the edge of the Lake District National Park in Cumbria, is an interesting case where villagers decided to use cooperatives in order to take control of two businesses that probably would have been forced to close down otherwise.

The first cooperative in the village was formed in 1999 to purchase the Hesket Newmarket Brewery, a micro-brewery which started its activity in the backyard of the local pub, 'The Old Crown', about ten years earlier. Since its opening, the brewery had proved to be a successful business: beers won awards at local and national beer festivals, and sales experienced a steady growth.

The pub and the brewery at Hesket Newmarket operated as two separate enterprises, although all beers served at the pub were produced in its own back yard. In 1995, the pub was sold and continued its business activities under new management. Four years later, in 1999, the owners of the brewery decided to sell the business. This was a crucial event for the villagers: although the brewery was privately owned, the local community feared that some large national companies would purchase and run it in an industrial way, causing the small brewery to lose its character and market independence. It was at this point that a few local residents started to think about a community action to buy the brewery. Julian Ross, a villager and one of the promoters of the cooperative initiative, said in an interview with the author:

> The idea was floated, of buying the brewery as a community . . . actually two ideas were floated: one was the idea of forming a cooperative and the other was the idea of forming a PLC . . . and it was done in a very scientific way, somebody hung an A4 on the wall of the pub and said 'if you're interested in buying, joining in trying to buy the brewery, stick your name down'! That's what my wife and I did, we just wrote our names down and never expected to hear any more . . . and sure enough we did, we were asked to vote whether we wanted to go down the PLC route or the cooperative route!

In the early days of December 1999, 57 people who agreed to the proposal of buying the brewery voted for the creation of a cooperative that could take over the business. The brewery is still owned by the cooperative, and Julian Ross is still one of the shareholders.

Meanwhile, the pub at Hesket Newmarket changed ownership twice, until the end of 2002, when the owner decided to sell it on the open market. Yet again, fears arose among locals and lovers of the pub that it might fall into the hands of a major national brewery or pub chain. The brewery, caught in a situation of economic difficulty – a foot and mouth outbreak was hitting Cumbrian farmers heavily at that time – could not make any offer to buy the pub. Hence, in November 2002, many villagers and brewery shareholders expressed interest in creating a new cooperative, although none seemed to have any idea about how to run a pub.

However, according to Ross, there were competences and capabilities available at a local level that could solve the problem related to inexperience. For example, a local businessman would provide free consultancy for financial planning, an important resource which helped to set up a viable cooperative scheme initiative. After taking advice from the brewery manager, who had previous experience of running a pub, the cooperative opted for leasing the pub to tenants. Cooperative shareholders did not know how to write a lease contract, but free support was provided by an external advisor who worked for a big firm in Manchester specialising in buying and selling pubs. In addition, a firm of solicitors based in Carlisle offered free consultancy, and this helped the cooperative to prepare the necessary legal documents. Public funding resources, made available by the particular situation the Cumbria economy was experiencing at that time, also played an important role. The committee formed for promoting the cooperative obtained £20,000 from the Cumbria Rural Regeneration Unit and an additional £15,000 from the National Park Sustainable Development Fund. These sums were in addition to the amount of funding that had still to be collected through the sale of shares.

Negotiations for acquiring the pub started at the beginning of January 2003, based on a price of £180,000. The money was mainly provided by shares purchased by 125 individuals who formed the cooperative, which was officially registered in March 2003. The purchase of the Old Crown was completed on 21 August 2003.

The two cooperatives at Hesket Newmarket are still in business. While the brewery makes most of its profit from beer production and sales, in the case of the pub the rent charged to tenants represents the only source of income for the cooperative, which decides how to invest it year by year. Ross indicates that, so far, most of the rent has always been reinvested in improving the building, or used to cover maintenance and insurance costs. For instance, in 2005 the building was extended and a new kitchen was made, but the investment was entirely covered in-house by the cooperative without borrowing a penny.

An important aspect to mention is the involvement of shareholders in the two cooperatives. In the case of the brewery, dividends have been growing steadily at an average of 3.5 per cent per year since its origin, reaching £100 per share in 2008 (quote from Julian Davey, chairman of the brewery, interviewed by the author). However, many shareholders do not cash their dividends and prefer these to be paid with two firkins of beer. With regard to the pub, at the beginning it was decided to reward the investment of £1,500 made by each shareholder with an annual 5 per cent return. However, due to initial costs that the cooperative had to face (i.e. purchase of new equipment, building refurbishment), shareholders did not receive any dividend for the first three years. From 2006, the cooperative started to pay dividends, mainly because costs related to the pub began to decrease. As with the brewery, the majority of shareholders of the pub cooperative do not cash in their dividends, which stay as finance available to the cooperative ready to be re-invested. Interestingly, shareholders are entitled to cash their share at the nominal price any time and without any penalty costs. This confirms that the utility shareholders receive from their membership transcends the mere economic value of the share they possess.

Ross affirms that the two cooperative initiatives proved to be successful because of the impressive involvement shown by the local community, and the rescues of both brewery and pub strengthen cohesion and mutual trust among villagers at Hesket Newmarket. In addition, the majority of local residents approached by the author agreed in saying that the survival of both brewery and pub avoided the closure of the village's other main retail business, a retail shop with post office facilities. In 2008, due to the owner's retirement, this small retail business was put on the market. Worried about losing their shop, villagers thought about creating another cooperative to purchase it. In the end, the shop was sold to a private buyer who is still running it.

The success registered by the Hesket Newmarket cooperatives inspired other villages to create cooperatives in order to rescue their pubs from closure. Similar initiatives started at Hudswell and Crosby Ravensworth, two villages located respectively in North Yorkshire and Cumbria. At Hudswell, the Hudswell Community Pub (HCP) was formed in early 2010 in order to re-open the village pub that had remained closed for more than two years. Unlike what happened at Hesket, this time the committee opted to sell shares at £1 each. An individual shareholder was entitled to buy any number of shares from 500 to 7,500.

In less than a month, the number of shareholders grew to 152, and the committee was successful in securing some financial support from public sector and development agencies (Key Fund Yorkshire, Yorkshire County Council, Business Link). The local pub was re-opened in June 2010. Since then the membership of the HCP has been constantly growing, and the cooperative managed to open the first shop in the village since the 1980s and to inaugurate an open-access library next to the pub's premises (Cabras, 2011).

In the village of Crosby Ravensworth, the initiative to form a cooperative to rescue the pub was promoted by the Lyvennet Community Trust (LCT), a non-profit organisation supporting charitable purposes for the benefit of local residents. In particular, LCT's main focus was the provision of affordable housing for people wanting to relocate within the parish of Crosby. When the pub was put on the market and was due to close in September 2009, the LCT started lobbying against its closure. In February 2010, LCT organised a public meeting in the village hall with the aim to propose the creation of a cooperative to buy the pub. The proposal was viewed favourably by local residents; soon afterwards, LCT put together a time-bound offer document to raise £215,000 in community shares towards the negotiated purchase price of £255,000, with the rest of the capital coming from grants or loans. Eventually, 297 people subscribed to the share offer launched in early 2011, raising a total of £300,000, which was enough to purchase and fully renovate the building. The pub reopened in August 2011 (Cabras, 2011; Community Shares, 2012).

Successful rural cooperatives in Britain can be found also in relation to other fields. Somerset Cooperative Services (2012) describes successful cases of cooperatives recently set up in the fields of wind energy (Watchfield, South Oxfordshire), construction (High Bickington, North Devon) and IT and Media (Wiveliscombe, Somerset). Similarly, Community Shares (2012) reports about newly formed rural cooperatives operating in retailing (Uley, Gloucestershire), hydro-electricity (Tutbury, Staffordshire) and broadband services (Alston, Cumbria). Other sources (The Plunkett Foundation, 2011; Cooperatives UK, 2012) indicate a constant increase in the number of cooperatives among community run shops registered in the past twenty years, from 33 in 1992 to more than 300 in 2012. Many of these shops are located in peripheral and remote areas of the country.

These cases demonstrate the great potential of rural cooperatives with regard to a number of aspects, e.g. preserving local businesses from closure, increasing the provision of services and developing multiple economic opportunities in the rural context, unlocking skills and resources at a local level, and increasing community cohesion and engagement in local communities.

Potential barriers and support available for rural cooperatives in Britain

While opportunities for cooperative businesses in rural areas appear significant, there are also challenges and barriers that may hold up the expansion of such initiatives. First, the challenges in securing financial support for cooperative start-ups (e.g. obtaining a loan from a bank or credit institute) still represents a significant task for many rural communities, in particular when a substantial financial injection into the project is required, as in the case of cooperative housing schemes or wind-energy farms (Plunkett Foundation, 2011). Second, the viability of the business may represent another significant issue. The majority of rural cooperatives are profitable businesses, but in some cases the main purpose tends to be the provision of a service rather than profit maximisation. This situation may prevent business diversification and expansion, leaving potential opportunities locked out. Third, the availability of entrepreneurial, legal and other skills at the local level represents a challenge for rural communities. Experienced and talented people can boost initiatives and facilitate processes within communities by acting faster and more efficiently, while other people would need some training either externally provided or 'gained on the job'. This could delay the development of a number of business initiatives, including rural cooperatives, resulting in missed opportunities or opportunity costs (Aiken *et al.*, 2011). Fourth, while rural cooperatives can enhance cohesion among communities, they still need to find a fertile terrain in order to develop. Setting up cooperatives in villages with very small populations may prove to be less challenging, since the levels of reciprocal knowledge and trust among residents may be higher in small villages than in larger ones. However, this may not always be the case: frictions and misunderstandings happen in small communities and can escalate and degenerate even faster and more dramatically than in large ones (Van Vugt and Hart, 2004; Van der Horst, 2008).

A possible barrier to cooperative ownership and initiatives in rural areas is represented by the level of support available, especially at a local level, which is significant but very fragmented (The Plunkett Foundation, 2011). There are several public sector bodies, national and regional agencies and rural support organisations (e.g., Rural Community Action Network, Cooperative Development Agency, The Plunkett Foundation, Department of Communities and Local Government) from which local communities can seek help and receive support. However, cooperatives are very diverse, and it may be difficult to provide tailored solutions for each single case (Plunkett Foundation, 2011). Probably an enhanced coordination among different agencies could improve the quality of support provided at a local level, by channelling efforts and resources in a more efficient manner and by reducing cases of overlapping among initiatives. For instance, agencies specialised in providing support to businesses and enterprises operating in specific sectors could work together with cooperative experts to elaborate more targeted solutions fitting their sectors of competence, for example, focusing on specific regulations, tailoring ad-hoc business strategies, and so on.

Timing is also important, as public financial support is frequently regulated by general economic conditions at local and national level and these conditions do not have to be necessarily positive in order to produce positive effects. In the case of Hesket Newmarket, a negative event for the local farming-based economy, namely the outbreak of foot and mouth in 2002, made significant public funding resources accessible for grants in support of socio-economic development initiatives. At the very same time, the villagers decided to create their second cooperative. This example shows that opportunities for successful cooperation can arise in both favourable and unfavourable economic conditions; decisions made by local authorities and governing bodies can expand potential benefits associated with those opportunities.

The role of volunteers in rural cooperatives needs to be considered. A significant number of rural cooperatives appear to be intrinsically connected with social entrepreneurship in the British rural context (Brown, 2008; Community Shares, 2012). Many of these businesses may need targeted strategies in order to attract and retain volunteers and – at the same time – fulfil their objectives in terms of mutuality and membership (Borzaga and Spear, 2004; Zeuli *et al.*, 2004). In such small communities, there is always the possibility that members and volunteers may disagree about the conduct of the business, with members in the role of 'right-holders' and volunteers as 'work-providers'.

Finally, cooperatives in rural areas can play an important role in the so-called 'Big Society', the Coalition Government idea which aims to move powers and responsibilities from the state to individuals and neighbourhoods by giving them more control over services supplied at a local level (Evans, 2011). However, 'Big Society' is used as an umbrella term to include a variety of organisations, from charities to non-profit and volunteering groups, from community interest companies to cooperatives and mutual societies. The Coalition Government itself intends to develop the Big Society by addressing three main broad agendas comprising the reform of public services, a more active citizenship, and transparency and accountability (Evans, 2011). Cooperatives in rural Britain can be instrumental to the Government plan, as they appear to combine mutuality and social purpose in a very effective manner. Moreover, the Localism Act (2011) strengthens opportunities for cooperative and mutual ownership in rural areas by giving local communities more control over managing and planning. This seems to indicate the intention of the Coalition Government to encourage cooperative initiatives in order to create business opportunities and economic development while, at the same time, targeting rural communities' needs. In the light of these considerations, it appears likely that the number of rural cooperatives in Britain will continue to grow.

Conclusions

The study presented in this paper has explored and examined cooperatives and mutual ownership and organisations in rural areas, by analysing points of overlap between cooperatives and communal ownership and by describing types and structures of cooperatives in detail. In particular, rural cooperatives have been investigated with regard to their role in the rural context and in local communities, where these businesses have a significant impact on community cohesion and social engagement, as well as generating positive effects on local economies and the supply chain.

Rural cooperatives in Britain have increased in number, size of membership and level of turnover since the early 2000s. They have proved to be important assets for rural communities, where mutual ownership frequently overlaps with communal ownership. In several cases, they work as a hub for their communities, and their objectives usually fall within those of social enterprises, especially when they are created in order to provide a new service or to save an enterprise from closure. The fact of being a community hub, combined with frequent inclusion within the social enterprise category (Borzaga and Spear, 2004), may generate a number of cases in rural areas of Britain in which mutual ownership developed as an extension of communal ownership, pursuing benefits for members of both cooperatives and the community.

While all cooperatives aim primarily to benefit their members, in the rural context they often aim also to benefit the communities in which they operate. While this situation should be treated as a positive externality and not as a priority (Zeuli and Radel, 2005), these two aspects never seemed to conflict with regard to the cases presented and discussed in this paper.

Targeting rural cooperatives with tailored programmes, by increasing their potential in terms of financial sustainability and raising the provision of skills needed to set up these businesses among rural communities, would generate benefits for local economies and supply chains too (Mayo and Ross, 2009). Policies and policymakers should then focus on the frequent overlap between cooperatives and social enterprises or related organisations operating within the rural context, in order to understand these businesses more clearly and support them more effectively.

References

Aiken, M., Cairns, B., Taylor, M., and Moran, R. (2011) *Community Organisation Controlling Assets: A Better Understanding*. York: Joseph Rowntree Foundation.

Bhunyan, S. (2007) The people's factor in cooperatives: an analysis of members' attitude and behaviour, *Canadian Journal of Agricultural Economics* 55: 275–98.

Birchall, J. (1997) *The International Cooperative Movement*. Manchester: Manchester University Press.

Borzaga, C. and Spear, R. (2004) *Trends and Challenges for Cooperatives and Social Enterprises in Developed and Transition Countries*. Trento: Edizioni 31.

Brewer M., (1979) In-group bias in the minimal group paradigm: a cognitive-motivational analysis, *Psychological Bulletin* 86: 307–24.

Brown, J. (2008) Community Investment: Using Industrial and Provident Society Legislation. Manchester: Cooperatives UK.

Cabras, I. and Reggiani, C. (2010) Village pubs as a social propellant in rural areas: an econometric study, *Journal of Environmental Planning and Management* 53(7): 947–62

Cabras I. (2011) Industrial and provident societies and village pubs: exploring community cohesion in rural Britain, *Environment and Planning A* 43: 2419–34.

Community Shares (2012) Community Led Planning Toolkit. Available at: www.acre.org.uk/Resources/ACRE/Documents/Community%20Led%20Planning/community%20shares.pdf (accessed 26 November 2012).

Cooperatives UK (2010) Community Shares: Practitioner's Guide to Governance and Offer Documents. Manchester: Cooperatives UK.

Cooperatives UK (2012) The UK Cooperative Economy 2012: Alternatives to Austerity. Manchester: Cooperative UK.

Craig, J. G. (1980). Member Commitment: A Thing of the Past or a Possibility for the Future. Cooperative FutureDirections Project. Working Paper no. 11. Saskatchewan: The Cooperative College of Canada.

Defourny, J. and Nyssens, M. (2006) Defining social enterprise, in M. Nyssens (ed.), *Social Enterprise: At the Crossroads of Market, Public Policies and Civil Society*, London: Routledge.

DTI (Department of Trade and Industry) (2002) Social Enterprise: A Strategy for Success. London: DTI.

European Commission, (2004) On the Promotion of Cooperative Societies in Europe. COM 2004/18. Brussels: European Commission.

Evans, K. (2011) 'Big Society' in the UK: a Policy Review, *Children and Society* 25: 164–71.

Fairbairn, B. (1994) The Meaning of Rochdale: The Rochdale Pioneers and the Cooperative Principles. Occasional Paper, University of Saskatchewan. Available at: *http://usaskstudies.coop/pdf-files/Rochdale.pdf* (accessed 22 July 2012).

Financial Services (2007) The Money Laundering Regulations. London: Stationery Office, No. 2157.

Girard, J. P. and De Bortoli, P. (2004) The solidarity cooperative in Quebec and social cohesion: Measuring and understanding the impact, in B. Fairbairn and N. Russell (eds), *New Directions in Cooperative Research and Practice*. Saskatchewan: Center for the Study of Cooperatives, University of Saskatchewan: 235–58.

Hechter M. (1986) The emergence of cooperative social institutions, in M. Hechter, K. D. Opp and R. Wippler (eds), *Paradox and Society: The work of Bernard Mandeville*, New York: de Gruyter.

Hind A. (1997) The changing values of the cooperative and its business focus. *American Journal of Agricultural Economics* 79: 1077–982

Mayo, E. and Ross, J. (2009) Calling Time on Pub Closures: The Cooperative Answer. The Plunkett Foundation, Woodstock. Available at: http://offline.cooperatives-uk.coop/live/images/cme_resources/Public/Publications/Calling-Time.pdf (accessed 2 July 2012).

Mingay, G. E. (1997) *Parliamentary Enclosure in England.* London: Longman.

Nilsson, J., Svendsen, G. and Svendsen, H. (2012) Are large and complex agricultural cooperatives losing their social capital? *Agribusiness* 28(2): 187–204

Parliament (2010) Cooperative and Community Benefit Societies and Credit Unions Act. London: The Stationary Office.

Parliament (2004) Companies (Audit, Investigations and Community Enterprise) Act. London: The Stationery Office.

Peredo, A. M. and Chrisman, J. J. (2010) Toward a theory of community-based enterprise, *Academic of Management Review* 31(2): 309–28.

Plunkett Foundation (2011) Review of Rural Social Enterprise in England. Woodstock: Plunkett Foundation.

Ray, C. (1998) Culture, intellectual property and territorial rural development, *Sociologia Ruralis* 38(1) 3–20.

Regulator of CICs (Community Interest Companies) (2012) Annual Report 2011/12. Presented to Parliament pursuant to section 27(8) and schedule 3, section 7 of the Companies (Audit, Investigations and Community Enterprise) Act 2004. Crown Copyright 2012.

Robb, A., Smith, J. and Webb, T. (2010) Cooperative Capital: What it is and Why Our World Needs it. Paper presented at the EURICSE Conference on Financial Cooperative Approaches to Local Development through Sustainable Innovation. Trento, Italy, 10–11 June 2010.

Somerset Cooperative Services (2012) Rural Cooperation. How Collaboration and Social Enterprise is Meeting the Needs of Communities in Somerset and the South Wales. Available at: www.somerset.coop/sites/default/files/Rural%20cooperation%20web.pdf (accessed 24 November 2012).

Somerville, P. and McElwee, G. (2011) Situating community enterprise: a theoretical exploration, *Entrepreneurship and Regional Development*, 23(5/6): 317–30.

Spear, R. (2005) The Community Interest Company: A New Form of UK Social Enterprise, Cooperatives Research Unit. Milton Keynes, UK: The Open University. Available at: www.mes-d.net/grupcies/boletin/Articulo%20I%20Edic%2029.pdf (accessed 30 July 2012).

Van der Horst D (2008) Social enterprise and renewable energy: emerging initiatives and community of practice, *Social Enterprise Journal* 4(3): 171–85.

Van Vugt, M. and Hart, C. M. (2004) Social identity as social glue: the origin of group loyalty, *Journal of Personality and Social Psychology* 86(4): 585–98

Woodin, T., Crock, D. and Carpentier, V. (2010) *Community and Mutual Ownership: A Historical Review*. York: Joseph Rowntree Foundation.

Zeuli, K. and Cropp, R. (2004) Cooperatives: Principles and Practices in the 21st Century. Madison, WI: University of Wisconsin Extension. Available at: www.community-wealth.org/_pdfs/articles-publications/coops/report-zeuli.pdf (accessed 23 September 2012).

Zeuli, K., Freshwater, D., Markley, D. and Barckley, D. (2004) Cooperatives in rural community development: a new framework for analysis, *Journal of Community Development Society* 35(2): 17–35

Zeuli, K. and Radel, J. (2005) Cooperatives as a community development strategy: linking theory and practice, *Regional Analysis and Policy* 35(1): 34–54.

5 Rural parishes and community organisation

Rebecca Herron, Jennifer Jackson and Karen Johnson

Introduction

Rural communities in England have changed continually over the centuries as cultural, economic, infrastructural and social factors have impacted on the physical and human landscape. In this chapter we are focusing on *how people change their own communities* – i.e. the processes by which people recognise and respond to local need (and opportunities) and the organisational structures that help shape and influence these processes in rural communities. In order to do this we present illustrations of change and development activities within two English communities that highlight aspects we have found particularly interesting and informative.

Through our personal experience and involvement in research with rural communities in England we became increasingly interested in the concept of 'The Parish' as an organising principle in rural communities – an idea which has encouraged us to look more closely at how actions in local communities are enabled and constrained by this concept.

Although arguably of Anglo-Saxon origin, the concept of *the parish* is still a meaningful contemporary concept in many rural communities with several (loosely interweaving) meanings of the term in use simultaneously. The *parish*, it seems, still suggests locally recognisable ties of space, social dependence, responsibility and identity – at a human scale. For example, in writing about the impetus to act on conservation issues, Mabey (1980) (quoted in Common Ground, 1987) reflected on the nature of a parish, highlighting its scale and properties:

'Conservation begins precisely where the pain and destruction of modern development are most keenly felt – in the parish, that "indefinable" territory to which we feel we belong, which we have the measure of' (ibid.: 248).

We reflect a little here on the long history of this concept and some of the apparent legacies of these cultural roots for the actions of modern-day rural residents. While our focus is on two (geographically separated) communities in England, we believe understanding the legacy and resilience of ancient social–organisational structures will have resonance in many rural communities in other countries. Details of agency and authority will of course change in different contexts but we believe that exploring and reflecting on community organisation in this way could make a valuable contribution to understanding the complexities of community experience and the restrictions and potential for change wherever these communities are located.

In this chapter we wish to highlight four qualitatively different uses of the term 'parish' we have identified through our research and some of the connections between these uses and the ability of people to take action on local social concerns. The distinct uses identified are (in chronological order):

1 a feudal/historical settlement – the bounded parish as an ancient or established place (and cultural space);
2 a religious/ecclesiastical parish (i.e. a parish church, its parochial church council, parish members and formal parish boundaries);
3 a secular civil/civic[1] parish council (with parish councillors, parish clerk and other officers, parish residents and formal parish boundaries);
4 a community planning process (sometimes referred to as *parish planning*, using some general notion of 'parish' boundaries, places and identities).

Each of these usages indicates a different organising principle. In some ways uses (2) and (3) may be thought to be linked as they are both *parishes of governance* (legally constituted organisational forms bearing specific legal identities, constitutions and domains). Similarly, (1) and (4) share some characteristics, being historically and socially constructed *parishes of place* and potentially self-organising forms of community organisation and decision-making (created and maintained by social forces and the continuing actions of the community members themselves).[2]

In order to illustrate some of these differences we present later in this chapter two examples of community-based planning and development in rural village contexts (one in Lincolnshire, the other in Cornwall). In the course of retelling these accounts we have drawn out several themes about how the different organising principles (i.e. the different forms of 'parishes' in use) shape the ways communities organise themselves, make plans for the future and take action on local needs. But before turning to these examples we feel it important to set the scene and discuss further the origins and notions contained in the idea of a parish.

The idea of a parish

The notion of a parish has continued resonance in the life of rural villages in twenty-first century England despite being an ancient concept with its roots in pre-Roman,[3] Anglo-Saxon, Norman English and early Ecclesiastical organisation. According to Pounds (2004), 'Even today, in rural areas, the parish council still retains vestigial functions which it has inherited from the Middle Ages.' Some authors go further and emphasise that even these mediaeval arrangements had their roots in much older, ancient, organisational territories:

'The age of many of our parish boundaries is astonishing. The Christian church even adopted some prehistoric estates for which the boundaries were visible and known in the landscape. Certainly many parish boundaries include prehistoric elements' (Common Ground, 1987).

As a concept linking religious organisation to a space and community, the idea of a parish was introduced by the Christian church in England in the seventh century when the Archbishop of Canterbury, Theodore of Tarsus, applied the term following the Council of Whitby (Bettenson, 1943; Stevenson 1957, 1983; Pounds, 2004). This concept of parish seems to have differed somewhat from the modern usage in that it referred primarily to the territory over which a *Bishop* had domain. For example, when discussing the ten particulars agreed by the English Bishops following the Council of Whitby, Bettenson gave the second particular as: 'no Bishop [may] invade the diocese (parochia) of another, but be content with the government of the people committed to him' (Bettenson, 1943).

Administrative and ecclesiastical boundaries set up by the church have undergone revisions and re-alignments over the centuries but some of the basic, original structure remains even to this today: 'The body of canon law drawn up under his [Theodore's] supervision, and his structure of dioceses and parishes, survived the turmoil of the sixteenth and seventeenth centuries and are substantially intact today' (Kiefer, 1999).

As well as providing community offices such as registering baptisms, marriages and deaths, historically, the ecclesiastical parish also had important civil roles in relation to justice and welfare (see Hindle, 2004; Pounds, 2004). For example, ecclesiastical parishes had a duty, enshrined in law, to provide relief for destitute members of their parish (see for example Bird, 1799).

With the growth of separate local government structures in the late nineteenth century (including new poor laws and the establishment of secular parish councils), many of the civil responsibilities of the church became shared by the new (secular) parish councils elected by the general public (with similar but not always identical parish boundaries and different roles and responsibilities). While the civic offices in these parish councils were (and still are) mostly unpaid positions the obligations of secular parish councils are inscribed in law (Charlesworth, 2010).[4] Parish councils thus form the most local level of government in England, with a long social, cultural and legal legacy.

The parochial church council (PCC) is a committee elected by those on a church's electoral roll.[5] PCCs within ecclesiastical parishes in the Church of England date from the 1920s, although 'Vestry Meetings' had been held annually before then.

The point we want to emphasise here is that each of these forms of parish contains within it a different notion of the identity of *The Parish*, the stakeholders involved and the agency of different actors. They also share related but different concepts of the parish boundaries and legal/ethical bounds and duties. Such responsibilities include caring for those identified as being in need within the parish. These were historically 'the poor' of the parish (Bird, 1799), but also now can be seen to include identified groups with particular needs such as younger and older residents, 'new-comers' and other groups. Throughout their history parish organisations can be seen to have had a wider social responsibility for meeting the needs of vulnerable people or those on the margins of society. Some of this responsibility has been inscribed in law while some comes from the internal motivations, priorities and common values of the community members themselves.

Both ecclesiastical and secular parishes are of more than just historical interest and can be found to be still active in many contemporary rural communities in England. According to the National Association of Local Councils (NALC) website, there are currently around 8,500 locally elected parish and town councils in England; 'over 15 million people live in communities served by parish and town councils nationally – this represents about 35 per cent of the population' (NALC, n.d.). These parish councils form a third tier of local government and frequently involve people who have detailed knowledge of a locality.

Many secular parish councils serve just one geographically bounded community while others serve two or more distinct hamlets or villages. In other words (to use the distinctions introduced above) different *parishes of place* can be brought together under a single *parish of governance.*

Similarly, according to its website, in 2012 the Church of England had more than 16,000 churches. While most churches serve a single parish, in some cases several parishes are grouped organisationally under the offices of a single parish priest or ministering team. Again it is possible to see in this the contrast between *parishes of place* and *parishes of governance.*

Both types of parish council (secular and ecclesiastical) can be seen as organisations with varying degrees of significance and influence in their own right. As local organisations and decision-making bodies, they are potential players in decision-making in rural communities. However, while there are shared characteristics of all English parishes, of either kind, the size and activity level of both ecclesiastical and secular parish councils vary widely, depending on their location, history and the individuals involved. Indeed, the size of a secular parish council can range from a very small rural village to a large town; and some councils are very active, while others show limited activity or involvement in community life.

A further use of the term parish has been introduced in communities in recent years in the form of community (or 'parish') planning (DETR, 2000). These community-based planning activities encourage local residents to join together to create plans for the development of the local area and to engage with local, district and county bodies and other agencies. According to a UK-based Parish Planning (n.d.) website: 'To date around 3,000 communities have produced a parish plan, either individually or by forming local clusters. These holistic documents comprise the socio-economic and environmental issues of a community and their proposed remedies'.

The point we want to emphasise here is that the concept of membership of *the parish* in this case is wider than that of governance-based definitions – and is often felt to include all those who live, work and use *a particular place*.

Parish planning (or *community planning*) committees are created during this process. These committees are separate from both secular parish councils and ecclesiastical parochial parish councils – although it is of course quite possible, sometimes even likely, that some committee members may be members of several of these councils.

On parish boundaries – physical and imagined

The concept of a parish is not exclusively rural but does have particular resonance and significance in rural contexts. One reason for this may be the frequent occurrence of distinct and recognisable parish boundaries in rural locations (both ecclesiastical and secular). Whereas urban parishes frequently blur into one another and overlay a complex physical and emotional geography of place and identity, in rural locations the identification with a particular parish may be much more apparent. Rural parishes may consist of a distinct settlement, such as a village, with clearly defined open physical space around it (for example, farmland or sea/rivers), and even where rural settlements are quite dispersed residents are still quite likely to identify with a named parish (perhaps as a recognisable point of reference).

Boundaries are important for maintaining all forms of parish. Formal records of them are kept by *parishes of governance*, while in *parishes of place* they tend to be more dynamic and permeable. Indeed the creation of marked boundaries and spaces of settlement and social organisation in England has an ancient tradition. In places parish boundaries can even be shown to relate to some of the first known settlement structures, bestowing (at least imaginatively) a deep history to some of our modern-day structures. In some rural communities the tradition of 'beating the bounds' is still practised as a means of reinforcing a sense of place and a physical reminder to subsequent generations of the bounds of a parish. This tradition[6] sees members of the community walking around the perimeter of the parish, stopping at established perimeter points and carrying out ceremonial functions.[7] It is a term also used figuratively to mean establishing and re-examining a place and one's relationship to it (see Miller, 2001, for a modern-day illustration of this idea).

But while it is interesting and informative to understand the *physical* extent of each domain, the focus on physical boundaries should not be the only consideration. As Mills (2001: 9) puts it: 'Although community often, even usually, implies place, the chief concern is nevertheless with people, with relationships.' Historically, rural parishes have often been described as places where people recognised each other: 'The traditional village was also a face to face society, in which persons knew each other in more than one role – or rather knew each other as persons as well as actors in particular roles; social relations were therefore characteristically many stranded' (Obelkevich, 1976).

Belonging, membership and knowledge of a space and place are also important in all of the identified organising principles of a parish. Parishes of governance not only have physical limits, marked as actual boundaries on maps (Crouch and Matless, 1996), but also have formal rules of membership and leadership (residency, registration of births and rules for election of officers of both kinds of parish). All parishes (either of governance or place), however, have an informal identity, with a sense of the norms and practices that define the character of each place.

The rights to be baptised, married and buried in your local parish church or the obligation to pay locally decided taxes are examples of the ways a person may be linked to a local parish through birth or residency. The legal identity of both ecclesiastical and secular parish councils, the voluntary nature of the offices within both forms of council, the levying of taxation, and the formal rules of decision-making on local expenditure all create and constrain the identity of parishes and their ability to create actions of certain kinds (see Bird, 1799; Pounds, 2004; and the National Association of Local Councils' website[8] for more information).

The physical spaces and other assets owned or initiated by parish organisations are also important to rural life. Rural communal life is often directly shaped by recognisable parish assets, particularly buildings (e.g. village/church schools, parish churches and civic/church halls) creating local meeting places and social spaces (DETR, 2000). The use of the word 'parish' is often reinforced through the naming of these artefacts – from the building of 'parish rooms' (also known as parish offices, civic halls and church halls), to the enactment of festivals, social events, fund-raising activities and the creation and distribution of 'Parish News' (both secular and ecclesiastical).

Similarly, the concept of a parish record is an element to consider – both as a part of building a unique identity for a parish and as a factor in organising changes in communities. The strength of various forces for preserving or changing the identity of a parish can affect planning and collective decision-making, and processes of record keeping can be interpreted as reinforcing both action and inaction in different ways. Formal processes for record keeping in parishes include minuted council records, parish reports, legal records and more informal processes such as recording 'parish memories' (e.g., Jackson, 2000).

A further form of identity is provided through the ongoing re-constitution of *community life*, an ongoing process shaped by the values, priorities, experiences and discourses within any given community. We recognise that different community organisations demonstrate varying levels of collective recognition of social concerns and responses to these. But in addition, we argue that the distinctive elements of 'parish' highlighted here exhibit legacies in the different ways in which communities identify their needs and the needs of others in their locality, make decisions about actions to take and generally direct and focus their energies and resources.

Two illustrations of community change generated within parishes

We are interested in the nature and interplay of these parish identities (in particular the notions of *parishes of governance* and *parishes of place*). In particular we are interested in the responsibilities each different form of parish organisation entails and the authority implied to act on behalf of, or in the interests of, other members within a rural community. Sometimes these parish identities interconnect or overlap, providing both potential for conflict of interests and opportunities for synergy and new ideas, 'un-thought of' outcomes and new capacities and perspectives.

We sketch here a couple of illustrative examples from different parts of England and contribute to wider reflections on the role of parishes within each case. These are drawn from our own personal experiences either through direct involvement or through direct connection to those involved.[9] Our main focus in retelling these accounts is not the notion of a parish as a historical/social phenomenon but on the different ways that this concept (and its historical/social legacy) *can help shape community organisation and change* currently in rural communities. This involves reflection on how action and resultant change are influenced by deep traditions and norms (often only partially visible to those involved). We are interested in how communities recognise the need to develop new actions (or maintain old ones) and how they muster and coordinate resources to do this. In other words, we are interested in understanding the role that all forms of *parish* play in the self-organisation of community life.

We present here examples of planning and development in communities from the viewpoint of two different kinds of parish (a parish of place and an ecclesiastical parish). We seek to highlight some of the differences embodied in the various concepts and illustrate some of their respective values as forms of organising practice within rural communities. The two examples are given as illustrations of how different notions of parish can shape very different approaches to making changes within communities.

The first illustration (from Lincolnshire): Branston Parish Plan, 2007–2010

Branston is a large village situated 4 miles to the south-east of Lincoln on the Sleaford Road within the boundaries of the heath and fen area that surround it. While it faces Lincoln, with the Cathedral dominating the skyline, it also has agricultural land and fields that distinguish and divide it from its urban neighbour. It is the centre of an ancient parish with evidence of its community roots and settlement going back to prehistoric and most notably Roman times.

From a tight knit agricultural community it rapidly grew in the nineteenth and twentieth centuries (from a population of 446 in 1801 to 1,337 in 1871 and 2,000 by 1951), to become what is often now considered a 'dormitory' village of Lincoln with a population of over 4,000.

As an agricultural community it was mainly self-sufficient with a range of craftsmen and shopkeepers working within the village. The Whites directory of 1892 recorded among its businesses: 4 grocers, 2 butchers and 1 baker, together with 4 blacksmiths, 2 tailors and drapers and 2 boot and shoemakers (Whites, 1892). With carriers getting from Lincoln what the community did not provide, residents could remain within the village boundaries for most of their needs.

Up until the middle of the twentieth century the village remained largely a 'face-to-face' society bound by social relations and interaction through daily commerce and regular community events. The setting up of the parish council in 1894 coincided with the beginning of rapid changes in the village's sense of place and community. An examination of the parish council minutes from 1894 to 1948 reveals how a small agricultural community had to respond to changes that were overtaking it and altering the nature of rural community life. The decision to half tar[10] the roads in 1911 mirrored this parallel world – a time when allowing both horses and cars to use the roads meant that the boundaries between the old and new worlds were colliding and the nature of being 'rural' itself was coming into question (Jackson, 2000).

In the early 1930s a debate within Branston about whether to install mains water not only demonstrated this divide, but also highlights how consultation was becoming part of rural government decision-making. A parish council survey from this period, which 'asked each house', found strong views among its residents, with only 44 households in favour of the proposed mains-water scheme; the others were fearful of costs and increased rates, with most of the residents being prepared to continue with the use of village pumps and wells. At a public meeting in May 1930 the community turned out in numbers to voice their continuing protest at the scheme, with only 27 voting for the water scheme and 200 against. The parish council minutes record the views of the dissenters, commenting, 'Mr Horsewood thought the Parish Council was trying to thrust the scheme on the village. . . . It was only the thin edge of the wedge and would mean increased assessments.'[11]

By the twenty-first century, like many other rural villages, Branston had grown to a scale beyond largely 'face to face' contacts and relationships in daily life,[12] commerce and decision-making. The parish council, though active in village issues and having open communication with its residents through routes of dialogue such as village groups, local newsletters and the Internet, still felt that there was further scope for resident participation (for example, often only three members of the public regularly attended parish council meetings).

The concept of the Parish Plan initiated by the Government's white paper of 2000 (DETR, 2000) therefore opened up an opportunity to consult and engage residents on what they saw as important in both the definition and development of 'place' and its rural context:

> Communities constantly grow and change and most people have strong views on whether this change is for the better or not, but unfortunately

> for the vast majority of individuals this is as far as their involvement goes. Parish Plans give everyone in the community the opportunity to influence and contribute towards the development of their parish by determining the issues which affect the community.
>
> (Branston Parish Plan, 2010, quoting and adapting DETR, 2000)

The intention was to achieve as wide an involvement as possible: 'It is not about the parish council or anyone else imposing their ideas, it is about giving everyone the opportunity to have a say and share their ideas, if they choose to do so' (Branston Parish Plan, 2010: 1).

In 2007 with a steering group composed of members of the parish council and interested members of the public the process of developing the parish plan began. While only 40 people turned up in the village hall to agree to its launch and give their views, a response to an extensive survey designed from the issues raised at the meeting received a response of approximately 35 per cent (640 households) from a village consisting now of around 2,000 households. In addition local businesses were consulted and importantly a group of sixth form students were involved to adapt the lengthy survey into a Youth Questionnaire.

The production of the 2010 Parish Plan (important for its process as much as the actual action plan that resulted) determined an evolving narrative about the nature of being part of a rural community and taking decisions about its future amid the dynamics of rural economies, social change and sense of belonging. For the parish council it has provided an extra understanding and continued dialogue about what the community wants. It proved the value of consultation and continues to be relevant to present village issues. For example, involving younger residents in the Plan and devising the Youth Questionnaire resulted in a Youth Council that now has the experience and confidence to participate and be included in decisions about the village (and is now regularly consulted by the parish council). The Parish Plan was therefore a vehicle for that involvement and a response to a problem identified by the Plan (i.e. that youth did not feel part of the community and that their issues were being subsumed among more general concerns).

The Plan itself revealed that residents have differing perceptions of the identity of the village: is it a commuter village or still a rural community? In particular, differences were perceived between older and younger residents. The general survey, for example, raised an overwhelming response among older and established respondents that 'residents value the rural village identity and are concerned that Branston could become a mini town – rapid expansion would affect village life' and that further housing should be 'small infill' to protect the 'village environment, curtilage and green belt'. In the youth survey, however, a need was expressed for small affordable houses and flats so that the younger generation could remain in the village. This is part of the ongoing dialogue.

The objective to develop a sense of community has not been achieved simply as a result of developing a plan and establishing an identified boundary around where people live. There were also gaps between what people said they wanted as a community and what they were prepared to do to achieve that. Community actions, such as cleaning up a nature area, were aspects residents had said they would be prepared to be involved with, but in reality only a few people took part. Similarly, the substantial support expressed in the survey for extending a neighbourhood watch scheme did not translate into numbers of volunteers coming forward to help with this.

Raising expectations by consultation was a further issue in that not all the desires contained in the survey responses were realistic or achievable (such as setting up the individual shops that had once been part of village life and community). However, in cases involving planning and applying for funding for capital projects, the parish council now have readily and easily available statistics which they can use to demonstrate need and prior consultation, which has helped raise funding for projects such as new village play equipment, the floodlit Astro Court and improvements to the Village Hall.

The Parish Plan opened up questions (as much as facilitating processes) about the nature of the village's rural identity. In many ways Branston has changed from the face-to-face community that it once was, but the fact that many of its residents still want to preserve a sense of belonging and distance from Lincoln is significant. For the parish council, the Plan provides a 'living document' by which they are continuing to consult and involve people. This process recognises that, while not everyone in the village may be willing or able to participate, involving as many residents as possible is important to the ongoing process of developing the village and to capturing and contributing to the continuing narrative of the village's identity.

The second illustration (from Cornwall): redeveloping the parish rooms at St Hilary Churchtown

The parish church of St Hilary near Penzance, Cornwall, provides an illustration of local (community-organised) development undertaken within the scope of an ecclesiastical parish. This rural parish church serves a small hamlet and scattered rural population and has a typical Sunday congregation of around twenty-five people. It has a distinctive artistic/cultural tradition and an ageing population. Until recently it also had a disused parish building on the edge of its grounds.

In previous centuries the parish church like many others had a 'parish house' nearby, which historically had a variety of functions including a place for meetings, and for brewing for parish feasts as well as serving as the Poor House for the village. In 1853 the church burnt down (all except the tower and spire) and was rebuilt in 1855. Having finished rebuilding the church, attention turned to the parish house. Deemed beyond repair, it was demolished and rebuilt using a large quantity of stone from a local disused mine-stack that was given to them for this purpose. The building has a lower and upper storey, is on the edge of the church graveyard and is maintained by the local church.

After the building had been completed a school (and Sunday School) was set up in it, and at one stage it was known that 70 boys were being taught there. The 'Old School' (as it is now known) was more recently used by church members as a meeting space. It also became the meeting place of the village's secular parish council.

By the 1880s another school had been built nearby and community members were using the building less. The church continued using it for various purposes (especially for the Sunday School which continued until the 1980s). The building gradually went out of use for both church and civil activities; and by the end of the twentieth century it was being used only for storage.

The conversion of the Old School building for modern use was an expensive consideration for a small parish congregation of very limited size (whose own modest immediate needs were sufficiently met by using the church itself or local school buildings). Importantly, though, the building was in the stewardship, both physically and imaginatively, of the local parish church. Members of this church felt the building could, and *should*, be developed, and invested energy into exploring opportunities for this. This activity started small and grew organically over a five-year period – starting from informal conversations with a local builder to the completion of the building, achieved by securing national grant funding, local support and volunteer input into the project.

In 2007 the newly appointed vicar and his wife (who was also a Reader in the church) were alarmed that the Old School building was at risk of becoming derelict. The Reader read the new Marazion and District Forum Community Plan and saw that local people were asking for a higher profile to be given to local history, language and culture and that there was a desire for a heritage centre[13] to be established (Marazion Forum, 2007; section 5). The idea was mooted that one of the two ground-floor rooms could perhaps be developed and used for this purpose,[14] so the Reader then attended local forum meetings to see what potential there might be in this idea.

When the initial idea of developing the building emerged, a decision was made by the church to create a subcommittee of the PCC to look into the possibility of restoring the Old School. Throughout its development work the building remained managed by the church's PCC, through this subcommittee. As the Old School project (as it was now rapidly becoming) developed it grew to include not only the preservation and restoration of the building, but also the appointment of a temporary curator (who provided expert historian input to the research, production of displays and professional networking as part of the development of a heritage room). This development had the secondary benefit (perhaps only fully understood later) of providing a point of reference and connection for the UK and international visitors that the church attracted each year (seeking links to their own family history or interested in the distinctive artistic and ecclesiastical history of the church).

The project made a conscious effort to build links to local schoolchildren, other residents and local artists and created a part-time (volunteer-run) tearoom in the upstairs space during summer months. These efforts to connect to wider community interests also included further consultations as part of its grant-funded commitments.

Several of the concepts of parish highlighted in this chapter may be seen as having helped to shape this process as it developed, in a variety of ways. For example, at the outset of the development the parish council and the parish church members were on remote (but friendly) terms. There was little formal connection between the two and little more in the way of informal connection. (They both appreciated the other's community roles and the physical overlay of their respective boundaries, but beyond that the connection was mostly historical.) As the work on the room started to develop, connections were strengthened. These links became productive, with the parish council seeming to recognise the positive momentum of the project and backing it both politically and practically. This culminated in the physical relocation of the secular parish council meetings back to the Old School in 2011. It seems on later reflection that the relationship between the two councils was important and had been a mutually supportive one. The links between ecclesiastical parishes and secular parishes can also be seen in the relationship between the local Parish Forum (and Plan) and the evolving use made of the (ecclesiastical) parish building.

The idea of the rooms being the responsibility of (or in the *stewardship* of) the parish church provided a particular kind of dynamic for the process. The implicit motivation was to create a resource that could be used by the parish as a whole, and not just by those using the church as a religious place of worship, within the wider remit of the parish church's responsibilities and relationship to the local community.

The initiator of the project and others on the PCC acted as a catalyst for the development of the rooms and activity within them. However, they were also very aware that ultimately the Old School had to be 'owned'[15] in common by the parish rather than by any particular individuals. This involved ensuring that, while the rooms were managed by the parish church and operated by volunteers from it, they were also recognised and valued (and in some wider sense even partially/imaginatively 'owned' or at least seen as a communal resource) by members from all the forms of parish, including the secular parish council, the local Forum and other residents – particularly local schools, local artists, local museums, District and County Council officers with related interests and those connected to other local interest groups. In short, the 'parish' was viewed as a *place* and social/cultural space not just as a form of ecclesiastical governance.

The identification of a point of mutual community interest (i.e. the concept of a local heritage centre) early on in the process provided a source of vision for the redevelopment and scope for accessing new forms of funding, not originally within the experience of the parish church. Support was provided in doing this and the project developed in new ways as a result. The wider support received (financial, practical and psychological) meant that the PCC committee were also mindful that it was important that the building be restored as a community resource and not just for use by church members. This also supported another aspiration of the church, to find ways to connect (and reconnect) to the wider community in which it sits.

Reflections on the different approaches to development and planning in parishes

The different forms of the concept of parish at work in our two examples can have very different implications for the processes of local development and planning in each and the management of any subsequent changes.

The rationale for planning change at a 'whole-parish' level (as in the Lincolnshire example) is usually to canvass opinion as widely as possible, to develop a range of viewpoints about what is needed (and desirable) in a location and then to enter a phase when potential directions for action can be collectively assessed and selected. This can be seen to involve both divergent and convergent phases of thinking, collecting wide-ranging ideas from different people and collectively evaluating these. It also involves the careful management of expectations by those organising the process; for example, through discussion, idea generation and the evaluation of proposals coming forward (see Friend and Hickling, 1997, for similar examples in planning and other contexts).

The intention here may be seen in some sense to get 'the whole system into the room' (echoing Churchman, 1971).[16] This type of process has often been adopted recently by secular parish councils wanting to improve the connection between themselves and the other members of their community. A basic starting premise must therefore be that the views of the wider parish[17] are valuable to the parish council (a representative body tasked with making decisions) and that through a structured process these local needs and aspirations can be articulated, shared and acted upon.

In the first illustration (from Lincolnshire), the scope for community involvement[18] and the subsequent range of potential developments to consider was wide. The government initiative (of parish planning) mentioned earlier in this chapter was viewed by Branston Parish Council as an opportunity to engage residents more widely and fully in the definition and development of 'place' and its rural context. Alternative ideas were generated from participants about future changes to the place, and then viable options were selected through a managed collectivised process. The resources (people, motivation, finance) were considered as part of the evaluation process.

In some cases the necessary linkages and resources were secured and subsequent actions resulted (such as acquiring an Astro Court) whereas in other cases (e.g. the clearing of a nature area) community aspirations were aired but not reflected in volunteers coming forward. As it is easier to imagine improvements than to bring them about, schemes have to find (as here) ways to manage the various expectations of participants. One advantage of going through this process is that it can produce information and develop relationships that add legitimacy to resulting immediate actions and longer-term planning.

In order to manage the expectations and complex interactions between all the various stakeholders potentially involved in 'getting everyone in the room', such planning processes often need to build in contingencies for conflict resolution or at least to anticipate differences of opinion on development priorities and to find ways to handle these. The underlying assumption is that, despite potential differences of opinion, this is a valuable process for community members to engage in. This kind of planning echoes the work of problem structuring theorists who seek to develop protocols for structuring problematic situations (Rosenhead and Mingers, 2001). This literature also highlights the need for awareness of the role of critical review and ethical reflections about what *should* be included in the process and where these (conceptual) 'boundaries'[19] should be drawn in practice (see Ulrich, 2003; Midgley, 2000).

In the second illustration (from Cornwall) a different model can be used to interpret the project. In this case the development of the original activity and the wider community ownership co-evolved through a sequence of events, which started with a small group of active community members and then, through an intentional process, incrementally widened to include other community members – in terms of the ownership, direction of development and usage of the developing project. This means that the choice of action was *not* open to the whole community at the outset, as the locus of control was provided by a small group of individuals (who incrementally widened their engagements to make more viable the new resource being created within the parish). The management of this project, however, was just as delicate, as people beyond the initial group were able to see something emerging and might be curious about (and could even be resistant or supportive of) its course. There is often a need to consciously act in ways that attempt to balance agency with community ownership (especially ownership in the longer term), as this is not ensured through the design of the process itself. A potential trade-off can be seen between, on the one hand, individual/group vision, motivation and agency, and, on the other, wider community buy-in and influence on the actions undertaken.

The two illustrations given here highlight different approaches to community planning, development and action, and some of the challenges each approach faces. Parish councils and parish churches (as in the Cornwall example) may well have long-established control mechanisms and decision-making processes (internal governance) but in order to act *within their communities* they also have to develop wider strategies for involving other community members (e.g., to validate or influence decisions). Conversely, it is possible to start from a broad position, attempting to engage the 'whole community' in a planning exercise (as in the Lincolnshire example) without an explicit initial agenda, and seek to come to a consensus on the concerns of those within the parish boundaries.

We do not wish here to promote any particular approach to rural community organisation and development, but rather to draw attention to the distinctiveness of different approaches. In particular, we wish to explore (through the notion of parishes) the ways in which historic organisational and imagined forms still play an important role in shaping the designs, decisions and actions for the future of many rural communities.

Parishes provide rich source material for exploring community organisation, rural identities, community imagination and performances (such as collective decision making, activity-planning and delivery and development initiatives). Despite the often derogatory use of the term 'parochial', *parishes* offer a fascinating example of a point where 'top-down' forms of governance meet 'bottom-up' forms of community (re)organisation. There is much scope to understand this interaction more and to explore further the organisational forms that generate very local decision-making and self-organised (and remarkably self-sustaining and resilient) community organisation.

Parishes have an extraordinarily long history (both physically and imaginatively) and are likely to reward a closer look for those interested in the future of rural communities.

Notes

1 Note: The terms civic and civil are used fairly interchangeably in this chapter as different community groups tend to use preferred forms that differ (e.g. when referring to Parish Councils). This is not to deny though that there are important differences between the two terms. Where possible we have used instead the term 'secular' to emphasise the distinction from 'ecclesiastical' parishes.

2 A further use of the concept of parish is found in the use of the (often derogatory) adjective 'parochial'; a term used to describe a perspective that focuses on local concerns without incorporating wider issues. As this is a state of mind rather than a space, place or process, it is not explicitly included in the above.

3 The term parish/parochial may also have appeared in use in Egypt *c.* AD 300 (Stevenson, 1957, 1983).

4 The Parish Clerk and other officers *may* be in paid positions, but the offices of the parish councillors are unpaid.

5 Anyone living within the parish, habitually worshipping in a church or with another association to it is eligible to be included on the church's electoral roll.

6 Practised in some ecclesiastical parishes but also with apparent pre-Christian roots and appealing to wider community adoption (for example, by those with environmental interests).

7 See for example the Wikipedia entry that tells us:

> *Beating the bounds* is an ancient custom still observed in some English and Welsh parishes. Under the name of the *Gangdays* the custom of going a-ganging was kept before the Norman Conquest. A group of old and young members of the community would walk the boundaries of the parish, usually led by the parish priest and church officials, to share the knowledge of where they lay, and to pray for protection and blessings for the lands.
>
> (http://en.wikipedia.org/wiki/Beating_the_bounds; accessed 1 November 2012)

8 See www.nalc.gov.uk.

9 In addition to this, a further person from each location contributed to drafting/checking these accounts.
10 Meaning that half the road would be tarred and used by motor-cars, and the other half would be left for use by horses and horse-drawn vehicles.
11 'Assessments' are a form of local taxation.
12 With many activities taking place outside traditional village boundaries (such as increasing levels of commuting to work, increased car ownership and use of facilities such as shops in other towns and cities).
13 Cornwall is the southernmost county of mainland Britain and has among other things a distinctive history of seafaring, mining/emigration and a minority Celtic language (recently revived). The church itself has an additional historical/religious and artistic history of wider interest, which draws a small but steady stream of visitors from across the UK and overseas.
14 The larger upstairs room was to be kept for community/social and church activities and meetings.
15 'Ownership' here refers to identification with and commitment to the Old School (legal responsibility remains with the church).
16 If considered this way, the 'system' under discussion can be thought of as the organisers' notion of what the local community consists of. This would be reflected in the choice of individuals and organisations involved and the 'boundaries' drawn (for example, does the planning process just engage residents of the place or those who work within it? Or does it go wider and consider other people with a relation to it – such as visitors or those who identify with the place for other reasons such as place of birth, heritage, etc.?).
17 As defined implicitly or explicitly through a collectivised planning process (see previous footnote).
18 People do not have to be active in these formalized planning processes to be involved in their communities and people can still be strongly attached to where they live without taking part in any formal processes. They may also be happy with other people acting on their behalf without feeling they have to do it for themselves. Formal organisations (such as parishes of governance) have often found this to be the case, with the more 'informal' activities (e.g. around parishes of place) seen as going some way to addressing the issue, but not completely.
19 Conceptual (systemic) 'boundaries' – a further use of this term explicitly discussed in this literature.

References

Bettenson, H. (ed.) (1943) *Documents of the Christian Church*. Oxford: Oxford University Press, reprint 1946.

Bird, J. B. (1799) *The Laws Respecting Parish Matters: Containing the Several Offices and Duties of Churchwardens, Overseers of the Poor, Constables, Watchmen and other Parish Officers: The Laws Concerning Rates and Assessments, Settlements and Removals of the Poor, and of the Poor in General*. Original publisher W. Clarke; republished 2005 (2nd edition): Farrington Hills, MI: Thomson Gale.

Charlesworth, L. (2010) England's early 'Big Society': Parish welfare under the old poor law, *History and Policy*, November 2010 (adapted from an article published in *Amicus Curiae* 81, Spring 2010). Available at: www.historyandpolicy.org/papers/policy-paper-108.html (accessed 4 January 2012).

Churchman, C. W. (1971) *The Design of Inquiring Systems: Basic Concepts of Systems and Organization*. Basic Books: New York.

Common Ground (1987) *Parish Maps*, adapted from Greeves (1987) *The Parish Boundary, Common Ground.* Available at: www.england-in-particular.info/parish maps/m-boundary.html (accessed 4 December 2012).

Crouch, D. and Matless, D. (1996) Refiguring geography: Parish maps of common ground, *Transactions of the Institute of British Geographers* 21: 236–55.

DETR (Department of the Environment, Transport and the Regions) (2000) Our Countryside: The Future – A Fair Deal for Rural England. Government White Paper. Department of the Environment, Transport and the Regions, HMSO.

Friend, J. and Hickling, A. (1997) *Planning under Pressure: The Strategic Choice Approach*, 2nd edition. Oxford: Butterworth-Heinemann.

Greeves, T. (1987) *The Parish Boundary.* London: Common Ground.

Hindle, S. (2004) *On the Parish? The Micro-Politics of Poor Relief in Rural England, c.1550–1750.* Clarendon Press, Oxford Studies in Social History. Oxford: Oxford University Press.

Jackson, J. (ed.) (2000) *Branston Remembered.* Branston, UK: Branston History Group.

Kiefer, J. (1999) Theodore of Tarsus, Archbishop of Canterbury. Anglican Resource Collection. Available at: http://justus.anglican.org/resources/bio/250.html (accessed 11 January 2012).

Mabey, R. (1980) *The Common Ground: A Place for Nature in Britain's Future?* London: Hutchinson.

Marazion Forum (2007) Marazion and District Community Plan, 2007–2027: For the Town of Marazion, and the Parishes of St Hilary, Ludgvan, Perranuthnoe, and St Micheal's Mount. Marazion and District Forum. Available at: www.cornwall.gov.uk/idoc.ashx?docid=992701f9-04a7-447a-950a-164bd50389fa&version=-1 (accessed 1 July 2013).

Midgley, G. (2000) *Systemic Intervention: Philosophy, Methodology and Practice.* Kluwer/Plenum: New York.

Miller, T. (2001) *Beating the Bounds, Walks and Rides in Lincolnshire in the Millennium Year.* Lincoln, NB: Nth Degree Publishing.

Mills, D. (2001) Rural Community History From Trade Directories, Aldenham, Local Population Studies. University of Hertfordshire.

Obelkevich, J. (1976), *Religion and Rural Society: South Lindsey 1825–1975.* Oxford: Oxford University Press.

Pounds, N. (2004) *A History of the English Parish, The Culture of Religion from Augustine to Victoria.* Cambridge: Cambridge University Press.

Rosenhead, J. and Mingers, J. (eds) (2001) *Rational Analysis for a Problematic World Revisited.* Chichester, UK: John Wiley & Sons.

Stevenson J. (1957, reprinted 1983) *A New Eusebius: Documents Illustrating the History of the Church until* AD *337.* London: SPCK Publishing.

Ulrich, W. (2003) Beyond methodology choice: Critical systems thinking as critically systemic discourse, *Journal of the Operational Research Society*, 54: 325–42.

Whites (1892) *Whites Directory of Lincolnshire 1892: (Descriptions of Every Place, Lists of Residents with Trades).* Lincolnshire: Whites.

Parish Records

Branston Parish Plan 2010, Branston, Lincolnshire.

Branston Parish Council Minutes (1894 to 1948), Branston, Lincolnshire.

Websites

Church of England (n.d.) 'Facts and Stats', www.churchofengland.org/about-us/facts-stats.aspx (accessed November 2012).

NALC (National Association of Local Councils) (n.d.) www.nalc.gov.uk/About_NALC/About_NALC.aspx

(accessed December 2011).

Parish Planning (n.d.) www.parishplanning.co.uk/background.html (accessed November 2011).

Part II

Represented rurality

6 English historical perspectives on rurality

Viewing the country from the city

Andrew Walker

Introduction

The dualism country/city is not a new one: it has a lengthy history dating back at least as far as the Greek Georgic poets. Within this pastoral poetry, initiated by Theocritus in the third century BC, it is evident that the view of the countryside evoked tends to be from the perspective of the town or court and often has little connection with the rural 'reality'. In many instances, the country is referred to as the innocent, unpolluted and uncorrupted, while the city is seen as the antithesis to this. The dichotomy is often seen particularly from the point of view of the large-city dweller, with the country constructed as an imaginary landscape, a place of refuge and escape from the demands of city life. As a consequence, the evocations of the country have often been romanticised, to such an extent that rural inhabitants might have difficulty recognising the representation of the landscape in which they have lived and worked.

The poetry of Christopher Marlowe epitomises the almost mythological rural world that many artists have celebrated over the centuries. In 1600, Marlowe wrote 'The Passionate Shepherd to His Love':

> Come live with mee, and be my love,
> And we will all the pleasures prove,
> That Vallies, groves, hills and fields,
> Woods or steepie mountain yeeles.
>
> And wee will sit upon the Rocks,
> Seeing the Sheepheardes feede theyr flocks,
> By shallow Rivers to whose falls,
> Melodious byrds sing Madrigalls.
>
> (Barrell and Bull, 1974: 77)

Such was the power of this rural imagery that wealthy landowners went to significant lengths to construct on the ground the archetypal landscapes evoked in poetry and art works. During the seventeenth and especially the eighteenth century, whole villages were destroyed and their inhabitants removed out of sight to be replaced by the picturesque, a landscape comprising follies, lakes and leafy arbours. From the generously sized windows of the landed families, some of whom made their money away from the country in commerce, could be appreciated unpopulated landscape views inspired by oil canvases hanging on the walls within these homes (Williams, 1973: 124; Barrell, in Pugh 1990: 19–40).

Over time, the preferred image of the rural consumed by the upper echelons of society changed, informed by the fashions of the day. During the later eighteenth and early nineteenth centuries, for instance, the Romantic movement, with its predilection for the 'noble savage' and the uncultivated, championed the awe-inspiring landscapes of the Scottish Highlands, the Lake District and the High Peak areas of Derbyshire and Staffordshire. From the evocation of the Peak District as an awe-inspiring place to visit in Jane Austen's *Pride and Prejudice* (Austen, 1813: 264), through the work of Romantic poets such as William Wordsworth and the championing of the Scottish Highlands through for instance Queen Victoria's renting and subsequent purchase of Balmoral Castle in 1852, the untamed landscape was, from the later eighteenth century until at least the mid-nineteenth century, a highly esteemed cultural phenomenon.

Constructing the rural in the nineteenth-century city

The romanticisation of the rural is a complex phenomenon, however. During the second half of the nineteenth and into the twentieth century, the cultural celebration of the rural was in part driven by a growing dissatisfaction with the urban, at a time of rapid city growth and the increasingly documented problems associated with urban living, be they associated with health, poverty, morality, political unrest, or transport difficulties. Following a number of decades during the mid-nineteenth century when it seemed that the means of tackling long-standing urban problems had been achieved, the later years of the nineteenth century saw a re-emergence of concerns about the condition of urban Britain, and particularly its lower classes. Much of this concern and anti-urban feeling crystallised around the experiences of London's poor. Many commentators emphasised the city's poor housing, low wages and unemployment, made worse by a trade depression coinciding with the long-term decline of established industries such as shipbuilding, metalworking and garment production. One influential work that drew significant attention to the plight of the city was Andrew Mearns's *The Bitter Cry of Outcast London*, first published in 1883 and serialised in the popular *Pall Mall Gazette* newspaper (Lees, 1985: 109). A whole sub-genre of publishing appeared to develop following the success of Mearns's study. One of the most prominent works in this field was produced by the founder of the Salvation Army, General William Booth, entitled *In Darkest England and the Way Out*, published in 1890. Booth's anti-urban views are expressed vividly in his text: 'As there is a darkest Africa, is there not also a darkest England? Civilization, which can breed its own barbarians, does it not also breed its own pygmies' (Lees, 1985: 110). As William Booth observed, the English slum resembled the African jungle in its 'monotonous darkness, its malaria and its gloom, its dwarfish, de-humanised inhabitants, the slavery to which they are subjected, their privations and their misery' (Lees, 1985: 110). William Booth's work advocated the construction of work colonies in the city, on farms and overseas as a means of eliminating poverty. Around the same time, Charles Booth was making a systematic attempt to plot the extent of the poverty experienced in London. His extensive seventeen-volume magnum opus, *Life and Labour of the People in London*, appeared between 1889 and 1903. Reflecting the contemporary rise of the eugenics movement, a number of influential commentators highlighted the ways in which the city was a potential cause of damage, not just to the city's poor, but also to its wealthier inhabitants. In an attention-grabbing book entitled *Degeneration amongst Londoners*, published in 1885, a London surgeon, Dr James Cantlie observed that 'city disease', or *urbomorbus*, affected all levels of society. Cantlie revealed that 'town air is bad, that everyone working in it must suffer after a time in health and stamina and that person must be blind who does not observe the effect on children born and brought up in towns, even if they belong to the upper and middle classes' (Lees, 1985: 137). The over-stimulation of town life was also considered to be a potential cause of mental ill health. One prolific late-nineteenth-century writer on health issues, J. Milner Fothergill noted that one unfortunate outcome of town living was the 'highly strung neurosal woman' (Lees, 1985: 137).

If such concerns with the city were not sufficient to prompt the celebration of the rural, an almost parallel anti-industrial vein of thinking also indirectly privileged the rural *modus vivendi* over the urban. Among an influential group of cultural commentators, considerable concerns were beginning to be expressed about the process of mechanisation and its impact upon those employed in industry. According to one such commentator, John Ruskin, the mechanisation of the workplace was deadening employees' souls. He argued that this brought about the 'degradation of the operative into a machine'. Ruskin lamented that 'We have much studied and much perfected of late the great civilized invention of the division of labour; only we have given it a false name. It is not, truly speaking, the labour that is divided but the men: – Divided into mere segments of men – broken into small fragments and crumbs of life' (Ruskin 1851: 163). Ruskin was a keen advocate of the work of a group of artists who formed the Pre-Raphaelite Brotherhood. He championed the work of, *inter alia*, Dante Gabriel Rossetti, William Holman Hunt and John Everett Millais in *The Modern Painters* published in 1860. The underpinning philosophy of the Brotherhood, in harmony with Ruskin's own views, was that there was a need to return to the Middle Ages for models of artistic production employed prior to the work of Raphael and other Renaissance painters who had supposedly introduced a range of techniques and a worldliness which had corrupted painting. The Pre-Raphaelites rediscovered what they viewed as a lost innocence of vision, which focused especially upon Nature. Their work was characterised by its close scrutiny of the natural, its celebration of every blade of grass and leaf detail (MacCarthy, 1994: 13). In many ways, the Pre-Raphaelites' championing of the natural in art was echoed in the Gothic architectural revival in which, through the work of architects such as George Gilbert Scott, A. W. N. Pugin and Alfred Waterhouse, many landmark Victorian buildings took on a form heavily influenced by the medieval, with detailed nature-inspired embellishments (Dellheim, 1982; Bradley, 2007). In some ways, both the Pre-Raphaelites and neo-Gothic architecture represented an attempt to escape the sullied, corrupt urban present for a spiritually and morally purer golden age, achieved through the glorification of nature.

Another key figure associated with the championing of romanticised notions of the rural in the later nineteenth century was William Morris. He has been described by one of his biographers, Fiona MacCarthy, as a social reformer, an early environmentalist, an educationalist, would be feminist and, latterly, a revolutionary Socialist (MacCarthy, 1994: vii). Similarly to John Ruskin, Morris's approach was informed by an anti-industrial standpoint. He, too, was closely associated with the Pre-Raphaelites and was an important figure within the Arts and Crafts movement. His philosophy was to 'have nothing in your houses that you do not know to be useful or believe to be beautiful' (MacCarthy, 1994: 185). His views on production echoed those of Ruskin. Morris declared that 'Nothing should be made by man's labour which is not worth making, or which must be made by labour degrading to the makers' (Robbins, 2010: 40). Today, Morris is perhaps best known for his wallpapers and fabrics, produced by his company, Morris & Co. Morris sought to retain significant control of the production process, championing *manu*facture over *machino*facture. As MacCarthy (1994) notes, his output was characterised by a celebration of the natural world. Pervasive vegetation appeared in all of the products of Morris & Co.: honeysuckles, tulips, marigolds, irises and carnations predominated (MacCarthy, 1994: 358–9).

In these anti-urban and anti-industrial cultural movements, however, glaring paradoxes existed. Among the keenest collectors of Pre-Raphaelite paintings were wealthy members of the industrial middle classes; and undoubtedly some of the most spectacular examples of Gothic architecture included town halls in northern manufacturing centres, such as Rochdale, Halifax and Manchester, and railway stations, perhaps most notably George Gilbert Scott's St Pancras station. Among the principal consumers of the output of Morris & Co. were the families of industrialists and businessmen. Morris himself had significant difficulties coming to terms with the fact that he was, in his own words, 'ministering to the swinish luxury of the rich' at a time when he was increasingly preoccupied with the concerns of the poor. He gained a reputation for his rudeness to customers and he regularly complained of the 'sadly stupid' and 'monstrously rich' customers with whom he conducted much business (MacCarthy, 1994: 412).

The privileging of the rural in cultural matters among Britain's industrial and business classes at the end of the nineteenth century has prompted much comment among economic and social historians. Martin Wiener, in an influential book, *English Culture and the Decline of the Industrial Spirit, 1850–1980*, has suggested that these middle-class tastes were in part to have a deleterious effect upon Britain's future economic performance. In a work that was in some quarters adopted as a Thatcherite text in the years immediately after its publication in 1981, Wiener argued that Britain's relative economic decline was due in part to the incompetence of its entrepreneurs, caused in turn by the low esteem accorded to industrialists especially. By the final third of the nineteenth century, Wiener argued that the prevailing anti-industrial cultural environment privileged the rural over the urban. To gain status within society, Wiener argued, land was necessary. Rather than investing industrial profit into further capital, conspicuous consumption often took precedence. A debilitating 'haemorrhaging' of talent occurred which both insulated the sons of the older elites against contact with industry and also gradually attracted sons of industrial and commercial families away from the occupations of their fathers (Wiener, 1981: 24). According to Wiener, the economic retardation experienced by Britain from 1870 onwards was due to the incompleteness of the country's Industrial Revolution. The social and cultural cachet that continued to be associated with landownership and the country's landed classes meant that the country's emerging industrialists sought to ape the aristocracy. The principal means by which the anti-industrial spirit was transmitted, argued Wiener, was the public school system. Wiener notes that few sons of industrialists and businessmen who entered this system followed the occupations of their fathers. Those who did, he argued, were 'civilized', that is detached from the single-minded pursuit of production and profit. For example, Isambard Kingdom Brunel, the well-regarded engineer, sent his two sons to Harrow (Wiener, 1981: 19). As Wiener observes they were as a consequence hardly likely to follow their father's profession, though in fact one of them, Henry Marc Brunel, did later become a civil engineer.

Wiener's thesis has been attacked, not least on chronological grounds: other historians such as Berghoff have demonstrated that the public school system did not educate more than a small fraction of the country's business and industrial community until at least the turn of the twentieth century (Berghoff, 1990). Others have suggested that the acquisition of a classical education, a recreational interest in the cult of the faerie and a passion for medievalism did not necessarily prevent individuals from single-mindedly pursuing profits in their professional lives. Notwithstanding these counter-arguments, Wiener's thesis has been widely advanced.

There are, however, other reasons why Wiener's argument and the pervasiveness of anti-urban sentiment in the later nineteenth century need to be considered cautiously. While the romanticisation of the rural appeared to be a central element of the tastes of the middle classes of the metropolis and large Midland and northern English provincial centres such as Birmingham, Leeds, Manchester, Liverpool and Sheffield, rather different views about the rural were prevalent in many smaller urban centres across the country.

Viewing the rural from the perspective of smaller urban centres: Lincoln, *c*.1850–1925

While the urban/rural dualism has been the subject of much historical debate, in recent years increasing emphasis has been placed upon the blurred boundaries between the country and the urban. Just as recent work has been undertaken exploring the edgelands (Farley and Symmons Roberts, 2011), it has to be acknowledged that, even though England has always been a relatively urbanised society in comparison to its European neighbours, for much of its history, the vast majority of its towns' centres were less than a ten-minute walk from surrounding countryside. In 1700, for instance, 80 per cent of England's towns were inhabited by fewer than 2,000 people (Clark and Slack 1976). Even by 1851, following a period of rapid urbanisation – although for the first time the majority of the English population was defined as urban – an urban centre was deemed to be one with a population of more than 2,500 (Steinbach, 2012: 14).

Somewhat little attention has been paid to the relationship between the urban and the rural from the perspective of relatively small-town England during the nineteenth and early twentieth centuries. While, from the standpoint of the metropolitan aesthete, the rural could be seen as unproblematically benign, as represented in the city's art galleries and many works of fiction, from the stance of the small-town middle-class inhabitant the rural could be perceived very differently. The remainder of this chapter will focus upon the experience of one town, Lincoln, and its authorities in seeking to maintain urban sensibilities in situations when rural incursions began to challenge respectable urban society's perceived notions of decorum and orderliness, which, since the passing of the Municipal Corporations Act of 1835, it had been possible to apply – at least theoretically – through extended mechanisms of local government (Hill, 1974: 38–62).

By the end of the nineteenth century and beginning of the twentieth century within the relatively small city of Lincoln, with a population of 48,784 in 1901, there were some traces evident of the romanticised notions of the rural, so popular among the metropolitan middle-class. A. W. N. Pugin's neo-Gothic St Anne's Bedehouses were at the vanguard of this cultural form within the city, being constructed in the early 1850s (Pevsner and Harris, 1989: 511; Trott, 2010: 30–32); and Bracebridge Hall, to the south of the city centre, completed in 1883 for one of the city's most prominent entrepreneurs, F. J. Clarke, was described by the clergyman A. C. Benson as 'a villa of flashy and new-fangled design' (Tann, 2011: 31). Pevsner and Harris described the Gothic mansion as a 'brash and chunky Victorian pile' (Pevsner and Harris, 1989: 527). The Swanpool Garden Suburb, built by 1919, was one of the later architectural manifestations of the romanticised evocations of the rural in the city. Only the first phase of this planned development was ever completed. It comprised a vernacular cottage-style estate, constructed for the workers of the engineering firm of Ruston and Hornsby, with tree-lined roads evoking the rural with names such as Almond Avenue and Cherry Grove (Pevsner and Harris, 1989: 526).

Notwithstanding these examples of the fashionable evocations of the romanticised rural within Lincoln, there is much evidence within the city's engagement with the rural that many of its inhabitants in the later nineteenth and early twentieth centuries were disinclined to lionise the rustic. Particular attention will be paid to two regular events in Lincoln's calendar when interactions between the urban and the rural were brought into particular focus: the annual horse fair and the more frequent animal markets.

The Lincoln cattle market

Historians, including Patrick Joyce and James Schmiechen, have recently placed emphasis upon the symbolism of the market and its location within the townscape. Joyce and Schmiechen have referred to the liminality of the market, which presented challenges to late Victorian corporations in their attempts to regulate markets, especially beast markets. Patrick Joyce has argued that markets were intermediary spaces – 'locations of transition, places which occupy a place on a boundary, marking off buyers and sellers, and particularly country and town' (Joyce, 2003: 81). In the marketplace the rules of the moral economy could be applied, where, on occasion, crowds applied customary law to secure 'fair' prices for goods. This sometimes involved the use of direct action by crowds in order to ensure the upholding of social norms and obligations and to maintain the 'proper' economic functions of various sections within a community, reminding those in authority of their responsibilities to society at large (Thompson, 1991: 188; 228).

During the late eighteenth century and early nineteenth century, according to James Schmiechen, the market place was, on occasion, a site of

> fraud, crime, adulteration, street fighting and . . . food riots . . . Fighting over prices, market tolls and selling space was common . . . The public market in short was seen as promoting bad habits, low morals, public disorder and an interruption in the town's food supply.
>
> (Schmiechen, 2001: 189)

As urbanisation grew rapidly in nineteenth-century Britain, increased regulation of public space became a particular concern of those in authority. In large towns and cities, such as the rapidly growing industrial centres of Sheffield and Manchester, significant social segregation occurred, with the middle classes vacating homes in urban centres and moving to peripheral areas as authorities struggled to regulate the centres of such towns and cities. As town authorities increased their powers, following the 1835 Municipal

Corporations Act, more concerted efforts were made to tame and order urban public space.

Lincoln's urban form in the early and mid-nineteenth century was largely pre-industrial in character. Unlike cities such as Manchester and Sheffield, which were marked by the development of socially segregated neighbourhoods, in Lincoln members of the city's working and middle classes continued to live cheek by jowl in the older part of the city. However, while Lincoln's urban form was relatively slow to change compared to larger industrial cities, the reordering of the city's market provision was uncharacteristically progressive. In 1846, a cattle and sheep market was opened in Monks Lane, on the eastern edge of the city. A site was purchased, partly owned by the Corporation and partly by the Ecclesiastical Commissioners. The land included an enclosure of three acres and was described as being 'fitted up with pens etc. and having a commodious inn at the entrance' (White, 1856: 104; White, 1872: 88). Prior to the opening of the new, enclosed (and therefore implicitly 'controlled') market place, the city's cattle markets and fairs took place in St Swithin's Square, off Broadgate. This was an open and relatively uncontrollable space (White, 1852: 104). Padley's 1819 map of the city shows that, although a sheep market was located immediately to the east of St Swithin's church and west of Broad Street, a separate 'beast market' was located next to the City Gaol at the intersection of Broad St, New Road, Clasketgate and Monks Lane (Mills and Wheeler, 2004: 30). The beast market's former home was indicated by the continued existence of public houses named the 'Bull's Head' on the corner of Clasketgate and Silver St, and the 'Brown Cow' virtually opposite, a little further south on the east side of Broad St, as represented in the 1851 Padley map of the city (Mills and Wheeler, 2004: 61). The new site of the market, therefore, removed the trading of farm animals from the city centre and relocated this to the urban margins.

Lincoln Corporation had been prompted to seek an alternative home for the city's markets, in part through a fear of unrest, an anxiety regarding traffic flows, and also because the extent of business meant that the market was outgrowing its existing site. According to the *Stamford Mercury*, on 5 May 1844, 'the site of the beast fair was bitterly complained of last Friday, it being so small that the cattle were strewed about far and wide from the top of the New Road down into Silver St' (*Stamford Mercury*, 5 May 1844). The account also outlined other advantages associated with the relocation of the event away from Lincoln's main streets: 'the high roads and streets of the city would then be left free and the pushing and driving and swearing now so prevalent would be prevented' (*Stamford Mercury*, 5 May 1844). Petitions from cattle dealers, butchers and 226 citizens persuaded the Corporation to develop the new site despite the opposition of some tradespeople who were worried that the relocation of the market would impact upon their business (*Lincolnshire Chronicle*, 8 May 1846).

The Marrat plan of Lincoln, revised in 1848 from an original produced in 1817, reveals how marginalised the new cattle market was, situated to the east of an old friary, and to the west of a vineyard (Mills and Wheeler, 2004: 39). Although the newly built railway line to Market Rasen passed relatively close by, there appears to have been no attempt initially to maximise this potential transport benefit.

By relocating the market to its new site on what was to become Monks Road, the Corporation aimed to control the market in a way that had not been possible previously. As long as the market occurred on a public thoroughfare, its control and regulation were difficult. This changed with the development of a new purpose-built market. The Corporation leased the cattle market to a series of individuals who had responsibility for ensuring orderly conduct on the site and who were accountable to the Corporation.

Regulations relating to the operation of the market grew significantly in the later Victorian period. This was due in part to the increasing intervention by the local corporation, but also as a consequence of the growth in central government-driven regulation. Directives from Westminster were particularly prominent relating to the attempts to prevent the spread of diseases such as foot-and-mouth and swine fever (e.g., under the Contagious Diseases Act [Animals], 23 February 1884). Market lessees' freedom was also curtailed by increasing regulations relating to the sale of goods and the recruitment of a series of inspectors. In 1882, for instance, following a complaint made by the Privy Council Inspector, the whole of the cattle pens had to be 'effectively paved and drained' (Markets and Fairs Committee Minutes, 21 December 1883).

The Corporation expressed concern over any contravention of the market regulations. The sale of inappropriate goods was a recurring subject within the Markets and Fairs Committee of the Corporation. In 1889, Mr Giles, the Corporation-appointed market inspector, was instructed to report on any sales held in the cattle market that were 'in opposition to the terms of the lease' (Markets and Fairs Committee Minutes, 13 September 1889). In November 1889, it was noted that 'the sale of hardware, ironmongery goods, also of harnesses, rugs, lines and brushes etc. are now held . . . are hereby forbidden' (Markets and Fairs Committee Minutes, 18 November 1889). At several points, the Markets and Fairs Committee threatened to take court action against the lessee, though very rarely did so. One councillor, Mr Page, declared that 'there appeared to be no backbone to the Markets Committee' (*Lincolnshire Chronicle*, 20 June 1890).

One of the advantages of the new semi-public site was that the market could be effectively policed. However, on a number of occasions, it was noted that gates were not closed when the market was not in use and that, as a result, it tended to be used for unsuitable purposes. In 1889, Mr Percy was informed that 'complaints have been made of boys using the pens and markets as a playground and that this, in his own interests, being liable to repairs, should be prevented' (Markets and Fairs Committee Minutes, 9 August 1889).

The city's chief constable was requested by the Markets Committee to instruct his men to prevent boys from using the closets and urinals in the market grounds on the days when markets and fairs were not being held (Markets and Fairs Committee Minutes, 3 September 1885).

Market days also required zealous policing. The Chief Constable was asked to take action by the Markets and Fairs Committee against those who sold unbranded pigs outside the cattle market (Markets and Fairs Committee Minutes, 3 September 1885). The treatment of animals in transit to market on occasion caused concern. Patrick Joyce has noted the rising sensitivities felt towards animals during the nineteenth century, which to an extent were addressed by the RSPCA, which was founded in 1824 (Joyce, 2003: 88). These concerns were often articulated most forcibly in urban settings. According to Joyce, in the 1850s and 1860s, 'the daily sight of sheep being pushed down the steps into basement abattoirs close to St James's church in Piccadilly was a cause of great upset at the time' (Joyce, 2003: 78). In Lincoln, the Chief Constable, Mr Mansell, was requested to direct the attention of the constable on duty near the market to the loading and unloading of sheep in order to ensure they were appropriately treated (Markets and Fairs Committee Minutes, 6 July 1885).

The instructions to the constable suggest that some of the animals traded at the market were brought in by waggons. In the middle years of the nineteenth century, though, many animals were still being led into the city by drovers. Francis Hill in *Victorian Lincoln* made reference to Edward Peacock, a countryman and farmer, who wrote in 1857 of the 'numerous droves of . . . cattle [which] pass daily through the streets leaving behind them unmistakable traces of their presence' (Hill, 1974: 2).

By the middle years of the nineteenth century, however, increasing use was being made of the railway as a means of bringing livestock to market. In 1849, the *Stamford Mercury* noted that many of the sheep brought into the city of Lincoln for the April Fair were conveyed by rail: the last train into Lincoln on 25 April 1849 comprised 30 Great Northern carriages full of sheep (*Stamford Mercury*, 4 May 1849). In 1887, the Market and Fairs Committee appointed Mr Howse as the Veterinary Inspector under the Contagious Diseases (Animals) Act of 1869. His weekly fee of £1.1*s*. was to be paid on his inspection of the cattle market twice weekly, all cattle and sheep fairs held within the city and the railway docks and pens once weekly (Markets and Fairs Committee Minutes, 5 December 1887).

Attempts were being made at the end of the nineteenth century to increase the use of the railway as a means of transporting livestock to market and thereby to reduce the inconvenience of processions of cattle through the city's streets. Lengthy discussions were conducted at both the Markets and Fairs Committee and at full council about the desirability of relocating the cattle market. By 1890, the site of the cattle market was deemed unsatisfactory, though the Corporation was unable to obtain a suitably large alternative site.

Thus, the cattle market remained on its existing site and a series of improvements to the facilities were undertaken. The most significant addition to the cattle market site was the construction of an abattoir. With a growing population, the city's need for slaughterhouses necessarily increased. The Council had attempted to build a temporary slaughterhouse in St Rumbold's Lane in 1894, but objections had been raised by the neighbouring Wesleyan Day School (Markets and Fairs Committee Minutes, 20 August 1894). Plans for a corporation slaughterhouse in the cattle market were drawn up by the City Engineer and this was constructed at the rear of the cattle market site, where it seems considerable earthworks were needed to accommodate the building. In April 1903, the new abattoir was officially opened by the Mayor (*Lincolnshire Chronicle*, 3 April 1903). The location of the abattoir was significant. Previously, the butchery had been situated in the heart of the city on a road unambiguously named Butchery St. This had been a relatively open site and no attempt appeared to have been made to conceal it. Alongside the corporation slaughterhouse on the site, several retail butchers had premises. Such spatial arrangements associated with the wholesale and retail meat trades were becoming relatively unusual by the end of the nineteenth century, however. While there was some debate among councillors about where the new abattoir should be located, it seems that all were agreed, according to the *Lincolnshire Echo* on 16 December 1897, that 'the Butchery was and remained a disgrace to the city of Lincoln.' The list of new corporation abattoirs visited by a deputation of Lincoln councillors prior to the development of the new facility included Derby, Manchester, Bolton, Blackpool, Accrington, Burnley and Birkenhead (*Lincolnshire Echo*, 16 December 1897). It seemed that the city did not wish to be left too far behind the civic developments undertaken elsewhere in this regard.

According to one anthropologist, Noelle Vialles, by the end of the nineteenth century, the slaughterhouse became a 'place that was no place' (Vialles, quoted in Joyce, 2003: 77). As Patrick Joyce identifies, 'Slaughter now took place in anonymous buildings . . . Slaughter became monitored, controlled, hygienised and punished if it did not measure up to its new science. Slaughter also became "humane". It also became large scale and industrial' (Joyce, 2003: 77). As Joyce indicates, something of the invisibility of the slaughterhouse is conveyed in the use of the euphemism for slaughterhouse – abattoir, which in French means 'to cause to fall, as trees are caused to fall' (Joyce, 2003: 77). Interestingly, in Lincoln, with the removal of the butcheries to the margins of the city centre, Butchery St was removed from the streetscape. In 1907, Ruddock's Lincoln directory still lists Butchery St, but by 1909, while entries for the street still exist in both Ruddock's and Kelly's directories, the reader is instructed to 'see Clasketgate' (Ruddock, 1907: 18) and informed 'now included in Clasketgate' (Kelly, 1907: 378).

Some of the problems associated with the city-centre location of the butcheries were removed, such as the occasional escape of runaway bullocks, recounted by one correspondent to the *Lincolnshire Echo* on 17 December 1897, who noted that an elderly gentleman narrowly escaped being knocked down in the incident. Despite the attempt to impose control and orderliness in the cattle market, inevitably some aspects were beyond human regulation.

References to the instatement of brick manure pits to accommodate 'sweepings and droppings' alluded to the constant battle to enforce order within the confines of the market (Markets and Fairs Committee Minutes, 14 February 1893).

By the end of the nineteenth century, significant attempts were being made to improve behaviour in the cattle market area by reducing the cultural centrality of the Cattle Market Hotel. Temperance provision was extended through the decade, partly as a result of the Church of England Temperance Society, which was able to provide a selection of non-alcoholic drinks such as tea, coffee and ginger beer. This facility in the cattle market was 'open the entire night for the convenience of herdsmen, drivers etc.' throughout the period of the April fair (Markets and Fairs Committee Minutes, 21 March 1893). The Markets and Fairs Committee also discussed providing those trading on the cattle market with a settling room. In 1891, at a council meeting, Councillor Ellis suggested the desirability of the Corporation building a 'settling house' at the cattle market. He stated that people purchasing stock had no other place to go to settle accounts but the public house, to which there were objections' (*Lincolnshire Chronicle*, 19 June 1891). By 1894, discussions were under way relating to the location of the new settling house on the cattle market (*Lincolnshire Chronicle*, 19 February 1894).

Lincoln Corporation's attempts to stress the increasing orderliness of the market were to a degree diluted by the decision to employ it as a location for the city's pleasure fairs, particularly that associated with the April horse and beast fair. Objections were made to this development, not least from a Mr Tennant, on behalf of the Privy Council (Markets and Fairs Committee Minutes, 1 August 1888). It was stated that markets being used as pleasure fairs 'brought a number of persons into contact with livestock which might have the effect of spreading disease and that it tended to prevent the cleansing of the market' (Markets and Fairs Committee Minutes, 1 August 1888).

Notwithstanding these reservations, and with the significant compensation generated by the rents received from the stallholders, the Corporation succumbed to the pressures applied from, among others, the local press and accommodated the fair on the cattle market site from the mid-1890s onwards. Before this, as the *Lincolnshire Chronicle* reported in 1891, the April pleasure fair tended to occupy the vacant ground on Monks Road to the east of the School of Art (*Lincolnshire Chronicle*, 24 April 1891). By 1898, however, the majority of the April pleasure fair was staged on the grounds of the cattle market. As the *Lincolnshire Chronicle* noted, 'So largely has the Corporation ground been taken up it is apparent the citizens will now take the lion's share of receipts from the fair. The wonder is that this source of revenue has been so long neglected' (*Lincolnshire Chronicle*, 29 April 1898).

The April pleasure fair quickly became established on the cattle market site. According to the *Lincolnshire Chronicle* in 1907, 'the pleasure fair was again situated on the usual spot on Monks Road and here citizens of all ages enjoyed themselves to the full' (*Lincolnshire Chronicle*, 26 April 1907). Before its move to the cattle market site, descriptions of the pleasure fair often referred to the lawlessness, or potential lawlessness associated with the event. Two-thirds of the *Stamford Mercury's* 1861 report of the April pleasure fair, for example, is dedicated to the crimes and policing associated with the event – with detectives being called upon from Manchester, Stoke, Birmingham, Leeds, Nottingham and Sheffield and reports of well-known thieves arriving for the event from Nottingham (*Stamford Mercury*, 26 April 1861). As the *Lincolnshire Chronicle* noted in its report of the 1867 April pleasure fair, 'The several trains were met at the stations by the detectives and persons known to be of suspicious character were quietly recommended to return home – a recommendation which was adopted in every instance' (*Lincolnshire Chronicle*, 27 April 1867). By 1907, the report of the fair is given over almost entirely to a description of its attractions. Among those listed are:

> roundabouts, cocoanut shies, with the former taking all forms varying from horses, cockerels and Venetian gondolas [and] so gaily coloured motor cars replete with rubber tyres, steering wheel . . . lamps and identification plates. The usual small stalls also found a place in the grounds.

As a postscript, it was added that the 'street traffic has been admirably controlled by the police under Chief Constable Coleman and his able staff . . .' (*Lincolnshire Chronicle*, 26 April 1907).

By the early twentieth century, therefore, Lincoln's cattle market appeared to be a relatively well-ordered space. Although originally cast out to the eastern margins of the city, in part so as to remove a potentially disruptive element from its centre, by the end of the nineteenth century, as the city continued to expand eastwards, the marginality of the cattle market diminished. Because of the sustained efforts to police and regulate the space occupied by the cattle market, through the implementation of government measures, local byelaws and self-regulation, the orderly terrain offered to the city by the cattle market was used to stage other events potentially challenging to the social order. By the beginning of the twentieth century, therefore, the threats to the city's economy and society, which had been perceived by many in association with the mid-nineteenth century cattle market, detailed by historians such as Joyce and Schmiechen, had been removed. Although constant vigilance was required, the Monks Road cattle market could now be regarded not as a site of social disruption where the rural and urban clashed, but one where interactions between the country and the city took place in a framework of regulation, hygiene and order.

The April horse fair

Lincoln's annual April horse fair was another event that brought together the urban and rural in potentially problematic fashion. At the end of the week-long event, which took place on the city's principal streets, including the High Street, according to one commentator 'the city's streets looked and smelt like a farm yard' (Elvin, 1967: 7). In contrast to the cattle market, where some form of *rapprochement* between rural and urban sensibilities enabled the market's continuance within an urban setting, the horse fair's end was regarded as more of an unambiguous triumph for the regulatory urban authorities.

The annual April horse fair, though, long resisted marginalisation within the city of Lincoln. The horse fair injected a substantial amount of income into the local economy for much of the nineteenth century, not least through the city's various inns and hotels, which did a brisk trade during the week of the fair. In 1869, some 5,000 animals were shown during the week (*Lincolnshire Chronicle*, 30 April 1869), the majority of them displayed on the city's streets, most notably the High Street and those adjoining it. The 1882 report of the fair, in the local newspaper, reveals a certain pride in the event. It noted that:

> By Monday morning there was a great influx into our city of breeders and dealers, several of the latter being from France, Germany, Austria and Belgium while the Irish breeders and dealers were largely represented.
>
> The various hotels and inns in the central part of the city were thronged with guests.
>
> (*Lincolnshire Chronicle*, 28 April 1882)

However, the same report also drew attention to the cultural clashes experienced in the city centre during the horse fair, when, it noted, 'as usual the men in charge [of the horses] have made these neighbourhoods particularly unpleasant to the occupants by reason of their unearthly yells and rough conduct' (*Lincolnshire Chronicle*, 28 April 1882). The sounds of the horse fair are much commented upon in press reports. In 1897, the *Lincolnshire Echo* referred to the 'loud-lunged individuals' who were in charge of the droves of young horses on the city's streets (*Lincolnshire Echo*, 20 April 1897). In 1893, a report described how:

> the thronged thoroughfares, cosmopolitan group of dealers . . . unusual tumults, hordes of exhuberant [*sic*] pleasure seekers and occasional rioters . . . converts the proud old city into a species of Nigni Novgerod and changes the High Street into a huge stable.
>
> (*Lincolnshire Echo*, 20 April 1893)

In addition to the offence caused to the urbane citizens of Lincoln by the influx of horse breeders and dealers, very real dangers presented themselves to passers-by as horses were put through their paces on the city's streets. The *Grantham Journal's* account of the 1864 April horse fair noted how 'Healey, a rat catcher was kicked violently over the arm which was broken and frightfully lacerated and many other persons were kicked but not seriously hurt' (*Grantham Journal*, 30 April 1864). The same report detailed how

Mr Toynbee, father of a city solicitor, 'was standing on High Bridge when a horse which was passing being cut with a whip swerved on one side and knocked Mr Toynbee down. He fell heavily on his forehead which was cut severely and bled profusely.' Nearly thirty years later, the *Lincolnshire Chronicle* commented, apparently rather light-heartedly, on the dangers of walking along Lincoln's streets during the horse fair. It noted that:

> The streets of the city have presented all these features of bustle and excitement so calculated to upset the nerves of the timid pedestrian who has proceeded along the thoroughfare with his 'weather' eye fixed with doubting gaze upon the heels of every animal within range; the 'horsey' man on the contrary has been in his element and has threaded his way amongst the animals regardless of iron-shod hoofs and with a contemptuous indifference to the fact that horses do sometimes elevate and extend their hind legs in a manner more forcible than pleasant to any unwary bystander.
>
> (*Lincolnshire Chronicle*, 29 April 1892)

Anxieties about the horse fair and the way in which it took over the city were becoming much more conspicuous in the early years of the twentieth century. While pride continued to be expressed in the event's significance, the uneasy disjunction between the rustic, dangerous, masculine, and relatively lawless world of the horse trader and the increasingly regulated, retail-orientated and feminized High Street became the subject of discussion. In 1903, for instance, the *Lincolnshire Chronicle* reported that there were enough horses at the fair 'to seriously interfere with vehicular traffic, to stop the trams . . . and to cause anxiety to nervous pedestrians who look askance at the business-like appearance of the hind-quarters of the hundreds of heavy animals backed up against the pavement' (*Lincolnshire Chronicle*, 24 April 1903). In 1903, such was the concern felt by some, that the City Council decided to consider the removal of the horse fair to the city's West Common (*Lincolnshire Echo*, 7 May 1903). This prompted considerable debate in the city. The Chamber of Commerce considered the matter and instituted a petition to retain the horse fair in the city centre, which, its members argued, was beneficial to trade, notwithstanding certain inconveniences that arose. As Mr G. Vickers, a member of the Chamber of Commerce commented, he did not think 'that there was much fear of the council taking any immediate action. They made projects at the commencement of one century and did not finish them in the next' (*Lincolnshire Chronicle*, 12 May 1903).

Although Mr Vickers's comments were perhaps overstated, longstanding discussions did take place among city councillors regarding the horse fair before significant actions were taken. Since the end of the nineteenth century, the city council had debated whether to regulate the event more stringently. In 1898, for instance, it was suggested that tolls should be charged for horses attending the fair; that the horses should be enclosed in one space; and that the horse fair should be removed from the High Street altogether. Such pleas continued into the third decade of the twentieth century before being heeded. Interestingly, during the first decades of the twentieth century, along with the challenges presented to the pedestrian, local papers again complained of the sounds associated with the horse fair – the 'lung power of the vendors' (*Lincolnshire Echo*, 26 April 1910); the 'raucous noises' (*Lincoln Gazette*, 26 April 1924). As the *Lincoln Gazette* declared in April 1922, 'A horse fair in the midst of a city crowded with modern traffic is simply an absurd anachronism' (*Lincoln Gazette*, 29 April 1922). The last horse fair on the city's streets took place in 1928, after which it was finally relocated to the city's West Common, where it diminished in significance until it ceased existence in 1952 (Elvin, 1967: 2).

Conclusion

As has been explored in the first part of this chapter, the romanticisation of the rural formed a recurring motif throughout much of the cultural output of later-nineteenth and early twentieth-century Britain, reflecting in part both a championing of the rural and a reaction against urban – particularly metropolitan – living. However, through the examination of the Lincoln case study and especially the analysis of the city's markets and horse fair, it seems that a more extensive examination of the interaction of the urban and rural in small- and medium-sized towns and cities at the turn of the twentieth century might suggest that the celebration of the bucolic was not as all-pervasive as some commentators might believe. This reluctance to lionise the rustic might have been particularly the case in smaller towns whose 'urban-ness' as a result of the town centres' proximity to the country was becoming somewhat questionable in a period when large urban centres were growing rapidly. Within Lincoln, although there remained awareness that economic benefit was derived from the close links with the rural hinterland, in the eyes of many law-abiding middle-class citizens the incursion of the rural population into the urban centre was a mixed blessing. A number of social and cultural historians have suggested that the nineteenth-century middle class was to some extent made in an urban context (Gunn, 1999: 12–29; Hill, 1999: 108). Within the developing administrative infrastructure of nineteenth-century urban society, largely populated by members of the middle class, their skills of political and social leadership could be tested and honed in an increasingly regularised public sphere. Within such a context, the relative disorder of the countryside could be seen to offer something of a threat in smaller market and county towns. Far from the idyllic rustic imagery which attracted the eye of the metropolitan sophisticate, to many inhabitants of smaller urban centres such as Lincoln, the 'rural' denoted inconvenience, disorder, lawlessness and the unwelcome smell of the farmyard.

References

Austen, Jane (1813) *Pride and Prejudice*. London: Penguin edition, 1972.

Barrell, John (1990) 'The public prospect and the private view: The politics of taste in eighteenth-century Britain', in Pugh, Simon (ed.), *Reading Landscape: Country, City, Capital*. Manchester, UK: Manchester University Press: 81–102.

Barrell, John and Bull, John (eds) (1974) *English Pastoral Verse*. London: Allen Lane.

Berghoff, H. (1990) 'Public schools and the decline of the British Economy, 1870–1914', *Past and Present*, 129: 148–67.

Bradley, Simon (2007) *St Pancras Station*. London: Profile Books.

Clark, Peter and Slack, Paul (1976) *English Towns in Transition*. Oxford: Oxford University Press.

Dellheim, Charles (1982) *The Face of the Past: The Preservation of the Medieval Inheritance in Victorian England*. Cambridge: Cambridge University Press.

Elvin, Lawrence (1967) 'The May Hirings', *Fireside Magazine*, 4(7): 4–7.

Farley, Paul and Symmons Roberts, Michael (2011) *Edgelands: Journeys into England's True Wilderness*. London: Jonathan Cape.

Gunn, Simon (1999) 'The public sphere, modernity and consumption: new perspectives on the history of the English middle class', in Kidd, Alan and Nicholls, David (eds), *Gender, Civic Culture and Consumerism: Middle-Class Identity in Britain, 1800–1940*. Manchester, UK: Manchester University Press: 12–33.

Hill, Francis (1974) *Victorian Lincoln*, Cambridge: Cambridge University Press.

Hill, Kate (1999) '"Thoroughly embued with the spirit of ancient Greece": Symbolism and space in Victorian civic culture', in Kidd, Alan and Nicholls, David (eds), *Gender, Civic Culture and Consumerism: Middle-Class Identity in Britain, 1800–1940*. Manchester, UK: Manchester University Press: 99–111.

Joyce, Patrick (2003) *The Rule of Freedom: Liberalism and the Modern City*. London: Verso.

Kelly's *Directory of Lincolnshire*, 1907. Lincoln Central Library.

Lees, Andrew (1985) *Cities Perceived: Urban Society in European and American Thought, 1820–1940*. Manchester, UK: Manchester University Press.

MacCarthy, Fiona (1994) *William Morris*. London: Faber & Faber.

Markets and Fairs Committee of Lincoln Corporation: minutes, 1883–94. Lincolnshire Archives (L1/1/20/1–3).

Mills, Dennis and Wheeler, Rob (2004) *Historic Town Plans of Lincoln, 1610–1920*. Lincoln, UK: Lincoln Record Society/Survey of Lincoln.

Pevsner, Nikolaus and Harris, John (revised by Antram, Nicholas) (1989) *The Buildings of Lincolnshire*, 2nd edn. London: Yale University Press.

Robbins, Edward (2010) '*News from Nowhere*: A Utopian Dream' in Hermansen Cordua, Christina (ed.), *Manifestoes and Transformations in the Early Modernist City*, London: Ashgate: 39–58.

Ruddock's *Lincoln City Directory*, 1907 and 1909. Lincoln Central Library.

Ruskin, John, (1851) *The Stones of Venice*, volume 2. London: Smith, Elder & Company.

Schmiechen, James (2001) 'The nineteenth-century British townscape and the return of the market place to Victorian history', in Shirley, Michael and Larson, Todd (eds), *Splendidly Victorian*. London: Ashgate: 187–201.

Steinbach, Susie L. (2012) *Understanding the Victorians: Politics, Culture and Society in Nineteenth-Century Britain*. London: Routledge.

Tann, Geoff (2011) 'From Bracebridge Hall to Grosvenor Hall', in Walker, Andrew (ed.), *South-East Lincoln: Canwick Road, South Common, St Catherine's and Bracebridge*. Lincoln, UK: Survey of Lincoln: 30–4.

Thompson, E. P. (1991) *Customs in Common*. London: Merlin Press.

Trott, Michael (2010) 'St Anne's Bedehouses', in Walker, Andrew (ed.), *Uphill Lincoln II: The North-Eastern Suburbs*. Lincoln, UK: Survey of Lincoln: 30–2.

White's *Directory of Lincolnshire*, 1852, 1856 and 1872. Lincoln Central Library.

Wiener, Martin (1981) *English Culture and the Decline of the Industrial Spirit, 1850–1980*, Cambridge: Cambridge University Press.

Williams, Raymond (1973) *The Country and the City*. London: Chatto & Windus.

7 Pits, pylons and posts

Writing under the English rural idyll

Catherine Parry

Literary criticism has tended to be culturally contextual and uninterested in the non-human world, and narratological theory in particular subsumes this world under the term 'setting' in fiction.[1] This configuration relegates the space of the fictional story-world to the status of an inert background to the human action of the novel; it is the means by which the plot is furnished with objects, or is the extrapolation and exterior metaphorical expression of human passions and cultural and social structures. 'Setting' becomes a humanised wordscape that forgets, as Timothy Clark says, that 'culture itself has a context' – the *meta-context* of the biosphere, land, water, air, or what we more commonly call 'nature' or 'the environment' (2011: 4). Emerging in the last twenty years, and contiguous with a 'material turn', ecocriticism is a form of literary criticism that has sought to retrieve this meta-context from the background to explore the poetics of its reproduction, representation and transfiguration, and the nature of humans in and with it. As Clark says, ecocriticism 'does not write as if human beings were sole occupants of the planet', and aims to 'open itself to a space in which fundamental questions about the human place in nature are at issue' (2011: 5).

The concept of rurality offers a framework in which to examine a mode of human inhabiting of the land, but one that assumes a degree of non-human, natural components to its condition; this perspective enables the development of a rich ecocritical approach to interrogating human relationships with the natural environment and the multiple forms of human crossings and penetrations of it. Literature has often been perceived as representing the English countryside via the trope of the rural idyll, a trope that has become part of a cultural discourse of a 'return to nature', ecological crisis, and simultaneous commodification of nature, and has often been criticised for participating in unreflective idealising. There is, however, a counter-discourse in English literature that resists this critical framework and narrates rural England in a self-reflexive fashion to produce a sub-landscape – a drop below the flat, idealised image of the rural landscape. This chapter offers ecocritically inflected readings of a representative sample of literary rural English landscapes: Kenneth Grahame's *Wind in the Willows*, Clive King's *Stig of the Dump*, Kazuo Ishiguro's *Never Let Me Go*, and Gareth Lovett Jones's

The Wind in the Pylons. It takes a deconstructive approach to exploring what suggests that a fictional, textual landscape is rural, and considers the significance of reflexive textualisations of human perceptual and experiential encounters with the non-human world.

In Britain (as in many other countries) rurality is legislatively defined according to human population density (Defra, 2011), delineating it as social spacing and a set of socio-political and economic conditions. In this way the word *rural* becomes a noun – a word associated with a deictic referent, and implying a self-evident object or concept that contains within itself its own definition and description; but as is frequently observed in the field of Rural Studies, *rural* has proved to have a meaning that is very difficult to pin down. This may well be because *rural* is an adjective and cannot therefore be reduced to an absolute value and the naming of specific conditions. The function of an adjective is to modify nouns, to be an agent of that noun's description, and to make propositions about it. An adjective is not, in itself, the subject of finite descriptive boundaries.[2] In the same manner as adjectives such as *beautiful*, *quaint*, *romantic*, *natural*, *sparse*, *peaceful*, the meaning of *rural* emerges as relative and subjective, and uncertain as to whether it is constituted by reality or social construction. The linguistic sign, *rural*, does not therefore refer to some fixed space, concept or object. Consequently, what is understood by *rural* varies a great deal as different agencies or politics have sought and continue to seek to assign particular values, ideals or problems, and differing and often conflicting attributes, to a particular ascription of a social, geographical, imaginary or abstract space. The cultural myth of rural England in particular is generated by imaginings of what type and degree of human presence is tolerable in the visual amenity of the landscape, and much of the conflict between the forces of development and those of conservation coagulates around these characterisations.

A rural landscape is one of domesticated nature, which Raymond Williams, in *The Country and the City* (1973), identifies as coming into conceptual being in opposition to the city, but the presence of nature in the equation implies that rurality is an intermediate zone between urbanness, as dense human land occupation, and wilderness, as an absence of human occupation in a land that is somehow perceived as 'virgin'.[3] The task, then, is to see the word for what it is – representative of a space of transaction, compromise and hybridity on a scale of human impact, a space shot through with both natural and human activity. A consequence of failing to do this is for the concept to exist as a normative claim, and an established and stable backdrop that makes natural some kinds of human activity while distorting and concealing others. Williams observes that the English ideal of rurality often had as its referent a countryside originating in the conscious design of landowners who sought 'a rural landscape emptied of rural labour and of labourers; a sylvan and watery prospect, with a hundred analogies in neo-pastoral painting and poetry' that operated as 'the expression of control and command' (1973: 124). These created landscapes, designed to be aesthetically pleasing views of an imagined version of nature rather than of indigenous wild systems, and distinct from working landscapes, became part of an archetype of England, which physically and discursively elided the unpicturesque (flat fields, middens, weeds, human poverty) from sight. Literature has often been complicit in perpetuating such a privileged, sentimental and unquestioning view of rural England in which the Miltonian 'happy rural seat of various view,' with its rich trees, golden fruit, and 'lawns, or level downs, and flocks/Grazing the tender herb' (Milton, 2000: iv. 247–53), sites Eden and the fantasy of an Ancient Greek Golden Age in a bucolic English landscape. It is possibly not so much that Milton imagined England looked like Paradise, but rather that he imagined Paradise looked like his vision of England, and this vision is rural, rustic and humanised rather than a wilderness.

The idea of England as an earthly Eden has had a tenacious grip on the literary imagination, as can be seen in *The Wind in the Willows*. The original 1908 edition of the novel had only one illustration – a frontispiece captioned 'And a River went out from Eden' (Robertson, 1995: 211), depicting three naked (sexless) children playing in a small waterfall. This created an explicit link between the domestic English countryside, in which *Willows* is set, and the myth of a rural, beatific eternity in Paradise. The pleasures, picnics and 'dusty lanes' (Grahame, 1993: 41) that typify the lives of the Riverbankers also reproduce some of the traditions of English pastoral, and suggest landscapes of rubicund simplicity that occlude the realities of history. Williams dismisses *The Wind in the Willows* as 'country-based fantasy' (1973: 258), and the imaginative residue of the novel is indeed of a nostalgic idyll of sun, leisure and comfort; but although the text perpetuates an ideology of middle-class privilege that seeks to preserve a particular version of England for the benefit of a minority in its mythic, rural world, it is not entirely unselfconscious about the disjuncture between creative, nostalgic narration and the original experience upon which this representation is based.

In a passage in which the Riverbankers tell stories around winter fires, they describe the river bank of the previous summer in 'scene-pictures' of purple loosestrife 'shaking luxuriant tangled locks along the edge of the river whence its own face laughed back at it', and recall dog-rose stepping 'delicately on the stage . . . [signalling] as if string-music had announced it in stately chords that strayed into a gavotte that June at last was here'. This effusive prose, complete with shepherd boys, nymphs and almost parodic flamboyance, is not, however, intended by the animals as mimesis. It is instead a conscious framing of the river bank in the pastoral literary tradition,[4] and the description of their fireside stories as a 'play' and as a 'rich chapter . . . [w]ith illustrations so numerous and so very highly coloured' (Grahame, 1993: 40–1) introduces brackets that suggest textual awareness of how an experience can be fictionalised and idealised in its retelling. The Mole, however, finds his friends' narrative extravagance unsatisfactory and, on an outing to the Wild Wood on a cold winter's day, discovers that:

> [t]he country lay bare and entirely leafless around him, and he thought that he had never seen so far and so intimately into the insides of things as on that winter day when Nature was deep in her annual slumber and seemed to have kicked the clothes off. Copses, dells, quarries and all hidden places . . . seemed to ask him to overlook their shabby poverty for a while, till they could riot in rich masquerade, and trick and entice him with the old deceptions . . . He had got down to the bare bones of it.
>
> (1993: 42)

Maureen Thum suggests that Grahame is exploring 'different modes of perception in their relationship to one another' (1992: 27), and the Mole, in perceiving the aesthetic effect of the metaphorical 'masquerade' of leaves and literary description, enjoys his best attempt at recovering an honest text of his own experience. He subverts the fantasy Eden and replaces it with what is for him, owing to its 'kicking off' of the 'clothing' of pastoral rhetoric, an infinitely more satisfying vision of England. In discerning the 'bare bones' of the land the Mole sees the solid and lasting matter previously concealed by pastoral words and summer leaves, and produces a self-reflexive understanding of his own role in the textualisation of Nature; but although he attempts to inhabit a space of 'hidden places' in a writing of nature, he fails. The Mole is to be commended for his efforts to articulate his sensing of an otherness and for understanding his complicity in its loss, but he remains an anthropocentric (so to speak) portly Edwardian gentlemole, limited to his own experience and unable to produce a poetics of non-human time and space. The Mole's focus is on a natural harmony made possible by stasis, a resistance to the taint of the modern and the urban (as symbolised by the Toad's love of cars and speed, a view shared by E. M. Forster's *Howard's End*), and to the containment and neutralisation of the unruly, uncivilised Wildwood. His wish for his beloved river bank is that it remains an ahistoricised, dematerialised dream space – a perpetual holiday that cannot take into account the dynamic relations and processes that constitute the ongoing reproduction and recreation of the land in time and space. The particular quality of the Mole's experience is, nevertheless, a subversion of the classically derived ideals upon which visions of rural England depend.

Stig of the Dump offers a far more compromised rural vision than *The Wind in the Willows*, and suggests that the rural landscape of post-World War II England in which *Stig* is set is difficult to typify as idyllic. Barney, the young hero of the story, is staying at his grandparents' house during the school holidays, and although the surrounding Kentish countryside is populated with the literary signposts of rural charm – lanes, copses, farm animals, orchards, hop gardens, villages and churches – a main road, a line of pylons, a cement works and a television mast are also visible in the same landscape. These modern intrusions suggest that the narrative rejects the traditions of pastoral and the rural idyll, instead embodying Paul Cloke's definition of the 'post-rural' in which rurality is conceptualised as 'characterised by a multiplicity of social spaces, overlapping the same geographical area' (2006: 19), with blurrings between country and city indicative of hybridisations, deterritorialisation and pseudo-rural landscapes. The Kent countryside that Barney can see from the top of the North Downs, with its mix of nature, longstanding human habitation, modern infrastructure and industrialisation, can certainly be described as hybrid; however, this literary landscape is not constituted from merely visible, superficial conditions or a two-dimensional formulation of multiple overlapping social spaces.

Barney encounters two environments that slip under the visible landscape, and which require a wider conceptualisation than a purely social framework. First, through his friendship with Stig, the eponymous 'caveman' dump-dweller, Barney makes a magical Midsummer-Night's-Dream-like trip back in time to (presumably) Neolithic England, and finds 'nothing but forest and heath' (King, 1963: 127), with only minimal marks of human presence in the landscape. Robert Pogue Harrison argues that forests exist in the cultural imaginary as mythological spaces that are 'antecedent to the human world' (1992: 1) and representative of the antithesis of civilisation and the rational human mind. This antithesis is made clear in the stark visual contrast between past and present landscapes as Barney makes an abrupt return at sunrise from the Neolithic forests to the misty early morning fields and roads of twentieth century England, invoking a sense of loss at the deforestation that has taken place in the intervening millennia. To Harrison and *Stig of the Dump* the loss of the forests marks the end of the enchanted world, and the emergence of the cement works and pylons from the mist is indicative of a mundane reality of which alterity is no longer a part.

Second, centuries of chalk-extraction have left a deep pit (now an informal dump) in the woods behind Barney's garden. As Barney stands at its edge for the first time the literal and metaphorical ground 'gives way' beneath his feet and he drops below the landscape – below the visible landscape, and below the cultural veneer that constitutes his habituation to and acceptance of his environment. This new orientation causes him to view the familiar furniture of the world from an unfamiliar angle as below the lived and worked Kent countryside is evidence of aeons of past lives that, until chalk-mining cuts into it, remains unseen and unnarrated. In describing 'lines of flints poking out like bones' (King, 1963: 8) from the sub-landscape of the pit's chalk walls, the narrative intimates a sense of the land, formations and organisms that precede and exceed human culture, and the solid chalk and flint geology that forms the Kentish North Downs invokes the vast stretch of time prior to a comparatively tiny period of human activity.[5] The hole left by land-removal is an untitled absence signifying a no-place status, and Barney observes that 'now [people] did not know what to do with this hole . . . they were trying to fill it up again. Anything people didn't want they threw into the bottom of the pit' (1963: 8). This suggests that in its reorientation as a rubbish dump the pit has become emblematic of an apparent necessity for society to conceal its wastefulness from itself. In this sense the pit could be conceived of as an outlier of industrial activity – a disconnected island of degenerated urban symbols skulking unseen and unconsidered beneath the discursive landscape; but although clearly a critique of thoughtlessness and the cycle of consumption that characterises modern urban life, the dump is not represented as an extra-urban wasteland. Among the broken furniture, old bottles and rusty nails are niche colonies of local flora and fauna as dynamic non-human life makes the most of a contaminated but relatively undisturbed space, and this adaptation to the penetration of industrialisation into rurality blurs conventional assumptions of a nature/culture divide, and exceeds a simple epitomisation of post-rural, overlapping social spaces. This environment is an enmeshing of material condition, abstract conceptualisation, and a space curiously composed not of human physical and social activity, but of its residue, and with 'nature' retaining a toehold. While the chalk strata revealed in the sides of the pit suggests that the past is more than just us, and that this narrative has a poetics of layers – layers of landscape composed of nature, pre-history, coccoliths, mines, forests, mists, villages and cement works – the pit also suggests that where once there was a landscape characterised by slow and continuous evolution, there is now disconnection, abruption and intrusion. The landscape no longer accumulates organically as a system in a constant process of change, exchange and infinite possibility, but contains elements such as pylons that are spontaneously imposed on the land as inert weight in the ecology and that cannot be accommodated by it.

Landscape and nature are key conceptual elements in an ecocritical evaluation of rurality. 'Nature', as is frequently observed, is a deeply complex word[6] denoting multiple aspects of the same concept; it is used to define the elements, land, sea, plants and animals as a single entity, and names something separate to humans which is *a priori* and given in existence. Therefore, using the word 'nature' invokes a domain occupied by the planet Earth and its elemental, organic and unconscious behavioural constituent parts. This domain includes the biological human body and some aspects of behaviour, but not human activity and its products – cars, cities, the internet, shopping – and seems a common sense distinction between what is assuredly natural and what is not. However, rurality proposes an environment in which this simple distinction is problematic, populated as it is by plants, landforms and animals that seem natural in essence and biology but that have habits, physical forms, and locations at least partly shaped by human intent (dairy cows, managed woodland, fields of wheat, pheasants, hedgerows, and so on). Creating 'nature' as the world that is 'not us' is an ontological conceptualisation that struggles to be meaningful in rurality. 'Nature' appears to refer to a concrete reality, but lacking a clear outline or palpable presence functions as a method by which humans can model, perceive and represent aspects of the world. It also bears a symbolic load – it is that from which humans try to escape, while also seeking to return to it as solace. This does not, however, mean that there is not a 'something' that can be referred to as nature.

The concept of landscape has proved to be similarly slippery in meaning, with disciplinary usages tending to revolve around treating it as the objective features of the land, or the way it is viewed, or, alternatively, incorporating these two approaches in order to recognise historical and geographical reality and the cultural and social construction of perspective. According to Bakhtin:

> when collective labour and the struggle with nature had ceased to be the only arena for man's encounter with nature and the world, then nature itself ceased to be a living participant in the events of life. Then nature became, by and large, a 'setting for action', its backdrop; it was turned into landscape.
>
> (1981: 217)

For Bakhtin, then, landscape is an intermediary layer between nature and human, an obscuring cultural superimposition resulting from human entry into an abstracted, alienated relationship with nature. Raymond Williams argues that landscape is a frame of representation – an idea that 'implies separation and observation' (1973: 120) – which produces (usually rural) scenery for the detached consumption of the powerful in society, while John Wylie suggests that '[l]andscape is both the phenomenon itself *and* our perception of it' (2007: 7). It is 'a *way of seeing things*, a particular way of looking and picturing the world around us. Landscapes are not just about *what* we see but about *how we look*' (ibid.). Our perspectives are conditioned by social and educational factors so that our gaze upon landscapes is 'always already laden with particular cultural values, attitudes, ideologies and expectations' that affect both the physical and the imaginative shaping of the land (2007: 7). David James offers a theorisation of literary landscape reproduction: literature offers a method of representing the perceptual experience that constitutes the human encounter with the land, and opens 'richly figurative spaces, where imagined and material zones coexist' (2008: 7). Landscape as a means of understanding how humans 'read' the land has, therefore, multiple configurations from which narratives of historical and lived relations can emerge; it signifies the complex interchanges between understandings and bracketings of naturalness and artificiality, and between imaginative representation and performance.

David Harvey observes that '[a]ll critical examinations of the relation to nature are simultaneously critical examinations of society' (1996: 1), and in both physical and literary terms landscape expresses and influences social conditions. Although the psychological, social and political landscapes of Kazuo Ishiguro's *Never Let Me Go* have provoked the most interest, the physical landscape its cloned children inhabit is significant not only as a 'setting' that illustrates their condition, but also as an instrument of their oppression and a factor in their exclusion from the 'proper' human life. Inhabiting a dystopian version of late twentieth-century England, the clones are bioengineered to produce replacement organs for 'natural' humans. Social, linguistic and cultural structures have emerged to enable 'real' humans to conceal from themselves the horror of the clones' physical suffering, but the biological condition of the clones – abstracted from phylogenetic development

– also bars them from immersion in the recursive historical development of humans and land. For the clones there is a close relationship between social structures and the concept of nature, and a conflict between the natural humanity they (the clones) express and the artificiality their contemporary culture uses to describe and exclude them. This is refracted through the rural environments they occupy and the condition of this occupation.

Kathy H. is the self-conscious self-narrator of *Never Let Me Go*, re-membering (or re-memorying) her life and friends to an unidentified narratee. Her childhood and teenage years are spent at a boarding school, Hailsham, and her memories of this period contain elements of what seems to be nostalgic happiness. She describes the school and its grounds in terms of its platial associations – places to be with friends, places to be alone, to have a private conversation. Place, says Lawrence Buell, is 'associatively thick' (2005: 63), and the thickness of individual and collective experience in the landscape is the conceptual means by which the social, political and economic intercourse that constitutes human history is imbricated with naturally derived topographical features such as woods and fields, and the built topographies of houses, roads or fences. Place has 'felt value' (Buell, 2005: 63) and ascribed meanings in its concrete locations, and is a concept that describes lived relations among and with stable, concrete 'things'. When Hailsham is dismantled by 'real' humans, who fear the creatures they have created but cannot let go, its concretised platial qualities vanish with it, leaving Kathy with no platial associations or loyalties. Her associations exist in a closed and entirely social system, and this system is imagined and connected through a place that now exists only in memory; it is as nostalgic as the past worlds of George Eliot and Thomas Hardy that the clones are encouraged to read.

Hailsham is sited in a secluded valley, which both screens the clones from public view and isolates them by obscuring their view of mainstream human life. The world beyond the occluding hills and trees is a 'fantasy land' (Ishiguro, 2005: 66) about which Kathy and her friends know almost nothing. In order to illustrate lessons about this unseen England their guardian, Miss Emily, uses photographs of the English countryside in calendars showing:

> little villages with streams going through them, white monuments on hillsides, old churches beside fields; if she was telling us about a coastal place, there'd be beaches crowded with people, cliffs with seagulls . . . and it's amazing, even now, after all these miles I've covered as a carer, the extent to which my idea of the various counties is still set by these pictures.
>
> (2005: 64)

However, as Kathy drives around England in later life, caring for other clones who have begun to donate their organs, these expectations are not met as she never finds the bucolic charm, friendly landscapes and visions of natural beauty offered by the calendars. The landscape Kathy moves across is populated with marshes, long roads, 'rows of furrowed fields' (2005: 113) and endless grey skies, and a trip to the seaside discovers a chilly wind and loneliness instead of 'ordinary', happy picnicking families. Kathy drives on the 'obscure back roads' (2005: 267) of a cold, grey England, apparently analogising her cultural alienation and exclusion with chill, empty and charmless backdrops, and reflecting her bioengineered unnaturalness, infertility and inability to challenge the cruel ontology that casts her as sub-human in reiterations of sterile dead trees and weak sun, and obstructively thick mud, boggy ground, weeds and thickets. In this sense the rural landscape is no more than a metaphor for the clones' cultural invisibility and helplessness, and the necessary background space in which they move, but such an interpretation ignores the quality of Kathy's experience of the land itself.

Kathy's descriptions of difficult boundaries or impassable ground are not made self-consciously or figuratively by her – she does not perceive dead trees as symbolic of her own lack of fertility, or barbed wire fences as an analogy of a cruel, exploitative and exclusionary system. Fences, ditches and mud are described by her as no more than the meaningless furniture of the land, practicalities to be overcome or to be defeated by, and metaphorical interpretations arise only in the negotiation between text and reader. As a created, bioengineered organism Kathy has no parents, cannot have children, has no discoverable place to call home once Hailsham is closed, no historical identity, no human or cultural ancestry to provide an ideological frame through which to make meaningful connections with the landscape. In much the same way as the cement works in *Stig of the Dump* are imposed onto rural fields, she is an irruption into a landscape that cannot assimilate her and into which she does not have permission to assimilate herself; she is not *of* it, but is an aberrant who cannot participate in the narrative of landscape – the story of the past that creates the human lives of the present. There is no sense of platial 'associative thickness' as the land constitutes only the geographical means by which Kathy's friends are scattered and disconnected. Hailsham's destruction ends affective platial connections, so that where those with privileged human status see themselves and their historical affiliations in the land*scape* as inclusive social and cultural representation, Kathy only travels across non-symbolic, meaningless *land* empty of emotional perspective. Although embodying human technological progress, her alienation also symbolises the exceeding by technology of our psychological and ethical capacities; in Kathy we see that we manipulate the material of the world beyond our ability to understand the effects on ourselves and the other life forms and matter concerned.

Although *The Wind in the Pylons* has a title which gestures towards parody its intention is not to lampoon its literary parent but to satirise an England that has succeeded and obliterated that found in *The Wind in the Willows*. Corporate power and greed, and the degraded social and material world engendered by an ethos of profit and growth, are the main targets for caricature and irony, but agri-business, modern politics, industrial animal farming and car culture, modern art and hunting are also in the firing line. Successors of the original *Willows* characters populate a novel in which there are only animals, or 'mals': Wyvern Toad is the smug, manipulative and ruthless CEO of a vast business, and has appropriated the laws of nature to explain the 'very very very short-term self-interest' of the Market, but he also manifests undercurrents of weariness at the effort to keep up with the ruthless society he has been instrumental in creating; Badger is an animal rights activist; Mr Rette is a highly stressed executive heading Toad's 'Global Corporate Degirthing Committee' (Lovett Jones, 2003: 73) (he makes people redundant), with status, a large house, and golf club memberships to support.

Only the Mole is retained in his original innocent and diffident form. *Pylons* is told from the Mole's perspective as, via the device of a time tunnel, he emerges unwittingly into the daylight above his home nearly one hundred years later than he might have expected. He is shocked to find that, outside his door where once there was 'a grassy meadow, close by a hedge . . . patterned over with the tiny white blooms of the blackthorn', there are now concrete posts, the shattered remnants of a hedge, and a vast ploughed field (2003: 16–17). The Mole is later uncomprehendingly horrified by immense out-of-town retail units and their attendant car parks, terrifying roads, bubbling yellow scum on his beloved River, a theme park at Toad Hall, sterile commercial forests, and small pockets of woodland designated as Conservation Areas kept for hunting. These landscapes are components of what their landowners (mainly Toads and Weasels) still claim as 'the Countryside' (2003: 208), a space in which Country mals describe themselves as the embodiment of everything worth calling nature in their control of what lives, grows or dies, so that 'malocentric' design deposes any sense of nature as some independent preceding and exceeding context. Rural countryside is a space shaped by class power and market forces, and has become post-rural – a space described by Cloke as one 'in which consumers of the rural realize that rurality represents an inauthentic pastiche of meanings and symbols but are nevertheless happy to go along with this postmodern condition' (2006: 22). The objects of *Pylons'* satire are those who, because social and career progress requires it, do indeed present the appearance of being 'happy to go along with' such an obviously constructed version of nature and rurality, but for many, including Mr Rette, who privately writes anguished poetic searches for otherness, there is anxiety and loss only just below the social veneer.

The brutal shock of *Pylons*' representation of rural England is created through the perspective of the Mole's unaccustomed eyes – eyes that were not exposed to the decades of cultural and ideological acclimatisation that intervened between his past and his present. Unable to accept the loss of his own Edenic England on the Riverbank of the past, the Mole simply cannot accommodate the post-rural commercial version of the idyll that confronts him. It is therefore possible that the Mole's perspective is exaggeratedly gloomy and alarmist, and this would allow his version of England to be rejected as an unrecognisable and purely speculative fiction. However, his wistful suggestion that more picnics and boating would solve many of the modern world's dissatisfactions, and a sudden jolt of doubt in his faith that everyone in Edwardian England was well-fed and happy, suggests that *Pylons*' perspective on the rural scene of *Willows* is not one of naivety, and that the contrast symbolised by pylons and willows involves something other than a nostalgic wish for a return to a fictional idyll. In an endnote Lovett Jones claims that '[w]ith the exception of a few imaginary details . . . the descriptions of landscapes, both rural and urban, in this novel are based on direct observation', and so insists that the damaged environment he portrays is not some alternative England intended only to highlight the paucity of the modern human condition. This rural England, says *The Wind in the Pylons*, is instead a real and profoundly problematic one in which everything – animals, plants, ecologies – that exists for purposes other than human industrial production and consumption is being physically and discursively overwritten, and subverted by landscapes of power and humanisation.

None of the novels under discussion renders mimetic representations of the world; anthropomorphic Edwardian animals, time travel, clone children, and a squirrel prime minister are components of fictional journeys into dreamy fantasy, horror and absurdity, but each of them is situated in an England which provokes an emotional response and a reflexive imaginative engagement both with the literary rural idyll and with an alternative to it. They explore the sub-landscape that purports to underlie aesthetic consumption and the search for meaning, and do not find meaning there; however, neither do they find some 'authentic', *a priori* rendition of England in their strategies of non-idealisation. Instead, what is revealed is an enmeshing of matter, discourse and symbol in which representation, interpretation and originary material are locked together in a dynamic embrace. The contemporary cultural/urban visualisation of rural England as a temporary utopian space becomes problematic in the literary juxtapositions and contrasts of 'natural' and human, producing texts which prevent the reader from moving through the textual landscape as if it is ambient and unproblematic, or as if writer, reader and critic are not implicated in its condition. These texts find aspects of contemporary rurality to be indicative of a troubled human relationship with the non-human world, and it is from this perspective that the concept of rurality offers literary criticism a field in which to explore the continuities, discontinuities, identifications with 'nature' and disavowals of a proposed connection of humans with the land as they emerge in literary representation. Equally, literary criticism offers a method with which to examine the complex of relationships that both produce and challenge the real and the imagined landscape.

Notes

1 Seymour Chatman (1978), for example, describes 'setting' as the story-space in which characters move. Principally, he says, setting ''sets the character off' in the usual figurative sense of the expression; it is the place and collection of objects

'against which' his actions and passions appropriately emerge' (p. 139), and contributes 'to the mood of the narrative' (p. 141).

2 See Guy M. Robinson (Robinson, 1990: xx) who notes that the term rural 'has proved an especially elusive one to define for purposes of academic study', and also Paul Cloke (Cloke *et al.*, 2006: 18), who argues that

> while cities are usually understood in their own terms, and certainly without any detectable nervousness about defining or justifying that understanding, rural areas represent more of a site of conceptual struggle, where the other-than-urban meets the multifarious conditions of vastly differing scales and styles of living.

3 'Wilderness' as a state of being is often considered to be irrelevant to England's densely populated, heavily farmed and altered landscapes, and whether this is a factual statement or not the idea of wilderness nevertheless persists variously in the imagination on a scale from an ideal condition of pure nature to land which has yet to be developed – a condition Heidegger termed 'standing reserve'.

4 See Rupert Hildyard's chapter, 'A Case Study in the Literary Construction of the Rural Idyll: The English Farm' (this volume), for a discussion of the pastoral tradition in English literature.

5 The chalk which forms the North and South Down of Southern England was laid down in the warm seas of the Late Cretaceous period. This chalk is a sedimentary formation composed of calcite from the shells of billions of coccoliths – tiny planktonic creatures – which once swam in the shallow waters covering what is now the British Isles (Holmes, 1978: 82; Lord *et al.*, 2002: 28, 44).

6 See Raymond Williams, *Keywords* (1976); C. S. Lewis (1967), *Studies in Words*; Kate Soper (1995), *What is Nature?*

References

Bakhtin, M. (1981) *The Dialogic Imagination*, ed. M. Holqist, trans. C. Emerson. Austin, TX: University of Texas Press.

Buell, L. (2005) *The Future of Environmental Criticism: Environmental Crisis and Literary Imagination*. Oxford: Blackwell.

Chatman, S. (1978) *Story and Discourse: Narrative Structure in Fiction and Film*. Ithaca, NY: Cornell University Press.

Clark, T. (2011) *The Cambridge Introduction to Literature and the Environment*. Cambridge: Cambridge University Press.

Cloke, P. (2006) 'Conceptualizing rurality', in P. Cloke, T. Marsden, P. Mooney (eds), *The Handbook of Rural Studies*. London: Sage.

Cloke, P., Marsden, T., and Mooney, P. (2006) (eds) *The Handbook of Rural Studies*. London: Sage.

DEFRA, 'Rural Definition and Classification'. Available at: http://archive.defra.gov.uk/evidence/statistics/rural/rural-definition.htm#defn. (accessed 14 October 2011).

Grahame, K. (1908) (1993) *The Wind in the Willows*. Ware, UK: Wordsworth Editions.

Harrison, R. P. (1992) *Forests: The Shadow of Civilisation*. Chicago, IL: Chicago University Press.

Harvey, D. (1996) *Justice, Nature, and the Geography of Difference*. Oxford: Blackwell.

Holmes, D. (1978) *Principles of Physical Geology*, 3rd edition. Middlesex, UK: Thomas Nelson and Sons.

Ishiguro, K. (2005) *Never Let Me Go*. London: Faber & Faber.

James, D. (2008) *Contemporary British Fiction and the Artistry of Space: Style, Landscape, Perception*. London: Continuum.
King, C. (1963) *Stig of the Dump*. London: Puffin Books.
Lewis, C. S. (1967) *Studies in Words*. Cambridge: Cambridge University Press.
Lord, J. A., Clayton, C. R. I. and Mortimore, R. N. (2002) *Engineering in Chalk*. London: CIRIA.
Lovett Jones, G. (2003) *The Wind in the Pylons*, vol. 1. Aylesbury, UK: Hilltop Publishing.
Milton, J. (2000) *Paradise Lost*. London: Penguin.
Robertson, G. (1995) 'And a river went out from Eden' (illustration), in J. Darcy. 'The Representation of Nature in *The Wind in the Willows* and *The Secret Garden*', *The Lion and the Unicorn* (2): 211–22.
Robinson, G. M. (1990) *Conflict and Change in the Countryside*. Chichester, UK: John Wiley & Sons.
Soper, K. (1995) *What is Nature? Culture, Politics and the Non-Human*. Oxford: Blackwell.
Thum, M. (1992) 'Exploring 'The Country of the Mind': Mental Dimensions of Landscape in Kenneth Grahame's *The Wind in the Willows*', *Children's Literature Association* 17(3): 27–32.
Williams, R. (1973) *The Country and the City*. London: Chatto & Windus.
Williams, R. (1976) *Keywords: A Vocabulary of Culture and Society*. London: Fontana/Croom Helm Paperbacks.
Wylie, J. (2007) *Landscape*. Abingdon, UK: Routledge.

8 A place for grazing livestock in defining rurality?

Stephen J. G. Hall

Concepts of rurality are necessary to underpin important practical matters such as policies for planning and rural development. Landscape ecologists have devised approaches based on multivariate statistics applied to environmental and socio-economic data (e.g. van Eupen *et al.*, 2012) while geographers have employed paradigms whereby rurality was 'equated . . . with particular spaces and functions' (Cloke and Thrift, 1994), but the use in policy documents of terms like 'intrinsic character' (see the Introduction) raises the question as to whether rural districts have emergent properties that are not captured by a purely statistical or formulaic approach.

At one level, rurality might be defined in negative terms as being the 'counterpart of urban' (Introduction), and a rural region being one where the factors defining the urban environment are absent or insignificant. Alternatively, rural districts might be defined as those where food is produced, yet under modern conditions it is very clear that farming and countryside have become 'disconnected' (Policy Commission on the Future of Farming and Food, 2002 – the 'Curry Report'). This chapter considers whether farm animals, specifically the grazing livestock (sheep and cattle), which are only kept indoors at limited times of the year, might contribute to a typology of the rural. I investigate whether livestock information, traditionally seen as productivist data of purely statistical interest, can give deep insights into the systems and cultures of which livestock are a part and can be indicative of rurality.

The British countryside is the product of centuries of development and a historical perspective is essential if it, and the livestock that use it, are to be understood. Reference is therefore made to certain aspects of the status of farm animals in the late eighteenth and the nineteenth centuries; the general background is given by Hall and Clutton-Brock (1988).

Although only 7 per cent of respondents in the study of Halfacree (1995) mentioned animals as a defining feature of the rural, the developing interest in animal geographies (Buller, 2004; Philo and Wilbert, 2000) provides an academic justification for this study. For some practical purposes, such as the planning of healthcare (Rousseau, 1995), socio-economic indicators are of prime relevance, but for environmental planning in the broad sense, the animal component is, I argue, of vital importance. Without grazing livestock, the characteristic British patchworks of fields, their boundaries, and traditional farm buildings would be threatened and land unfit for crops would be taken over by scrubland or forestry. While today livestock production only accounts for a small proportion of national income (Policy Commission on the Future of Farming and Food, 2002), in the 1930s, 90 per cent of agricultural land was devoted to growing food for livestock, and half of agricultural workers were involved in one way or another with livestock (Astor and Rowntree, 1939: 126), and the physical and cultural relics of this predominance remain with us.

Livestock culture is also embodied in Britain's farming families, very many of whom have long histories as tenants or freeholders. Of 260 respondents to a preliminary survey in 2006–8 of British livestock farmers, 174 (67 per cent) could trace the involvement of their families back at least 150 years. Respondents were from 51 of the 59 non-metropolitan '1974 counties' of Great Britain (Hall, unpublished).

Farm animals have not been prominent in academic rural studies in spite of this importance. They are a component in most people's notion of the countryside, as evidenced by the media coverage and political consequences of the foot and mouth outbreak of 2001 (Woods, 2008). Perhaps theoretical interest is currently directed more into concepts of rurality that appear most relevant to 'post-productive' patterns of use (Halfacree, 2006). However, in view of an emerging and rather less cavalier attitude towards UK food security (prompted by rising world demand for food and biofuels) one might question the durability of a post-productivist approach to the countryside. The livestock that have featured in recent academic discourse have predominantly been the rare breeds (Evans and Yarwood, 2000; Yarwood and Evans, 1998; but see Yarwood and Evans, 2006) and little awareness has been evident of previous work on the geography of the minority and commercial breeds (as reported, for example, by Carlyle, 1979; Hall, 1996; Hall and Ruane, 1993; Walton, 1984; Wiener, 1954, 1961). The importance of a geographical approach has become better appreciated recently (Bertaglia *et al.*, 2007; Carson *et al.*, 2009), but academics from outside the animal science community often have difficulty in understanding livestock biodiversity, partly because of the sheer number of breeds involved, but also because most livestock extant in Britain are crosses between various pure breeds. The easily accessible publicity and educational materials focus on the pure breeds and disproportionately (in terms of gross contribution to rural livelihoods) on the rarest breeds.

Because breeds owe their origins and persistence to the interactions of many factors (genetic, cultural, commercial and historical), the definition of the term 'breed' has inspired much discussion. In the UK, the operational definition of livestock breed used by Defra is: 'an interbreeding population of husbanded or formerly husbanded domesticated animals of consistent genotype and phenotype with a recognized history and administrative framework' (Defra, 2011). Worldwide, and regionally, the number of breeds in a given country is correlated with present-day human population sizes and this is evidence that breeds were developed to fill specific commercial or cultural niches that are most diverse in numerically strong human societies (Hall and Ruane, 1993).

Local breeds arose throughout the British Isles and their distinct identities began to be recognized, documented, and indeed celebrated as contributing to regional pride at the time of major agricultural innovation that was well under way by the mid-eighteenth century (Hall and Clutton-Brock, 1988). Within each breed, higher-performing animals were selected for breeding, on the basis of their own characteristics or of their relatives or ancestors. By 'higher-performing' is meant animals which are better able to respond to improved conditions of husbandry, and this improvement is of most value if it is heritable. This is the basic principle of animal breeding, whose application, together with advances in management, have improved food security and living standards across the globe (Hall, 2004).

Changes in market requirements and developments in veterinary and livestock science have led to great changes in British livestock. Today the dairy cattle sector is dominated by the Holstein Friesian cow and the beef industry by crossbred animals derived from insemination of dairy cows by bulls of beef breeds, mainly of continental European origin; the sheep sector is more complex (Pollott and Stone, 2003). End results have included the numerical contraction of most of the traditional British cattle and sheep breeds (Hall and Clutton-Brock, 1988).

The sheep and cattle industries are based on complex patterns of interdependence and specialization of farms mediated by a wide range of marketing systems. This diversity has recently acquired new prominence through the analyses of trading networks conducted after the foot and mouth disease outbreak of 2001 (Mansley *et al.*, 2003).

Thus the commercial herd or flock at pasture is the visible expression of a set of relationships, conditioned by commercial reality and historical context. The hobby farm of a few purebred animals of a rare breed (Yarwood and Evans, 2000) is also part of a network but one which is much less complex, generally focusing on a specific fellowship of enthusiasts and maybe a particular abattoir and farm shop and usually with a relatively recent history.

Before considering the role of grazing livestock in defining rurality as it exists today it is worth considering two of the ways in which livestock contributed to the perception of the rural in the late eighteenth and early nineteenth century (Georgian period) and the later, Victorian, period.

At least so far as many rich people were concerned the ownership of land served multiple functions, including the assertion of social status, and grazing livestock played their part in this. The media for this assertion included social events, for example, the Holkham sheep shearings (Wade Martins, 2009) and national and regional agricultural shows (Goddard, 1988, 1989). Portraiture often featured depictions of owners or their residences as well as their prize animals. The emphasis on animal pedigree has been claimed (Ritvo, 1990) to parallel the assertion of continuity of ownership of the land. Though it has not been formally studied, it seems likely that this process is being paralleled today with rural gentrification (Heley, 2010; Stockdale, 2010), fuelling at least some of the current interest in rare and exotic breeds of livestock.

English landscape painting of the eighteenth and early nineteenth centuries was an especially significant contribution to Western art (Pevsner, 1956). Payne (1993) points out how artists of this period were relatively unlikely to be working to a commission and depended for sales on their works appealing to the purchaser, by conforming to particular aesthetic or moral precepts. Popular themes for pictures of the rural tended to be crops, because of the opportunities to draw moral lessons. Barley tended not to feature as a subject, apparently because of its principal use, namely brewing. Particularly numerous are scenes of the wheat harvest (which drew attention to morally elevating hard work providing the staff of life to the nation, largesse of the farmer towards gleaners, etc.) and hay mowing (men at work scything, women turning the hay, wholesome rustic flirtation under the late summer sun). In contrast, depictions of people interacting directly with their animals – milking cows, shearing sheep, or leading draft oxen – are much scarcer than relatively formal portraits of animals, with or without their proud owners (see for example Spargo, 1988). But livestock were used in many paintings of lofty genre, apparently to give discreet guidance as to how a landscape should be perceived; '[s]heep are beautiful, goats are picturesque, but bulls are sublime' (Bicknell, 1981). This is particularly clear in the work of James Ward R. A. (Grundy, 1909). A very different market was catered for by the naive genre paintings of prize animals (see for example Moncrieff *et al.*, 1996), which were so popular at the same time as the emergence of the sporting picture.

It was not just representations of livestock that carried a message about rurality. The landed interest were deeply involved in pedigree breeding of livestock, particularly cattle (Ritvo, 1990). Although it was claimed that the general livestock population of the country was improved by this activity, this was probably not the case (Walton, 1986, 1999), and the performance factors of interest were often dictated by fashion and were of no relevance to market requirements (Ritvo, 1990).

Studies on the geographical affinities of pedigree livestock breeds have mainly considered the more moneyed sectors of society principally because the herd and flock books and breed society records focus on only the elite section of each breed. But the same principles applied to owner-occupiers and tenantry, and all 260 respondents to the informal survey cited earlier were able to specify the breeds of livestock with which their families had been associated.

For many, perhaps most people, an important part of personal identity is a connection with a particular location and for land-based society, connection with farm animals used to be particularly significant, giving personal satisfaction and pride of ownership. In the words of Rudyard Kipling:

At the gate beside the river where the trouty shallows brawl,
I know the pride that Lobengula felt,
When he bade the bars be lowered of the Royal Cattle Kraal,
And fifteen miles of oxen took the veldt.
From the walls of Bulawayo in unbroken file they came
To where the Mount of Council cuts the blue . . .
I have only six and twenty, but the principle's the same
With my Sussex Cattle feeding in the dew!
(Alnaschar and the Oxen: 1924)

For at least some owners, along with social aggrandizement went the satisfaction of advancing the cause of Improvement by upgrading one's tenants' stock (Watson and Hobbs, 1951).

The underlying complexity in the social contexts of different livestock breeds in the nineteenth century is shown by a preliminary analysis where the herd book lists of owners of cattle of each breed (for the year nearest to 1881) were matched with the names of the principal British and Irish landowners (Bateman, 1883).

Table 8.1 Differences among UK and Irish cattle breeds in percentage of pedigree herd owners who were substantial landowners, early 1880s

Breed	*Total number of UK and Ireland owners in herd book volume consulted*	*Number of owners in Bateman (1883)*	*As percentage*
Kerry and/or Dexter	96	29	30
Red Poll	69	20	29
Sussex	102	19	19
Highland	183	35	19
Devon	35	6	17
Shorthorn	636	98	15
Aberdeen Angus	182	20	11
North Wales Black	41	4	10
Jersey	1,199 (and another 396 owners in Jersey itself, not considered here)	114	10
Galloway	71	6	8
Ayrshire	90	5	6
Hereford	146	7	5
South Devon	96	3	3
Lincoln Red	185	2	1

Source: Hall, unpublished.

Evidently some breeds were of particular interest to the bigger proprietors; reasons presumably included geography, breed marketing and royal patronage. Queen Victoria herself was a member of the breed societies for Devon, Dexter, Jersey, Hereford, Shorthorn and Aberdeen Angus cattle, and Dorset Horn sheep.

Probably less in the British Isles than in continental Europe, local distinctiveness and patrimony may be expressed in food and drink. Livestock breeds often appear to contribute to local identity though an inferred association with some local food, usually meat or a dairy product. However, it is often not clear whether the local affinity is with the breed or with the product. Jersey milk and butter are from cows of the Jersey breed, and (away from Jersey itself) are most unlikely to have come from the island. In 2010 an application was turned down for conferment of Protected Designation of Origin status on butter from the island (Defra, 2010).

Indeed, it is the island of Jersey (116 km^2 in area, human population 89,000; about 2,000 milking cows) that provides a contemporary example of how a livestock breed can be enfolded into local culture. The Jersey breed of dairy cattle has become the second most numerous dairy breed worldwide (Hall and Clutton-Brock, 1988). Yet on its native island, the breed has declined in numbers in parallel with the restructuring of the island's dairy industry, and the export market for breeding stock vanished, the growing demand for young cows being met by the daughter populations primarily in Denmark, the USA, Canada, New Zealand and the UK, which have been subject to intense selection for commercial attributes. The island herd had been kept as an isolated pure breeding population, with imports of live cattle, semen and embryos having been banned since, by some measures, 1789. This genetic isolation is paralleled by isolation from commercial competition, as the importation of liquid milk into Jersey is only permitted under licence, a barrier to free trade instituted to protect the island dairy industry from competition.

Jersey's dairy herds have been under increasing commercial pressure in recent decades and a need has been voiced for productivity of the island's cattle to be improved. It has also been argued that the island could, and should, regain its former position as a source of breeding stock for herds elsewhere. In principle, selection within the island herd could lead to genetic improvement; in practice, importation of semen from more productive Jerseys elsewhere in the world would give a much more immediate improvement following an upgrading process. One reason why the political and community commitment to the Jersey dairy industry is so striking is that the liquid milk needs of the island could (apparently easily) be met by one or two bulk road tankers arriving every day on the ferry from Weymouth. The breed society in 2009 repeated its petition to the States of Jersey to annul the import ban and this was agreed after intense public scrutiny and interest. The full story is yet to be told (Hall, in preparation); an outline of certain aspects has already appeared (Holloway and Bear, 2011). The discussion raised issues of food security, political independence, sustainability of agriculture, and protection of a major 'tourist icon'. My reason for this example is not so much to start a debate on whether Jersey possesses rurality, as to emphasize that the presence of grazing livestock is one of the defining features of the culture, in the broadest sense, of the island.

The foregoing examples and discussion have probably not shown that the presence of grazing livestock is necessary or sufficient as a definition of rurality, but some pointers have been given to how animal geography can contribute to rural studies. The historic and current status of grazing livestock may contribute to the finer-detailed classification of regions already defined as rural on some socio-economic set of criteria. While van Eupen *et al.* (2012) subdivided rural regions according to their 'accessibility' and 'economic density', I would suggest that an alternative approach might be to subdivide on some set of criteria derived from the area's livestock.

These criteria will need a historical dimension. A recent discussion (Gamborg *et al.*, 2010) about nature conservation and habitat restoration is relevant here. Two contrasting views are termed the 'historical' view and the 'end-state', or 'consequentialist', view. Verbatim,

> To say what is good and right judged by end-state principles, we do not need any information about the way this state of affairs [restoration of a habitat] was brought about. On historical principles, by contrast, legitimacy or acceptability depends entirely on past developments. Here information about events of the past is not merely relevant, or interesting, but essential to the determination of moral value.
>
> (Ibid.: 70)

Applied to the rurality discussion, 'end state principles' would mean that a former coal mining area, restored and now grazed by livestock, might be considered as being 'rural to a certain degree', while by 'historical principles' it would probably be less so.

One might argue that areas where farming has become least disconnected from the countryside possess the emergent properties of rurality to the highest degree, and it is the persistence of traditional livestock husbandry that is most clearly indicative of this connectivity. Thriplow Farms in Cambridgeshire (Walston, 2009) provides an illustration. Today this might to the outsider appear the ultimate 'industrial agriculture' estate. In 2008 the farm was purely arable, employing one or two men full-time and producing (among other crops) about 4,400 tonnes of wheat a year, and it was here in the late 1970s that what must have been among the longest furrows in the country (just under one mile) were ploughed. But its history is one of mixed farming. In 1953, 90 people were employed on 2,000 acres, of which area three-quarters were cropped and the rest grazed by 250 Jersey dairy cows, 175 Aberdeen Angus beef cattle, while 300 Large White pigs, between 2,000 and 3,000 poultry and 30 riding horses (Arabs) were also kept.

Thriplow today might, because of its livestock history, possess rurality in a higher degree than, say, a former coal mining area rehabilitated and converted to woodland, or a tract of former arable land re-engineered and re-vegetated in order to resemble pristine wetland, because Thriplow is an area that historically possessed grazing livestock and, indeed, in 2011 the return of beef cattle to Thriplow was announced (Thriplow Farms, 2011).

Livestock geography has much to contribute to discussion on rurality. This is a fertile field of study, richly manured by agricultural writers over two centuries, from where the rural specialist can expect to reap a bountiful harvest.

References

Astor, Viscount and Rowntree, B. S. (1939). *British agriculture: The principles of future policy*. Harmondsworth, UK: Penguin Books.

Bateman, J. (1883). *The great landowners of Great Britain and Ireland: A list of all owners of three thousand acres and upwards, worth £3,000 a year; also, one thousand three hundred owners of two thousand acres and upwards, in England, Scotland, Ireland and Wales, their acreage and income from land, culled from the modern Domesday Book; also their colleges, clubs, and services. Corrected in the vast majority of cases by the owners themselves*, 4th edition. London: Harrison.

Bertaglia, M., Joost, S., Roosen, J., and Econogene Consortium. (2007). Identifying European marginal areas in the context of local sheep and goat breeds conservation: A geographic information system approach, *Agricultural Systems* 94, 657–70.

Bicknell, P. (1981). *Beauty, horror and immensity: Picturesque landscape in Britain 1750–1850. Exhibition selected and catalogued by Peter Bicknell. Fitzwilliam Museum, Cambridge, 7 July–31 August 1981*. Cambridge: Cambridge University Press.

Buller, H. (2004). Where the wild things are: The evolving iconography of rural fauna, *Journal of Rural Studies* 20: 131–41.

Carlyle, W. J. (1979). The changing distribution of breeds of sheep in Scotland, 1795–1965, *Agricultural History Review* 27: 19–29.

Carson, A., Elliott, M., Groom, J., Winter, A. and Bowles, D. (2009). Geographical isolation of native sheep breeds in the UK: Evidence of endemism as a risk factor to genetic resources, *Livestock Science* 123: 288–99.

Cloke, P. and Thrift, N. (1994). Introduction: refiguring the ‘rural’, in P. Cloke, M. Doel, D. Matless, M. Phillips and N. Thrift (eds), *Writing the rural: five cultural geographies* (pp. 1–5). London: Paul Chapman.

Defra (2010). Application to Protect the Name ‘Jersey Butter’ as a Protected Designation of Origin (PDO): Decision Letter. Available at: http://archive.defra.gov.uk/foodfarm/food/industry/regional/foodname/products/documents/jerseybutter-decisionletter-101111.pdf (accessed 9 October 2012).

Defra (2011). Definition of a Breed for the Purpose of the UK National Inventory. Available at: www.defra.gov.uk/fangr/2011/03/17/national-inventory/ (accessed 9 October 2012).

Evans, N. and Yarwood, R. (2000). The politicization of livestock: Rare breeds and countryside conservation, *Sociologia Ruralis* 40: 228–48.

Gamborg, C., Gremmen, B., Christiansen, S. B. and Sandøe, P. (2010). De-domestication: Ethics at the intersection of landscape restoration and animal welfare, *Environmental Values*, 19, 57–78.

Goddard, N. (1988). *Harvests of change: The Royal Agricultural Society of England 1838–1988*. London: Quiller Press.

Goddard, N. (1989). Agricultural literature and societies. In G. E. Mingay (ed.), *The Agrarian History of England and Wales. Volume VI. 1750–1850*. Cambridge: Cambridge University Press: 361–83.

Grundy, C. R. (1909). *James Ward, RA: His life and works with a catalogue of his engravings and pictures*. London: Otto.

Halfacree, K. (1995). Talking about rurality: Social representations of the rural as expressed by residents of six English parishes, *Journal of Rural Studies* 11: 1–20.

Halfacree, K. (2006). Rural space: constructing a three-fold architecture. In P. Cloke, T. Marsden, and P. Mooney (eds), *Handbook of Rural Studies*. London: Sage, 44–62.

Hall, S. J. G. (1996). Human ecology and the evolution of livestock, *Anthrozoos* 9, 81–4.

Hall, S. J. G. (2004). *Livestock biodiversity: Genetic resources for the farming of the future*. Oxford: Blackwell Science.

Hall, S. J. G. (unpublished). Spreadsheets available from author.

Hall, S. J. G. (in preparation). Manuscript in preparation.

Hall, S. J. G. and Clutton-Brock, J. (1988). *Two hundred years of British farm livestock*. London: British Museum (Natural History).

Hall, S. J. G. and Ruane, J. (1993). Livestock breeds and their conservation: A global overview, *Conservation Biology* 7: 815–25.

Heley, J. (2010). The new squirearchy and emergent cultures of the new middle classes in rural areas, *Journal of Rural Studies* 26: 321–31.

Holloway, L. and Bear, C. (2011). DNA typing and super dairies: Changing practices and remaking cows, *Environment and Planning A* 43: 1487–91.

Mansley, L. M., Dunlop, P. J., Whiteside, S. M., and Smith, R. G. H. (2003). Early dissemination of foot-and-mouth disease virus through sheep marketing in February 2001, *Veterinary Record* 153: 43–50.

Moncrieff, E., Joseph, S., and Joseph, I. (1996). *Farm animal portraits*. Woodbridge, UK: Antique Collectors' Club.

Payne, C. (1993). *Toil and plenty: Images of the agricultural landscape in England, 1780–1890*. New Haven, CT, and London: Yale Center for British Art and Yale University Press.

Pevsner, N. (1956). *The englishness of English art*. London: The Architectural Press.

Philo, C. and Wilbert, C. (2000). *Animal spaces, beastly places: New geographies of human–animal relations*. London: Routledge.

Policy Commission on the Future of Farming and Food (2002). Farming and Food: A Sustainable Future. London: Cabinet Office. Available at: http://webarchive.nationalarchives.gov.uk/20100807034701/http:/archive.cabinetoffice.gov.uk/farming/pdf/PC%20Report2.pdf (accessed 12 June 2013).

Pollott, G. E. and Stone, D. G. (2003). The Breeding Structure of the British Sheep Industry 2003. London: Defra. Available at: http://archive.defra.gov.uk/evidence/economics/foodfarm/reports/documents/pollott2003.pdf (accessed 12 June 2013).

Ritvo, H. (1990). *The animal estate: The English and other creatures in the Victorian age*. London: Penguin.

Rousseau, N. (1995). What is rurality? *Occasional Paper Royal College of General Practitioners* 71(September), 1–4.

Spargo, D. (1988). *This land is our land: Aspects of agriculture in English art*. Stoneleigh, Warwickshire, and London: Royal Agricultural Society of England and Mall Galleries.

Stockdale, A. (2010). The diverse geographies of rural gentrification in Scotland, *Journal of Rural Studies* 26: 31–40.

Thriplow Farms (2011). Thriplow Farms Ltd. 2011. An expansive and expensive year. Available at: www.thriplow-farms.co.uk/annual/2011.pdf (accessed 9 October 2012).

van Eupen, M., Metzger, M. J., Perez-Soba, M., Verburg, P. H., van Doorn, A. and Bunce, R. G. H. (2012). A rural typology for strategic European policies, *Land Use Policy* 29: 473–82.

Wade Martins, S. (2009). *Coke of Norfolk 1754–1842: A biography*. Woodbridge, UK: Boydell Press.

Walston, O. (2009). *Thirty-five harvests 1974–2008*. Thriplow, UK: Thriplow Farms.

Walton, J. R. (1984). The diffusion of the improved Shorthorn breed of cattle in Britain during the eighteenth and nineteenth centuries, *Transactions of the Institution of British Geographers* NS 9: 22–36.

Walton, J. R. (1986). Pedigree and the national cattle herd circa 1750–1950, *Agricultural History Review* 34: 149–70.

Walton, J. R. (1999). Pedigree and productivity in the British and North American cattle kingdoms before 1930, *Journal of Historical Geography* 25: 441–62.

Watson, J. A. S. and Hobbs, M. E. (1951). *Great farmers*. London: Faber & Faber.

Wiener, G. (1954). Migration of pedigree Ayrshire cattle in Great Britain, *Journal of Agricultural Science, Cambridge* 45: 476–80.

Wiener, G. (1961). Population dynamics in fourteen lowland breeds of sheep in Great Britain, *Journal of Agricultural Science, Cambridge* 57: 21–8.

Woods, M. (2008). *New labour's countryside: Rural policy in Britain since 1997*. Bristol, UK: The Policy Press.

Yarwood, R. and Evans, N. (1998). New places for 'Old Spots': The changing geographies of domestic livestock animals, *Society and Animals* 6: 137–65.

Yarwood, R. and Evans, N. (2000). Taking stock of farm animals and rurality. In C. Philo and C. Wilbert (eds), *Animal spaces, beastly places*. London: Routledge, 98–114.

Yarwood, R. and Evans, N. (2006). A Lleyn sweep for local sheep? Breed societies and the geographies of Welsh livestock, *Environment and Planning A* 38: 1307–26.

9 A case study in the literary construction of the rural idyll

The English farm

Rupert Hildyard

Interpreting rurality means understanding that rurality is, among other things, a cultural construction with a history and a politics. But if we are to assess how the rural imaginary operates now in the twenty-first century it is arguably useful to look back on what happened to the rural imaginary in the twentieth century. The aim of this chapter is to focus on one aspect of rurality, the romanticisation of the English farm. It will be argued that this image is of much more recent, twentieth century, provenance than is usually assumed – namely the inter-war period – that it flourished in the immediate post-war period from 1945 to the 1970s and has been under threat for reasons that are probably too familiar to require stating since the 1980s. This paper discusses two key texts in the construction of the popular image of the English Farm, both bestsellers at the time of publication though largely forgotten since, *Corduroy* (1930) by Adrian Bell and *The Story of a Norfolk Farm* (1941) by Henry Williamson. It seeks to relate these 'farm texts' to the larger and longer tradition of pastoral in English literature, and in particular to the work of two great ruralists of the canonical English literary tradition, Thomas Hardy and D. H. Lawrence. Second, it argues that these inter-war farm texts participated in and helped inaugurate a cultural celebration of the English farm and farming especially in children's literature and visual and material culture after World War II that has more recently been superseded. Third, it suggests that the key characteristics of these 'farm texts' can offer insight into the persistence and meaning of rurality in the twenty-first century.

The pastoral tradition in English literature

The idea of the rural idyll long precedes the idyll of the English farm. It goes right back to the ancient classical world – quite literally as rural comes from the Latin for country, *rus*, as opposed to the city, *urbs*. 'Idyll' means 'little picture' and is the title given to his poems by the inventor of 'pastoral', Theocritus who wrote poems in the second century BC about Sicilian shepherds, cowherds and nymphs for the benefit of a sophisticated urban Greek readership in Alexandria, Athens and the cities of the Hellenistic world. Pastoral always implies a strong contrast between the innocent simplicity of country life and the decadent sophistication of the city, yet carries the contradiction of being addressed to and enjoyed by an urban audience – indeed a celebration of country life cannot exist until urban civilisation is invented. It is a nice example of the deconstructive trope – or literary device – that what we think is the prior term in a 'hierarchised' binary opposition (like nature/civilisation) is actually a product of its secondary 'supplement'. It is not the country that comes before the city, it is the city that produces the country.

The pastoral tradition was carried on in Latin verse, in for instance Virgil's *Georgics* (about farming) and the *Odes* of Horace, and was revived in the Renaissance as part of the larger humanist rediscovery of classical thought and culture. The idea that country life was more simple and harmonious and natural became a powerful trope of European culture. Terry Gifford has suggested three definitions of pastoral (Gifford, 1999: 1–2): most strictly, a particular specialised genre of poetry (as Leo Marx put it 'no shepherds, no pastoral'); more generally, any idealised representation of country life and, third, pejoratively, an artificial and false representation of rural life. This debate goes back a long way: Gifford's definitions of pastoral can be illustrated by two famous Elizabethan poems, Christopher Marlowe's exemplary pastoral 'The Passionate Shepherd to His Love' (*c.*1592) and Walter Raleigh's witty, realistic and proto-feminist rejoinder 'The Nymph's Reply' (1596).

In English culture the idealisation of country life accomplished through pastoral carried particularly strong connections with the landowning class. From Tudor times to the early twentieth century, political power and social status as well as much of the economic resources of the nation were increasingly concentrated in the hands of the landowning class to a much greater degree than was the case in other European states such as the city states of Renaissance Italy, the absolute monarchies of Catholic France and Spain or autocratic Russia (see Somerville, this volume, on the English gentry). The political and economic power base of the English ruling class was in the country (the land), and pastoral idealisation centred on the country house (the mansion and estate of the family) as an expression of strength, stability, continuity and harmony. Visual and material culture such as the country house itself, the picturesque landscape and landscape painting by such as Gainsborough, Morland and Constable can all be seen to make use of pastoral to exalt the values of the landed class. In literature Spenser, Sidney, Shakespeare, Marvell, Herrick, Pope, and Gray all contribute to the genre. Jane Austen's novels, ending as they do with heroines taking simultaneous possession of a husband and a desirable country residence, represent the epitome of the identification of pastoral felicity with the values of the landed gentry. Many critics (notably Raymond Williams (1973), Frank Kermode (1952), John Barrell (1972), Greg Garrard (2004)) have pointed out how pastoral lends itself to the legitimation or, to put it more tellingly, 'naturalisation' of a class hierarchy and the celebration of the values and interests of the landowning class.

But though there is sometimes genuine attention to farming and agricultural practices little of this pastoral literature focused on 'the farm' as such, probably not least because, until the transition from collectively managed open field farming, the farm, as an isolated economic and social unit, was not the dominant economic entity in English agriculture in quite the way it became after the parliamentary enclosure process. Parliamentary enclosure typically involved, through much of lowland England, not just the parcelling up of the township's land and the replacement of communal management by individual enterprises but the 'planting' of new farmsteads out in the new holdings created, in place of farms located in the nucleated village – that is, a new physical distinction between farms and villages (see for instance Pryor 2011; Rackham 1986).

The revolution of Romanticism (*c.*1790–1830) was contemporaneous with the peak of the parliamentary enclosure movement and marks a decisive development in thinking about the rural. Famously, Wordsworth and other Romantics see for the first time, and in explicit contrast to urban civilisation, a deeper meaning in Nature, 'something far more deeply interfused' (from Wordsworth's 'Tintern Abbey', 1798) than a mere background to human activity. At the same time there is a reaction against the artificiality of pastoral ('anti-pastoral') and substitution of more realistic and often bitter representation of country life in the poetry of Crabbe, Burns, Wordsworth himself and pre-eminently John Clare.

In the nineteenth century the increased reverence for nature that, as is the way with ideology, ironically accompanied more efficient economic exploitation of natural resources and a growing distance from natural processes for much of the population, coincided with a new genre, nature writing, inspired by the nature worship of the Romantic poets, exemplified by Gilbert White, W. H. Hudson and Richard Jefferies as well as the continuation of the Romantic tradition in the poetry of G. M. Hopkins, A. E. Housman and Edward Thomas.

But it is only with Thomas Hardy and D. H. Lawrence that the farm begins to make a significant appearance in fiction. Up to that point it is natural beauty and the country house that is celebrated, not the domestic and economic entity of the farm. There is a complete contrast between the distant view of Abbey-Mill Farm from Knightley's park in Austen's *Sense and Sensibility* (1811) or the rather closer but more sarcastic attention to Dagley's farm in George Eliot's *Middlemarch* (1871) on the one hand and on the other the sheep shearing in *Far From the Madding Crowd* (1874) or the dairy in *Tess of the d'Urbervilles* (1891) by Thomas Hardy. The life of Hagg Farm in *Sons and Lovers* (1911), Marsh Farm in *The Rainbow* (1915), Bailey Farm in *The Fox* (1923) plays an integral not an incidental part in the story. For Hardy and Lawrence the farm has become not just a setting – as even Wuthering Heights is for Emily Brontë's dramatis personae – but a significant and meaningful destination in the life of the characters. Perhaps particularly there is a sense in, for instance, *Far From the Madding Crowd* and *The Rainbow* that the life on the farm represents an ideal way of life superior both to urban employment and to gentry leisure. This shift from a more genteel, distanced and purely contemplative view of the rural to what could be called a hands on engagement with farming life is another decisive moment and a critical one in the genesis of what could be called the twentieth-century 'farm text'.

The Story of a Norfolk Farm – Henry Williamson

Henry Williamson wrote *The Story of a Norfolk Farm* on the eve of World War II, and it was published in early 1941. It tells the story of how, disenchanted with Devon and tired of writing after the success of *Tarka the Otter* (1927), the author came to the decision to buy 235 acres of land in Norfolk and take up farming. The book covers the period of four years from 1935 when, up from Devon on a visit to his publisher's country cottage, he first came across the farm, to August 1939 at the end of his second year farming, with an epigraph written in June 1940. It tells of his struggle over the decision and problems over buying the land; the challenge of setting up the farm and moving his family, restoring cottages for them to live in, the first year farming, buying livestock and getting in crops; the indecisive results of the first harvest and eventual success at the end of the second year.

What is the appeal of the book? The story is first of all a narrative of heart-warming triumph over adversity, in which the initial simple hook – will he get the farm and make a success of it – is eventually answered in the affirmative after a struggle with a succession of obstacles such as the decision, the vendor, his own family, traditional attitudes, bad workmanship, the weather, government policy, the economics of farming, and so on. In particular the story follows a sort of Robinson Crusoe template, in which Our Hero bravely and patiently builds up a little homestead in the wilderness from which the settler can efficiently and productively exploit the resources around him. Like Defoe, Williamson offers a detailed and meticulously recorded do-it-yourself manual for the aspirant farmer (or the middle class urban reader of pastoral) on setting up your own farm – instruction and information on how a farm is bought and sold (and how it changes occupation as well as ownership); how to repair buildings and roads; how to buy machinery and stock; how to plough a field with a tractor; or care for a sick bullock, and so on.

The other less often remarked, but essential, pleasure of the text is the emphasis on manual labour and practical knowledge – both *Robinson Crusoe* (1719) and *The Story of a Norfolk Farm* are books that tell you how to do things – build a road, plough a field, design a house, and tend a sick animal in Williamson's case. It is a model that many other twentieth-century 'farm texts' have followed. It is also a strikingly individualistic text. Williamson very ably communicates the loneliness of making the decision to buy the farm, of pitting himself against the professional experts – lawyers, surveyors, valuers – against the locals, against his workforce, against the economy, against the weather and of course against nature. He typically represents himself as alone, or, if with others, as holding out against or forth to strangers and only much more rarely as part of a cosy circle.

Although no critics, outside Williamson's still passionate circle of fans, have claimed it as great literature, *The Story of a Norfolk Farm* is worth comparing to what is often regarded as the timid British literary fiction published between the wars that is still typically found on university English Literature courses (such as the novels of Waugh or Greene). Quite apart from its interest as a 'farm text' or rural writing, what is engaging about the book is the sheer headlong reckless rush of the story, from the opening as the author speeds up to London in his open top sports car to the epigraph where he lays his pen down in the midst of the fall of France in 1940. It is clear that Williamson, by his own account, was an extraordinarily active man, taking on the huge task of buying and organising a farm at the same time as two building projects, moving his large family from Devon to Norfolk, doing much of the manual work on the farm and all the business, engaging in politics, birdwatching, shooting and socialising as well as turning out articles and books in order to pay for it all, at a time when the technology of transport and communication that we now rely on was much less efficient.

The headlong rush is not just a matter of what happens. One of the pleasures of the book is the way it is made up of a torrent of diverse discourses, insouciantly packed together in a way that today would be labelled postmodern in its transgression of established generic boundaries. Life writing, political comment, family drama, natural history, social observation, a practical introduction to buying, setting up and running a farm are all fluently and furiously braided together.

In this mixture of discourses the last one – what might be called the DIY manual of how to start farming – is obviously the mainstream of the book. It offers to the usual urban reader of pastoral, on one hand the intricacies of the business of farming – from valuations and 'tenant right' to buying stock, hiring labour and selling your corn – on the other the physical work of ploughing, putting in a gatepost or working a seed-drill – how to do it and how it feels to do it. One question that arises is how and why these details of agricultural working practices should be intrinsically interesting to twentieth-century readers, and more so than those of say, running a shop, or house building or motor mechanics.

Of the other discourses, the simplest element to explain is the attention to nature. Williamson often breaks off an account of farm work or some human problem to notice, say, a pair of plovers trying to protect their nest, the aerodynamics of a sand-wasp or the behaviour of turkeys in a flood. One of the most telling examples is his note of how the local Norfolk shooters will kill any bird that has no obvious benefit with the stupid saying 't'aint no use is it?' (Williamson, 1982: 376). Similarly his appreciation of the Norfolk landscape, the pinewoods, saltmarshes, sea-lavender, sunsets, with the occasional pointed comment about pollution of rivers or indiscriminate industrial development, is at least proto-ecological in that it implies biophilia, which is to say the love of the living world that E. O. Wilson (1984) and others argue is an inherent and vital part of our make-up.

But, from a twenty-first-century and ecocritical perspective, a key interest in the text is the contradiction between Williamson's love of nature and his espousal of modern farming practices. This contradiction is one of the fault lines in the text. Despite Williamson's evident ecological sympathies his principal aim as a farmer is to master the land, to clean it of thistles and weeds, restore its fertility and bring it back into good heart. When he arrives, what he sees at the farm is evidently agriculturally unkempt but in ecological terms a cornucopia of biodiversity. It would be anachronistic to equate the improvement of 'derelict' land in the 1930s with ecological malpractice or to expect an appreciation of the biodiversity of the land in those pre-agrochemical days, though this is in effect what he gives in one of his first accounts of the farm. But one can see that Williamson's enthusiasm for new roads, drainage, improved buildings and the elimination of untidiness and weeds is entirely consonant with the post-war modernisation of agriculture after the war and quite alien either to rural nostalgia or to the ecological sensitivities he professed.

This contradiction is confirmed by Williamson's enthusiasm for machinery. It is his shiny new grey Ferguson tractor (closely followed by the Alvis Silver Eagle) that inspires the greatest passion in the text (far more than either his long-suffering wife, barely concealed mistress or overlooked children), and he frequently acclaims new technology and progressive scientific agricultural practices. The infatuation with speed and powerful machines connects not only with claims to aggressive virility but with the Futurist idolisation of technology. He comments derisively on his youthful naivete about machinery when talking about ploughing by horse in comparison to tractor.

At a deeper level, the text is essentially a narrative of the author's own experiences and developing consciousness: it is what is nowadays called 'life writing'. *The Story of a Norfolk Farm* is, as Williamson himself says, the story of the Norfolk farmer. It begins with his disenchantment with Devon, his exhaustion with writing, and represents among other things his gradual mastery of the business and practice of farming, his changing relationships with his family (his mother, his wife, his brother-in-law, his son), his developing political views, his feelings about the land and about manual labour. The attraction of life writing depends on an ultimately Romantic or Wordsworthian belief that what is most important in life is our inner development as human beings, that the epic human narrative is not the outer story of war or politics or money-making but the coming-into-being of the self. The farm is clearly a stage in a sort of Lawrentian quest for Williamson to find himself and to find a 'right' relationship both with those immediately present to him – his family, his workers, his neighbours – and with wider society.

Having said that, we can note that this 'life writing' aspect of the book is not as fully developed as it might be. Again Williamson is curiously wooden in this area – he is occasionally gruffly apologetic about the hardships his wife Loetitia endures or nauseatingly sappy about the eldest son (largely ignoring his four other children). The family are there but curiously absent from the story. Questions arise particularly about relationships with his family and others. Reading between the lines, one cannot help asking, who is Ann? Surely conditions on the farm must have been quite horrible for Loetitia? Why did Sam leave so abruptly? Was it really necessary to enter into the endless, acrimonious and expensive legal dispute with the previous tenant Strawless? Williamson is quite honest and open about all these events – he notes 'life in the new cottages was not easy for Loetitia' for instance (Williamson, 1982: 239) – but perhaps not honest and open enough: in many cases it sounds as if there might be more to the story, as indeed we may learn from other sources, there was.

It is noticeable too that the narrator frequently ends by blaming various mistakes and fiascos on his own weakness in accepting the advice of others. A constant refrain is that he will in future trust his own instincts and stick unyieldingly to his own convictions. The impression of a very angry man that can be read between the lines is confirmed by other biographical information: Williamson seems to have been often unpleasant and unpopular if not impossible (Henry Williamson Society, n.d.). The dictatorial tendencies of his behaviour are a matter of ideology as well as personality: *The Story of a Norfolk Farm* is very definitely a gendered text. With the exception of Miss Gunton, a land agent who makes a brief seductive appearance, the few female characters who appear (i.e., his mother, wife, daughter) do so only to underline the subordination or exclusion of women from the world of the farm. The text appears deaf to any feminine let alone feminist voice – and, though it is not a very companionable text, what companionship there is, is invariably masculine – the wildfowler, the labourer, the auctioneer, the builder. Much of the text is a projection of a masculinity that is at once romantic and individualistic but at the same time patriarchal and commanding.

This in turn leads to the unshirkable question of his politics. Williamson became an out and out fascist and admirer of Hitler at just the time he was starting the farm and writing the book. He was briefly arrested during the war, and present-day British fascists claim he never renounced or mitigated his views (Mosley, n.d.). The advocacy of modernisation and idolisation of technology, along with his gender politics and increasingly autocratic behaviour all fit the fascist pattern. But apart from an Author's note, dated 11 November 1940, saying he had made excisions on his publisher's advice or insistence there is no evidence of directly fascist sympathies in the text (Williamson 1982: ii).

This is not to say there are no politics in this text – quite the contrary. But they are the sort of anti-capitalist and anti-war politics to which many on the left in the twenty-first century would happily sign up. One set piece in the middle of the Norfolk pastoral is his account of Christmas 1914 in the trenches. Most of the politics is strictly agricultural and rural: the swamping of the market by cheap foreign produce, financial investment in agriculture abroad when it should be in Britain, the lack of controls on pollution, the absence of sanitation and decent housing. There is nothing here in the text that can be seen as itself fascist.

The issue of whether rurality itself, the appeal to nature and to a more authentic organic way of life, is contaminated by its significance in Nazi ideology is a much larger debate (discussed for instance in Bramwell 1989; Bate, 2000;,Clark, 2002) that needs to be addressed at proper length. But three preliminary points might be made. First, if we are to proscribe any early twentieth-century texts because their authors were fascists, we shall have a long list that will include major literary figures such as T. S. Eliot, W. B. Yeats, D. H. Lawrence, and Ezra Pound. Second, Fascism was a contradictory mishmash of ideologies – nationalism, socialism, modernisation, technophilia, social Darwinism, and so on – as well as rural-ism or nature love (it also differed wildly in its national variants). To pick out nature-worship as its key feature is implausible and arbitrary. Finally, it might be said that perhaps the most important shared characteristic of fascism and rural organicism from an early twenty-first-century perspective, at a time when there has been another failure of the financial infrastructure of free market capitalism, is that both are clearly attempts to respond to the insecurity and destructive character of capitalist modernity.

More immediately relevant to rural studies is what Williamson made of the farm text. Whatever else he was, he was nothing if not bold. His construction of *The Story of a Norfolk Farm*, even where flawed and unfulfilled, is an unprecedentedly interesting and potent combination of different genres and discourses: life writing, the farming manual, nature writing, political comment, family drama – and this in turn can give us an insight into the construction of the rural idyll in the twentieth century.

Corduroy – Adrian Bell

It is worth contrasting *The Story of a Norfolk Farm* with a simpler and earlier text, *Corduroy* by Adrian Bell, published in 1930 and set ten years earlier in 1920 when Bell, at the age of just nineteen (though for some reason he says twenty), arrived on his motorcycle one late afternoon in October at a farm in Suffolk. His father, a socialist and republican journalist, had sent him to public school but, according to Adrian's son the journalist Martin Bell, refused to pay for him to go to university because he regarded it as a playground for the privileged rich (Bell, 1982: v) (a curious reversal of later assumptions about public schools and university), and was equally sceptical about Adrian's aspiration to be a writer. Insisting he did not want an office life, it was arranged that a Suffolk farmer should 'for the usual premium' (Bell, 1982: 2) (i.e., as in an apprenticeship) give the young man a training in agriculture.

The book covers the twelve months he spent on the farm, following the agricultural year through the seasons and ending the following October with his decision to become a farmer himself. Bell's narrative is therefore rather different from Williamson's – it is a *Bildungsroman*, a young man's self-discovery, rather than mid-life crisis, and an education rather than a Crusoe-type self-establishment (which he covers in the sequels to *Corduroy*). Much of it concerns the actual labour of farm work – how to harrow or plough, to thresh a stack or pull mangolds, to milk a cow or feed pigs. Equally he discovers the mental work of running a farm – planning rotations, making decisions about the day's work for a team of up to ten men, horses and implements, keeping accounts and records, buying and selling. The persistent refrain is the surprising complexity and sophistication of even the most basic practices (such as feeding cattle) in what is supposed to be an elementary and simple way of life. On his first morning he says, 'I returned to breakfast with an inkling of the complexity of farming, and a burdening consciousness of my own ignorance' (Bell, 1982: 15).

Another dominant theme is Bell's induction into the farming community – on the one hand the Suffolk labourers with whom he worked and whose dialect at first he could not even understand, on the other hand the extended family and friends of Mr Colville, the farmer. He is taken shooting and fox hunting, to Sunday lunch, the market and the Agricultural Show, to dances, the cinema and family parties. Coupled with this are his own feelings about farming and the arty life in Chelsea he has left behind back in London. Unlike Williamson, Bell says little about the economics and politics of agriculture. Virtually the only reference to the agricultural depression is a parenthesis in Chapter 7: '(Had they but known how far it was to fall in ten years, and that most of them standing there talking half seriously of 'no profit' would then be bankrupt and facing a portionless old age!)' (Bell, 1982: 140).

On the other hand he tells us much about social customs and practices that had survived from pre-war days and the contrast between the old Suffolk country life and the new England he sees on his trip to the seaside with the Colvilles. The village cobbler and blacksmith, the miller with a working windmill, horse drawn gigs and oil lamps are still there at the same time as bicycles, the cinema and the bus were beginning to change rural life. Above all, he gives a detailed description of the largely pre-mechanised agriculture dominated by horsework that was fast disappearing even seventeen years later when Williamson was writing. Equally, though he shows perhaps less interest in the individual creature than Williamson does for say his cat or the woodcock owl, in that respect already a hardened farmer, one of the strengths of the text is its aesthetic appreciation of the countryside – the end of the day pulling mangolds, or threshing in a winter's dawn or a harvest moon – and it is one that is characteristically embedded in labour. It is clear that again unlike Williamson what Bell is choosing is a way of life, and a key part of that is awareness of the 'more-than-human' world we inhabit.[1]

A big difference from Williamson is Bell's diffidence – rather than arriving like the older man as a celebrity in East Anglia, determined to make his mark and convinced of his own abilities and opinions, Bell presents his younger self as a dreamy naive incompetent who conscientiously does his best despite his embarrassment over his ignorance. This is endearing, particularly as he occasionally lets on that he generally turns out to do a good job. At the end of his second day on the farm, pulling mangolds, he is told 'You done wonderful well, sir, considerin'' (Bell, 1982: 34) and after his first bout at ploughing with horses is told, 'That ain't half bad for one who ain't never touched a plough afore,' adding 'I too was secretly pleased . . .' (Bell, 1982: 133). He respects both the farmer and the labourers. Again the attitude to class is quite different – where Williamson evidently sees himself as the equal of the gentry, is supercilious of the professionals and scathing about the ignorant villagers and labourers, to the metropolitan Bell from arty Chelsea the world of the well-to-do farmers is as alien as that of the labourers. He is as interested in the ploughman, the ferreter, the blacksmith. One of the things he notices in this part of Suffolk is the gulf between gentry and yeomen and the absence of the gentry since the war.

Corduroy is a much gentler and more humane example of the farm text. He shows for instance none of Williamson's masculine indifference to women. Bell is sharply aware of nearly every woman he encounters – Mrs Colville, the girl at the pub, Mrs Jarvis, the general's wife, Dick's sixteen-year-old daughter are each given a vivid thumbnail sketch, but not, the reader will sense, because his interest is predatory, but because he is interested in them and likes them.

The value of *Corduroy* is that it attaches a different set of meanings to the English Farm: conviviality, community, cooperation, hard work, stability, continuity. Like all versions of pastoral it gets its meaning from its opposition to urban civilisation – the drawing rooms of Chelsea full of 'nervous significances' and 'hurtful probing into personality' – but whereas Williamson's text is an act of wilful self-assertion against a world he perceives as wrong, at Benfield the narrator learns to subdue himself to communal endeavour and practical work. It is to these sometimes competing, sometimes complementary meanings of the farm text that we now turn.

The literary construction of the English farm

One important aspect of this essay is simply to draw attention to a specific form of rural writing: what I have called the 'farm text'. This genre or sub-genre has produced many examples other than *The Story of a Norfolk Farm* or *Corduroy* in the twentieth century. Perhaps most important has been its influence on children's literature of the twentieth century and the iconography of visual and material culture – examples include inter-war railway posters, the engravings of Clare Leighton, the work of J. E. Tunnicliffe for Ladybird Books and of Frank Newbould (a classic example being the latter's image of the South Downs for the wartime campaign 'Your Britain: Fight for it now'). But these two books are key examples of the literary construction of the English farm, and they tell us something about the appeal of the concept and the resonance of the farm in twentieth-century English culture. Let us summarise our findings.

The connection was noted with one of the earliest, most famous and strangest texts in modern English fiction: Defoe's *Robinson Crusoe*. It has become a commonplace of literary criticism to note how Defoe's proto-novel mirrors (or rather re-draws, re-imagines, re-presents) the position of the bourgeois individual in a capitalist free market economy in his struggle to accumulate property (see, e.g., Novak, 1961; Eagleton, 2005). It is also rather more obviously a portrait of the colonial settler in a strange land. Both scenarios are reproduced in the farm text. So too the protagonist of the farm text seeks to establish an independent, secure and comfortable steading and he too is settling into a strange land with alien people and habits. Given that this remains one of the basic narrative patterns of life in a free market society there is no doubting the obvious and enduring appeal of an imaginary representation of the situation of every individual's relationship to the market. Whether or not they are rural migrants, most readers will identify with and reproduce this hopeful narrative of progressive establishment of an (illusory) secure and comfortable settlement in the unpredictable chaos and anarchy of a free market society based on economic competition.

Closely related to this is another aspect of the dominant ideology of individualism. The farm in a modern (i.e. post-enclosure) economy is unquestionably an individual enterprise in which the businessman takes on the rest of the world. A farmer is an extreme example of the opposition of individual and society in that he is not only economically but (often) physically isolated on his own land from the rest of society. This can be mitigated in a traditional farming community, but that of course is less the case for incomers like Williamson and Bell. One of the differences between them is that Bell's story relates his gradual integration into the farming community: the isolation of the farm is less stark in *Corduroy*. As such farm texts again provide a satisfying imaginary representation of the situation of every individual's relationship to the market and to civil society in a capitalist economy – re-imagining the individual as independent and autonomous but in dramatic opposition to the forces that would overwhelm him.

Clearly too, both texts express an alienation from urban modernity and the masses, whether that is represented by the drawing-rooms and studios of Chelsea or the corrupt business and politics of inter-war Britain.

On the other hand, the farm text simultaneously provides, within its protective shell against the outer world, a fantasy of authentic relationship and community – the 'family' (including sometimes those that work there) that occupies the farm in relations of mutuality, intimacy and affection in contrast to the impersonal forces of competition and struggle that rule outside. Again there is a striking difference here between Williamson's solipsism and Bell's exemplification of the self-in-relation. But both texts in their different ways point to the possibility of imagining the self in satisfying relation to others in the farm text.

Most fundamentally, the farm text is clearly a variant of life writing. Both texts are essentially a narrative of the author's own experiences and developing consciousness. Once again this has its significance for the meaning of rurality that nearly always carries with it the promise of self-actualisation.

We have also seen that the farm text offers instruction and information on how a farm is bought and sold and changes occupation; how to repair buildings and roads; how to buy machinery and stock, how to plough a field or care for a sick bullock. But this is more than an instruction manual. Much of the appeal and resonance of the farm text must be that in some sense readers (perhaps rightly) feel that working all at once with our hands, with animals, with machinery, with plants, the soil and the weather is profoundly authentic and connected in a way or to an extent that other work or practices do not.

Finally, despite Bell's eschewal of nature writing or animal sentiment, both writers show a respect for the 'more-than-human' world, an interest in nature and closeness to the non-human that is arguably proto-ecological.

The 'rural idyll' remains a key and contested concept in the discussion not just of cultural values but in very practical debates on public policy in terms of planning and economic development. The value of a literary perspective on rurality is that literary criticism can give detailed and empirically based attention to the meaning of the 'rural idyll' – or simply a different sort of attention to its meaning than is produced by more sociological or theoretical analyses. Discussion of the 'rural idyll' can too readily fall into the habit of seeing it as merely an artificial construct, a middle class fantasy originating in hierarchical class culture and sustained by media representations, that is a vehicle for reactionary or at best nostalgic politics. All this is true, as far as it goes, but the aim of this discussion of early twentieth-century farm texts that contributed significantly to contemporary constructions of the rural idyll, has been to argue that they represent other more substantial and powerful anxieties and desires that are real and cannot be dismissed.

A clue to the significance of the 'farm text' is provided by that much-borrowed term invented by the French philosopher Michel Foucault in a posthumously published essay called 'Of other spaces': heterotopia. He says in the essay:

> There are also, probably in every culture, in every civilisation, real places – places that do exist and that are formed in the very founding of society – which are something like counter-sites, a kind of effectively enacted utopia in which the real sites, all the other real sites that can be found within the culture, are simultaneously represented, contested, and inverted. Places of this kind are outside of all places, even though it may be possible to indicate their location in reality. Because these places are absolutely different from all the sites that they reflect and speak about, I shall call them, by way of contrast to utopias, heterotopias.
>
> (Foucault, 1986: 24)

He mentions ships, cemeteries, prisons, boarding schools, museums and motels as exemplars. Heterotopias are real but other, part of the society but separate, and have a utopian element to them: the farm, at least as imagined in the farm text, may be considered as another example of heterotopia in contemporary modern society.

What is clear from the two texts is that, as Foucault's hypothesis suggests, the 'farm text' contains a mixture of elements that are both utopian and ideological: in its space appears a confused mixture of the dreams and fears of twentieth-century English society. On the one hand, among the clearly utopian elements to be found in both texts are the potential for self-actualisation; respect for, interest in and closeness to the natural world; more holistic forms of labour, above all manual work, but also mechanical and mental skills; and personal and communal relationships that go beyond the cash nexus and are reciprocal, nurturing and respectful. At the same time, some of the conflicted ideology of twentieth-century society is powerfully present, most obviously in Henry Williamson's autocratic personality and obnoxious behaviour to others, and his adulation of technocratic efficiency. But even in the gentle Adrian Bell, the farm text is a vehicle for an implied distaste for modernity, the masses and urban culture; a longing for stability and continuity; an acceptance of social inequalities as inevitable; and perhaps above all an ideology of individual fulfilment that is deeply enmeshed in capitalist modernity. Negative or positive, utopian or ideological, these are meanings of the 'farm text' that remain powerfully relevant to rurality in twenty-first-century Britain.

Note

1 The term 'more-than-human' is used by David Abram (1997) and others to challenge the simplistic definition of Nature as the non-human and enforce the point that 'Nature' both includes and goes beyond the human.

References

Abram, D. (1997) *The Spell of the Sensuous*. New York: Vintage.

Barrell, J. (1972) *The Idea of Landscape and the Sense of Place*. Cambridge: Cambridge University Press.

Bate, J. (2000) *Song of the Earth*. London: Picador.

Bell, A. (1982) *Corduroy* (first published 1930). Oxford: Oxford University Press

Bramwell, A. (1989) *Ecology in the Twentieth Century: A History*. New Haven, CT: Yale University Press.

Clark, T. (2002) *Martin Heidegger*. London: Routledge.

Eagleton, T. (2005) *The English Novel: An Introduction*. London: Blackwell Wiley.

Foucault, M. (1986) 'Of other spaces'. Available at: http://web.mit.edu/allanmc/www/foucault1.pdf (accessed 30 March 2013).

Garrard, G. (2004) *Ecocriticism*. London: Routledge

Gifford, T. (1999) *Pastoral*. London: Routledge

Henry Williamson Society (n.d.) 'Biography'. Available at: www.henrywilliamson.co.uk/biography/ancientsunlight (accessed 30 March 2013).

Kermode, F. (1952) *English Pastoral Poetry*. London: Harrap.

Marx, L. (1964) *The Machine in the Garden*. New York: Oxford University Press.

Novak, M. E. (1961) 'Restoration and eighteenth century', *Studies in English Literature, 1500–1900*, 1(3): 19–29.

OswaldMosley.com (n.d.) 'Henry Williamson'. Available at: www.oswaldmosley.com/henry-williamson (accessed 30 March 2013).
Pryor, F. (2011) *The Making of the British Landscape*. London: Penguin.
Rackham, O. (1986) *The History of the Countryside*. London: Dent.
Williams, R. (1973) *The Country and the City*. London: Hogarth.
Williamson, H. (1982) *The Story of a Norfolk Farm* (first published 1941). London: Clive Holloway Books.
Wilson, E. O. (1984) *Biophilia: The Human Bond with Other Species*. Cambridge, MA: Harvard University Press.
Wordsworth W. (1798) 'Tintern Abbey', in *Lyrical Ballads* (reprinted 1992). Ithaca, NY: Cornell University Press.

10 Horncastle Brass Band

Revising the banding myth from the edges of rurality

Sue Frith Grau

> In this country we tend to think of brass in terms of the traditional 'brass band' movement rooted in the colliery villages and industrial towns of northern England, Scotland and South Wales. Rightly so; those magnificent ensembles have been powerhouses of musical virtuosity for more than 150 years. And they flourish still, even if the mines and mills that sponsored them have largely disappeared.
>
> (Richard Morrison, *The Times*, 5 July 2008)

Brass bands, although considered by some to be a national institution, do not have a strong presence in the British national press. Whenever their activities are reported, any mention is likely to combine a sense of tradition, of the North and of industrialisation. Yet, as the excerpt from *The Times* shows, brass bands still thrive even though the understood conditions of existence have been largely undermined. This chapter tries to develop some explanation for the continued survival of the brass band in Britain today, and to argue the case for the cultural importance of the rural brass band, examining the historical operating structures and community involvement of a prosperous band maintained in a rural market town in the middle of one of the largest rural shires in England, namely Lincolnshire. Horncastle Brass Band was chosen as a suitable subject for study not only because of the nature of its rural geography, but also because it endures up until the present day, which gives an indication of the strength of the organisational structures underpinning the group. This band has outlasted some of the biggest, best-recorded and most well-funded brass bands of all time. Comparisons are made not only with the perpetuated myth of the industrial brass band, but also with other musical ensembles. The first section of this chapter deals with the rather uneasy concept of modernity that underpins the discourse of the brass band and how the brass band could actually be seen as as much a symbol of the rural as of the urban. Indeed, in the opening ceremony of the London Olympic Games 2012, we would have been just as ideologically comfortable to see a brass band playing music on the village green during the dancing round the maypole as round the iron smelting furnaces in the factories. The middle sections of the chapter provide some more in-depth reading of the brass band as a movement and how historical events have shaped the rural brass band in general, before leading into a case study of Horncastle Brass Band.

Although this chapter deals specifically with a case study from a particular region of England, it is known that brass bands sprang up in all kinds of communities all over Britain around the same time in the nineteenth century. For the purposes of this study, 'rural Britain' should be taken generally to encompass rural areas of Scotland and Wales as well as England. With the continued existence of bands such as the Peebles Silver Band, founded in 1834, which has a heritage dating back to before the 1st Peebleshire rifle volunteers into which the band was incorporated for a while (Mackie, 2012), it could be suggested that similar groundswells of rural banding activities were as evident in Scotland as in England. Certainly the Creetown Silver Band, was established through a rural community effort; local villagers raising enough funds to buy the first set of instruments in 1880, and with the exception of a small hiatus in activity during World War I, and another during World War II, has been thriving ever since (Creetown Silver Band, 2011). The situation in Wales is less clear, however. There is evidence of rural bands existing in the late nineteenth century, but their longevity comes into question. Ruthin band, for example are recorded as having won the contest at Corwen on 2 August 1881 (BrassBandResults [n.d.]) and then at some later date disbanded, eventually reinventing themselves in 2008. Newtown Band, Powys, on the other hand, has an impressive record of existence since its establishment by a few local players in the 1870s, even persevering through World War II, training and teaching the women and children left behind by conscription (Pugh, 2005). Undoubtedly more research could be undertaken in this area.

The general and academic brass band discourse carries overtones of the stereotypical image of the industrialised regions of Yorkshire and Lancashire: a discourse and ideology that would appear to be mediated through the concept of modernity. Very few studies investigate the contribution of the brass band to the rural communities around Britain. Horncastle, a small market town in the very centre of rural Lincolnshire is the setting for this chapter, which explores the context of a town band, both in the wider political and economic sphere and in the largely preconceived notions of brass banding in general. Although the Brass Band Movement (to be discussed in further depth later in the chapter) contributed immensely to the populating of all areas of the British Isles with local brass bands, it has also, through the meticulous attention to contesting and competition, inevitably introduced a hierarchy of value which has led to regional identification of brass bands with the North of England. By default, then, more rural areas around Britain have become secondary in terms of brass banding status within the Movement and therefore have assumed less worth as a field of study. This may be particularly relevant because of the rural association with agrarianism, thereby weakening the Movement's connection to modernity. In effect much of the brass band phenomenon has become invisible through lack of documentation rather than lack of interest.

The aim here is to represent an average community brass band as an integral cultural entity within a small market town. Potentially this representation could be much more the norm than would be understood from the intertwined discourse of industrialisation and 'Northernness'. Dave Russell, who has consistently included brass bands in his books and articles about music making in England, appropriately recognises the limitation of the inherently understood wisdom of brass bands' association with 'Northernness' (Russell, 1987) but then continues to perpetuate the discourse through his writing on 'Looking North' (Russell, 2004), arguing, again appropriately, that the national decline of the brass band in the 1950s had an impact on the representations of the 'Old North' (227–8). In fact it is likely that the vast majority of brass bands had very little to do with heavy industry, or particular regional geography. Russell (cited in Herbert, 2000: 69) quotes Wright and Round as having estimated that there were up to 40,000 brass bands in Britain in 1889. Even taking into account that there was no discernible method of registering band numbers at the time (and that such numbers may be wildly misreported), it is inconceivable that the majority of the brass bands would have been affiliated with the industrial North or that they would all have been supported by funds from coal mines or steel mills. Most must have been in more rural areas. The numbers of brass bands at any one time, however, is at best vague. In the early days it probably depended on how one defined a brass band as to whether it was counted or not. Even investigations in more recent years, such as Finnegan's 2007 edition of *The Hidden Musicians*, show that there is no real way of cataloguing exactly how many brass bands exist due to fluctuations in player loyalties and regional boundaries. An estimated several thousand of these brass bands inevitably therefore comprised local musicians in all areas meeting together, without intervention from large companies or funding from heavy industry.

The motivation for counting up the bands in the British Isles may have stemmed from the obsession of the brass band Movement of pitting their musical abilities against each other. Band contests are thought to have been infrequent (and possibly spontaneous) events from the early decades of the nineteenth century, but by the middle of the century, the Belle Vue contest in Manchester became an annual event, establishing rules and patterns for contesting at other venues in the future. The impact of launching a contesting structure was to be far reaching. In the beginning, it enabled bands to compare their abilities with each other and, with the relative ease of travel enabled by the blossoming train service, allowed bands from relatively further afield to become much more aware of each other and their status within a sub-culture of banding. Over time, the contest arena led to a coming together of bands in what became known as 'The Brass Band Movement'. The bands who came to represent the Movement in the public eye were inevitably the ones who performed well at national contests, and these bands tended to be the ones with the most funding for instruments and the most time off work for the players. One could be forgiven for immediately recognising the importance of the Yorkshire colliery or Lancashire factory brass band in this scenario. However, most contesting was (and continues to be) done at a much more local level. Scores of smaller events have been held around the country since the middle of the nineteenth century.

It would seem rather presumptuous to assume that the Horncastle Band is so unusual that recorded activities of contesting as early as the early 1860s were almost totally out of kilter with the normal banding sphere, as would be suggested if most contesting bands were from Yorkshire and Lancashire. This particularly does not seem to be a sensible conclusion to make since there is evidence of an annual contest held in Boston, Lincolnshire, in which there was a prize for the 'Best Lincolnshire Band'. This suggests two things at least; that there was more than one contesting Lincolnshire band and that there were bands arriving to contest at Boston from outside of the Lincolnshire region. Boston itself, being a port, although industrial does not have the usual profile of the widely perceived brass band hinterland. The brass band phenomenon, then, could probably be seen as a distinguishable, more inclusive entity which was not confined to the brass band Movement, which is the emphasis of many previously published academics. This is almost certainly the understanding that Russell intends to imply when he says: 'The absolute heartland of the pre-1914 movement was undoubtedly formed by the West Riding of Yorkshire, especially the textile district, and industrial Lancashire' (Russell, cited in Herbert, 2000: 72).

Around the 1850s, at a time when the interest in brass banding really became quite intense, the maltings business became quite significant for Horncastle, largely due to the good transport and communications provided by the nearby rivers and many of the local inhabitants from the town and the nearby villages would have been occupied in this type of business. The change in working hours primed the way for many great changes in living conditions, particularly those associated with culture, the arts and social circumstances. With the increased leisure time came the possibility to use the extra hours productively, making time for pastimes in the arts and, of particular interest to this study, in music. It was at this time when the first documented evidence of the existence of a town band in Horncastle can be seen (Robinson, 1983: 12), appearing on a flyer for an outing on the new canal on the 'Boston Packet', a boat hired by the band for a day trip. Denis Mills studied some of these far reaching effects of increased leisure time on Lincoln and the surrounding villages during the years between 1850 and 1950 (Mills, cited in Drake 1994).

Mills noted that alongside the nationwide effect of the Ten Hours Act, agricultural employment especially in arable areas (such as Lincolnshire) declined dramatically, which was also the time of the sweeping implementation of labour-saving machinery, in step with the Industrial Revolution. Populations in the regions of the coalfields increased at the same time as the local rural population in Lincolnshire were in the midst of a difficult period of change involving their labour force and their communities. The general decline in the farming industry continued, even in better times. The shape of Britain's farming communities was evolving and the meaning of 'rural' became subject to flux. By contrast, the improvements in urban living during the same period were impressive. The Victorian city was in the ascendancy and probably overshadowed accomplishments in the declining rural areas, which may lead us to develop some explanation of why the brass bands in rural regions such as Lincolnshire became somewhat underreported and underrated.

In the first quarter of the twentieth century the transport system, stimulated by the increase in urbanisation and subsequent densities of population, became an increasingly significant phenomenon. Whereas most urban amenities did not extend to the more rural areas, the train network combined with a new bus system worked to mobilise the more rural population, allowing them to work in nearby towns while still living at home, thus fracturing the stability of the insulated rural communities. This certainly would have increased the mobility of bandsmen and enabled them to attend rehearsals, although even up to the mid-1900s, the cost of transport was a severely curtailing factor in attendance and membership. At Horncastle Band the weekly subscription for several years around the mid-1930s was two old pence, which was waived for young learners and those who had heavy transport costs to bear (as may have been the case for many in the large rural shire). Thus, in areas in Lincolnshire, as in other highly rural shires, the change from a largely working-class land-labouring workforce to a predominantly urban working class (even those who did not actually live in urban centres) became more and more prevalent. The difference in Lincolnshire (and particularly in Horncastle, possibly) at that time was that there was very little major urbanisation. Consequently, the conditions in which the Horncastle Town Band has flourished have remained remarkably consistent throughout the years.

Horncastle has over the years become somewhat more urban, but still remains on the periphery of urban society. Wright (1982) barely mentions Horncastle in his work on *Lincolnshire Towns and Industry*, an omission that speaks to the lack of impressive industry during the years 1700–1914. Even in the data gathered regarding population, Wright doesn't label Horncastle with either the large or small town status. From the beginning of the twentieth century the population of the town remained relatively stable at around 4,000, which again suggests that very little has changed in terms of manufacturing industries that might require a large workforce. Horncastle has always been, however, an important trading centre with its ideal location between two rivers. This emphasis on trade is what has characterised the town even more than revolutions of any kind. Both Wright (1982) and Robinson (1983) suggest that leather working has been an important part of the working life of the town, the success of which has waxed and waned over the course of the eighteenth and nineteenth centuries. However, even when the larger shoe and boot making companies were moving into the more commercial centres of Lincolnshire like Lincoln and Boston, Horncastle retained two independent boot and shoe making concerns in the town; an indication of the independent and self-reliant nature of the market town. The town is the largest one for at least fourteen miles in all directions and was a very important centre for commerce for many years, hosting the famed horse fair, which at the beginning of the twentieth century was on the decline after hundreds of years of thriving business. In more recent years, Horncastle has built up an international reputation for being the centre of the antiques trade. The town has evidently reinvented itself several times, but continues to thrive on the old standard of local tradesmen and small businesses. These businesses form the foundation of Horncastle society, and it is from here that societies and organisations are formed.

In rural areas, the role of the military in the evolution of brass bands should not be overlooked or underestimated. Many bands were initiated through the formation of the voluntary corps that saturated the entire British nation during the nineteenth century. French military strength, it could be suggested, helped to give rise to a phenomenon that is a defining living symbol of British culture. Galvanising the populace against the enemy inevitably encouraged a powerfully connected shared memory. Bands were at the forefront of parades and military functions, occupying the pole position for photographs, ensuring their place in the reporting of community rituals and the subsequent recollections of involvement and community spirit.

David Robinson (1983), a well known local historian, varies in his estimation of the age of the Horncastle band, which is unsurprising since there are discrepancies in the reporting of the definitive date of formation of the 'G Company' Volunteer Corps (ranging from 1859–1861), from which it is claimed that the band emerged. However, Tweed (1936: 5) suggests that the band existed much earlier and was a facet of the original Volunteer Corps established in 1803. Tweed provides convincing anecdotal evidence (1936: 5–7) that a band from Horncastle was contesting around 1860. Not only were they contesting, but were successful in a consistent fashion. A prize drum was won by the Horncastle Band in a Boston Contest, supposedly worth 20 guineas. Unfortunately, the band did not consider the drum to be worth the full 20 guineas and successfully sued the promoters of the contest in the County Court. The following year the Horncastle Band were again placed first in the same competition and received another drum, which allegedly may still survive and the plaque attached to the side lists the names of the eleven members of the band who won it. There was another brass plaque attached when the drum was lovingly restored by George Jobson and Frank Bell, relatives of two of the original bandsmen. Legend has it that Shaw, the drummer in the conquering band of 1861 was so elated that he strapped himself to his own drum and banged it throughout the town without waiting for the rest of the band to accompany him. This evidence is also supported somewhat through an extract from the 'Daily Herald' dated 7 February 1949, entitled 'New cup joins an old drum', which identifies that it was 88 years previously (1861) that the drum was won and had remained in the bandroom ever since (quoted in Sonin, 1949). The article claims, 'This band of agricultural workers, which included 11-year-old Gordon North (cornet) and

Bandmaster Turner's 18-year-old daughter, Alwyn (horn), competed against 18 bands – and won.' Presumably the terminology 'agricultural workers' in this instance is more a commentary on the location of the band headquarters rather than on the complement of the band, which appears (from the band meeting minutes) to have been made up at this time of mainly shopkeepers, tradesmen and retired servicemen. In particular it is unlikely that an eleven-year-old boy would have been a full time agricultural worker. By contrast, the Lincolnshire Echo on the same day (with perhaps a rather more accurate understanding of the demographic of Lincolnshire brass bands) also reported the 88-year lack of success in contesting, but only found the one woman in the band worthy of mention, with no claims to assume an agricultural element.

Tweed's rendition of history suggests that the drummer of the band appears to have been a very well regarded position, probably stemming from the military activity in which the band may have had its origins. Marching to a drum would have been a high profile activity at the time. The Horncastle Parish Clerk of 1865 was also a drummer in the band for a short time, but was seemingly deposed of this high-ranking position by a rigged voting system whereby the lucky winner of the position of drummer actually had the casting vote. One might suggest (although Tweed does not actually do so) that the subsequent washing of the drum in 'Sot's Hole' may well have been revenge under the cover of sabotage. Certainly the drum became strangely heavy, and, on 19 April 1867, Mr John Coates Osborne, the Parish Clerk, wrote the resignation of the drum. Tweed (1936: 5) notes an excerpt from Osbourne's diary:

> March 17. Went into the Exchange Hall to see Tom Baker's traps removed. Espied threepenny bit on the floor – nailed it. At a Band Committee meeting to-night elected drummer in band by casting vote of Tom Shaw. . . . Not a very triumphant result.
>
> March 27. Practice night for the Rifle Corps. Took drum to 'Sot's Hole' 'Washed it'
>
> April 5. . . . Band practice after church. Had the drum on and marched in the room. It appears very heavy and I don't much fancy I shall manage it comfortably.
>
> April 6. . . . Officers' parade to-night at 6.30; a very fair muster. The Captain announced Rd Clitherow's resignation as lieutenant, appointed Rt Armstrong in his place. The ensigncy in abeyance between Dr George and W. Jeffery.
>
> April 19. Wrote resignation of drum
>
> April 21. Poor Mr. Nicholson appeared to be shocked at the music used on Sunday to go to church with. I explained that they were bound to have quick-steps to march to. I think there is often some rummer music inside the church then any the band ever plays.

From Tweed's recollections (1936: 17), the band appears to have led the celebrations at the end of the Boer War in 1902, but this seems to have been the turning point for the collaboration of the bandsmen and the military. In 1903 the band was disbanded due to the lack of a bandmaster. A band re-emerged in 1905 (probably largely constituting the members of the old 'G' Company) under the baton of Mr F. Blyth, called the Town and Volunteer Band (Tweed 1936: 19). Although it was stipulated at this time that the band should play for the company when required, there is no readily available documentary evidence that they ever did so. By 1911, the band was reported as playing in the Coronation Parade Service in Woodhall Spa under the name of Horncastle Town Band (Tweed 1936: 22).

Tweed does not really clarify whether the Horncastle Town band was effectively the same band as the Volunteer band, but deeper investigation of the paratext of Horncastle society provides further clues in terms of the band's links with the wider community. This also gives a great deal of insight as to the composition of the band; the type of person who was a band member and how they were situated within the structures of Horncastle society. Morton's Almanack of the year 1938 shows Joseph Kirk who resigned from the band aged 80 years. Kirk was born and bred in Horncastle and is noted as having joined the band when it was the band of the old Horncastle Volunteers, suggesting first that he had been a military man and second that the band was actually a fairly continuous entity during the 50 years of his membership.

Brass bands tend to occupy what is a privileged but uncomfortable position somewhere between high culture and popular culture in both social status and cultural 'value'. In consequence, whether they are loved or loathed, bands tend to have some relevance to most sections of society, and a total acceptance only from the brass band community as a whole. To the lover of classical music, brass bands offer affordable and local renditions of some of the most revered canons of orchestral arrangements, satisfying the values placed on musicianship and artistry that is commanded by the classically musically educated. On the other hand, brass bands have the ability to transcend genre barriers and can replicate the big band sounds and also cover the more current 'pop' sounds of the era. It would seem sensible then to challenge, or at least question, the notion that brass bands were an entirely working class phenomenon at any time. While the general consensus of opinion might be that brass bands are not quite the 'real thing' in terms of serious classical music, the supporting cast of Horncastle Town band is most impressive. The lack of industrial connections is notable and firmly situates the patronage of the band in the military realm. Taken from the 1932 Morton's Almanack we can see that the officials of the Horncastle Town band were as follows:

> President, Mr H. C. Haslam MP,
> Vice Presidents: Lieutenant Colonel Sir A. G. Weigall, K.C.M.G,
> Major A. A. Ellwood, D. S. O. and Mrs W. Achurch

The general running of the band fell to the day-to-day members who established themselves into a committee, the minutes of which would place the members into the tradesmen and local businessmen category. In comparison, the officials of the Horncastle Amateur Orchestral Society consisted of a much less notable (though no less worthy, surely) line-up of local business people as follows:

> Honorary Conductor and Honorary Secretary: Mrs W. Achurch, L.R.A.M.,
> Honorary Treasurer: Mr A H Harris
> Honorary Librarian: Mrs U. Spratt
> Committee: Messers Jason Elam, H. W. Kemp, W.Bell and J. Taylor.

It is worth noting that Mrs W. Achurch appears on both committees and was a qualified female conductor who did eventually become President of the Town Band in later years. Interestingly it was that band which withstood the test of time and indeed provided the music at the funeral of Mrs Achurch in the 1970s (while the orchestra has not enjoyed the same longevity). Lieutenant Colonel Weigall, by comparison was a very wealthy military man who lived with his wife Lady Weigall (whose daughter married into the aristocracy) in Woodhall Spa, a village close to Horncastle that has strong military connections and was the headquarters for the Dambusters 617 squadron during World War II. Weigall himself had held the government position of Governor of the State of South Australia in 1920–21. This type of patronage evokes an ideological position quite at odds with the discourse of Northernness and industry. It is also worth noting that although Weigall was more than happy to add his name to the band's honorary committee, there was no funding on offer at any time. Indeed it was more likely that the band would play for garden parties held by Weigall as a favour to their Vice-President, which is in stark contrast to the more paternalistic style of funding for bands from industrial centres.

Photographs from Morton's Horncastle Almanacks are very revealing in terms of family involvement in the band and in cross involvement between the band and the Orchestra. It has already been mentioned that Mrs Achurch held positions in both the band and the orchestra at different times, but some individuals also appear to have been players in both organisations. A photograph of the volunteer company in 1887 at Tumby Swan (Morton's Almanack, 1932) enables the identification of members of the band as well as the other volunteers. The name of C. Elam appears here as well as in other photographs at Thornton Abbey near Horncastle, where he is seen with his brother Jason Elam. Jason Elam also appears in photographs of the local orchestra where he is evidently seen as a double bass player. The Elams were obviously a family of the area who were significantly involved in the town's social and cultural life. A closer look shows that many names represented here are typically Horncastle names, which evidences the tightness of the community from where the players were derived. Lammyman, Taylor, Frith, Daubney, Woolley and Chatterton are all names that are still found in Horncastle today. Significantly many of these names are associated with trades and businesses, which would seem to argue with widely held beliefs that bandsmen belonged to a section of society categorised by a working class status. However, this may not be particularly unusual in bands that have a military background. Bands of the volunteer Corps recruited those men who were not in the regular army, which may well have particularly applied to those who were in a trade or running their own businesses. Captain Murray (in Herbert, 2000: 38) of the 16th Middlesex Rifles insisted that the volunteers were, 'As to position in life . . . of the tradesmen and respectable artisan class'. Horncastle's Jason Elam was a good example of such respectability having a full-page advertisement in the Morton's Almanack in 1935, evidencing his status as businessman and tradesman in the Town. His establishment was found on East Street, which was a major thoroughfare of the town, just adjacent to the main Bull Ring area, signifying perhaps that he was indeed rather well-to-do even among the business sector of the town. Furthermore, the town's media (Morton's) felt that his wedding anniversary was of sufficient interest to townsfolk to be included in the yearly Almanack (1935). It may be that the band's constitution of tradesmen gives us a clue to some of the resilience that has enabled a continued longevity when other bands have ceased to exist.

The demographic and composition of the band members may have had an impact on the general running of individual organisations. In order to further explore the impact that cultures, funding arrangements and composition of the organising teams have had on bands, we can compare some of the functional and managerial aspects of Horncastle Town Band with those of the Rossington band. The Rossington band belonged to the Rossington Colliery. Situated on the outskirts of Doncaster and just over 50 miles away from Horncastle, this was a band with all the stereotypical traits of the heartland of brass banding. Rossington band enjoyed corporate funding from the Rossington Miners' Welfare Scheme for many years whereas the Horncastle Town band relied on more modest income from concerts, functions and fetes to swell the bank balance. Both bands have documented evidence of the difficulties of purchasing an entire set of new instruments. The approach and resulting satisfaction of these purchases could be said to indicate some of the flaws in the funding processes of welfare schemes.

The funding for the Rossington Band included the purchase in 1924 of a new set of instruments from Hawkes by the Welfare Committee at a cost of £300. In fact, the Welfare Committee oversaw the running of the band in its entirety, having six members of the Welfare Committee on the Band Committee, and the original moniker of the band was The Rossington Miners' Welfare Band. There was much documented wrangling during the next two years over the cost of and dissatisfaction with the Hawkes instruments. Coupled with the changing business face of the organising committee, the result was what appears to have been a difficult, corporate approach to external suppliers. There were also insecurities over whether the band was eventually responsible for the outstanding payment, or whether agreements made by the Welfare Committee belonged to the corporation. In its heyday, the Rossington band, supported by the colliery, was among the best in the land but, sadly, it eventually folded when Polypipe (the most recent sponsor) was taken over and the funding was no longer forthcoming.

By contrast, we can see through historical documents and correspondence that Horncastle Band had a problem with Boosey and Hawkes instruments that also ran the span of at least two years from 1971 to 1973 but showed a very different approach to the issue (information taken from letters belonging to Horncastle band). The person from the Horncastle band who was in contact with Boosey and Hawkes was the Band Secretary, Mr Kemp (a furnisher and funeral director), who, it appeared, had taken delivery in 1971 of a full set of instruments at his shop in Horncastle, having negotiated a 5 per cent discount by using his own firm as a guarantor. Some hard bargaining appears to have taken place and Mr Kemp secured another 2.5 per cent discount for payment in full over two years (at a rate of 0 per cent interest). However, it seems that this payment was never forthcoming from the band. Eventually in 1973, Mr Kemp received a letter asking for an explanation of why there had been no payment. Mr Kemp's response was swift and curt:

> We think the best thing is for you to start at the beginning, and send an invoice, with a Credit Note for the old instruments; then your Statement can follow, from which we shall deduct our agreed commission, and you can then have full and final settlement without any messing about . . . we are sure the Band Committee will be glad to know that at long last the instruments belong to them.

Further correspondence suggests that Mr Kemp drove the bargain even harder and secured another discount for his company's 'handling charges'. The difference in approach to what in effect is a similar problem in both bands is clearly one of the fundamental factors in the functional organisation of the band. Mr Kemp from Horncastle was a member of the band, elected to the position of secretary and who took full responsibility of that position. He was also the director of his own company and a businessman, skilled in the ways of negotiation. The committee of the Rossington band did not have such a vested interest in their own band. They were accountable not only to the band members but also to those who controlled the very generous financial support, who also happened to be their own employers. That would have been a much more difficult position to negotiate. However, the point must be made that, throughout its history, Horncastle Band has never enjoyed the contesting success or the acclaim within the Movement of bands such as the well funded and geographically well placed Rossington Miners' Welfare Band.

In conclusion, this chapter has set out to establish the brass band as a national and potentially a rural phenomenon rather than a regional or class embedded symbol of Britishness. Symbolic representation of national institutions such as the brass band tends to provide a hegemonic image of a shared identity that works to portray a community in a favourable light. The images that are most favourable within the dominant discourse are given the most encouragement through whatever mass communication is available, creating aspirations of belonging to representational groups in society. This is evident in the representation of the Movement by those bands that have been recognised as the most successful. The Brass Band Movement has created a value system by nature of contesting and league tables that tend to draw a veil over the majority of rural brass bands, since it is difficult for a self-funding band to compete in excellence with organisations supported by funding from heavy industry. Consequently, little is known about the internal community of rural brass bands, but that is not to assume that there is nothing to say. It is the emphasis on the industrial centres in both popular understanding and in academic writing that renders the rural brass band community invisible. The Movement has been unintentionally complicit in the othering of rural brass bands by identifying the 'norm' as the elite bands from the Yorkshire collieries and the Lancashire factories. It is from this selective dialogue that the idea of what it means to be a brass band is honed and refined, almost into simplistic stereotypes of that which is, in reality, many and varied. It is inevitable that such symbols and representation, when highly developed and well documented through the arts, mediated through disparate academic disciplines and through oral traditions, may appear to be exclusive. By investigating a rural brass band, we can begin to challenge these assumptions of the norm. Horncastle is a small town with very little to connect it to industrial lifestyle of the nineteenth century, but the activities of rural life are not totally incompatible with industrialised centres, and the same is true in reverse. It is in this problematic area of sub-culture versus geography that the brass band quietly maintains some of its strongest roots. Exploring the background and underpinning of a rurally based brass band with a long history shows us that a brass band is a communal endeavour that can span the oppositional creations of the rural as well as the industrial urban areas. Through investigations of the nature of family belonging to a region and a community, of relationships with the rural society and the underpinning of the organisation, it is possible to see that, although there are certainly differences between the establishments of a rural or urban brass band, there are many more similarities than differences. The structures of the urban and the rural brass band are remarkably similar, due to the rules governing the Movement but it is the people who operate within those structures who make the differences which we perceive as statements of academic and cultural value. The rural brass band is a thriving artefact of both British history and British culture today, at least as enduring as and arguably more enduring than many bands of the industrial North and various other forms of musical ensemble.

Acknowledgements

Grateful thanks are extended to Banovallum Brass Band in Horncastle and to Mrs Betty Morton for allowing access to their personal archives, without which this research could not have been achieved.

References

BrassBandResults (n.d.) Ruthin town, BrassBandResults, www.brassbandresults.co.uk/bands/ruthin-town (accessed 2 February 2013).

Creetown Silver Band (2011) Band history, Creetown Band. Available at: www.creetownband.org.uk/band-history (accessed 6 February 2013).

Drake, M. (ed.) (1994) *Time, Family and Community. Perspectives on Family and Community History*. Oxford and Malden, MA: Blackwell.

Finnegan, R. (2007) *The Hidden Musicians Music-making in an English Town*. Middletown, CT: Wesleyan.

Herbert, T. (ed.) (2000) *The British Brass Band: A Musical and Social History*. Oxford: Oxford University Press.

Kemp, E. J. (1936–49) *Horncastle Town Band Brass Band Minute Book*.

Lincolnshire Echo (1949) Horncastle Band 1st – After 88 Years, 7 February.

Mackie, D. (2012) *History of the Band 1834–1897*. Peebles Burgh Silver Band. Available at: www.peeblessilverband.com/7.html (accessed 06 February 2013).

Morrison. R. (2008) It's a blast – BRASS 2008 brings massed bands to Durham. *The Times*, 5 July.

Morton's (1932) *Lincolnshire Almanack with Horncastle and Woodhall Spa*. Horncastle, UK: W. K. Morton & Sons.

Morton's (1935) *Lincolnshire Almanack with Horncastle and Woodhall Spa*. Horncastle, UK: W. K. Morton & Sons.

Morton's (1938) *Lincolnshire Almanack with Horncastle and Woodhall Spa*. Horncastle, UK: W. K. Morton & Sons.

Pugh, D. (2005) History of the band. Newtown Silver Band. Available at: www.newtownsilverband.co.uk/history.php (accessed 6 February 2013).

Robinson, D. (1983) *The Book of Horncastle and Woodhall Spa*. Buckingham, UK: Barracuda Books.

Russell, D. (1987) *Popular Music in England 1840–1914, A Social History*, Manchester, UK: Manchester University Press.

Russell, D. (2004) *Looking North. Northern England and the National Imagination*. Manchester, UK: Manchester University Press.

Rossington Miners' Welfare Band Minutes (1924–1926) Available from Lincoln Archives, Lincoln.

Sonin, R. (1949) New cup joins an old drum. *Daily Herald*, 7 February, as reported in the Horncastle Town Brass Band Minute Book.

Tweed H. R. (1936) *A History of the Horncastle Detachment, 4th Battalion The Lincolnshire Regiment (Territorial Army): From the Raising of the Original Volunteer Corps in 1803 to the Present Time*. Horncastle, UK: W. K. Morton & Sons.

Wright N. R. (1982) *Lincolnshire Towns and Industry, 1700–1914*. Lincoln, UK: Society for Lincolnshire History and Archeology.

Part III

Contested rurality

11 Dairy farming and the fight for ownership of the concept: 'rural'

Alison Moore

In this chapter, I use cultural studies methods and concepts to consider two questions: what is the impact of the concept 'rural' on how rural issues are played out? And who and what define what rural means, in concept and in fact?

These questions are addressed through discussion of a controversy that emerged from the 2009 proposal for an 8,100-cow 'mega-dairy' at Nocton in Lincolnshire: the notion of whether cows belong in- or outside. In the Nocton plans, which were based on the US 'super-dairy' model, the cows were to be housed in 450-animal sheds and to be 'zero-grazed': i.e. the animals were to be kept inside for the majority of the time (Nocton Dairies, 2010: 6, 8). The Nocton Dairies' plans and their ultimate rejection in an environment of high profile 'no' campaigns came at a time of increasing difficulties for UK dairy producers. A squeeze on profits and rising costs had led to many smaller farms disappearing; in this environment more intensive methods became increasingly attractive. Yet in a 2009 study, 95 per cent of participants said they found the notion of cows being housed permanently indoors unacceptable (Ellis *et al.*, 2009: 271) and a recent opinion poll found that 61 per cent of the public would not buy milk that came from 'large, indoor dairies' (WSPA/Ipsos Mori, 2010). This gap between cultural acceptability and economic expedient has clear implications for UK dairy farming. The job of cultural studies then is to ask what role popular culture plays, and might continue to play, at this time of change, through its representations of dairy production.

The dairy cow placidly chewing its cud in the field is perhaps the quintessential signifier of British rurality, so changes in the way this beast is kept inevitably affect the way the rural is understood. And since the rural exists both through discourse and through physical form, each of which impacts on the other (Woods, 2011: 200), then both ideas about the dairy cow, and the beast's material situation, contribute to the meaning of rural. Analysis is thus carried out here using examples from both cultural text and cultural practice: advertising and the farm visit respectively. While other genres such as children's literature (Bunce, 2003; Horton, 2003; Parry, this volume) and broadcast texts (e.g., Jones, 1995; Phillips *et al.*, 2001) have been dissected in relation to rural signification, advertisements have been overlooked: John Urry seems to be alone in specifically mentioning their influence (2002: 89). As for the farm visit, cultural analysis is completely lacking, surprising given that many farmers depend on this leisure pursuit for their continued economic viability. Nonetheless, it is generally recognised that mass-media and popular culture do play a large part in representing the rural (Laing, 1992; Fowler and Helfield, 2006). Certainly, according to Michael Woods, 'the media is now the means by which the majority of the population comes to "know" the rural' (2011: 35). Also widely recognised is that mediated representations of the rural often portray an idyllic or pastoral scene (e.g., Short, 1992; Cloke, 2003a). For some, mediated representations of varied rural settings result in their having a 'composite idea' of the rural that they expect of their own local countryside (Phillips, 2008, in Woods, 2011: 37).

If we are to understand rural change therefore we need to grasp how it is both conceived and practised. In farming terms, change has been the source of much difficulty. Farming is seen as symbolic of rural values (Holloway 2004: 203; Woods, 2011: 22), but issues such as 'changes demanded by the globalised food industry' (Cloke, 2003b: 2) and BSE (Muecke, 2005: 61–2) have challenged this image. In particular, farming industrialisation has caused tensions between farmer and non-farmer (Short, 1992: 1- 2; Seymour *et al.*, 1997: 71) to the extent that for residents both concept and experience of the countryside has been marred (Seymour *et al.*, 1997: 71). Given this context, the Nocton controversy may seem to be more of the same traditional-versus-industrial discourse. However, neither representation nor practice of dairy farming is so easily categorised. With this in mind, I now outline the cultural studies tools used here to explore this tangled web.

According to Raymond Williams, culture is an expression of 'meanings and values' (1961, 2001: 57), and cultural analysis should clarify what those meanings and values are. Williams also emphasises that cultures are fluid; meanings change and analysis of such changes can offer insights into cultural change in general. This scholar's focus on meaning and change thus make his work ideal for the matter of this chapter.

Williams conceptualises culture as having three primary elements which he terms 'dominant', 'emergent' and 'residual'; these he uses to help explain the 'dynamic interrelations' involved in cultural change (1977: 121–2). The dominant culture is 'a central system of practices, meanings and values' (Williams, 2005: 38) that prevails as the norm. Residual elements are ideas from the past that in some way are 'still active in the cultural process' (1977: 122). Emergent elements are 'new meanings and values, new practices, new relationships and kinds of relationships' (123). In any period one can identify the interplay of the three forms at work. Key to Williams's ideas is the notion of incorporation, whereby selected residual and emergent elements are incorporated into the dominant culture in such a way as to preserve the overall status quo (2005: 39–40). Thus the dominant culture maintains hegemony by reference to parts of its past and by acceptance, within certain bounds, of new ideas, meanings and values. It becomes clear then that hegemony is 'highly complex' and constantly developing as competing elements bed into and break out of its bounds.

The above concepts offer the tools whereby ideas that form the current hegemony around dairy may be recognised through the identification of strands of continuity and change. We begin to consider these strands now by situating Nocton Dairies' ideas about a cow's proper environment in the context of current dairy practice and Williams's concepts. In a *BBC Lincolnshire* interview in March 2010, Nocton co-director Peter Willes, while trying to make the Dairies' approach to cow husbandry clear, asserted that 'Cows do not belong in fields'. This boldly stated claim acted as a red rag to the project's many opponents. Yet on most UK dairy farms, herds already do spend several months a year indoors anyway (NFU, 2010: 6). This fact is not widely recognised beyond dairy farms themselves, however (Pullar, 2011), and as a result, there is a public perception that cows are always outside, which popular cultural representations do little to counter and much to encourage.

According to Williams, there are forms that are truly emergent and forms that are 'merely novel' expressions of the dominant mode (Williams, 1977: 123). In theory terms, we might see Nocton Dairies' proposal as the latter, given that it appears to simply extend current practice. Yet because keeping cows inside permanently is widely *perceived* to be different to current UK practice, it is arguably an emergent form, in that it calls upon the public to adopt 'new meanings and values [and] new relationships' (1977: 123) in accepting that the cow has no need for access to the outside. While in the following analyses I take the latter view, this example does raise the question of what exactly to consider when applying these concepts, when practice and perception differ so widely.

The divergence between the real and imaginary lives of dairy cows can be illuminated though analysis of dominant conceptions of dairy cows created in popular cultural texts. The Anchor Butter advertisements of the eighties (discussed further below), where cows waxed lyrical in lush green meadows[1] perhaps come most readily to mind among readers of a certain age, but a more recent TV advert for Müller yoghurt is also a case in point. 'From farm to yogurt in 24 hours' (Muller Dairy UK Ltd, 2008) features a single glassful of milk represented as hand-milked in the field from a lone cow, then passed from person to person until it reaches the dairy. The advert contains no modern rural paraphernalia: the glass is taken by foot, push-bike, go-cart, donkey, rowing boat and old-fashioned tractor to the dairy, and all set against a backdrop of lush sunlit countryside settings. The sunlight itself is often hazy and slightly sepia-tinged, prompting a feeling of nostalgia.

This arguably is an example of a post-modern rural landscape that erases the modern and anything unpleasant from view (Urry, 2002: 88). It is a mythical rural, a representation of timelessness and is typical of the way that dairy products are promoted by setting the cow outside in an idyllic landscape. The advert promotes the dominant view of dairy produce (healthiness, freshness, goodness), but we can see here how residual notions are incorporated. That there is a cow milked by hand outside in a field refers back to a time when for each family this may have been the practice, at once connoting simplicity and closeness to 'nature', while keeping milk tied to the domestic sphere. Here then is an example of Williams's 'selective tradition' (2005: 39), wherein residual elements are drawn upon in the dominant culture: 'certain meanings and practices are chosen for emphasis, certain other meanings and practices are neglected and excluded' (ibid.). From a whole history of cow-milking and cow-keeping practices, much has been excluded, and this specific rural notion is selected to support and reinforce the dominant idea of what dairy ought to be about.

While the residual reference is commonplace in advertising, the dairy cow has also in recent decades been conceptualised as more progressive of habit. Nocton Dairies co-director Robert Howard inadvertently identified this tendency when discussing resistance to Nocton's plans: 'Campaigners think cows should be like in the Anchor Butter advert, with 50 to 100 cows dancing in a field,' he claimed, 'It is a lovely idea, but not the reality' (in Derbyshire, 2010).[2] While we might credit the campaigners with more common sense than Howard claims, his comment does not simply re-emphasise the problems caused when material and conceptual diverge so wildly. It also points to the common aspect of advert cows, that they are both active and aware: they know what their milk is used for and have a sense of ownership of it. Early examples of this were indeed those eighties Anchor adverts where cows sang of their butter quality. This trope of self-awareness is still apparent today though. A 2010 Anchor Butter commercial playing on the tag line 'Made by Cows since 1886' (Arla, 2010) shows cows in the factory checking the production line, working the computers and moving stock about. A series of adverts for Cravendale milk with the tagline, 'So good, the cows want it back' (Arla, 2005) features cows plotting to break into a supermarket. Müller extends this idea: in 'Thank you cows' (Müller Dairy UK Ltd, 2010), a cow stands on an empty beach, while the voiceover intones, 'Müller Fruit Corner would like you to meet Mary: she's always dreamt of being a horse'. As the cow runs along the beach, the voice-over continues: 'and to thank her for all the natural dairy goodness she gives us, we made her dream come true . . . go on girl, gallop . . . let the stallion within run free.'

There is nothing new about animals talking, singing or represented as complicit in their own exploitation (e.g., see Baker, 2001: 172), thus we can say these representations are conceptually part of the dominant mode. What is new in conceptual terms is a discourse that frames cows as aimful, business-like or aspirational. The more contemporary cows yearn: the recent Anchor cows do business, the Cravendale cows plot and plan, and Müller's 'Mary' has ambition. All of these require a sense of identity. These representations draw on current self-actualisation models related to people, and since they present a shift away from the traditional cow conceptualisation, we can see they are emergent aspects incorporated into the dominant advertisement–cow model.

Given the above representations, it is easy to see how the Nocton proposal to take this apparently active, desiring, individual cow from its sunlit idyll and confine it in great numbers would be anathema. With this in mind, we now consider two examples that in their very different ways are strategies to manage the perception of cows in relation to the zero-grazing method of dairying. The first example is Compassion in World Farming's (CIWF) *Cows Belong in Fields* campaign, begun in response to Nocton Dairies' plans. The campaign adverts simply read, 'Cows belong in fields. Say no to the mega-dairy' (CIWF, n.d.). While the problems that mega-dairies might cause in terms of welfare and environment are multiple,[3] the slogan limits the discourse so as to focus attention on this one issue. In theory terms this exclusive framing can be read as an effort to bar a perceived emergent practice from incorporation through the use of linguistic boundary lines that constrain public perception of the mega-dairy. Williams argues that dominant modes are exclusionary, such that they commandeer 'the ruling definition of the social' (1977: 125). We see this in action here, the words 'cows belong in fields' employed to retain the current definition of 'dairy cow', premised on this one facet of the creature's existence and excluding other facets from thought. Here, then, CIWF is acting as hegemonic arbiter, policing the acceptable edges of meaning.

While the CIWF campaign saw much support, Nocton Dairies themselves owned that their PR campaign was ropey (Driver, 2010a): their attempts at discussing where cows belong were little short of disastrous. But managed differently, the permanent housing of cows inside and indeed in great numbers has elsewhere been made palatable to the public. This is the case with our second example – Fair Oaks Farm in Indiana, USA – which was the model for the Nocton proposals (Driver, 2010a), and wherein the visitor centre is one of the most popular leisure destinations in Indiana (Driver, 2010b). Gordie Jones, a key figure in the development of Fair Oaks, was one of Nocton's advisors, and had things gone to plan, Nocton would have had its own visitor centre (Willes, in Davies, 2010).

Fair Oaks' success resides in the way it is conceptually managed. At its visitor centre, people are bussed through the free-stall barns in which many hundreds of cows live permanently together (Cooley, 2012); they view the cows being milked on the rotary milker, watch births in a specially designed theatre and see newborn calves in the 'nursery' (Campbell-Gibbons, 2010). In short, Fair Oaks foregrounds the enclosed lives of the cows while presenting it as good for them, and appears to make the whole dairy process available for scrutiny. Thus the facility's material construction and its processes contribute to a discourse that normalises the inside-based lives of the cows.

Fair Oaks is an example of incorporation in progress. It has aspects of the dominant culture in that it builds on the traditional farm or dairy visit. And for the audience, the tour's birthing theatre and rotary milker position the cows as performers (albeit unwitting), and so arguably as complicit as advertisers' singing cows. On the other hand, Fair Oaks lacks aspects of the dominant culture discussed earlier: it does not romanticise cows as creatures of green ever-sunlit fields or as individuals with specific human-type yearnings. There is no confusion here between concept and practice: the cow is presented as a creature of the internal domain, and a new relationship is constructed between scrutinising public and dairy animals. The emergent method of dairying has here been incorporated into the mainstream.

Concrete implications for the dairy beast emerge from this moment of collision of the cow image with modern dairy reality. At the very least, there is a heightened awareness within the dairy industry of the need to improve communication with the public about current dairy practices (e.g., see Chartered Institute of Marketing, 2011), focusing on the cow itself. It was no coincidence that Fair Oaks was on the itinerary of UK dairy representatives who, partly in response to the Nocton issue, went to the US to investigate super-dairy functioning and PR management in 2010 (Driver, 2010b). Nor indeed that one of the priorities of the Dairy Cow Welfare Strategy includes the aim to be proactive in providing information to consumers about welfare standards and to increase 'consumer knowledge of dairy farming' (NFU, 2010: 23) through websites, educational and promotional materials. In light of these intentions, it is worth exploring briefly what potential currently exists for re-representation of the dairy cow in the UK.

In terms of the farm visit, it's not news that many UK farms already diversify into tourism (Phelan and Sharpley, 2010). Indeed, given the current state of economic affairs, it is likely that this trend will increase. There is thus an opportunity at dairy farms that are, or intend to be, open to visitors, to deliberately focus on re-presentation of the way that cows currently live. This is not about getting the PR right so that the zero-grazed cow might become acceptable; it is about restoring reality and transparency to a cultural practice that has become clouded with misrepresentation. One example of different representation is New Gokul, part of a Hare Krishna complex in Hertfordshire. New Gokul is unusual in that it operates a no-kill policy, the cows are hand-milked, and calves suckle from their mothers for many weeks (Bhaktivedanta Manor, 2012a). As with the majority of UK dairy farms, New Gokul cows are kept inside in winter, but at a special 'Letting the Cows Out Day' event, people are invited to watch the cows go into the fields for the first time after their winter inside (Bhaktivedanta Manor, 2012b). Visitors are thus with little effort made aware of the farm's current herd housing practice and the rationale behind it. A more conventional example is Gorstage Green Farm, Cheshire, home of 'Farmer 4 a Day', where visitors assist the farmer as he goes about his ordinary dairy work (Farmer-4-a-Day, 2012). Farmers like these, who show and discuss with visitors where and how cows are actually housed – not just at visiting time, but all year round – clearly go some way towards removing the myth of the ever-outside cow. However, those dairy farm attractions that limit information to the milking process and give no explanation of, or opportunity to see, the rest of the cows' experience in current dairy farming, are equally culpable in perpetuating the myth.

In relation to theory, there are two interesting points here. First, those conventional farmer–tourist hosts who inform the public about their dairy cow husbandry resolve the dissonance between the cultural representation and cultural practice that made a plan like Nocton's such an issue. Notably, however, they never leave the dominant culture in doing so. The New Gokul example provides a useful contrast to this. It is at once very different to the norm ideologically, but in terms of cow accommodation, very normal. Therefore despite marked differences, it can be read *in theory terms* as on a par with Fair Oaks: that is, it incorporates the genuinely emergent into the dominant culture successfully. Williams's concepts deployed here allow us to see how apparently divergent forms actually perform the same societal function.

While individual farmer–tourist hosts can go some way towards redrawing the dairy cow, they are limited in their public reach. In contrast, of the advertisers discussed earlier, Müller spent £20 million on advertising in 2011 (AHDB, 2012: 3) and in 2010 Arla allotted a £10 million marketing budget to Cravendale alone (*The Grocer*, 2010). Taking into account TV, cinema and internet marketing, mail drops and other promotions, the potential to change views about cows' contexts arguably resides with these major suppliers.[4] Yet it is difficult to imagine one might see a change of representation here: it is not really in their interest to change it. David Barnes, the Nocton director, may have claimed that advertising represents an unreal view of the situation of the dairy cow (in Derbyshire, 2010), nonetheless these images seem thought to be reliably profitable, and in a risky economic climate, certainty matters. It is unlikely that Müller, or indeed any of the 156 dairy producers Müller draws from (AHDB, 2012: 4), would insist that advertisers use images of winter-shed-based dairy cows to help sell their products (although anything is possible in advertising). The same can be said for Arla and its 1,400 'farmer members' (AHDB, 2011: 2).

For those responsible then for a great deal of the advertisement representation of dairy, whatever other perhaps more transient tropes feature, no move from that useful residual/dominant representational cow identified earlier is likely to occur on a long-term basis. What we can see from this and the dairy visit is the way in which the hegemony regarding the dairy cow's representation is to a great extent driven and governed by the economic contingencies prevailing in this sector. One farmer, in face-to-face touch with a visiting public, may be able to see both the benefits and means of developing new dairy cow representations; the very different priorities of a large dairy company make it less likely to do so. As we have seen, though, from the Fair Oaks example in the US, a scale of farming much larger than exists in the UK, combined with a strong PR strategy and a large budget, has made another representation widely acceptable.

Analysis of the kind deployed in this chapter demonstrates the value of a cultural studies approach. Williams's concepts allow us to see the workings of hegemony in this arena: the clear connection between the representation in, and of, a cultural artefact or practice, and the ideological and economic factors driving the representations. Culture is not created in a vacuum divorced from the real world, but by people who have the motivation, and importantly, the means and tools to create it. As Williams himself contends, 'whatever purposes cultural practice may serve, its means of production are unarguably material' (1981: 87). Those who have more ownership and control of material forms control more of the culture.

This chapter sought to consider the impact of the concept 'rural' on how rural issues are played out. The choice to focus on the changing context of the dairy cow, a widely recognised, fondly imagined signifier of rurality, has allowed us to see 'rural' as a mesh of representations, processes and forms that impact on the real lives of the animals living therein. Consideration of where dairy cows are understood to belong has demonstrated that popular culture representations about dairy production, and the materiality of production, are often at odds. The furore over Nocton Dairies' plans for this bovine bearer of rural meaning was in part impelled by industry-accepted popular culture representations that have ironically been their own worst enemy. Were these images not so ubiquitous, were they not tied in so effectively to a complex web of nostalgic, traditional and contemporary concepts, the real dairy cow may not have sustained the same place in the public imagination and heart. Willes's comments may well have then passed unnoticed and the Cows Belong in Fields campaign never taken off. Here we also need to recognise that the rural conceived through the cow-in-field icon arguably represents in the UK a uniquely British rural in the public psyche, and one which it has been seen is not likely to be laid aside. Thus, we see the power of this image: although we have argued it is a residual element in the dominant culture, deployed as a rhetorical device, the British public view it as a vital part of their rural future.

The chapter's second concern was about who or what defines the meaning of 'rural'. The scattering of examples given here demonstrate that multiple discursive sources – national and international, individual and corporate, trivial and earnest – operate in concert and conflict to forge hegemony over what constitutes rural practice and meaning. In material terms, both the thwarted Nocton Dairies and successful Fair Oaks can be seen as attempting redefinition through employment of the mega-dairy method. In representational terms, the language and imagery of advertiser and pressure group try to tie down the meaning of 'dairy cow'; dairy organisations can be seen to be attempting to adjust that meaning.

Finally, all of the above are seen here through the lens of discipline, so rural becomes defined by cultural studies generally, and by this academic in particular. Cultural study recognises that meanings, values, and practices pertain to particular times and places, and acknowledgement of change is essential, so 'rural' is continually redefined. As an academic with both professional and lay interest in animals, I recognise that to speak of rural is to include the beasts that make it what it is. The elasticity of Williams's deceptively simple concepts offers the freedom and range to explore changes in definition and the effects on, and of, the beast. Williams's claim that hegemony is internally complex (2005: 38) is certainly borne out when considering the interplay of elements here and the struggle for dominion, through the dairy cow and the dairy farm industry, over what rural means.

Notes

1 When these ideas were presented as a paper, Dr Jonathan Cooper (University of Lincoln) quite rightly made the point that the New Zealand-based 'Anchor cows' actually would spend most of their time in fields. However, my argument is about audience reception: the impression formed would be that all cows live like this.
2 See Hanbury-Tenison, 1997: 92 (in Woods: 2011: 37), for similar comments on Disney.
3 Full expert background to these problems is of course provided by CIWF in its literature. See www.ciwf.org.uk.
4 Space does not permit, but an examination of other stakeholders such as supermarkets in relation to dairy and popular culture would also be highly relevant.

References

AHDB (Agriculture and Horticulture Development Board) (2011) Company Review: Arla. Kenilworth: AHDB.

AHDB (Agriculture and Horticulture Development Board) (2012) Company Review: Müller. Kenilworth: AHDB.

Arla (2005) Cravendale – cows break into supermarket. TV Advert [MPEG Video]. Available at: creativeclub.co.uk (accessed 23 August 2011).

Arla (2010) Made by cows since 1886. TV Advert [MPEG Video]. Available at: creativeclub.co.uk (accessed 23 August 2011).

Baker, S. (2001) *Picturing the Beast: Animals, Identity and Representation*. Champaign, IL: University of Illinois Press.

Bhaktivedanta Manor (2012a) The five principles of cow protection. Available at: http://bhaktivedantamanor.co.uk/newgokul/index.php/cowprotection/ (accessed 28 March 2012).

Bhaktivedanta Manor (2012b) New Gokul. Available at: http://bhaktivedantamanor.co.uk/newgokul/ (accessed 28 March 2012).

Bunce, M. (2003) Reproducing rural idylls. In P. Cloke (ed.), *Country Visions*, Harlow, UK: Pearson Education: 14–30.

Campbell-Gibbons, H. (2010) US dairy trip – 'Dairy farming super-sized'. NFUonline.com. Available at: www.nfuonline.com/News/US-dairy-trip--%E2%80%98dairy-farming-super-sized%E2%80%99/ (accessed 23 October 2011).

Chartered Institute of Marketing (2011) Dairy marketers must milk issues strategy. Available at: www.cim.co.uk/news/pressrelease/newsreleases/2011-02-17.aspx (accessed 20 January 2012).

CIWF (n.d.) The 'mega-dairy' campaign got back on the road for Christmas! Available at: www.ciwf.org.uk/cows_belong_in_fields/lincolnshire_bus_thank_you.aspx (accessed 24 October 2011).

Cloke, P. (ed.) (2003a) *Country Visions*. Harlow, UK: Pearson Education.

Cloke, P. (2003b) Knowing ruralities? In P. Cloke (ed.), *Country Visions*. Harlow, UK: Pearson Education: 1–13.

Cooley, W. (2012) A 21st Century Family Farm. *Progressive Dairyman*. Available at: www.progressivedairy.com/pd/features/2007/0607/0607_fairoaks.html (accessed 24 January 2012).

Davies, J. (2010) 'We're not the bad guys' – Nocton Dairies farmer speaks out. *Farmers' Guardian*, 13 August. Available at: www.farmersguardian.com/home/livestock/livestock-news/%E2%80%98we%E2%80%99re-not-the-bad-guys%E2%80%99-nocton-dairies-farmer-speaks-out/33676.article (accessed 15 June 2011).

Derbyshire, D. (2010) Battery farm for cows: 8,000 animals to be housed in milk factory. *Mail Online*, 01 March. Available at: www.dailymail.co.uk/news/article-1254467/Battery-farm-cows-8-000-animals-housed-milk-factory.html#ixzz10R9Rqsrq (accessed 29 September 2010).

Driver, A. (2010a) Nocton Dairies: Super dairy could be a cow heaven – David Barnes. *Farmers' Guardian*, 18 November. Available at: www.farmersguardian.com/home/hot-topics/super-dairies/nocton-dairies-super-dairy-could-be-a-cow-heaven-david-barnes/35635.article (accessed 15 June 2011).

Driver, A. (2010b) Why 'super dairies' must get PR right. *Farmers' Guardian*, 18 June. Available at: www.farmersguardian.com/home/livestock/livestock-news/super-dairies-must-get-pr-right/32669.article (accessed 15 June 2011).

Ellis, K. A., Billington, K., McNeil, B. and McKeegan, D. E. F. (2009) Public opinion on UK milk marketing and dairy cow welfare, *Animal Welfare*, 18(3): 267–82.

Farmer-4-a-Day (2012) Welcome to Farmer4aday. Available at: http://farmer4aday.co.uk/ (accessed 28 March 2012).

Fowler, C. and Helfield, G. (eds) (2006) *Representing the Rural: Space, Place and Identity in Films about the Land*. Detroit, MI: Wayne State University Press

Holloway, L. (2004) Farms. In S. Harrison, S. Pile, and N. Thrift (eds), *Patterned Ground: Entanglements of Nature and Culture*. London: Reaction Books: 203–5.

Horton, J. (2003) Different genres, different visions? The changing countryside in postwar British children's literature. In P. Cloke (ed.), *Country Visions*, Harlow, UK: Pearson Education: 73–92.

Jones, O. (1995) Lay discourses of the rural: Developments and implications for rural studies, *Journal of Rural Studies*, 11(1): 35–49.

Laing, S. (1992) Images of the rural in popular culture 1750–1990. In B. Short (ed.), *The English Rural Community: Image and Analysis*, Cambridge: Cambridge University Press: 133–51.

Muecke, S. (2005) Country. In T. Bennett, L. Grossberg and M. Morris (eds), *New Keywords: A Revised Vocabulary of Culture and Society*, Oxford: Blackwell: 61–3.

Müller Dairy UK Ltd (2008) From farm to yogurt in 24 hours. TV Advert [MPEG Video]. Available at: creativeclub.co.uk (accessed 28 September 2010).

Müller Dairy UK Ltd (2010) Thank you cows. TV Advert [MPEG Video]. Available at: creativeclub.co.uk (accessed 28 September 2010).

Nocton Dairies (2010) *Cow Welfare and Management Statement for the Nocton Dairies Proposal*. FWI. Available at: www.fwi.co.uk/gr/Cow%20welfare%20and%20management%20statement.pdf (accessed 22 October 2011).

NFU (2010) *Dairy Cow Welfare Strategy*, NFU. Available at: www.eblex.org.uk/documents/content/returns/chawg_dairy_cow_welfare_report__2010.pdf (accessed 26 June 2011).

Phelan, C. and Sharpley, R. (2010) Agritourism and the Farmer as Rural Entrepreneur: A UK Analysis. Unpublished paper presented at 'NeXT Tourism Entrepreneurship' Conference, Wilfrid Laurier University, Waterloo, Canada, 26–27 April. Available at: http://clok.uclan.ac.uk/1677/1/Agritourism_and_the_Farmer_as_Rural_Entrepreneur_A_UK_Analysis.pdf (accessed 28 March 2012).

Phillips, M., Fish, R. and Agg, J. (2001) Putting together ruralities: Towards a symbolic analysis of rurality in British mass media, *Journal of Rural Studies* 17(1): 1–27

Pullar, D. (2011) How big is a herd of dairy cows? *Dairy 2020*, 12 July. Available at: http://dairy2020.com/how-big-herd-dairy-cows (accessed 12 October 2011).

Seymour, S., Lowe, P., Ward, N. and Clark, J. (1997) Environmental 'Others' and 'Elites': rural pollution and changing power relations in the countryside, in P. Milbourne (ed.), *Revealing Rural 'Others': Representation, Power and Identity in the British Countryside*, London: Pinter: 57–74.

Short, B. (1992) Images and realities in the English rural community: An introduction. In B. Short (ed.), *The English Rural Community: Image and Analysis*, Cambridge: Cambridge University Press: 1–18.

The Grocer (2010) Cravendale keeps it pure with new look. *The Grocer*, 10 April. Available at: www.thegrocer.co.uk/fmcg/cravendale-keeps-it-pure-with-new-look/208596.article (accessed 28 March 2012).

Urry, J. (2002) *The Tourist Gaze*, 2nd edition. London: Sage

Willes, P. (2010) Interview with Peter Levy. *BBC Lincolnshire*, 17 March. Available at: www.youtube.com/watch?v=0ht1741iqlM&feature=related (accessed 20 September 2011).

Williams, R. (1961, 2001) *The Long Revolution*. Letchworth, UK: Broadview Press.

Williams, R. (1977) *Marxism and Literature*. Oxford: Oxford University Press.

Williams, R. (1981) *Culture*. London: Fontana.

Williams, R. (2005) *Culture and Materialism*, 2nd edition. London: Verso

Woods, M. (2011) *Rural*. London: Routledge

WSPA/Ipsos MORI (2010) WSPA/Ipsos MORI Survey June 2010. Available at: www.ipsos-mori.com/Assets/Docs/Polls/WSPA_dairy_Topline_140610.pdf (accessed 20 January 12).

12 Contested attitudes towards wildlife in Britain

Sue Bestwick

The terms city and country can evoke powerful images and have very different meanings to particular social groups within society. Raymond Williams explains some of the positive interpretations: 'On the country has gathered the idea of a natural way of life: of peace innocence and simple virtue. On the city has gathered the idea of learning, communication, light' (Williams, 1985: 1). However, Williams also argues that there are negative associations with the city and the country: 'On the city as a place of noise, worldliness and ambition; on the country as a place of backwardness, ignorance and limitation' (ibid.: 1). These ideas, though, are much generalised views that have been in existence for a long time; and after industrialisation the differing views became even more distinct because of the rapid growth of towns and cities resulting in unsanitary, overcrowded conditions during the nineteenth century. Anti-urbanism was a popular sentiment in this period, as the poet William Cowper commented: 'God made the country and man made the town, the former had made a pretty good job of it and the latter a frightful mess' (Woodell, 1985: 168). So, the relationship between the city and the country has been subject to the changing values and ideals of society from pre-industrial Britain to the twenty-first century and this in turn has impacted upon rural and urban views towards the countryside and British flora and fauna.

In this chapter I intend to examine rural and urban attitudes as well as intrinsic value judgements towards two of our most common mammals, the grey squirrel and the fox, chosen, because they both live equally successfully in the city and the country.

The fox and the squirrel are subject to widely differing opinions as to their perceived 'value': are they 'pests' that need to be controlled by trapping, shooting or hunting, or do they have a 'worth' to humans, economically, aesthetically or even as an amenity value? The historical context of both mammals is very important to the rural/urban debate even though they have had very different if not indeed chequered histories; this will give an essential dimension to the discussion, as their relationships with man over the centuries have been somewhat complicated.

The fox, symbol of wild nature or continual persecution?

Of all British mammals it is perhaps the fox that generates the most vociferous debate as to its 'worth' or indeed its place as the most destructive 'pest' or 'vermin' in need of extermination. As Lovegrove argues,

> Throughout the passage of time no animal in Britain has suffered a more schizophrenic relationship with man than the fox. On one hand it has been vilified since time immemorial and persecuted as one of the most despised of predators while on the other hand it has been protected with passion for man's pleasure.
>
> (Lovegrove, 2007: 209)

The fox has been hunted relentlessly for hundreds of years and it could easily have suffered the same demise as the lynx, bear and wolf, which were totally eliminated from the British Isles from the Roman period to the 1600s, the wolf being the last to disappear. However, the fox has survived mainly due to man's penchant for the chase; hunting the animal for sport was popular in the middle ages and has continued unabated until the hunting ban came into force in 2005. The implementation of the hunting ban has been extremely contentious and has only served to highlight the widely differing views of the city and the country, which will be examined in more detail a little later.

Fox hunting has always been considered as essentially a 'country pursuit', and in the nineteenth century it was mainly country 'gentlemen' who took part in the sport. It was the perceived reputation of the fox as creating mischief and thievery that has ensured its place as vermin in the eyes of man. These doubtful traits justified the pursuance of the animal, as Thomas comments: 'The fox was a subtle, "pilfering foe", a "conscious villain" and the highly organised sport of fox hunting could be seen as just vengeance on the midnight thief' (1983: 163). As well as being hunted the fox was (and still is) persecuted by farmers and gamekeepers with snares, shooting, poison and trapping, but even in the nineteenth century the animal did have its champions in the form of a professor of modern history, Edward Augustus Freeman. As a learned intellectual in 1869, Freeman attacked supposedly 'civilised' country gentlemen for the hunting and killing of foxes. In a now famous article Freeman supported his argument for the banning of fox hunting with the notion of the 'march of civilisation' and the changes in sensibilities towards cruelty to animals; in order to decry field sports, he also had to deconstruct cruelty as well as redefine the concept of manliness. The perceived masculine virtues of skill in riding, appreciation of good company and fresh air were denounced as 'the functions of a butcher' by Freeman (cited in Boddice, 2008: 15) who proceeded to say: 'The manly sport of fox hunting seems to me not to be manly at all, but to be at once cowardly and foolhardy' (ibid.). So, the seeds of discontent towards hunting with dogs were sown in the mid-nineteenth century by historians such as Freeman with the difference in attitudes between town and country already in evidence. The sport still continued, though, with unbridled enthusiasm, and measures were even taken to ensure a steady supply of foxes for the chase such as importing 'bagmen', whereby foxes were brought into an area to be released and cubs were protected, and foxes were imported from France to establish new coverts. Also, of paramount importance was that the fox was only killed during the chase, while the curious act of vulpicide (killing the animal by other means than hunting) was very much frowned upon by the aristocratic hunting elite. As Thomas comments, 'vulpicide became one of the greatest moral offences a country gentleman could commit' (1983: 164). These sentiments were entirely at odds, however, with those of farmers and other country dwellers whose chickens and young lambs may have been destroyed. It would seem, therefore, that class was significant in terms of attitudes towards the fox in the eighteenth and nineteenth centuries.

Although from 2005 hunting with dogs was made illegal, fox hunting now takes place in a different form but it is still essentially a country pursuit and is open to more than just the aristocracy. However, some city dwellers would argue that class is still a divisive issue with only the 'toffs' participating in this sport. The meaning of fox hunting can be constructed in a variety of ways, and class is a predominant feature according to the urban anti-hunt fraternity who argue that: 'it is still a matter of class privilege, a question of whether or not the advantaged few should be permitted to continue a tradition that offends the majority (town and city dwellers)' (Wallwark *et al.*, 2004: 27). Before the hunting ban came into force, the rural population as represented by the Countryside Alliance were beginning to mobilise protests against what they saw as a threat to their 'country way of life' in 2001, followed by 400,000 people who marched through London in 2002. Although hunting was top of the agenda, there were many other issues at stake such as rural employment, the closing of post offices in villages and the often inadequate transport system in the countryside, so the official stance was: 'A march for Liberty and Livelihood'. The divide between the city and country appeared to be growing ever wider at this time and the Countryside Alliance set out some of the more contentious issues in a charter which:

> says that country people need a countryside movement because their way of life is now under siege, opponents of country ways and values take issue with all aspects of the countryside's management of animals, including live animal transport, hunting, livestock husbandry, shooting, fishing and national hunt racing.
>
> (Howkins, 2003: 225)

The claims for the retention of fox hunting by the Alliance ranged from the control of vermin, the provider of rural employment and other leisure activities involving up to one and a half million people a year as well as its role in the construction of a national identity. This was in stark contrast to urban anti-hunt people who saw hunting as a barbarous 'sport' involving extreme cruelty to a wild animal. The 'value' of the fox in this context is that of a sublime wild mammal that is not harmful to humans, and to city dwellers the fox is actually a source for the observation of nature at close quarters, as opposed to having a 'value' in terms of sporting activities in the countryside.

As well as being an essential provider of 'sport', the fox was used by the Countryside Alliance as a symbol of national identity. The discourse of the relationship between British national identity and the timeless 'rural idyll' has a long history, and has been associated with allegedly essential British values such as social cohesion, continuity, and harmony. Especially in times of crisis, as in the two world wars, the British countryside was seen as 'what we are fighting for'. The Alliance attempted to use these values to foster the tradition of fox hunting as essential to a 'country way of life', so: 'hunting can be deemed part of the very essence of nation, because . . . 'country', in the sense of nation, is closely bound up with 'country' in the sense of green fields' (Wallwark *et al.*, 2004: 27). In this context fox hunting is seen as a national pursuit, which is the right of the 'English countryman' and: 'by implication, supporters of the "Hunting with Dogs" bill are cast not merely as anti-hunting, but also, more heinously, as anti-British' (ibid.: 28). So, it appears that it is a kind of 'moral geography' that necessitates the control of the fox as 'vermin' in order to preserve a national way of life involving not just sport and leisure activities but sound economics in terms of providing much needed jobs in the countryside.

However, urban attitudes towards the fox are in some ways even more complex. Even though anti-hunt groups still protest vociferously against hunting, the idea of the animal being a 'cuddly creature' (visions of Basil Brush perhaps or Roald Dahl's 'Fantastic Mr Fox') is being somewhat dispelled in the present day. Recent media reports have fuelled a sense of 'moral panic' about the activities of the urban fox. In June 2010 *The Guardian* juxtaposed the urban fox with its country counterpart as a

> Scruffy looking, bin raiding, lawn wrecking monster [who] is developing a different pattern of behaviour to its fluffier, warier country cousin. We have created a stereotype of the urban fox; while rural foxes are bushy tailed red beauties, the city dweller is a mangy, malnourished beast that emits blood curdling screams at night.
>
> (*The Guardian*, 2010)

This kind of representation by the media has been fuelled by the attacks in 2010 on two children in London who both needed hospital treatment, and since then there have been further attacks, one where a kitten was killed by a fox, and another where a woman, again in London, claimed that she was awoken when a fox 'sank its teeth' into her ear (*The Daily Telegraph*, 2010a). These media reports created moral panics among people living in towns and cities, particularly London, to the extent that a recent survey by 'Opinions Matter' in association with London WildCare Trust revealed that: the fox has become the second least popular (after the magpie) wild creature in the city as 'almost one in five said that foxes were a menace, vicious, and carried disease' (*The Daily Telegraph*, 2010b). It would appear that the urban fox is now a much maligned creature, and conservationists are concerned that people, 'have become afraid of nature, especially in towns and cities where foxes have been blamed for making mess and noise' (ibid.). So, the cultural or aesthetic 'value' of the fox as a sublime symbol of wildlife and nature in town and city gardens has diminished to the extent that some city dwellers now see the animals as 'pests' which should be trapped and killed.

The grey squirrel: alien, destructive tree rat or friendly image of wild nature?

Unlike the fox the grey squirrel is a fairly recent import. It was brought to Britain from the United States, the earliest recorded introduction being a pair of squirrels that were kept caged at Henbury Park in Macclesfield, Cheshire, in the nineteenth century and released in 1876 when the novelty value waned (Middleton, 1931: 17). However, there are several other unrecorded introductions and subsequent releases such as in Montgomeryshire in 1830, and Denbighshire in 1828 (ibid.: 15). But by far the most important releases of the grey squirrel that contributed to its becoming established in Britain took place at Woburn Park in Bedfordshire; ten were released in 1890 (ibid.: 18), and the increase of the animals was very rapid as the British climate and environment proved to be an ideal habitat. It was the unprecedented success of the establishment of the grey squirrel in Britain that began to cause concern even as early as 1931 when the first comprehensive study was carried out by A. D. Middleton at Oxford University. He was particularly concerned with what he saw as the noxious habits of the grey squirrel: 'The grey squirrel's attack on birds is certainly carried out chiefly in the nesting season, by the destruction of eggs and young birds' (ibid.: 51). However, damage to woodland is perhaps one of the most destructive habits of the grey squirrel; deciduous trees such as English Oak are destroyed when: 'very large patches of bark are peeled, frequently girdling the tree and resulting in the death of the top or the whole of the tree' (ibid.: 47). Another common site of damage is actually inside the roof spaces of houses where the squirrel is very adept at gnawing through quite thick pieces of timber such as roof joists as well as destroying electric cables, thus causing quite serious damage, hence it acquired the name of a 'tree rat'. However, the grey squirrel is also charged with destroying not only British flora but fauna in the form of the indigenous red: 'grey squirrels are believed to be carriers of parapoxvirus, and, although the virus has no effect on grey squirrels, it causes disease that is invariably fatal in red squirrels' (Tompkins *et al.*, 2002, cited in Gurnell *et al.*, 2004: 27). However, there can be other reasons for the scarcity of the presence of red squirrels such as habitat loss and, as Kean argues, 'frequently the demise of the red squirrel was linked, incorrectly, to the spread of the grey squirrel' (Kean, 2001: 165). Also, what must be considered at this point is that the native red squirrel was charged with much the same destructive habits in the nineteenth and early twentieth centuries. As Lovegrove argues, the red squirrel 'was regarded as a serious problem in regenerating woodlands and plantations' (Lovegrove, 2007: 96). It was recorded that up to 2,200 red squirrels were killed annually in the New Forest from 1880 onwards. Squirrel clubs were formed such as the Highland squirrel club in 1903 and were responsible for killing some 82,000 red squirrels on thirty to forty highland estates in the first thirty years (of the twentieth century), the price paid for tails varying from 3 *d.* to 4 *d.* (ibid.: 96). What a difference a century makes, as the red squirrel is now the subject of massive conservation efforts in the relatively few small areas where it can still be found in Britain today, and ironically Scotland is one of the last enclaves where the red squirrel can be found.

City and country dwellers can have markedly different perceptions of both species of squirrel, especially the grey. Even before the last war, the grey squirrel was viewed quite differently in the town and the country. In magazines such as *The Field* and *Country Life*, a very caustic attitude was taken towards the animal, with *The Field* suggesting: 'We are confronted today, in short, with the opening stages of a plague; in a short time the whole face of England will have been invaded by a foreign rodent' (quoted in Kean, 2001: 168). These attitudes intensified in later decades, and the Ministry of Agriculture and the Forestry Commission were instrumental in fuelling a campaign of extermination of the animals by offering financial incentives to farmers and others to kill greys. Every method was used, even explosives, against 'a non native animal and a half-breed at that' (ibid.: 169). It was the apparently sentimental attitude of city dwellers that was at odds with country perceptions, as Kean argues:

> It was the very presence of grey squirrels in towns, that led, some argued, to their endorsement by those possessing that apparent city characteristic of sentiment. The grey squirrel was both alien, destroying the indigenous culture, and liked – [but only] by people who lived in towns and the suburbs.
>
> (Ibid.: 169)

Unlike the fox the grey squirrel has no real 'value' in terms of sport, but it could be argued that the animal has economic value, especially if killed for its meat; there are now a growing number of organic meat companies specialising in squirrel meat, with even first-class restaurants offering squirrel dishes. This is of course at odds with the very people in cities who abhor the culling of the animal that they suppose is cute and furry, as these top-class restaurants are invariably situated within an urban setting.

Similarly to the fox, the red squirrel has been associated with the idea of nation and more specifically Englishness rather than Britishness, and has been used to represent the myth of the 'rural idyll'. Beatrix Potter's tale of Squirrel

Nutkin epitomises the English idyll of Cumbria and the Lake District where she lived until her death in 1943. In the early 1960s another national icon was born when Tufty the red squirrel was invented by the Royal Society for the Prevention of Accidents. The Tufty Club was a road safety initiative for the under fives; by 1972, however, its membership had reached two million, with older children included.

It would appear that city and countryside attitudes towards both the red and the grey squirrel are extremely complex: the red is now an endangered species and almost revered as a national symbol, whereas the grey is recognised by some as the 'alien tree rat' with only destructive intentions. It was the apparently sentimental perception of the grey squirrel in towns and cities that angered many country dwellers and further highlighted: 'the division between town and suburb and the country' (ibid.: 167). A correspondent for *The Field* reported 'seeing a group of six grey squirrels being admired by a crowd of people in London's Russell Square [and] when I ventured to suggest that I should kill them with my stick the whole crowd seemed horrified' (ibid.: 167).

What is the future for the fox and the grey squirrel?

It could be argued that human perceptions of both the fox and the grey squirrel are very contentious, as they are the inevitable consequence of the differences between urban and rural society. These differences began in the late eighteenth century when the Romantics idealised the English countryside and this was mainly due to anxiety about rapid industrialisation that reached its zenith in the nineteenth century. Criticism of the 'dark satanic mills' and the need to return to a supposedly pre-industrial 'rural idyll' was promoted by poets such as Shelley, Keats, Clare, Blake and, most of all, the lake poet Wordsworth. Historically both animals have been subject to changing attitudes that have depended upon the social and cultural mores of society at a given point in time. Even the red squirrel suffered the same fate as the grey squirrel does today, as tens of thousands were shot for alleged destruction of forests. The fox and the red squirrel have contributed to the national identity debate, and the country 'sport' of hunting is seen by country dwellers as a continuation of 'traditional values' that they believe belong to a timeless English past. This is of course in stark contrast to some urban perceptions of a class divisive rural pursuit that exists only for rich people who are intent upon promoting extreme cruelty to a wild animal.

The question of the future for these two animals, which are an integral part of the urban and rural British landscape, is probably best answered by referring to the concepts of 'use' and 'delight', which were first coined by the environmental historian, Christopher Smout. It is the perceived 'value' of the fox and the grey squirrel that raises more complex issues. Smout used the seal culls in Scotland and Europe during the 1970s to explain how the public viewed them to be too delightful for use and destruction. However, countries such as Norway continued with seal culls on the grounds of so-called 'traditional custom', but 'their skins eventually became unsalable' (Smout, 1983: 35), mainly due to high-profile media publicity. According to Smout:

> seals have developed an iconic appeal as a source of delight [which] is very real and highly politicised but, as is often the case, those who show 'delight' are not those who are affected by policies to control or prevent 'use'.
>
> (Ibid.: 34)

This contradiction between 'use' and 'delight' can be seen to apply to the fox and the grey squirrel in Britain. Foxes have a 'use' to country dwellers as a means of following an apparently 'traditional sport' as opposed to some urban perceptions of foxes as delightful images of wild nature. The same could be said of the grey squirrel, 'use' being the culling for meat (sold at Budgens supermarket in London) as well as being a 'delightful' image of nature for city people to enjoy.

Smout's observations sum up the highly sensitive and problematic issues concerning the perceived 'value' of all wildlife, particularly by the opposing sides of the city and the countryside, as he states: 'Nature is contested ground because the relationships and the confrontations between "use" and "delight" are real because one side's totem is the other side's pest and not all the arguments are on one side' (ibid.: 36).

However, in the future, maybe it will not just be the fox and the grey squirrel engendering these complex differences in attitudes between the countryside and the city, because other wildlife such as the muntjac deer, the mink and the badger also provoke fierce debate from both sides. Two of these animals (the muntjac and the mink) are imported, and are accused of destroying flora and fauna, but the indigenous badger is assumed guilty of an even more serious crime, that of carrying the deadly and highly contagious TB virus and transmitting it to cattle.

Attitudes towards badgers are of course very much in the news because of the proposed cull, which is due to take place in the autumn of 2012. The debate as to whether the animals carry the deadly TB virus has been ongoing for some time. Defra are committed to the implementation of the cull as they argue that: 'The disease forced the slaughter of 25,000 cattle in 2010 alone and will cost taxpayers around £1 billion over the next ten years if not effectively dealt with' (Defra, 2012). Statements such as this are very contentious. Even though they are apparently 'science based' (according to Defra), there are scientists who disagree with these views:

> Defra said costs could spiral to £1 billion over the next ten years if no action is taken, but more than 30 prominent scientists have signed a letter, published in the Observer, claiming the planned killings will actually increase bovine tuberculosis among British cattle (and these include) eminent scholars such as Professor Sir Patrick Bateson, president of the Zoological society of London.
>
> (*The Daily Mail*, 2012)

So, it would appear that there are serious doubts about the claim that the badger spreads the TB virus to cattle. However, there are obvious problems for beef and dairy farmers, as a high incidence of the disease can affect their livelihoods. As *The Daily Telegraph* reported (2012), one farmer was forced to watch dozens of his calves being shot because of bovine tuberculosis, and he lost more than a tenth of his herd. Non governmental organisations such as the RSPCA, RSPB and Rural England are not convinced of the effectiveness of a controlled cull of badgers, but interestingly this highly charged debate is not confined to rural against urban, it is also centred upon farmers *for* and *against* the cull, which has created an unusual fundamental disagreement between farmers in different parts of the country. These opposing views within the rural community are exemplified by a farmer in Gloucestershire whose farm is just outside the area of the proposed 'pilot badger cull'. David Purser is not persuaded by government intervention in sanctioning a cull; he argues that he and other farmers: 'were very concerned that a cull would actually increase the disease through the "perturbation" effect where infected badgers fleeing the culling spread the disease to surrounding areas' (*Farmers Weekly*, 2012).

This proposed cull of an instantly recognisable indigenous mammal has succeeded in dividing not only urban and rural but extraordinarily, has also divided farmers within rural communities. Man's relationship with wildlife has been complex and subject to change for centuries but whether we are 'capable of finding acceptable balances to satisfy human interests' (Lovegrove, 2007: 301) as well as ensure the sustainability of all of our native wildlife only time will tell.

References

Boddice, R. (2008) Manliness and 'The morality of field sports': E. A. Freeman and Anthony Trollope 1869–71, *The Historian* 70(1): 1–28.

Defra (2012) Pilot areas confirmed. Press release, 19 January 2012. Available at: www.defra.gov.uk/news/2012/01/19/pilot-areas-confirmed/ (accessed 16 October 2012).

Farmers Weekly (2012) Gloucestershire farmer speaks out against badger cull, written by Phillip Case, 12 October. Available at: www.fwi.co.uk/articles/12/10/2012/135728/gloucestershire-farmer-speaks-out-against-badger-cull.htm (accessed 16 October 2012).

Freeman, E. A. (1869) 'The morality of field sports', *Fortnightly Review* (new series) 6: 353–85.

Gurnell, J., Luc, A., Wauters, P., Peter, W., Lurz, W. and Guido, T. (2004) Alien species and interspecific competition: Effects of introduced eastern grey squirrels on red squirrel population dynamics, *Journal of Animal Ecology* 73: 26–35.

Howkins, A. (2003) *The Death of Rural England, A Social History of the Countryside since 1900*. London: Routledge.

Kean, H. (2001) Imagining rabbits and squirrels in the English countryside, *Society and Animals* 9(2): 163–75.

Lovegrove, R. (2007) *Silent Fields, The Long Decline of a Nation's Wildlife.* Oxford: Oxford University Press.

Middleton, A. D. (1931) *The Grey Squirrel: The Introduction and the Spread of the American Grey Squirrel in the British Isles.* London: Sidgwick & Jackson.

Smout, T. C. (1983) *Nature Contested, Environmental History in Scotland and Northern England since 1600.* Edinburgh: Edinburgh University Press.

The Daily Mail (2012) Top scientists blast planned badger cull as 'mindless' and call for ministers to call off the killings, written by Sam Webb, 14 October. Available at: www.dailymail.co.uk/news/article-2217545/Top-scientists-blast-planned-badger-cull-mindless-ministers-killings.html#ixzz2QKc2iswS (accessed 15 October 2012).

The Daily Telegraph (2010a) Fox bites woman's ear as she sleeps, written by Peter Hutchinson, 10 September.

The Daily Telegraph (2010b) Fox attack leaves 1 in 5 afraid of wildlife, written by Louise Gray, 2 September.

The Daily Telegraph (2012) The badger cull is not just a shot in the dark, written by Cole Moreton, 13 October.

The Guardian (2010) Invasion of the urban foxes, written by Patrick Barkham, 7 June.

Thomas, K. (1983) *Man and the Natural World, Changing Attitudes in England 1500–1800.* London: Penguin Books.

Tompkins, D., Sainsbury A. W., Netteleton, P., Buxton, D. & Gurnell, J. (2002) Parapoxvirus causes a deleterious disease of red squirrels associated with UK population declines. Proceedings of the *Royal Society B* 269: 529–33.

Wallwark, J. and Dixon, J. A. (2004) Foxes green fields and Britishness: On the rhetorical construction of place and national identity, *British Journal of Social Psychology* 43: 21–39.

Williams, R. (1985) *The Country and the City.* London: The Hogarth Press.

Woodell, S. R. J. (1985) *The English Landscape, Past, Present and Future* (Wolfsen College Lectures 1983). Oxford: Oxford University Press.

13 Changing social relations in the English countryside

The case of housing

Peter Somerville

Introduction

This chapter looks at the changing character of social relations in the countryside, with a view to understanding the prospects for rural housing development today. Starting with a brief review of the history of these changes, the chapter goes on to consider the issue of rural gentrification and then provides an analysis of the politics of rural housing development. Policies and proposals for rural housing are evaluated and conclusions drawn. Throughout the chapter, the focus is primarily on land because the availability of land is crucial for housing development.

Historical background to rural housing in England today

Howard Newby described the two main social classes in the countryside as follows:

> a comparatively affluent, immigrant, ex-urban middle class and the remnants of the former agricultural population tied to the locality by their (low paid) employment, by old age and by lack of resources to undertake a move. The former group lives in the countryside mostly by choice (and this includes the majority of farmers and landowners) and has the resources to overcome the problems of distance and access to essential services. The latter group, by contrast, has become increasingly trapped by lack of access to alternative employment, housing and the full range of amenities which the remainder of the population takes for granted.
>
> (Newby, 1980: 273–4)

This serves to highlight that the issue is not a simple one of 'locals' versus 'newcomers'. Rather, it is a case of a coming together of 'old' landed and 'productivist' interests centred mainly on agriculture with 'new', so-called 'post-productivist' interests based on a middle-class search for the rural idyll (Murdoch, 1995) – or perhaps a bourgeois colonisation of rural heterotopia (Halfacree, 2009), or maybe an expansion of the (urban) 'space of flows' into the (rural) 'space of places' (Castells, 1996, 1997, 1998; Reed, 2008), or a more complex and dynamic concatenation of material, social and cultural forces (Parry, this volume). Meanwhile, the original 'locals' have become a shadow of their former selves due largely to the mechanisation of agricultural labour and the decline of domestic service.[1]

Right up to the eighteenth century, Britain and Ireland were overwhelmingly rural and such towns as they had, with the notable exception of London and a number of ports that were reliant on international trade, were what is now called 'market towns', being situated at the centre of local and largely agricultural market operations. In the nineteenth century, some of this rural land became urban as a result of industrialisation. The remainder, however, continued to be dominated by large family estates, which were the power base of a landed gentry (the old ruling class, still represented in the House of Lords), many of whom could trace their ancestry back to Norman times. Then, in the first half of the twentieth century, many of these large rural estates (particularly in Eire) were broken up and sold to sitting tenants, resulting in what Newby (1987: 153) called 'a new breed of owner–occupier commercial farmers'. In the second half of the twentieth century and up to the present day, this process has continued but, in addition, large estates have been recreated through agglomeration into corporate landholdings. Cahill (2010), for example, notes that, over this long historical period, the key change has been from family estates to corporate estates, with the largest single ones being the Forestry Commission, the National Trust, and the Defence Estates. Even so, the monarch (through the Crown Estate) still has one of the largest landholdings in Britain, and more than a third of the total land (urban and rural) continues to be owned by aristocrats (most notably, the Duke of Buccleugh and Queensberry, the Duke of Atholl, the Duke of Cornwall and the Duke of Westminster).

The importance of this history for understanding rural problems today has been highlighted by Spencer (1997). He distinguished between two different types of rural area: 'closed parishes', which have 'a long history of domination by a principal estate proprietor or a small number of landed agriculturalists' (Spencer, 1997: 78 – I take him to mean something like 'gentlemen farmers', the gentry typically being owners of large tracts of agricultural land) and 'open parishes', where there is a much greater diversity of ownership within the area. This distinction seems to have arisen in the first half of the twentieth century. In closed parishes, the big landowners restricted new housing development, while in open parishes such development was more likely to occur, presumably because of the lack of strong organised opposition to it. The planning system instituted by the Town and Country Planning Act 1947 then effectively set this distinction in stone by allowing local authorities dominated by landed interests (known colloquially as 'squirearchies') to designate small settlements in closed parishes as non-growth areas, thus restricting new development to the open parishes, now designated as 'key settlements'.[2]

If this explanation is correct, it means that key characteristics of the British countryside today derive from the opening up of landownership that occurred largely in the years from 1918 to 1948 (though it continues up to the present day). Many of the former closed parishes have seen a change from an aristocratic landlord to a public landlord but this does not seem to have led to any reduction in the emphasis against (non-agricultural) development, and many other closed parishes continue to be dominated by traditional landed gentry. On the other hand, many (and unfortunately there seems to be no way of knowing how many[3]) open parishes have become dominated by agri-businesses, who are not necessarily any more interested in non-agricultural development (except for their families and friends) than landowners in closed parishes. Consequently, with the exception of those open parishes designated as key settlements, much of the countryside is effectively closed to new development that is not required for agricultural purposes.

It seems to be generally accepted that the social composition of the countryside has changed radically over the last hundred years or so (see, for example, Williams, 1965). Many of the old family estates remain, but they do not dominate the national picture as they once did. Agriculture has become far more intensive and more capitalised, still taking up huge tracts of land but employing only a fraction of the labour force that it used to. New employment in the countryside has nowhere near made up for the loss of agricultural jobs (for the most recent confirmation of this, see Gallent and Robinson, 2011: 304 – 'the lack of quality jobs in the villages was a recurring theme'). At the same time, most rural areas have grown in population, mainly due to an influx of commuters and retirees. This has increased demand for housing in these areas while at the same time new housing development has been restricted because of the bias towards agricultural interests. The result has been a long-term failure to provide sufficient affordable housing for those who need it outside of certain key settlements.

Satsangi *et al.* (2010: 185) are clear that the problem has always been, and continues to be, the system of landownership in the country(side): [4]

> Land allocated for housing in rural areas has been concentrated in larger settlements, often within or adjacent to designated key settlements in the past, and market towns today (Cloke, 1979; Parsons, 1980; Cameron and Shucksmith, 2007), focusing the process of middle class gentrification in locations – often village locations – where development has been generally discouraged or where speculators bid for the high end of the market.

Consequently, and ironically in view of the ideology of rural conservation, it is the smaller rural settlements (understood in this chapter to mean those with a population of less than 3,000) that have experienced the greatest social change. At the same time, counter to this ideology, the growth of agri-business has seen the greatest destruction of traditional rural environments, habitats and ways of life (Harvey, 1998). The issue of gentrification is discussed separately in the next section.

Rural re-gentrification

The concept of gentry embodies a unity of (rural) production and consumption. In the English tradition, a 'gentleman' was a man of leisure, earning income not from his labour but from his ownership of land (his 'lady' also lived on unearned income but did not originally own property in her own right unless she inherited it from her husband when he died) (Cannon, 1997; Coss, 2003). He did not work, exactly, but he consumed the countryside, typically conspicuously, through so-called 'field' sports (hunting, shooting, fishing, etc.) and grandiose projects of building, excavation, landscaping and other rural 'improvement' such as deer parks. Arguably, this continues to be true of an elite of landowners today, who are overwhelmingly male[5], often do not work (at least not in the countryside) and pursue the same 'gentlemen's' sports (see, for example, Heley, 2010, on the 'new squirearchy'). Whether they are exploiting the countryside through agri-business, or 'protecting' it from non-agricultural development, or consuming huge swathes of it with their leisure activities, the effect seems to be the same, namely that the countryside works for the benefit of themselves and to keep the landless in their place or to exclude them altogether. In this long-term historical endeavour, the traditional 'upper class' aristocrats have now been joined by large numbers of 'middle class' bourgeois *parvenus*.

Given the above concept of gentry, gentrification can be defined as a process of changing the social composition and material, social and cultural practices of an area so as to ensure the (continuing or renewed) dominance of the gentry. This definition includes all four primary shifts identified by Darling (2005): changes in the rural class structure, post-productivist rural capital accumulation, and changes in rural agents, as well as changes in rural housing composition. In support of this argument, it seems to be generally agreed that the spatial pattern of gentrification, at least in part, reflects historic structures of landownership (see, for example, Phillips, 2005), with a long-term process of replenishment of the gentry from an upwardly mobile section of the middle class (Mingay, 1976: 5; see also Thompson, 2001). Rural gentrification in particular arose as a consequence of urbanisation, which lowered the value of rural property (land and buildings) relative to urban property, making it more affordable for new purchasers to develop or improve (Little, 1987; Phillips, 1993). The wealthiest of these purchasers, typically owner–occupiers but also second home owners, have become 'new gentry', taking over from but also adding to the existing gentry. The others, however, consist primarily of two groups: commuters, living mainly nearer to urban areas, and working in a range of occupations, which can broadly be described as 'service class', serving either the gentry or the state; and retirees, tending to reside in more remote areas and coastal resorts (see, for example, Boyle and Halfacree, 1998).[6] Both of these groups see the countryside as largely a place of consumption, and the effect of their activity, whether intended or not, is to support and reinforce the position of the gentry – hence the term 're-gentrification'.[7]

Rural gentrification has its supporters, who point to the fact that it has achieved the valorisation of rural areas generally, both key settlements and small villages and hamlets – the former, for example, by improved local services, and the latter by bringing disused agricultural properties back into use (for example, the classic 'barn conversion' – see discussion in Phillips, 2002: 286–7). On the other hand, however, Spencer (1997) suggests that gentrification has been greatest in non-growth areas or closed parishes and least in key settlements or open parishes (for example, in South Oxfordshire). If correct, this is an important finding because it shows, first, that the major expansion of key settlements since 1947 has not been dominated by any particular social class, and second, that it is the social composition of non-growth areas that has changed most radically, so that they are now dominated by middle-class commuters, retirees and second-home owners. Moreover, the combination of restricted housing supply and the increased housing demand from incomers results in the exclusion of lower-income households from access to housing in these areas, either because the latter cannot afford the housing that comes available or because they were themselves the occupiers of this housing and have been 'persuaded (or forced) to move away' (Spencer, 1997: 89).

Partly confirming Spencer's findings, Phillips (2005: 484) found that in North Norfolk the middle classes were most concentrated in the smallest parishes. He studied two closed parishes in particular (Shotesham and Thornage), and found an interesting difference. Shotesham was dominated by a single (aristocratic) landowner until 1919, after which the structure of property ownership became more open and consequently ready for gentrification from the 1970s onwards, with many of the owner–occupier farmers and smallholders selling off parts of their holdings for residential infill development, and from the 1980s selling off farm buildings for conversion to residential use – all to incoming households or 'to professional agents of gentrification such as local builders and property companies' (Phillips, 2005: 489). Thornage, in contrast, had a more open property structure but still had one large (aristocratic) landowner, whose estate was not broken up until the 1970s, when the housing was sold largely to middle class incomers and non-residential property was vacated and converted into residential use. New-build development was more restricted in Thornage, however, because of the expansion in agricultural landholdings outside the village (it seems that the traditional lord of the manor had 'rationalised' his assets into an agri-business) (Phillips, 2005: 490). Phillips (2005: 491) concluded that the two villages had been *made ready for gentrification* in different ways, at different periods and through different sets of agencies, resulting in Shotesham appealing to those desiring a 'community idyll' and Thornage having the character of a 'peaceful pastoral'. Other researchers have made similar observations in a variety of rural contexts. Stockdale (2010: 38), for example, found that, in rural Scotland, more affluent in-migrants were more likely to reside in isolated rural dwellings and the smallest settlements, while less affluent ones moved to larger settlements.

The relationship between gentrification and agricultural intensification is an interesting one. The planning system created in 1947 drew a sharp distinction between agricultural and non-agricultural land, giving free rein to farmers to use the former as they saw fit provided that the use was for agriculture only. In practice, this meant that most of the land in rural areas could not be developed for non-agricultural purposes unless the farmer/developer could get permission for change of use, which tended to be given only when agricultural use ceased or became economically unviable. Rural gentrification, therefore, occurred either in relation to the land that was not zoned as agricultural or as a result of agricultural land being made ready for gentrification because it was no longer 'needed' for agriculture. The result has been a division between two kinds of exclusive landed estate, according to which residential 'islands of gentrification' (Satsangi *et al.*, 2010: 4) are surrounded by land that is reserved for agricultural use.

Effectively, then, there are potentially two (overlapping) gentries in the English countryside, loosely associated with 'productivist' and 'post-productivist' constructions of the rural (and, *pace* Murdoch *et al.*, 2003, with 'modernist' and 'pastoralist' narratives). The first is largely *in absentia*, consisting of the owners and shareholders of agri-businesses, the traditional so-called nobility, and large public and voluntary sector landowners. The second comprises the more affluent middle class newcomers, who are concerned mainly with protecting and preserving their particular versions of the rural idyll. It could be argued that the gentry have become more 'differentiated' (Murdoch *et al.*, 2003), between agricultural and non-agricultural landowners (see Sutherland, 2012, on specifically agricultural gentrification in England and Scotland, both through incomers and of existing farming households). According to Murdoch *et al.* (2003), the relationship between these two also varies on a *regional* basis. In much of south-east England, occupied mainly by middle-class commuters, pastoralism predominates, producing what Murdoch *et al.* call the 'preserved' countryside, while in areas such as Northumberland, where large private estates and big farms predominate and the middle-class population is small, there is more evidence of modernist narratives (the 'paternalistic' countryside). In other areas such as Devon, agricultural interests are powerful, but are strongly contested by incoming middle class workers and retirees (the 'contested' countryside). This research suggests that there may be two gentries or more, with very different and indeed incompatible interests and views.[8]

Arguably, however, production and consumption are two sides of the same coin. A productivist approach to agricultural land is perfectly compatible with a consumptionist approach to non-agricultural land. The post-war planning system of land zoning therefore makes possible the protection of one kind of land for productivist agriculture while making ready another kind of land for gentrified consumption. Paradoxically, the elimination of the traditional countryside by the expansion of agri-business goes hand in hand with its re-creation, from their imagination, by incoming gentrifiers. Furthermore, the large agricultural landowners and the rich owners of non-agricultural land do not constitute clearly identifiable separate groups and have similar interests in ensuring that the countryside is both productive and, so far as possible, idyllic (though with these functions being, to some extent, spatially separated).[9]

A key issue in relation to gentrification is whether it is associated with the displacement of residents from the gentrified areas (as claimed by Spencer, 1997, quoted above). For theorists of urban gentrification such as Neil Smith (1996), this is central to their argument that gentrification represents a form of revanchism or 'taking revenge'. In the context of residential change, revanchism is a process by which the rich and their allies and supporters repossess spaces inhabited by the poor. As a form of revanchism, gentrification specifically involves the displacement of the poor from the areas where they have traditionally lived and their replacement by middle-class incomers and consumers. This issue of displacement of the poor has been a long-standing concern also in relation to rural areas (Shucksmith, 1981, 1991). Gallent and Robinson (2011: 299) have recently argued, however, that the picture is more complex than this, with something of a disjuncture between economic and social perspectives:

> Economically, displacement expresses a state of disequilibrium between property supply and demand (Sumka, 1979; Lee and Hodge, 1984), narrowing market opportunity . . . And yet, the process of social change may begin as an expression of taste and only later becomes a question of economics. Pioneering gentrifiers (Dangschat, 1991) may move into run-down urban areas or into villages that, because of local economic restructuring, are in decline. In urban and in rural areas, lifestyle aspirations are the trigger, and social change is a product of contrasting priorities (Atkinson, 2000; Newman and Wyly, 2006), with existing households moving elsewhere in search of jobs (for economic reasons, young people are often 'committed' to leaving rural areas rather than 'committed' to staying: Ford *et al.*, 1997 [see also Rugg and Jones, 1999; Jamieson and Groves, 2008]) and newcomers taking advantage of surplus housing supply to meet their lifestyle aspirations rather than having a primary investment motive.

This is an interesting argument. It seems to be saying that, at least initially, rural gentrification does not displace existing households, because the latter are moving away primarily for employment reasons ('employment is as big a driver of out-migration among the young as the cost of housing – and in fact bigger in many instances' – Gallent and Robinson, 2011: 304), and the new residents are then simply moving into housing that might otherwise lie empty and are contributing to the regeneration of the area.[10]

This analysis seems to miss the link between direct displacement through housing changes and indirect displacement arising from other changes, particularly in employment. As Hamnett (2003: 2424) has pointed out in connection with London, gentrification involves 'the gradual replacement of one class by another, rather than large-scale direct displacement', and this comprises 'major changes in industrial, occupational, earnings and income structures' as well as related changes in the housing market. The reduction of employment opportunity in gentrified rural areas (as also in some urban areas) is in fact mostly, if not entirely, due to the actions of the gentry themselves: first, of agri-businesses in maximising the yield from their landed assets, and second, of both agri-businesses and the 'new gentry' in attempting, with the able assistance of the planning system, to exclude unwanted new development from the areas that they control, resulting in serious housing shortages in many rural areas and corresponding rises in rents and house prices. It is the annihilation of jobs that comes first, displacing the population that had or could have had those jobs. An influx of better-off households into non-growth areas then occurs, which reinforces and exacerbates this residential displacement in a number of ways. First, and most obviously, it places additional pressure on house prices, making housing less affordable for local people. Second, at least in more remote areas, the incomers seem to provide little new employment that matches the skills of local people, so that: 'In England, areas of "sparse" rural settlement, together with more peripheral districts, have consistently underperformed in terms of levels of "gross value added", job creation, productivity and new business formation (CRC, 2008)' (Satsangi *et al.*, 2011: 50). Third, rather than investing in local businesses and services, incomers tend to be more concerned with developing and adding value to their own property. Fourth, in the case of commuters, much of their consumption does not take place in the community in which they live, and mainly for this reason gentrification has not prevented (and has even contributed to) the continuing loss of traditional rural amenities and services (see, for example, Rural Coalition, 2010). Finally, many incomers attempt to secure their privileged position by supporting restrictions on both new business and new housing. All of this sounds remarkably similar to Smith's urban narrative of employment extinction and revanchism.[11]

The politics of rural housing development – sustainability contested, homelessness, and so on

The history of policy affecting rural housing in England, at least since World War II, has been mainly one of support for agricultural 'improvement' and restrictions on residential development.[12] One of the key reasons offered in more recent years for further restricting such development is that it is said to be both economically and ecologically unsustainable (see, for example, Breheny *et al.*, 1993; Williams, 2000). Economically, it is argued that there are economies of scale in the provision of a range of services (both private and public), which means that it makes sense to concentrate development in 'key settlements' (large enough to support, for example, a primary school, a range of shops and public amenities – and, not least, a sufficient variety of jobs) (Cameron and Shucksmith, 2007). Ecologically, development in non-growth areas is seen as unsustainable, not so much because of the carbon emissions associated with such development as because of the increased travelling that results from it – to work and to shop and to other facilities, often several miles away (Hoggart and Henderson, 2005: 190).

There are a number of problems with these arguments, however, especially that they serve to write off thousands of small villages and hamlets as already unsustainable. Rather than allow these villages to grow at their own pace and therefore become more sustainable, they are condemned either to die a slow death or to be exclusive spaces for the affluent. Those living in these non-growth areas are forced to rely even more than they do already on private cars as the only available means of transport (the implications of this for older people are discussed by Key, this volume; see also Bevan *et al.*, 2006). The corresponding increase in the consumption of fossil fuels indicates that restricting growth in smaller rural settlements does not, after all, necessarily make them more environmentally friendly.

Whatever the balance of arguments in relation to economic and ecological sustainability, it seems clear that restrictions on rural development are not *socially* sustainable, if this term is taken to mean socially mixed, in social class, income, ethnicity and age. The question is starkly posed by Satsangi *et al.* (2010: 28): 'in many parts of Britain, rural communities are whiter, more middle class, more affluent and contain more retired people than at any time in the past. Is this the sustainable future that Britain wants or its countrysides need?' The question is of course rhetorical. Gallent and Robinson (2011: 305), however, argue that the key requirement is not for social mix as such but for 'a balance between younger residents, families and older people', in order to ensure the reproduction of the life cycle. Most people would probably agree that a community whose young people are moving away and not coming back is at risk of extinction in the longer term, and that local housing provision has a role to play in ensuring that this does not happen (Gallent and Robinson, 2011: 304–5). Yet in Britain rural young people are indeed increasingly leaving the village in which they grew up, for example, in order to go to university, and not returning to live there permanently (Champion, 2007). This is no doubt due primarily to lack of local employment and housing opportunities, particularly in the private rented sector (Satsangi *et al.*, 2010: 177). So once again, the defence of a policy of no-growth areas on grounds of sustainability fails to convince. In the actions of government, social sustainability, at least in rural areas, has been subordinated to the drive for economies of scale and, to a lesser extent, to environmental needs (Hoggart and Henderson, 2005: 194). What counts as a social 'balance' is, in any case, contested, particularly in terms of what constitutes a balance between long-standing indigenous populations and incoming households (Gallent and Robinson, 2011: 305), with an over-emphasis on the former running the risk of leading to stagnancy and stasis, while too much of the latter can result in fragmentation and instability.[13] It could also be argued that even if overwhelmingly middle-class communities are socially sustainable (in Gallent and Robinson's, 2011, sense) they are not socially desirable, but this is an argument for another paper.[14]

Official statistics indicate that homelessness in England is less prevalent in rural areas than in urban areas (see, for example, CRC, 2008). This chapter has argued, however, that affordable housing is greatly lacking in many rural areas,[15] and the link between this lack and homelessness seems to be well established (Satsangi *et al.*, 2010: 199). The lower level of rural homelessness, therefore, contradicts what one would reasonably expect to see. Cloke *et al.* (2000, 2002) suggest that this is because rural homelessness is culturally and politically denied as being incompatible with the rural idyll and that many homeless people leave the countryside and make their way to urban areas (see also Robinson, 2004; Milbourne, 2006). Studies have also indicated that homelessness in rural areas is much more likely to be 'hidden' (Jones, 1999), with people sleeping rough in isolated buildings and areas (Evans, 1999) and in far greater numbers than those recorded in official counts (Robinson and Reeve, 2002). It also seems significant that in a rural local authority (Craven District Council) two-thirds of homeless people stayed with family or friends after becoming homeless, compared with only 4 per cent in Sheffield (Robinson and Coward, 2003), suggesting that there were fewer alternatives available to the rural homeless. Services for homeless people also continue to be lacking in many rural areas (Milbourne and Cloke, 2006), with significant local opposition to the provision of services to young homeless people (Oldman, 2002), who are particularly likely to feel isolated and socially rejected (Evans, 1999). The exclusion of homeless people from the countryside also, of course, serves the interests of home owners in preserving the value of their property (Shucksmith, 1990). Overall, therefore, this looks like it could be another example of revanchism.

The politics and policy of rural housing is, as this chapter has suggested, largely focused on the 'protection' of the countryside, understood in terms of restrictions on non-agricultural development, in order to make it safe for producer-driven agriculture and consumer-driven gentrification. As thoroughly documented in Satsangi *et al.* (2010), a plethora of commissions, reviews, initiatives and laws have failed to bring about any significant change to this policy emphasis and have mostly reinforced it. Absurdly, in some rural areas, policies have been introduced that aim to meet local need for affordable housing but actually have the opposite effect because they place further restrictions on any development that does take place, typically by requiring that a proportion of the new housing must be for local need. Such restrictions result in fewer houses being built, increased competition for existing housing, higher house prices and a greater problem of housing affordability (Satsangi *et al.*, 2010: 141–7).[16]

Over the years, there have also been a number of attempts by governments to levy a tax or charge on the gain in land value that results from a grant of planning permission (e.g., the Community Land Act 1976 and the Planning

Gain Supplement proposed by the last Labour government). It is not clear how any of these attempts would have increased the provision of rural affordable housing but they all failed due to a combination of pressure from landed interests and the excessively cumbersome character of the governmental proposals. The latest such attempt is the Community Infrastructure Levy (CLG, 2011a), which allows for different levels of charge in different areas, with a requirement that a 'meaningful proportion' of the revenues raised by this charge in any particular area should be allocated back to that area, to pay for a wide range of infrastructure. It is too early to say what the effects of such a charge will be but it is not at all clear how this policy could increase affordable housing provision. The general principle remains that a tax on development acts as a disincentive to develop, so this does not look like a departure from traditional rural housing policy.

The Community Infrastructure Levy has been proposed as an alternative to the locally negotiated planning gain approach, which emerged in the 1970s. Under the Town and Country Planning Act 1971, local authorities were allowed to make agreements with developers, giving them planning permission in return for their making a contribution to the community – and this contribution could be in the form of affordable housing. Since then: 'The basic approach has been to use the development control process to negotiate, with private interests, for the inclusion of affordable homes within speculative developments' (Satsangi *et al.*, 2010: 128). These so-called s106 agreements, however, appear to have been reached almost entirely in relation to key settlements and market towns. Affordable housing contributions via s106 are rare in settlements with less than 3,000 residents, and become increasingly rare as the size of the settlement decreases (John Mather, Rural Housing Enabler, Lincolnshire, personal communication, 25 November 2011). If Lincolnshire is in any way representative of rural areas in England, this means that the contribution of this policy to the provision of affordable housing in villages and hamlets has been negligible.

The other element of the locally negotiated planning gain approach is the rural exception sites policy. This involves the local authority granting planning permission for housing on land that is not normally released for such use. In this case, normally all the housing is affordable, typically housing association rented accommodation. It relies on the landowner being willing to release the land at less than the full development value. This is now the main way that affordable housing is provided in small rural settlements in England (Hoggart and Henderson, 2005: 185), and one can see how it might appeal to those who are not opposed to affordable housing as such but only to 'substantial' housing development that threatens the character of an area and/or has no accompanying infrastructure or service provision (Gallent and Robinson, 2011: 304; see also, for example, Phillips, 2002: 298–303, on objections to proposals for 'out of character' housing developments in rural Berkshire). There are problems with this policy, however. The very fact that the sites are 'exceptional' means that they are outside the 'normal' planning process, which means that local planners are not very supportive of them (Hoggart and Henderson, 2005: 190), and this results in little provision (Gallent, 2009; Taylor, 2008), often in segregated locations (Hoggart and Henderson, 2005: 191). The numbers completed are tiny (only 122 in the whole of Lincolnshire in 2010 – a not untypical year). Some local housing authorities, however, are now allowing some housing for private sale to be included in exception sites developments, with the surplus from the sale being used to cross-subsidise the affordable housing provision (for example, West Lindsey District Council Local Plan Policy Res 7). This has the potential to stimulate a growth in the number of developments coming on-stream but it seems unlikely that the total number of dwellings built will increase substantially, and there is a risk that it could encourage speculative over-provision of non-affordable housing (as may have happened in the Selby area of Yorkshire – Gallent and Robinson, 2011: 304).

Realistically, therefore, it seems that planning gain approaches are never going to result in adequate affordable housing provision, particularly in small rural settlements. When land prices are rising, landowning developers are inclined to develop for sale at market prices. When land prices are falling, they tend to sit on their landholdings until such time as prices start rising again. Neither scenario is conducive to their developing affordable housing. Consequently, a planning gain approach is unlikely ever to lead to the identification of sufficient private land to meet the need for affordable housing. Even where suitable land is identified, the difficulties in ensuring the viability of individual schemes are extreme. Where property values are low, the cost of building a house can exceed its sale price. But where property values are high, the price of land is high too. In both cases, agreement on price between landowner and housing association can be very difficult to achieve (John Mather, 25 November 2011). Such considerations strongly suggest that the failure to provide sufficient affordable housing in small settlements has, as Hoggart and Henderson (2005: 188) found in their research in Norfolk, 'less to do with local opposition to exceptions homes than to the unwillingness of key "development" agencies to promote exceptions options.'

The most obvious alternative to reaching agreements with landowners/ developers is direct public funding for social renting.[17] However: 'The history of developing social renting in rural areas can be summed up in two words: inertia and resistance' (Satsangi *et al.*, 2010: 156). Although research reveals considerable variation from one area to another, not only in the amount of provision but also in the reasons for a given amount of provision (Newby, 1979; Dickens *et al.*, 1985; Long, 2005 – all stemming from differences in social class relations and political culture), the most striking feature in most rural areas is the meagre supply of social housing, particularly in recent years (Hoggart and Henderson, 2005: 186 – an average of one new home per small settlement per decade; Bramley and Watkins, 2009). As Satsangi *et al.* (2010: 158) point out, the situation has deteriorated 'as supply has abjectly failed to keep pace with sales' under the right to buy, and resold council housing has gone to middle class incomers and second home owners (Chaney and Sherwood, 2000). An increasing number of small settlements contain no social housing at all, with the consequence that these areas have become the exclusive preserve of the 'new' gentry. This does not look like revanchism so much as a long, slow decline produced by a system of more or less benign neglect (though by no means in all rural areas – for example, Long, 2005, contrasts the supportive paternalism of Waveney with the parsimony of Fenland) – or, more hypocritically, by a concern to meet the housing needs of known 'local people on local wages', but only by rehousing them away from the villages in which they may have lived all their lives (Gallent and Robinson, 2011: 305). Whatever the local 'culture', however, the result is much the same, namely the exclusion of poorer households from many of the more rural areas.[18]

In this context, it can be seen that the current affordable housing programme run by the Homes and Communities Agency is likely to produce even less housing than ever in rural areas (under this programme, only 82 properties are due to be completed in rural Lincolnshire by 2015 – John Mather, 25 November 2011). There is potential for new community-led schemes to supplement this provision, for example, through the vehicle of a Community Land Trust (by an estimated 40 properties per year in Lincolnshire – John Mather, 25 November 2011), such trusts being set up specifically to enable communities to develop new affordable housing and to ensure that this housing will remain affordable in perpetuity. Many village residents have reported that they would be more willing to support such community-led affordable housing developments (Gallent and Robinson, 2011: 305). However, if Lincolnshire is in any way typical, the numbers of new homes anticipated as being provided under this vehicle are considerably lower than the already insufficient numbers being achieved through the rural exceptions sites policy (in Lincolnshire, 40 homes per year compared with 122 homes per year).

Parish councils have an important role to play in the provision of affordable housing. With support from Rural Community Councils, many parish councils have produced their own parish plans, some of which focus on the need for affordable housing. Parish surveys of housing need, however, have been criticised on a number of grounds – most commonly for implying that young people want to stay in the area when actually they may prefer to move away (Hoggart and Henderson, 2005: 189), but also because they tend to reinforce existing settlement patterns, with people being deemed to need to live in a particular area only if they already have connections of some kind with that area. Not surprisingly, given the extent of gentrification in many small rural settlements, far more residents in such areas are worried about the possibility of new housing than about the lack of affordable housing (e.g. in rural Breckland and South Norfolk – Hoggart and Henderson, 2005: 189), and unfortunately, this results in many parish councils being opposed to new housing development in their areas (Bevan *et al.*, 2001). Currently, however, it is argued that housing needs surveys are persuasive in identifying a growing need for affordable housing in many parishes. Respondents self-declare if they are in affordable housing need, if they want to continue to live in the parish, and if their need is immediate or anticipated. They are also asked if they know the contact details of any former residents of the parish who wish to return, and these people are then included in the survey. The financial and personal circumstances of all respondents are assessed in order to determine that they are in fact in need of affordable housing.

In spite of the evidence from parish surveys, the new gentry continue to insist that other people do not 'need' to live in the places that the gentry themselves have made exclusively their own, and can be housed satisfactorily and even more appropriately (e.g. in terms of housing costs and access to services) in larger 'key settlements' (for the latest evidence on this, see Gallent and Robinson, 2011: 302, especially in the commuter-dominated parish of Slaugham, Sussex).[19] The consequence of accepting such an argument would be a permanent residential segregation along lines of social class, with country estates for the gentlefolk and townships for the landless poor. Unfortunately, the logic of housing association provision tends only to reinforce this situation because it focuses primarily on the quality of housing provided, irrespective of location, and on the provision of a range of housing-related services. As Hoggart and Henderson (2005: 193) put it: 'associations can be expected to respond to rural housing need if they feel these are best satisfied in villages. For many this is not the case.' In general, in the assumptive world of housing association officers, as with planners, small-scale provision of social housing in small villages is seen as *unsustainable*. Fundamentally, they do not understand that such development is precisely what is required in order for such villages to be sustainable (at least in the sense advocated by Gallent and Robinson, 2011, of a balance between different types of household).

Conclusion

The future for affordable rural housing in England looks very uncertain, and the policy situation seems unlikely to change to any significant extent (see, for example, Satsangi *et al.*, 2010: 207). This chapter has attempted to identify an explanation for this recalcitrance, as lying primarily with the system of land ownership, in particular its extreme inequality, the coincidence and mutuality of productivist and consumptionist interests in the countryside, and the buttressing of that system by planning law and practice, particularly since 1947, but continuing right up to the present day. The 'traditional' landed gentry (owners of country estates and 'gentlemen' farmers) may have declined (though on the whole this decline has been exaggerated), but their class has been reproduced and rejuvenated by prosperous financiers, businessmen (and I say 'men' advisedly) and 'professionals' of various kinds (including some academics). This chapter has argued that the commonalities between these groups outweigh the differences, resulting in what Shucksmith (2000) fairly described as an *exclusive* countryside (and even more exclusive now than it was then). The power of this landed class in the countryside is so great, so entrenched and taken for granted over so many generations, that few people even recognise it, let alone question it. Its salience is not so much a product of revanchism (though signs of this can be detected, as in Heley, 2010) as of uninterrupted and unchallenged hegemony. It is perhaps in relation to housing, however, that the harmfulness of this power can be most clearly seen, because the system of land ownership effectively prevents the provision of sufficient housing to meet the need that exists in so many rural parishes.

Optimists might argue that the Localism Act 2011 contains a number of provisions to facilitate an answer to the rural housing question (Satsangi *et al.*, 2010). These provisions include a community 'right to build' and a presumption in favour of development where most of the community agree (CLG, 2011b). There are no doubt a number of parish councils, parish partnerships and other rural community groups that will want to take advantage of these measures in order to ensure the provision of affordable housing in their parishes (Gallent and Robinson, 2011: 306). On the whole, however, it seems appropriate to strike a more cautionary note, for three reasons. First, the experience of developing parish plans in the past does not necessarily prepare an organisation for the land use and spatial planning that will now be expected – that is, for evaluating 'proposals for what development should happen where' (Bishop, 2010: 620 – see also 621, 623). Second:

> the key difficulty (after building community support, which is a significant challenge in itself) is the acquisition of land: this will derive either from highly unpredictable patterns of philanthropic gifting, the transfer of land from public ownership (which is rarely an option in rural areas) or community subscription and purchase, which is still likely to rely on the goodwill of a landowner, selling land to the community at less than market value.
>
> (Satsangi *et al.*, 2010: 218)

As we have seen in this chapter, such landlord philanthropy and goodwill are only rarely forthcoming, and the Localism Act 2011 does not change the situation in this respect. Third, there are many serious – indeed overwhelming – difficulties in collaborating across parishes, not only in the provision of affordable housing but also in transport planning, the location of schools, sewage works, and infrastructure more generally (Bishop, 2010: 621). For all these reasons, there will be a need for many more rural housing enablers (Bishop, 2010: 620–1), and for greater support from all relevant local authorities (Satsangi *et al.*, 2010: 211), if the rural housing question in England is ever to be positively answered.

Taking into account all of these considerations, it seems clear that current housing and other policies do little or nothing to counteract the exclusive character of much of the English countryside in terms of residence. Powerful rural landowners such as the National Trust (which has over three million members), for example, continue to support exclusive developments for the rich (e.g. Cliveden Village, Taplow, in Buckinghamshire – restricted to owner–occupiers over 55 years old) while opposing any expansion of affordable housing provision. What is needed is a more determined and systematic attempt by national government to tackle the issue of lack of affordable housing in small rural settlements, using a variety of methods, for example: removal of the bias within housing and planning policy and practice against new housing in such settlements; increased funding from the Homes and Communities Agency for new social housing developments in these areas, based on local housing needs surveys (mandatory for district councils, with parish councils being obliged to cooperate in conducting them); and increased government support, including funding, for bodies such as Community Land Trusts. The increased funding here could be, at least in part, raised from new taxes on land values and on wealth. The idea of land value taxation, which is more economically efficient than traditional property taxation (Smith, 2001), goes back to the physiocrats of the eighteenth century and is perhaps best known from the work of Henry George (1879). Maybe the time has come for a revival of such approaches if the current dominant political mindset is to be shifted.

Acknowledgements

This chapter is based upon an article previously published in IJLBE Issue 5(2) 2013, and appears here by kind permission of the journal's editors and Emerald Group Publishing.

Notes

1 For an historical account of the changing relations between middle and working classes in one village, see Ambrose (1974). On the (further) decline, dilution and (partial) disappearance of the rural working class in England and Wales, see, for example, Hoggart (2007).

2 Restrictive spatial regimes in rural areas are, of course, not peculiar to England or the UK but also exist in Spain, Norway, Sweden, France, the Netherlands, and other countries (de Groot *et al.*, 2012: 304). Even in key settlements and designated growth areas, what Short *et al.* (1987: 37) called the anti-development 'voice of the stopper', which is 'the voice of middle class, middle aged owner–occupiers seeking to protect their physical and social environments', is typically very loud. For similar evidence of overwhelmingly anti-development opinion in rural Berkshire, see Phillips (2002: 299). This suggests that, in the view of many rural residents in designated growth areas, the restrictive spatial regime is not restrictive enough. Who these residents may be is discussed in the next section.

3 DEFRA keeps a register of landholdings but this register is not available to the public.

4 Satsangi (2007) highlights the crucial role played by landownership on the isle of Gigha in Scotland, where the purchase of the island by its residents from a single, private landowner (traditionally, the laird) fundamentally reshaped economic, social and political relationships governing housing provision.

5 Following an ancient tradition of patriarchy in rural areas – see Davidoff *et al.* (1976).

6 Drawing upon Caulfield (1994), Phillips (2002: 301) suggests that gentrification is driven, in part, by a dislike of suburbia. If this is correct and applicable to England, then the commonly used term 'counter-urbanisation' seems inadequate for making sense of the process of middle-class migration to the countryside. Halliday and Coombes (1995), for example, identified three kinds of counterurbanisation: anti-metropolitan, driven by house price differentials on a regional scale; anti-urban, involving a rejection of city living; and pro-rural, which is a selection of the rural idyll. All of these could involve gentrification but it is impossible to know because their case study of Devon looked only at motivations for moving, not the effects of moving. Stockdale (2010: 35) rightly points out that counter-urbanisers are not necessarily gentrifiers, but unfortunately her research in rural Scotland defines gentrifiers purely in terms of their income, irrespective of their intentions, actions and effects.

7 Since the gentry were traditionally rural, it is not surprising that the term 'gentrification' evokes a rural imagery (Redfern, 2003). So, given that the English countryside was already historically gentrified, the term 're-gentrification' seems more appropriate to describe the processes discussed here.

8 In his study of Panten in Germany, Duenkmann (2010) comes to a similar conclusion in relation to the perceptions of rurality within the village, namely agricultural productivist views (which he calls 'anti-conservationist') and consumptionist or 'idyllic' views (the rural idyll in Germany seems remarkably similar to that in England). Interestingly, however, he also identifies a third view, which he calls 'reform-oriented', which is conservationist but seeks to move agri-business towards a multi-functional model of agriculture.

9 Phillips (2002: 300) provides a neat illustration of this combination of productivist and consumptionist interests in a quote regarding a planning application to West Berkshire Council, in which the village of Boxford is seen as an idyll of productive agriculture and beautiful (consumable) landscape, which needs to be protected from the ravages of planners and money-grabbers. One can almost hear the sound of drawbridges being raised.

10 For a similar argument, see Hoggart (2007), who accepts at face value that 'working class' people choose to move either out of or into rural areas. More recently, longitudinal research in the Netherlands has found that, even controlling for income, rural residents intending to move within their area (local movers) are more likely to realise their location preference than those intending to move to a rural area outside their current area of residence (non-local movers). The authors conclude that 'rural residents are not systematically excluded from the countryside' (de Groot *et al.*, 2012: 311). However, both their argument and their conclusion are flawed: the argument rests on a false assumption of preference equivalence (between the preferences of local movers and those of non-local movers – in reality, non-locals may be likely to be more willing than locals to consider moving to areas other than their 'preferred' location), and the conclusion ignores the role of system factors other than housing, in particular employment. It could be, therefore, that even in the Netherlands local residents have been displaced from rural areas – not directly, by one class of people supplanting another, but systematically, through the operation of the housing and employment markets.

11 This should not be taken to imply, however, that the rural working classes are in decline. As Hoggart (2007: 314) shows, they are remarkably resilient, dynamic and 'more adaptable in achieving their housing needs than the literature implies'. Still, this adaptability has its limits – for example, those people on low incomes who move out of rural areas tend to go only short distances up the rural settlement hierarchy (Milbourne, 2007: 383). Researchers have also pointed out that low-income groups continue to move to rural areas in a number of developed countries,

including the UK (most notably recent migration from Eastern and Central European Accession States), but they mostly do not move into areas of gentrification (Milbourne, 2007: 383). Interestingly, however, Stockdale (2010: 37) suggests that some in-migrants to rural areas, including areas of rural gentrification, may have been displaced by *urban* gentrification processes.

12 I say 'mainly' because there have been some notable exceptions, but these relate entirely to designated growth areas, for example, New Towns, market towns, larger settlements, and villages outside of green belts but within commuting distance of large conurbations (for example, central Berkshire – Short *et al.*, 1987).

13 This is by no means inevitable, however – for example, the incomers may be stable households and may adapt well to their new circumstances (see, for example, Phillips, 1986, on 'mucking in', and the 'move-in and join-in' settlers described by Cloke *et al.*, 1995, 1998, and by Phillips, 2001, 2002).

14 The literature on the role of housing in developing mixed sustainable communities suffers from a lack of clarity concerning the meanings of 'sustainable', 'mixed' and 'community'. For a critique of this literature, see Cheshire (2007). Research shows that many people living in new developments are not keen on having neighbours who are much better-off or worse-off than themselves (Bretherton and Pleace, 2009). Somerville (2011: 195) concludes that: 'The concept of a mixed-income community is not based on any proper understanding of community or community development' and is 'yet another example of a neo-colonial and managerial mentality.'

15 In Breckland, for example, Hoggart and Henderson (2005: 187), found that most households with at least one manual worker and most households with at least one person aged 16–24 were dissatisfied with affordable housing provision in the area.

16 The worst case scenario was that of the Lake District Special Planning Board in 1980 (Satsangi *et al.*, 2010: 146–7). Interestingly, however, the argument applies to all cases where extra restrictions are imposed on development. The (initial!) popularity of such counter-productive policies can be explained on the basis that they are acceptable to those who are opposed to development (while also salving their consciences, if they have any, by allowing them to think that they are indeed promoting housing for local need) while at the same time the policy makers can point to concrete achievements because at least some needy local people (though possibly fewer than before) do get housed through such policies (Satsangi *et al.*, 2010: 148–9).

17 Satsangi *et al.* (2010) also discuss shared ownership, HomeBuy and low cost home ownership. I can recommend this discussion for readers who are interested in these policies. For the purposes of this chapter, however, it is probably sufficient to point out that none of these schemes is targeted at poorer households or at smaller rural settlements. The schemes therefore entirely fail to address the key rural housing problem identified in this chapter.

18 As if this were not bad enough, the Coalition government's policies, particularly relating to housing benefit, are set to make life far more difficult for lower-income rural households (for an up-to-date appraisal, see Clarke and Monk, 2012).

19 The researchers found that rural residents' attitudes towards affordable housing provision depended on three factors: their perception of the proximity of urban areas – the more mobile and affluent commuters assumed that others would share their level of mobility, so believed it was reasonable to provide affordable housing for those who needed it in a 'nearby' urban area rather than in their home village; the size of the settlement in which they lived (the larger the settlement, at least in poorer rural areas not near to urban areas, the greater the acceptance of new housing provision); and, for those living in smaller settlements, their desire to protect their rural 'oases' (Gallent and Robinson, 2011: 303).

References

Ambrose, P. (1974) *The Quiet Revolution: Social Change in a Sussex Village 1871–1971*. London: Chatto & Windus.

Atkinson, R. (2000) 'Measuring gentrification and displacement in greater London', *Urban Studies* 37(1): 149–65.

Bevan, M., Cameron, S., Coombes, M., Merridew, T. and Raybould, S. (2001) The Role of Social Housing in Rural Areas. Coventry, UK: Chartered Institute of Housing.

Bevan, M., Croucher, K., Fletcher, P., Rhodes, D. and Riseborough, M. (2006) The Housing and Support Needs of Older People in Rural Areas. CRC 26. London: The Countryside Agency.

Bishop, J. (2010) 'From parish plans to localism in England: straight track or long and winding road?' *Planning Practice and Research* 25(5): 611–24.

Boyle, P. and Halfacree, K. (1998) *Migration into Rural Areas*. Chichester, UK: Wiley & Sons.

Bramley, G. and Watkins, D. (2009) 'Affordability and supply: the rural dimension', *Planning Practice and Research* 24(2): 185–210.

Breheny, M., Gent, T. and Lock, D. (1993) Alternative Development Patterns: New Settlements. London: HMSO.

Bretherton, J. and Pleace, N. (2009) Residents' Views of New Forms of High Density Affordable Living. Coventry: Chartered Institute of Housing/Joseph Rowntree Foundation.

Cahill, K. (2010) 'Who really owns Britain?' *Country Life*, 19 November. Available at: www.countrylife.co.uk/property_news/article/506200/Who-really-owns-Britain-.html (accessed 12 June 2013).

Cameron, S. and Shucksmith, M. (2007) 'Market towns, housing and social inclusion', in Powe, N., Hart, T. and Shaw, T. (eds), *Market Towns: Roles, Challenges and Prospects*. London: Routledge: 81–92.

Cannon, J. (ed.) (1997) *The Oxford Companion to British History*. Oxford: Oxford University Press.

Castells, M. (1996) *The Rise of the Network Society*. London: Blackwell.

Castells, M. (1997) *The Power of Identity*. London: Blackwell.

Castells, M. (1998) *End of the Millennium*. London: Blackwell.

Caulfield, J. (1994) *City Form and Everyday Life: Toronto's Gentrification and Critical Social Practice*. Toronto: University of Toronto Press.

Champion, A. G. (2007) Reviewing Rural Futures: Population Projections and Migration across the Urban–Rural System. London: Rural Evidence Research Centre, Birkbeck, University of London. Available at: www.rerc.ac.uk/findings/documents_demography/Proj_Ests_ReportsA_F.pdf (accessed 15 February 2013).

Chaney, P. and Sherwood, K. (2000) 'The resale of right to buy dwellings: a case study of migration and social change in rural England', *Journal of Rural Studies* 16: 79–94.

Cheshire, P. (2007) *Segregated Neighbourhoods and Mixed Communities*. York, UK: Joseph Rowntree Foundation.

Clarke, A. and Monk, S. (2012) Rural Housing at a Time of Economic Change. Cambridge: Cambridge Centre for Housing and Planning Research, University of Cambridge.

Cloke, P. (1979) *Key Settlements in Rural Areas*. London: Methuen.

Cloke, P., Phillips, M. and Thrift, N. (1995) 'The new middle classes and the social constructs of rural living', in Butler, T. and Savage, M. (eds), *Social Change and the Middle Classes*, London: UCL Press: 220–38.

Cloke, P., Phillips, M. and Thrift, N. (1998) 'Class, colonisation and lifestyle strategies in Gower', in Boyle, P. and Halfacree, K. (eds), *Migration in Rural Areas*. London: Wiley: 166–85.

Cloke, P., Milbourne, P. and Widdowfield, R. (2000) 'Homelessness and rurality: "out-of-place" in purified space?' *Environment and Planning D: Society and Space* 18: 715–35.

Cloke, P., Milbourne, P. and Widdowfield, R. (2002) *Rural Homelessness: Issues, Experiences, and Policy Responses*. Bristol, UK: The Policy Press.

Commission for Rural Communities (CRC) (2008) State of the Countryside 2008. Cheltenham, UK: CRC.

Communities and Local Government (CLG) (2011a) Community Infrastructure Levy: An Overview. London: CLG.

Communities and Local Government (CLG) (2011b) Localism Act. London: The Stationery Office.

Coss, P. (2003) *The Origins of the English Gentry*. Cambridge: Cambridge University Press.

Dangschat, J. (1991) 'Gentrification in Hamburg', in Van Weesep, J. and Musterd, S. (eds), *Urban Housing for the Better Off: Gentrification in Europe*. Utrecht, The Netherlands: Stedelijke Netwerken: 63–88.

Darling, E. (2005) 'The city in the country: wilderness gentrification and the rent gap', *Environment and Planning A* 37: 1015–32.

Davidoff, L., L'Esperance, J. and Newby, H. (1976) 'Landscape with figures: home and community in English society', in Mitchell, J. and Oakley, A. (eds), *The Rights and Wrongs of Women*. Harmondsworth: Penguin.

De Groot, C., Daalhuizen, F., van Dam, F. and Mulder, C. (2012) 'Once an outsider, always an outsider? The accessibility of the Dutch rural housing market among locals and non-locals', *Journal of Rural Studies* 28: 302–13.

Dickens, P., Duncan, S., Goodwin, M. and Gray, F. (1985) *Housing, States and Localities*. London: Methuen.

Duenkmann, F. (2010) 'The village in the mind: applying Q-methodology to re-constructing constructions of rurality', *Journal of Rural Studies* 26: 284–95.

Evans, A. (1999) *'They Think I Don't Exist': The Hidden Nature of Rural Homelessness*. London: Crisis.

Ford, J., Quilgars, D. and Burrows, R. (1997) *Young People and Housing*. Salisbury, UK: Rural Development Commission.

Gallent, N. (2009) 'Affordable housing in "village England": towards a more systematic approach', *Planning Practice and Research* 24(2): 263–83.

Gallent, N. and Robinson, S. (2011) 'Local perspectives on rural housing affordability and implications for the localism agenda in England', *Journal of Rural Studies* 27: 297–307.

George, H. (1879) *Progress and Poverty*, 4th edition (1920). New York: Doubleday, Page & Co.

Halfacree, K. (2009) '"Glow worms show the path we have to tread": the counterurbanisation of Vashti Bunyan', *Social & Cultural Geography* 10(7): 771–89.

Halliday, J. and Coombes, M. (1995) 'In search of counterurbanisation: some evidence from Devon on the relationship between patterns of migration and motivation', *Journal of Rural Studies* 11(4): 433–46.

Hamnett, C. (2003) 'Gentrification and the middle-class remaking of inner London, 1961–2001', *Urban Studies* 40, 12: 2401–26.

Harvey, G. (1998) *The Killing of the Countryside*. London: Vintage.

Heley, J. (2010) 'The new squirearchy and emergent cultures of the new middle classes in rural areas', *Journal of Rural Studies* 26: 321–31.

Hoggart, K. (2007) 'The diluted working classes of rural England and Wales', *Journal of Rural Studies* 23: 305–17.

Hoggart, K. and Henderson, S. (2005) 'Excluding exceptions: housing affordability and the oppression of environmental sustainability?' *Journal of Rural Studies* 21: 181–96.

Jamieson, L. and Groves, L. (2008) Drivers of Youth Out-migration from Rural Scotland: Key Issues and Annotated Bibliography. Edinburgh: Scottish Government.

Jones, A. (1999) 'No cardboard boxes, so no problem? Young people and housing in rural areas', in Rugg, J. (ed.), *Young People, Housing and Social Policy*. London: Routledge: 145–58.

Lee, B. and Hodge, D. (1984) 'Social differentials in metropolitan residential displacement', in Palen, J. and London, B. (eds), *Gentrification, Displacement and Neighborhood Revitalization*. Albany, NY: State University of New York Press.

Little, J. (1987) 'Rural gentrification and the influence of local level planning', in Cloke, P. (ed), *Rural Planning: Policy into Action?* London: Harper & Row: 185–99.

Long, I. (2005) 'Fiscal conservatism versus local paternalism: divergent experiences of public housing decline in rural areas of England during the 1980s', *Journal of Rural Studies* 21: 111–29.

Milbourne, P. (2006) 'Rural housing and homelessness', in Cloke, P., Marsden, T. and Mooney, P. (eds), *The Handbook of Rural Studies*. London: Sage: 427–44.

Milbourne, P. (2007) 'Re-populating rural studies: migrations, movements and mobilities', *Journal of Rural Studies* 23: 381–6.

Milbourne, P. and Cloke, P. (2006) 'Rural homelessness', in Milbourne, P. and Cloke, P. (eds), *International Perspectives on Rural Homelessness*. London: Routledge: 79–96.

Mingay, G. (1976) *The Gentry: The Rise and Fall of a Ruling Class*. London: Longman.

Murdoch, J. (1995) 'Middle-class territory? Some remarks on the use of class analysis in rural studies', *Environment and Planning A* 27: 1213–30.

Murdoch, J., Lowe, P., Ward, N. and Marsden, T. (2003) *The Differentiated Countryside*. London: Routledge.

Newby, H. (1979) *Green and Pleasant Land? Social Change in Rural England*. Harmondsworth, UK: Penguin.

Newby, H. (1980) 'Urbanisation and the rural class structure: reflections on a case study', in Buttel, F., Buttel, F. and Newby, H. (eds), *The Rural Sociology of the Advanced Societies*. London: Croom Helm.

Newby, H. (1987) *Country Life: A Social History of Rural England*. London: Weidenfeld & Nicholson.

Newman, K. and Wyly, E. (2006) 'The right to stay put, revisited: gentrification and resistance to displacement in New York City', *Urban Studies* 43: 23–57.

Parsons, D. (1980) Rural Gentrification: The Influence of Rural Settlement Planning Policies. Brighton, UK: Department of Geography Research Papers no 3, University of Sussex.

Oldman, C. (2002) Support and Housing in the Countryside: Innovation and Choice. Wetherby, UK: The Countryside Agency.

Phillips, M. (1993) 'Rural gentrification and the processes of class colonisation', *Journal of Rural Studies* 9: 123–40.

Phillips, M. (2001) 'Class, collective action and the countryside: a perspective on class formation in late twentieth century Britain', in Van Gyes, G., de Witte, H and Pasture, P. (eds), *Can Class Unite? The Differentiated Workforce, Class Solidarity and Trade Unions*. Aldershot, UK: Ashgate: 247–74.

Phillips, M. (2002) 'The production, symbolisation and socialisation of gentrification: impressions from two Berkshire villages', *Transactions of the Institute of British Geographers, New Series* 27(3): 282–308.

Phillips, M. (2005) 'Differential productions of rural gentrification: illustrations from North and South Suffolk', *Geoforum* 36: 477–94.

Phillips, S. K. (1986) 'Natives and incomers: the symbolism of belonging in Muker parish, North Yorkshire', in Cohen, A. P. (ed), *Symbolising Boundaries: Identity and Diversity in British Cultures*. Manchester, UK: Manchester University Press.

Redfern, P. (2003) 'What makes gentrification "gentrification"?' *Urban Studies* 40(12): 2351–66.

Reed, M. (2008) 'The rural arena: The diversity of protest in rural England', *Journal of Rural Studies* 24: 209–18.

Robinson, D. (2004) 'Rough sleeping in rural England: Challenging a problem denied', *Policy and Politics* 32(4): 471–486.

Robinson, D. and Coward, S. (2003) *Your Place, Not Mine: The Experiences of Homeless People Staying with Family and Friends*. London: Crisis.

Robinson, D. and Reeve, K. (2002) Homelessness and Rough Sleeping in North Lincolnshire. Sheffield: Centre for Regional Economic and Social Research, Sheffield Hallam University.

Rugg, J. and Jones, A. (1999) *Getting a Job, Finding a Home: Rural Youth Transitions*. Bristol, UK: The Policy Press.

Rural Coalition (2010) The Rural Challenge: Achieving Sustainable Rural Communities for the 21st Century. Available at: http://ruralcommunities.gov.uk/wp-content/uploads/2010/08/RuralCoalitionWEB_MH.pdf (accessed 21 November 2010).

Satsangi, M. (2007) 'Land tenure change and rural housing in Scotland', Scottish Geographical Journal 123(1): 33–47

Satsangi, M., Gallent, N., and Bevan, M. (2011) *The Rural Housing Question*. Bristol, UK: The Policy Press.

Short, J. R., Witt, S. and Fleming, S. (1987) 'Conflict and compromise in the built environment: housebuilding in central Berkshire', *Transactions of the Institute of British Geographers, New Series* 12(1): 29–42.

Shucksmith, M. (1981) *No Homes for Locals?* Farnborough, UK: Gower Press.

Shucksmith, M. (1990) *Housebuilding in Britain's Countryside*. London: Routledge.

Shucksmith, M. (1991) 'Still no homes for locals? Affordable housing and planning controls in rural areas', in Champion, T. and Watkins, C. (eds), *People in the Countryside: Studies of Social Change in Rural Britain*. London: Paul Chapman: 53–66.

Shucksmith, M. (2000) *Exclusive Countryside? Social Inclusion and Regeneration in Rural Areas*. York, UK: Joseph Rowntree Foundation.

Smith, J. J. (2001) Property Tax Shift Success. Available online at: www.progress.org/archive/geono05.htm (accessed 12 June 2013).

Smith, N. (1996) *The New Urban Frontier: Gentrification and the Revanchist City*. London: Routledge.

Somerville, P. (2011) *Understanding Community: Politics, Policy and Practice*. Bristol: Policy Press.

Spencer, D. (1997) 'Counterurbanisation and rural depopulation revisited: Landowners, planners and the rural development process', *Journal of Rural Studies* 13(1): 75–92.

Stockdale, A. (2010) 'The diverse geographies of rural gentrification in Scotland', *Journal of Rural Studies* 26: 31–40.

Sumka, H. J. (1979) 'Neighborhood revitalization and displacement: A review of the evidence', *Journal of the American Planning Association* 45(4): 480–7.

Sutherland, L.-A. (2012) 'Return of the gentleman farmer? Conceptualising gentrification in UK agriculture', *Journal of Rural Studies* 28: 568–76.

Taylor, M. (2008) Living, Working Countryside: The Taylor Review of Rural Economy and Affordable Housing. London: Department for Communities and Local Government.

Thompson, F. (2001) *Gentrification and the Enterprise Culture, Britain 1780–1980*. Oxford: Oxford University Press.

Williams, J. (2000) 'Tools for achieving sustainable housing strategies in rural Gloucestershire', *Planning Practice and Research* 15: 155–74.

Williams, R. (1965) *The Long Revolution*. Harmondsworth, UK: Penguin.

14 Rural crime and policing

Angus Nurse

This chapter considers questions of rurality in the context of rural crime. Legal and criminology scholars debate rural crime definitions, in doing so adopting sometimes conflicting perspectives on whether rural crime is purely subject to a strict legalistic classification of being acts defined as such by the criminal code, or a moralistic or social legal one sometimes found in environmental or species justice discourse (Situ and Emmons, 2000; Wise, 2000). Rural crime is thus defined differently in legal and policy debates, and its practical enforcement affected by philosophical differences on the nature of rural crime and its enforcement requirements. This chapter critically evaluates different perspectives on rural crime and its law enforcement and policy imperatives.

Defining rural crime

The introduction to this book indicates the difficulties of measuring rurality and its classification according to a combination of population density and distance from major settlements. Problems also occur in the socio-legal classification of rural crime, in part because rural crime has been neglected as an area of criminological study (Donnermeyer *et al.*, 2006) but also because practitioners and policymakers with different operational parameters adopt different classifications. Thus, no consistent definition of rural crime exists across the criminological or policy literature. Instead, rural crime is defined according to a range of demographical, economical, social or cultural factors according to the ideological perspectives of different rural crime enforcement or policy bodies. These include NGOs, statutory law enforcers, policymakers, campaigners and think tanks, and the classification employed can determine whether a particular crime is the responsibility of a state's justice department or its environment department. One definition of rural crime employed in criminal justice policy analysis is that of 'small towns, farming communities and the open countryside' (Donnermeyer, 1995), classifying rural crime according to the crime's location within a countryside or non-urban perspective. UK police definitions, however, are population density based; partially on operational policing concerns with the number of crimes committed per head of population, which can determine how resources are allocated, but also, according to the distinction between inner-city and 'other' crime (Marvell and Moody, 1996; Machin and Marie, 2005), can determine the policing approach applied to a particular crime problem. However, the British Crime Survey (which measures citizens' experience and fear of crime) uses a classification of residential neighbourhoods (ACORD), a more detailed crime classification based on demographic, employment and housing information, analysing housing by its rural, urban or inner-city status (Taylor *et al.*, 2010).

A further criminological definition of rural crime situates it within the nature of the crime itself, considering rurality as a specific crime characteristic. Criminology often classifies rural crime within the subgenre of green criminology according to White's (2008a) notion of animal rights and species justice, which deals with animal abuse and suffering (including crimes impacting on animals in the wild or at least living predominantly away from urban conurbations, and cruelty or welfare offences involving farmed animals), or as environmental or ecological crimes, considering environmental justice in relation to the use of natural resources in defined geographical areas (White, 2008b). Rural crime is thus interpreted and classified as part of a green perspective (South, 1998), which considers crimes that affect the environment and biodiversity as requiring a criminal justice response that reflects environmental, ecological justice, or animal rights concerns, and an increased sensitivity to crimes causing environmental harm. In accordance with notions of species justice, rural crime can include animal abuse offences consisting of 'socially unacceptable behaviour that intentionally causes unnecessary pain, suffering, or distress to and/or death of an animal' (Ascione, 1993: 228) and wildlife crime offences against animals that exist in a wild state (Nurse, 2011). The former definition incorporates crimes against feral or stray animals living in a semi-wild state (Schaffner, 2011) and those 'liminal' wild animals who live 'in close association with humans' (Donaldson and Kymlicka, 2011: 156), but who are nevertheless primarily non-domesticated, such as urban foxes, squirrels and gulls. The terms wildlife crime and rural crime are thus used interchangeably and with considerable crossover but without coherence, reflecting multiple definitions employed to suit specific policy agendas. The UK's National Gamekeepers Organisation (2004) defines poaching as significant wildlife crime (a classification accepted by the UK Government's environment department, Defra), while UK environmental and animal protection NGOs primarily define wildlife crime as crimes against *wild* flora and fauna and not including crimes affecting game birds or animals that do not live in a natural wild state as these are effectively captive species specifically reared for game purposes. More varied definitions exist in other jurisdictions such as the US where such distinctions between game and wildlife are less marked, thus poaching of game and killing of wildlife may constitute both rural and wildlife crime (Eliason, 2003). Consistent with this, green criminology considers rural crimes against animals (whether wild or domestic) to fall within a wider definition of environmental or green crimes of a rural nature, which are defined in part due to their violation of existing rules and environmental regulations and their origins in human action (Lynch and Stretesky, 2003: 227). This incorporates a moral perspective on environmentalism employed by some NGOs, which argues that while some green crimes may not contravene any existing law, where they result in or possess the potential to result in environmental and human harm, they should be classified as crimes.

Rural crime may thus be classified according to where it takes place, via an operational policing perspective that defines rural crime as simply any crime that happens in a rural area, but may also be classified according to its rural-specific nature (e.g. poaching or wildlife crimes such as badger baiting). In part, jurisdiction-specific rural crime definitions reflect the types of crimes that occur within the countryside and this determines both the legislative and policy approach to specific rural crime problems. However, these definitions are not consistently applied either in the policing or in the policy (legislative) response to rural crime.

Rurality and policing perspectives

Police perspectives generally view rural crime as less serious, in terms of both intensity and type of crime, than urban, and particularly inner-city crime, predicated on perceptions that rural areas require less intensive policing (Muhammad, 2002) and a more informal community-oriented approach to policing. Law enforcement policy and official crime statistics predominantly focus on lower-working-class 'street crime' (Lea and Young, 1993: 89) dictating this as a policing and media priority in criminal justice, although wildlife and environmental crimes continually attract media attention due to the efforts of NGOs. Research consistently shows that the core areas of policing (violent and serious crime) tend to be less prevalent in rural areas perhaps in part because the nature of rural communities often means there are fewer recorded crimes per capita. Sorokin, Zimmerman and Galpin (1931) concluded that crime in the rural context of the United States and numerous European countries was much lower than urban crime rates, albeit they focused primarily on rural arrest rates and paid little attention to differences in rural and urban crime statistics' recording practices. Their findings have been replicated in more recent research: Weisheit *et al.* (1994) commented that 'most research concludes that crime is less frequent in rural areas', based on the data of uniform crime reports that present crime by type and population group (1994: 1). In the UK, the 2009/10 British Crime Survey and Police Recorded Crime data for England and Wales concluded that 'crime rates were higher in areas classified as predominantly urban than in areas classified as predominantly rural' (Flatley *et al.*, 2010: 165). While more recent research indicates that rural crime has risen in some areas (Which?, 2011), it still remains at lower (per capita) levels than urban crime. In part this reflects the diverse nature of rural areas with wider, less densely populated areas, offering less opportunity for traditionally numerous crimes of burglary and other property crimes. But it also reflects the fact that rural areas may define and record crime differently and are generally served by fewer criminal justice agencies (Weisheit *et al.*, 2006) and have less formal surveillance.

Reiner (2000) identifies that the police classify crime according to both its merits and its cohesion with accepted notions of policing; 'cop culture' defines some crimes as 'rubbish' and not worthy of police time while other crimes are classified as having value, that is, the sort of thing that both police managers and operational officers consider they should be doing. Rural crime classifications that include such activities as theft/damage to farm equipment, rural drug use and poaching with the association of 'good class' or 'mainstream' villains that the police are there to apprehend are likely to be accepted, while 'lesser' offences such as fly-tipping and wild animal theft are not. Muhammad (2002) identifies that rural officers generally work with comparatively fewer resources and lower budgets than their urban counterparts, taking into account crime volumes and perceived seriousness of offences (Nurse, 2008, 2012; Wellsmith, 2011), with rural policing often considered a 'soft' option requiring a more community driven social support service by police managers (Weisheit *et al.*, 1994) unencumbered by media-driven violent crime images of city policing (Young, 2010). However, rural officers are generally better respected than their urban colleagues in part because they are often required to have greater links with their community (Fenwick *et al.*, 2011; Muhammad, 2002). Kowalewski *et al.* (1994) identified that respect for individual rural officers was predicated on their perceived toughness and professionalism to a greater degree than that of urban officers.

Rurality impacts on communities differently depending on population size, geography, social mix, specific community context and culture (Small and Supple, 2001), which influences both responses to and tolerance of rural crime. However, research consistently shows that rural areas generally have a greater level of informal control and closer social bonds that facilitate social (informal) policing of selected crimes, aided also by the relative stability of the population (Wilson, 1991), producing generally lower levels of recorded crime (Smith, 1980). The nature of rural communities, which can be more close-knit than urban ones, emphasises informal control in part because of shared notions of external pressure and need to preserve the community. Cohen (1982) argued that rural communities sometimes adopt a positive orientation to their collective distinctiveness by regulating their social behaviour so that the reality of difference is mediated by 'the appearance of similarity' (1982: 13). In this context, rural police officers are often highly visible, identifiable and known to the community, with their actions being subject to greater public scrutiny. Consequently, they may have less discretion to dispose of some kinds of offences than their largely anonymous urban colleagues (Eisenstein, 1982).

Challenges to the legitimacy of hunting and angling regulations are common in the US, UK and several other jurisdictions (Eliason, 2003; Nurse, 2009). Studies have found that rural hunting communities consider hunting and killing of wildlife to be their right irrespective of legislation (Bristow, 1982; Pash,

1986), and enjoy the challenge of outwitting enforcement agencies who they not only see as outsiders seeking to impose controls on their way of life, but actively engage with as the enemy (Forsyth and Marckesc, 1993). For example, an area where game shooting takes place may publicly appear to be intolerant of wildlife crime, but reliance on the estate for employment or housing, and the influx of urban income into the local economy, can mean that residents turn a blind eye to illegal activity occurring on an estate in order to continue enjoying the economic and social benefits of a successful shooting operation. Thus policing in rural areas and particularly in relation to wildlife crime can represent a model of policing imposed on a community who have historically engaged in 'traditional' forms of sport or recreation where killing of animals is acceptable and specific 'rural' notions of crime may exist (Meagher, 1985; Marshall and Johnson, 2005). This contrasts with the environmental radicalism of town dwellers and enforcers who increasingly engage with the countryside yet find many of its practices problematic.

NGO perspectives

NGOs are not usually involved in practical law enforcement, but in rural crime (broadly defined) various NGOs assist the police and prosecutors actively detecting, investigating and prosecuting crime. NGOs have traditionally collated information on the amount of rural crime that exists (albeit with a focus on wildlife crimes), while the statutory enforcement authorities (police, Customs, etc.) have only recorded crime data on an ad-hoc basis (Conway, 1999; Nurse, 2008). One consequence of this is that NGOs have, traditionally, been in a better position than the statutory authorities to assess rural crime policing and criminal behaviour problems, particularly those affecting wildlife. This gives NGOs considerable influence in directing the law enforcement agenda to their areas of specific interest and in which they have acquired considerable expertise. In effect, rural crime allows for the study of 'private policing' in an area of criminal justice policy where a considerable amount of law enforcement activity is still carried out on a voluntary basis by private bodies in the UK such as the RSPCA's uniformed Inspectorate (in respect of animal welfare crimes and wildlife cruelty crimes such as badger baiting and badger digging) or the RSPB's Investigations Section which takes the lead on the investigation of some wildlife crime cases before they are taken over by the Crown Prosecution Service (CPS). The League against Cruel Sports has also taken a lead on monitoring the effectiveness of the 2004 Hunting Act, providing assistance and advice to the police and taking prosecutions to ensure the law is being used. Thus whereas in some areas, such as street crime, police functions are being privatised with the introduction of private security patrols, police community support officers (PCSOs) and street wardens (Fielding and Innes, 2006), rural crime is an area where the policing function has traditionally been carried out by NGOs where it involves non-standard offences, and it is only recently that the police have become active in operational law enforcement of wildlife and environmental offences, remaining under pressure from NGOs to become more involved. Given the lack of centralised expertise in rural crime, especially that involving wildlife, police and prosecutors in a range of jurisdictions still rely heavily on NGOs. Thus US citizens have come to understand and expect that NGOs like the Sierra Club, Defenders of Wildlife and Earthjustice will take action where federal government agencies fail to do so. This picture is replicated in other countries.

However, the role of NGOs as enforcers or campaigners varies according to the types of crime involved, with different policy perspectives pursued in respect of game offences and poaching, habitat destruction and pollution of rural environments, or offences involving domestic/farm animals and animal welfare and cruelty offences. The relationship between NGOs and policymakers also varies so that, for example, game offences are considered to be effectively policed within the UK's strong game and anti-poaching legislation, with good cooperation between police and game rearing staff over poaching, but the same is not true of wildlife offences. Game rearing staff regularly report poaching offences (which directly affect their livelihoods and the rural economy) to statutory agencies but may be reluctant to have the same involvement in wildlife offences such as bird of prey prosecution, where game rearing staff are often suspects and may be in conflict with the police and conservationists over the appropriateness and legitimacy of enforcement action and rural crime policy.

Complex attitudes to rural crime exist within rural communities where resistance to legislation to control or criminalise traditional rural field sports continues, while NGOs sometimes pursue an abolitionist agenda on moral grounds seeking to criminalise or regulate rural activities such as shooting and fishing. The campaign against the 2004 Hunting Act was often characterised as 'town versus country' (Burns *et al.*, 2000), and debates concerning regulating traditional field sports and hunting activities reveal perceptions that affluent sections of society seek to impose their will on poorer rural members of society and pursue an idealised notion of rurality. There is, however, arguably a three-way divide between the rural poor actively involved in rural pursuits, the gentrified rich who are involved in both a managerial and participatory capacity, and the new urban/cosmopolitan middle classes who seek to influence the classes above and below them. Lowe and Ginsberg (2002) concluded that the US animal rights movement has a disproportionately well-educated membership reflecting what Parkin (1968) called 'middle class radicalism'. Certainly the major UK wildlife crime NGOs, while not all pursuing policies from an animal rights perspective, represent a professional movement comprising large professional organisations (comparable with medium to large businesses) rather than being a grass roots or 'activists' movement. Figures for certain major wildlife or animal protection NGOs show annual running costs typically in excess of £50 million per organisation (see for example RSPB 2010, RSPCA 2006). The organisations' considerable public support (the RSPB has over a million members), together with the resources available for campaigning and political lobbying, allows the main environmental NGOs to take the lead in promoting rural crime as an issue of importance. It also places the organisations in a position to employ expertise, for example, specialist investigators and political lobbyists, promoting their policy objectives and adopting a dominant policy or scientific position, while their socio-economic position allows them to exploit that perceived expertise and dominate the policy debate on rural crime.

Rural criminality

Smith (2010) argues that 'we only have a fuzzy notion of the stereotypical rural criminal and find it difficult to acknowledge the existence of a rural criminal underclass' (2010: 373). Yet the opportunities provided to rural criminals make it likely that specific types of offending endemic to rural areas exist, multiple classifications of rural crime notwithstanding (Enticott, 2011; Nurse, 2011). Research on wildlife crime identified distinct types of offender involved in those rural crimes containing a wildlife element, concluding that, in addition to the 'traditional' criminal who commits offences for financial gain, other specific offender types exist (Nurse, 2011). The dictates of countryside employment, particularly in the game rearing industry, create three types of criminals. First, *economic criminals* commit wildlife crimes as a direct result of particular economic pressures (e.g., direct employer-pressure or profit driven crime within their chosen profession). In some cases their offences are determined by the demands of competing within a rural economy that is under both economic and political threat. *Masculinities criminals* commit offences involving harm to animals. They are drawn to the countryside where their quarry (e.g., game or wild birds, badgers, hares) can be found and where their criminal behaviour exhibits a stereotypically masculine nature (Groombridge, 1996; Kimmel *et al.*, 2005). This is expressed both in terms of their exercise of power over animals and the links to sport and gambling involved in such activities as hare coursing, badger baiting and badger digging. Finally, *hobby criminals* commit crimes for which there is no direct benefit or underlying criminal 'need', such as collecting wild birds' eggs or dead wild animals for taxidermy purposes. They attract a criminal justice reaction which is often disproportionately severe, for example via a consistent approach to prosecuting even 'minor' or 'technical' offences and the use of large numbers of officers for search warrants even where neither the offence nor offender are considered to be serious. This can in part be due to the involvement of NGOs and the need for public condemnation of particular offences seen as morally repugnant (Nurse, 2013a: 311–13).

Analysis of documentary evidence, case reports and interviews with practitioners (Nurse, 2011), together with previous research (Kemmerer, 2004; Eliason, 2003), identifies that offenders involved in the exploitation of wildlife, farm animals or the rural environment commit their crimes for the following main general reasons:

- profit or commercial gain;
- thrill or sport;
- necessity of obtaining food;
- antipathy towards governmental and law enforcement bodies;
- tradition and cultural reasons.

Certain specific types of offending can only take place in rural areas as they are inherently reliant on countryside species (e.g. hare coursing, badger baiting, illegal fox hunting). Thus a form of rural criminality has either emerged in a rural setting due to the opportunity to commit specific crimes or adapted to it so that some offenders specifically travel to rural areas to commit their offences.

The challenge of policing rural crime

The majority of policing theory and literature is based on a model of social organisation that sees crime as primarily dealt with through community engagement and a combination of proactive and reactive policing. However, Mawby (2007) comments that the 'crime prevention issues [in rural areas] may be qualitatively different from those facing criminal justice agencies in the cities', as crime occurs in a changing social landscape 'affected by demographic changes, changing crime trends and by the introduction of new policing practices' (Smith, 2010). While some common crimes such as theft and violence occur in both rural and urban areas, rural areas have some inherently different problems, such as wildlife crime. Other problems that are often more pronounced in rural areas include those of illegal migrant workers, fly-tipping, mass trespass (associated with music festivals and other countryside gatherings), crop and timber thefts, and unlawful use (and theft) of off-road vehicles. In addition, rural specific crimes such as wildlife crime or poaching present specific challenges for rural police forces frequently lacking in both the expertise and resources necessary to deal with non-standard policing challenges, that is, matters that officers do not routinely encounter and may not be trained to deal with (Nurse, 2012; Kirkwood, 1994).

The effects of geography alone can have significant impacts on rural justice, by negatively influencing the availability of resources, response times and the speed with which support services can be provided. Thus NGOs, identified by White (2012) as integral to environmental enforcement according to regulation theory (which dictates that environmental enforcement cannot be carried out by statutory policing agencies alone), become increasingly important in rural crime enforcement.

Rural cultures may also employ a mistrust of government and outsiders, especially where there is a perceived lack of understanding on the part of policymakers or enforcers of the specific needs of rural communities. There may also be a reluctance to share internal problems, providing difficulties for investigators pursuing enquiries into rural crime issues (Nurse, 2012), particularly NGO investigators. As a result rural crime develops increased significance to enforcers who see rural communities as actively resisting legitimate law enforcement activity while enforcers seem increasingly intrusive to the rural community, creating polarised positions (an 'us and them' situation) where effective enforcement becomes difficult to achieve. A specific notion of rurality as lawlessness, and the significance of rural crime as an indicator of the anti-social nature of rurality and rural communities, are reinforced and perpetuated, although perception and reality may differ.

As a result, when rural crime does occur it sometimes receives disproportionate attention. Mingay (1989) suggests that the image of the countryside as a safe place to live is an important social construction such that when crime occurs in the countryside its threat value is perceived as greater. As a result the attention of outside agencies including NGOs, particularly in the areas of wildlife crime and perceived 'cruel' field sports, may result in aggressive policy and enforcement activity, influenced by a sense of outrage, which are actively resisted by a community that does not recognise the legitimacy of the enforcer.

An inclusive approach?

While politicians and other policymakers operate according to a definition of rural crime as crime occurring in rural areas and affecting the wider rural community, NGOs and some practitioners view rural crime as predominantly crime affecting wildlife and biodiversity. The reality is that demographic, economic, social, and cultural characteristics all influence the nature of criminality (Marshall and Johnson, 2005), the required policing and policy response to rural crime, and the type of offences that make up rural crime. They also affect who may be responsible for dealing with an offence, whether statutory or voluntary agency or whether criminal justice or environment department. Thus the range of factors that determine the conception of rurality involved are relevant for understanding a rural crime's position within the justice system.

Rural crime not only attracts individuals wishing to exploit a rural setting (and resources) necessary to the commission of their crimes, but also creates opportunities for those involved in criminal activity to adapt their offending to the opportunities offered by the availability of wildlife, farm equipment and the relatively lower level of policing resources. The Countryside Alliance (2012) sampled 27 police forces in England and Wales and concluded that, on average, rural areas within police forces in England and Wales had fewer police officers, PCSOs and specialist officers per head than urban areas (2012: 1). However the lack of resources relates not solely to numbers of officers but also the lower level of practical investigative resources and expertise allocated to rural policing, particularly where rural specific crimes such as wildlife crime are concerned. Roberts *et al.*, (2001) identified that enforcers and regulators working in the area of wildlife crime 'often lack resources and expertise' (2001: 1), while Nurse (2012) and Wellsmith (2011) both identified a continued lack of resources to deal with environmental and wildlife crime problems, with Wellsmith noting that several police forces had reduced or eliminated their Wildlife Crime Officer (PWCO) role due to austerity cuts (2011: 7). ACPO evidence to the 2003/04 House of Commons Environmental Audit Committee noted that, in respect to wildlife crime, 'we receive no messages from government indicating that these matters should have resources directed towards it. Few Chief Constables are therefore prepared to dedicate resources toward areas they are not asked to concentrate on' (House of Commons, 2004: 25). Thus police managers acknowledge that resources are not always allocated to tackle such crime problems. As a result, the specific challenges of rural policing (generally lower resources both per capita and in relation to the seriousness of crimes, complexity of enforcement issues and generally wider geographical areas to cover) remain both operational policing and policy problems.

Addressing these multiple problems requires a new integrated policy and policing definition of rural crime, recognising rurality in the context of rural crime as encompassing both crime that takes place in non-urban areas (both rural and semi-rural) and crime of a distinctly rural nature involving wildlife, liminal or farmed animals, the natural environment and the specific problems of a non-urban environment. Defining rurality is a central issue in deciding how crimes should be policed and whether they should be the responsibility of a justice ministry or an environmental department. Currently, rural crime in the context of 'mainstream' crime occurring in a rural area is the responsibility of justice departments of government in the US and UK. But rural crime, which is considered to be distinctly environmental or wildlife crime, is the responsibility of the environment department and is seen as being outside the remit of mainstream statutory policing. In the US this means that it is dealt with by the Department of the Interior and specialist bodies like the Environmental Protection Agency or US Fish and Wildlife Service, and in the UK it is substantially left to NGOs to enforce even though there is often overlap between such offending and other offences (Nurse, 2011; 2012).

Thus this chapter argues that rural crime should be redefined as incorporating both crimes of a distinctly rural or environmental nature and mainstream crimes that take place in rural areas. This new conception of rural crime includes both countryside specific crimes that can only take place in non-urban environments, such as the theft of farm machinery, and natural environment crimes predominantly located in geographically rural or semi-urban environments, for example natural water course pollution. In adopting this geographical 'non-urban' definition, the distinction between wildlife and game offences becomes redundant. Instead it is more pertinent to consider a subclassification of rural animal crime that affects 'wild', 'game', 'farm' or 'companion' animals within a broader definition of rural animal crime.

For rural crime policy and law enforcement to succeed, rural crime must come to mean both countryside specific and 'ordinary' crime taking place in rural locations, with the application of mainstream criminal justice techniques (e.g., situational crime prevention, use of forensic techniques) to a countryside and non-inner city environment (Nurse, 2012; Wellsmith, 2011). This requires adequate resources to be provided for rural policing rather than continued reliance on NGOs, so that theft or violence in rural areas are considered no less serious than inner-city crime, are comparatively no worse resourced despite their seemingly lower prevalence (Nurse, 2012; Weisheit *et al.*, 2006), and are seen as being the responsibility of mainstream criminal justice agencies. NGOs are an important component of some enforcement activity (e.g., as expert advisers), yet continued NGO enforcement of rural (including wildlife and other environmental) crimes is undesirable where NGOs adopt the role of lead enforcer. While in principle NGO involvement is necessary when public enforcement falls down, in practice NGOs often lack the resources and practical experience of the full range of policing techniques to fully investigate and prosecute crimes; thus NGO enforcement becomes primarily based on apprehension and punishment rather than incorporating required crime prevention techniques (Nurse, 2013a; Wellsmith, 2011).

Given limited resources and the fact that law enforcement is rarely a priority for NGO resources (Nurse, 2013a), decisions must also be made on which enforcement priorities should be pursued by NGOs. This risks enforcement becoming subject to the private interests and campaigning objectives of an NGO and implemented selectively, rather than being conducted in the public interest and in accordance with public policy priorities. White (2012) also notes that some NGOs justify using illegal means to achieve particular aims, particularly where enforcement is allied to an ideological position on law enforcement or rural crime, for example a fundamental opposition to the lawfulness of game shooting or field sports. This can make effective collaboration between NGOs and official law enforcement agencies problematic (White, 2012) and risk undermining the legitimacy of enforcement action. NGOs operate their enforcement activities from a particular perspective (Nurse, 2013a), so that some enforcement action may be intended to achieve a campaigning objective, some might be approached from a moral perspective, seeking to punish activities that the organisation disapproves of, and some might be pursued in order to highlight inadequacies in current law (Nurse, 2013a: 311–13). Thus rural policing might be pursued from an ideological rather than a 'pure' public protection perspective. While this does not imply criticism of any particular NGO, the interests of law and order should be paramount in rural policing.

Rural crime, in all its different conceptions, constitutes a social problem that requires statutory not voluntary policing (Nurse, 2012, 2013b; Wellsmith, 2011), so that such crimes are seen as part of an overall criminal profile, and not just as an environmental issue as certain rural crimes (e.g., those involving animals and which are seen as natural environment issues) are currently defined.

References

Ascione, F. R. (1993) 'Children who are cruel to animals: A review of research and implications for developmental psychopathology', *Anthrozoos* 6: 226–47.

Burns, L. Edwards, V. Marsh, J. Soulsby, L. and Winter, M. (2000) Committee of Inquiry into Hunting With Dogs in England and Wales. London: HMSO.

Bristow, A. P. (1982) *Rural Law Enforcement*. Boston, MA: Allyn & Bacon.

Conway, E. (1999) The Recording of Wildlife Crime in Scotland. Edinburgh: Scottish Office.

Cohen, A. P. (1982) *Belonging: Identity and Social Organisation in British Rural Cultures*. Manchester, UK: Manchester University Press.

Countryside Alliance (2012) Help the Beat Go On: Rural Areas Need the Help of Police & Crime Commissioners. London: Countryside Alliance

Donaldson, S. and Kymlicka, W. (2011) *Zoopolis: A Political Theory of Animal Rights*. Oxford: Oxford University Press.

Donnermeyer, J. F. (1995) 'Crime and violence in rural communities', in S. M. Blaser, J. Blaser, & K. Pantoja (eds), *Perspectives on Violence and Substance Use in Rural America*. Oakbrook, IL: North Central Regional Education Laboratory (NCREL): 27–63.

Donnermeyer, J. F., Jobes, P., and E. Barclay (2006) 'Rural crime, poverty, and community', in W. S. DeKeseredy and B. Perry (eds), *Advancing Critical Criminology*. Lanham, MD: Lexington Books.

Eisenstein, J. (1982) 'Research on rural criminal justice: A summary', in S. Cronk, J. Jankovic and R. K. Green (eds), *Criminal Justice in Rural America*, Washington DC: US Department of Justice: 117.

Eliason, S. L. (2003) 'Illegal hunting and angling: The neutralization of wildlife law violations', *Society and Animals* 11(3): 225–43.

Enticott, G. P. (2011) 'Techniques of neutralising wildlife crime in rural England and Wales', *Journal of Rural Studies* 27(2): 200–8.

Fenwick, T. Dockrell, R. Slade, B. and Roberts, I. (2011) Rural Policing: Understanding Police Knowledge and Practice in Rural Communities. Scottish Institute for Policing Research Summary No. 10. Dundee, Scotland: Scottish Institute for Policing Research/University of Dundee.

Fielding, N. and Innes, M. (2006) 'Reassurance policing, community policing and measuring police performance', *Policing and Society* 16(2): 127–45.

Flatley, J. Kershaw, C. Smith, K. Chaplin, R. and Moon, D. (eds) (2010) Crime in England and Wales 2009/10: Findings from the British Crime Survey and Police Recorded Crime. London: Home Office.

Forsyth, C. J. and Marckesc, T. A. (1993) 'Thrills and skills: A sociological analysis of poaching', *Deviant Behavior*, 14(2): 157–72.

Groombridge, N. (1996) 'Masculinities and crimes against the environment', *Theoretical Criminology* 2(2): 249–67.

House of Commons Environmental Audit Committee (2004) *Environmental Crime: Wildlife Crime*. London: The Stationery Office.

Kemmerer, L. (2004) 'Hunting tradition: Treaties, law, and subsistence hunting', *Animal Liberation Philosophy and Policy Journal* 2(2): 1–20.

Kimmel, M., Hearn, J. and Connell, R. W. (2005) *Handbook of Studies on Men & Masculinities*. London: Sage.

Kirkwood, G. (1994) *The Enforcement of Wildlife Protection Legislation: A Study of the Police Wildlife Liaison Officers' Network*, Leicester, UK: De Montfort University.

Kowalewski, D., Hall, W., Dolan, J. and Anderson, J. (1984) 'Police environments and operational codes: A case study of rural settings', *Journal of Police Science and Administration* 12(4): 363–72.

Lea, J. and Young, J. (1993 revised edition) *What Is To Be Done About Law & Order?* London: Pluto Press.

Lowe, B. M. and Ginsberg, C. F. (2002) 'Animal rights as a post-citizenship movement', *Society and Animals* 10(2): 203–15.

Lynch, M.L. and Stretesky, P. B. (2003) 'The meaning of green: Contrasting criminological perspectives', *Theoretical Criminology*, 7(2): 217–38.

Machin, S. and Marie, O. (2005) Crime and Police Resources: The Street Crime Initiative. IZA Discussion Paper no. 1853.

Marshall, B. and Johnson, S. (2005) Crime in Rural Areas: A Review of the Literature for the Rural Evidence Research Centre. London: Jill Dando Institute of Crime Science, University College London.

Marvell, T. B. and Moody, C. E. (1996) 'Specification problems, police levels, and crime rates', *Criminology* 34(4): 609–46.

Mawby, R. I. (2007) Editorial, *International Journal of Rural Crime* l(1): 2–20.

Meagher, M. S. (1985) 'Police patrol styles: How pervasive is community variation?', *Journal of Police Science and Administration*, 13(1): 36–45.

Mingay, G. E. (1989) *The Rural Idyll*. London: Routledge.

Muhammad, B. (2002) Rural Crime and Rural Policing Practices (Multicultural Law Enforcement). Detroit, MI: Detroit Police Department.

National Gamekeepers Organisation (2004) Wildlife Crime: Evidence to MP's on the EAC Sub-Committee. Darlington, UK: National Gamekeepers Organisation.

Nurse, A. (2008) *Policing Wildlife: Perspectives on Criminality and Criminal Justice Policy in Wildlife Crime in the UK*. Birmingham, UK: Birmingham City University

Nurse, A. (2009) 'Dealing with animal offenders', in A. Linzey (ed.), *The Link Between Animal Abuse and Human Violence*. Eastbourne, UK: Sussex Academic Press, 238–49.

Nurse, A. (2011) 'Policing wildlife: Perspectives on criminality in wildlife crime', *Papers from the British Criminology Conference* 11: 38–53.

Nurse, A. (2012) 'Repainting the thin green line: The enforcement of wildlife legislation', *Internet Journal of Criminology*, October 2012.

Nurse, A. (2013a) 'Privatising the green police: The role of NGOs in wildlife law enforcement', *Crime, Law and Social Change*, 59(3): 305–18.

Nurse, A. (2013b) 'Species justice: The future protection of wildlife', *The Monthly Journal of the International Green Criminology Working Group*, February 2013.

Parkin, F. (1968) *Middle Class Radicalism: The Social Bases of the British Campaign for Nuclear Disarmament*. Manchester, UK: Manchester University Press.

Pash, P. (1986) 'Poacher wars', *Illinois Department of Conservation: Outdoor Highlights*, 14(1) 3–9.

Reiner, R. (2000) *The Politics of the Police*, Oxford: Oxford University Press.

Roberts, M., Cook, D., Jones, P. and Lowther, D. (2001) *Wildlife Crime in the UK: Towards a National Crime Unit*. Wolverhampton, UK: Department for the Environment, Food & Rural Affairs/Centre for Applied Social Research (University of Wolverhampton).

RSPB (Royal Society for the Protection of Birds) (2010) Birdcrime 2009: Offences against Wild Bird Legislation in 2009. Sandy, UK: RSPB.

RSPCA (Royal Society for the Prevention of Cruelty to Animals) (2006) Annual Review 2005: Royal Society for the Prevention of Cruelty of Animals. Horsham: RSPCA.

Schaffner, J. E. (2011) *An Introduction to Animal and the Law*, Basingstoke, UK: Palgrave Macmillan.

Situ, Y. and Emmons, D. (2000) *Environmental Crime: The Criminal Justice System's Role in Protecting the Environment*. Thousand Oaks, CA: Sage.

Small, S., and Supple, A. (2001) 'Communities as systems: Is a community more than the sum of its parts?', in A. Booth and A. C. Crouter (eds.), *Does it Take a Village? Community Effects on Children, Adolescents, and Families*. Mahwah, NJ: Erlbaum: 161–74.

Smith, B. L. (1980) 'Criminal victimization in rural areas', in Barbara Raffael Price and Phyllis Jo Baunach (eds.), *Criminal Justice Research: New Models and Findings*. Beverly Hills, CA: Sage.

Smith, R. (2010) 'Policing the changing landscape of rural crime: A case study from Scotland', *International Journal of Police Science and Management*, 12(3): 373–87.

Sorokin, P., Zimmerman C. C. and Galpin C. J. (eds) (1930–32) *A Systematic Source Book in Rural Sociology*. Minneapolis, MN: University of Minnesota Press.

South, N. (1998) 'A green field for criminology? A proposal for a perspective', *Theoretical Criminology*, 2(2): 211–33.

Taylor, J., Twigg, L. and Mohan, J. (2010) 'Investigating perceptions of antisocial behaviour and neighbourhood ethnic heterogeneity in the British Crime Survey', *Transactions of the Institute of British Geographers*, 35: 59–75.

Villiers, P. (2009) *Police and Policing*. Hook, UK: Waterside Press

Weisheit, R. A., Falcone, D. N., and Wells, L. E. (1994) *Rural Crime and Rural Policing*. (Research in Action). Washington DC: US Department of Justice, National Institute of Justice, NCJ 150223.

Weisheit, R. A., Falcone, D. N. and Wells, L. E. (2006) *Crime and Policing in Rural and Small-town America*, 3rd edition. Prospect Heights, IL: Waveland Press.

Wellsmith, Melanie (2011) 'Wildlife crime: The problems of enforcement', *European Journal of Criminal Policy and Research* 17(2): 125–48.

Which? (2011) Rural Crime on the Rise, London: Which? Available online at: www.which.co.uk/news/2011/08/rural-crime-on-the-rise-261461 (accessed 26 March 2013).

White, R. (2008a) 'A green criminological perspective', in E. McLaughlin and T. Newburn (eds), *The Sage Handbook of Criminological Theory*. London: Sage.

White, R. (2008b) *Crimes against Nature: Environmental Criminology and Ecological Justice*. Devon, UK: Willan.

White, R. (2012) 'NGO engagement in environmental law enforcement: Critical reflections', *Australasian Policing* 4(2): 7–12.

Wilson, T. C. (1991) 'Urbanism, migration, and tolerance: A reassessment', *American Sociological Review*, 56(1): 117–23.

Wise, S. M. (2000) *Rattling the Cage: Towards Legal Rights for Animals*. London: Profile.

Young, A. (2010) *The Scene of Violence*. Abingdon, UK, and New York: Routledge.

15 Gypsies and Travellers in modern rural England

Margaret Greenfields

Introduction

If asked in a survey to articulate the characteristics of a 'typical' English rural resident (if such there can be claimed to be), it is highly likely that the majority of respondents would paint a picture of a relatively unchanging, predominantly mono-cultural society where farmers and young families co-mingle with a number of middle-class incomers who seek refuge in a rural idyll from the challenges of urban life, and a smattering of ageing eccentric rural 'characters' and a squire or two may be encountered in the village pub or store.

In fact, a picture might emerge that (other than the extraordinarily high number of homicides in televisual portrayals) bears some resemblance to the remarkably successful rural crime series *Midsomer Murders*, a programme that became embroiled in controversy in March 2011 when the creator indicated in an interview with the *Radio Times* that he had deliberately excluded visibly different ethnic minority characters from the series on the grounds that a programme that represented the 'last bastion of Englishness' and that relied on 'English genteel eccentricity' would not offer an accurate portrayal of such a community if ethnic diversity were to be shown (see Easton, 2011). Indeed so strong is the concept of a homogenised population in rural locales that Agyeman and Spooner (1997) argue that ethnicity has been conflated with 'visible minorities' to the extent that an *'invisibility of whiteness as an ethnic signifier'* (1997: 199; original emphasis) exists, leading to a widespread failure to recognise the diversity of minority ethnic populations present in rural settings or to problematise the role of 'place', 'space' and community relationships between members of different ethnic or national groups.

While in recent years an increasing body of work has been produced on the economic situation and integration (or not) of White Eastern European minority communities in rural areas (e.g., Bailey, 2011; Markova and Black, 2007; White, 2011; Williams, 2007), Gypsies and Travellers have remained consistently marginalised from most discourse on rural ethnicity and racism, with but few authors (e.g., Halfacree, 1996; Holloway, 2003, 2005; Mayall, 1988, 1995; Sibley, 1997) commenting on the tensions that exist in relation to these populations' use of, and residence in, rural locales.

Despite the centuries-long historical connection between Gypsies and Travellers and rural land-work in Britain (Greenfields, 2010; Mayall, 1988, 1995), popular anti-Traveller rhetoric (frequently fuelled by hostile media reporting of unauthorised encampments or sites 'set up over a weekend' – see Morris, 2000; Richardson, 2006) and the growth of campaigning groups determined to 'defend their areas' from 'inappropriate [Gypsy site] developments' (Erfani-Ghettani, 2012) have led both to a resurgence of rural racism against Gypsies and Travellers and a revisionist approach to local history, whereby populations who have lived and worked alongside sedentary residents for centuries are air-brushed out of narratives of rural life and presented as alien to the landscape in which they wish to settle. This process, according to Powell (2007: 112), is one of 'dis-identification' and 'stigmatisation' fuelling everyday conflict and antagonism between populations within a single locality. In this chapter, I set out to explore how this artificial narrative that endangers community cohesion has grown, as changing socio-economic circumstances have diminished employment opportunities for many Gypsies and Travellers and public awareness has been lost of the varying social and employment roles they have occupied over time, as well as of the familial and residential interrelatedness of previous generations of rural dwellers.

As common memories of shared employment in the fields have become endangered by the 'drift from the land' and the increased use by farmers of Eastern European gang labour to fulfil 'picking' work previously undertaken by rural labourers alongside Gypsy/Traveller migrant workers, casual social contacts between communities have become less explicitly and spatially ethnicised. Thus the trend to separation (and lack of awareness that one's neighbouring field worker is a Gypsy or Traveller) has grown, as housing has taken the place (for many Gypsies/Travellers) of horses and caravans (Greenfields and Smith, 2011), clothing worn by both communities is purchased from the same high-street outlets, and even patterns of speech and use of slang move closer together, making it harder (other than for an experienced observer) to tell Gypsy apart from *gorjer* (sometimes *gorja*), or Irish Traveller from an Irish 'countryman'.[1] Accordingly, the result, when this apparent consensus of homogeneity is destroyed – whether by sudden identification of a housed neighbour as a member of a largely despised ethnic group (Greenfields and Smith, 2010) or by the presence of an enclave of caravan dwelling Travellers – is typically increased stereotyping of an entire ethnic group as alien, dangerous 'space invaders' associated with 'land-grabs' and the unauthorised occupation of Green-Belt land (regardless of whether it has been purchased by the would-be site dweller), which is itself increasingly conceptualised in terms of the moral category of an unchanging rural idyll (Halfacree, 1996).

Holloway (2005) reports that, even in situations where sedentary populations have a vested interest in the continued presence of a visible Gypsy population (for example, in her exploration of the relationships between residents of Appleby, site of the large horse fair which has been described as 'the rural equivalent of Notting Hill Carnival' (2005: 354), and the Gypsies who bring both money and a large influx of curious tourists to the locality to view this cultural and economic gathering), there is a marked ambivalence towards the temporary nomadic population. Gypsies and Travellers are perceived on the one hand as a source of economic benefit to the local community (and some local pride associated with a relatively unique event with clear historical provenance), but on the other as a group who in their wake bring criminality, dirt and risk – characteristics seen as concomitant with the presence of nomads in popular discourse (Richardson, 2006) and associated darkly with any alien or 'stranger' who adheres to differing social mores or who is perceived as disconcertingly cosmopolitan and 'different' from their sedentary neighbours, especially if their appearance or linguistic skills vary from that of the mainstream community (see further Simmel, 1971).

Holloway noted, however, that Appleby local residents emphasised repeatedly that their relationships with Gypsy visitors to the Fair were not uniformly negative or disrespectful, with a number of respondents attributing positive moral categories to 'real Romanies' in contrast to the 'hangers on' who were perceived as 'not like' older generations of Travellers, inauthentic, and perhaps only tenuously connected to the Gypsy/Traveller community, and in the main marked out (negatively) by perceptions of their likely undesirable behaviour while in the locality. In turn, respondents' discourse tended to rely upon physical markers (skin colour, dress style, etc.) to determine who was or was not 'genuinely' a Gypsy, with participants keen to ascribe to those Gypsies seen as 'authentic' more positive characteristics than were attributed to the dangerous strangers who moved among them – a mode not far removed from the rhetoric (and harsh legal penalties) pertaining to 'counterfeit Egyptians' or vagrants who mimicked the ways of 'genuine Romanies' in Tudor England (Mayall, 1995).

Greenfields (2010: 253) found too, in her study of Gypsies' and Travellers' *own* perceptions of ethnic identity markers, that a clear consensus of opinion existed on specific cultural traits, behaviours and appearances that marked an individual out as a member of the community, as someone who could be automatically identified by other Gypsies and Travellers even if able to 'pass' to outsiders. Thus phrases such as 'you know one as soon as you see another Traveller – see him walking out that shop? He's one, and her over there' were common. Accordingly, markers of identity and performance of such behaviours were jealously guarded, with respondents speaking animatedly about fluency in Cant/Gammon or Romani,[2] the extent to which they, their parents or grandparents 'travelled', and the quality, age and style of jewellery or other adornments that could confer status on an individual or alternatively lead to indications of 'gorjification' and 'undesirable' blurring of boundaries between populations living in close proximity.

As can thus be seen, the apparent external lack of differentiation between entwined communities (other than at moments of tension) *and* the popular stereotype of 'outsider' Gypsies can both mask complex, dynamic sets of social relationships and local narratives, effectively excluding recognition of the changing nature of rural communities and the impact of 'affluent incomers' on creating and reifying notions of 'authentic' (acceptable) Gypsies (typified by painted, horse-drawn wagons, which ironically are more commonly used by 'New Travellers' who may benefit from the picturesque nature of their accommodation – see Greenfields, 2010). Accordingly, uninformed attempts to pigeon hole members of these communities into a 'place' (geographical and social) in rural England can thus impact on the lived reality of long-established rural communities where Gypsies and Travellers (both housed or sited) and their sedentary neighbours may 'have knowed each other since we was kids' (see further Smith and Greenfields, 2013).

Gypsies, Travellers and changing community patterns

As alluded to above, in many ways the nub of traditional interactions between Gypsies, Travellers and their sedentary neighbours has been the mutually beneficial symbiotic relationship that existed between the communities, despite the enactment of centuries of legislation that sought to curtail nomadism and enforce sedentarism upon travelling people (Mayall, 1995). Romany Gypsies were first recorded in Britain in the early sixteenth century, and Irish Travellers were noted as traversing mainland Britain and working as itinerant pot-menders (*tinklers*, from which the derogatory term 'tinkers' was derived) by the mid-seventeenth century (Kenrick, 2004). Gypsies and Travellers are therefore among the oldest minority ethnic communities in Britain (Clark and Greenfields, 2006), traditionally occupying a position of accepted, additional rural labour during harvest time, and moving on when their labour was no longer required.

Until the mid-twentieth century, the majority of Gypsies and Travellers (across not only Britain but also most of Europe) resided in tents or wagons and travelled for work purposes, the most important being trading (e.g., of horses, scrap metal, clothes and carpets), the provision of entertainment (for example, traditional roles included working as musicians and fortune tellers) and engaging in the seasonal agricultural work that was so crucial to pre-industrial society. Such activities – and specifically land work – were a major source of employment for Gypsies and Travellers until the post-war development of new technologies largely eliminated the need for manual field labour.

In addition to the traditional travelling life of nomadic Gypsies there is a long history of housed Travellers residing in urban (and peri-urban/semi-rural) working-class areas, with many such families travelling in the summer and spending the winter lodging in small towns or on the semi-permanent camps that grew on the edges of urban centres. In time such settlements became incorporated into towns and cities (Birmingham, London, Bristol and Southampton had well defined 'Gypsy' areas for example) as development swamped isolated hamlets, until by the late nineteenth century (Mayall, 1988) many Gypsies and Travellers lived in close proximity to both small towns and great urban conurbations, as more families were travelling smaller distances for shorter durations, thus blurring the residential boundaries between tent and caravan dwellers and the rural and urban poor.

In the late nineteenth century and throughout the early twentieth century the relationship between Gypsies, Travellers and their neighbours was often characterised by limited spatial and social/moral distance: distinctions between nomadism and sedentarism were often less clear cut than today, with Gypsies merely one element of a wide range of peripatetic groups that included 'navvies', itinerant artisans, 'tramps' and (after the failure of the potato crop in the 1840s) large numbers of destitute Irish. In addition to the above groups could be found the travelling 'brush and basket makers, horse dealers, tinkers, cheapjacks, miscellaneous hawkers, travelling potters, fairground people and the like' (Fraser, 1995: 216).

Accordingly, for Gypsies and Travellers, as well as a significant number of the semi-itinerant working classes who were 'on the tramp' for work, an annual cycle might involve obtaining lodgings in a market town (typically rooms shared with extended family members) or negotiating with a farmer who was agreeable for a household to 'winter up' on his land in a barn, or to 'pull' their caravans on his land in exchange for the provision of help with livestock as required for the winter months. Once the warmer weather arrived a period of seasonal nomadism would begin, perhaps obtaining work in farms or on market gardens in Sussex or Surrey (conveniently near to the major markets of London) and then beginning the circuit of harvesting throughout the summer and early autumn months – following the various harvests on a well-trodden route, where known and respected families would return again and again to work for a familiar farmer, with the relationship persisting through the generations as a farmer died or passed the land to his son, and the families of Gypsies in turn would continue to work the land as their older people passed away or became too frail to be of significant help in undertaking field work.

The huge benefit of such systems for both farmers and Gypsies/Travellers was that the entire family would work together – frequently alongside local villagers (or, in the case of the Kent hop-fields, itinerant Londoners who would come out from the East End for several weeks, living and working alongside their Romany neighbours) – maximising the income for the extended group, as everyone from small children upwards participated in the labour, with the harvest typically paid for by the weight or measure rather than on a daily rate. Consequently, movement between country and town and in and out of lodgings (if there was no place to pitch a bender tent or station a caravan) or campsites (where such existed) was dictated largely by demands for labour and agricultural cycles (Samuel, 1973). The presence of areas where Gypsies and Travellers could winter up, utilise a traditional 'halting place', or retain a semi-permanent presence are still well attested by the plethora of Gypsy Hills, Romany Roads and Tinkers' Lanes across rural (and indeed urban) settings, and indicate that in earlier decades nomadic people were widely accepted as part of everyday life.

Unsurprisingly, in circumstances of such propinquity, interpersonal relations developed (in much the same way as Greenfields and Smith (2011) identify for twenty-first-century Gypsies and *gorjas* co-resident on local authority housing estates), with Mayall (1988) noting that marriage between Gypsies and *gorjas* was not uncommon in the eighteenth and nineteenth centuries, becoming more frequent with the increasingly urban/peri-urban presence of Travellers as the century drew to a close and winter work opportunities were more likely to be town based.

Essentially, therefore, while increasing relationships with town based employment and the growth of urbanisation even in hitherto rural areas meant that Gypsies and Travellers might – during certain periods of the year – have been less likely to be performing purely rural/farming activities, it is clear that a significant percentage of this population were actively resident in, and closely engaged with, rurality and rural populations until large-scale, rapid economic and social change after World War II rendered many itinerant jobs obsolete. The simultaneous development of mechanised harvesting equipment and wide-ranging government legislation, aimed at 'tidying up' the hitherto essentially unregulated housing anomalies (which meant that large numbers of bombed out urbanites and returning soldiers lived in caravans, buses or accommodation devised from old chicken-sheds and railway carriages alongside their Traveller neighbours), resulted in profound changes in the traditional economic practices and nomadic lifestyles of Gypsies and Travellers (see Belton, 2005; Smith and Greenfields, 2013). Subsequent policy initiatives speeded up the pace of change, and a number of long-standing semi-rural 'mixed' communities were demolished with startling speed as families were forcibly moved from sites and caravans into newly built housing estates, where regulations proliferated and the comforts of running water and modern living standards failed signally (for many) to compensate for the loss of community and a traditional way of life (Kenrick and Clark, 1999).

Over a relatively few years (recalled in a number of recently published oral histories, e.g., McKinley, 2011; Richardson and Smith-Bendall, 2012; and narratives collected by Smith and Greenfields, 2013), a nomadic lifestyle became increasingly difficult to retain, with interviewees noting the rapid pace of regulation, which meant that a physically hard life, but one that was overwhelmingly recalled in retrospective narrative as happy and with a degree of spontaneity and freedom, was curtailed by: increasing demand for building and agricultural land; a decline in stopping places; stringent planning laws; and successive policies that to all intents and purposes outlawed nomadism and sought to settle the travelling population either on permanent caravan sites or into housing. Indeed, Kenrick and Clark (1999) estimated that half of every generation of Romany Gypsies has made the transition into housing throughout the twentieth century as a result of draconian planning laws and a shortage of sites, and, as is graphically illustrated by the findings of a series of Gypsy Traveller Accommodation Assessments (GTAAs – required by law under the 2004 Housing Act[3]), the high level of conflict over the development of unauthorised Gypsy caravan sites, which plagues rural community relations, is rooted in a long-term persistent failure of local authorities to provide or permit developments of caravan sites for Gypsy/Traveller communities, who stubbornly resist their forced assimilation and cling to a determination to travel and live a sited life as did their parents and grandparents before them.

This chapter does not seek to provide an overview of successive planning policies (see instead Clark and Greenfields, 2006; Kenrick, 2004; Cemlyn *et al.*, 2009). Rather, we are concerned with how employment opportunities and social practices have been ruptured following these abrupt social transitions, leading to disruption of long-standing relationships and contested use of place within rural communities.

Indeed, as one elderly Gypsy male expressed forcibly during a focus group undertaken for research carried out by Greenfields and Smith into the experiences of housed Gypsies and Travellers:

> See what you've got to understand, is that our people kept the countryside, we kept them fields, grew new crops, kept the farms and fed this country through two world wars. By rights, as we never always got paid for the work, that countryside is ours and we get very upset when we drive through and see obstructions like housing estates rather than the willow tree. The hassle [Hazel] tree and the old cobnut tree have all been uprooted for monstrosities these settled folk choose to live in.
>
> (Smith and Greenfields, 2013: 97)

Employment changes and the impact on inter-ethnic rural contact

As has been described above, the enforced sedentarisation of Gypsies and Travellers (and the loss of the ability to 'just get up and go when you've had enough of a place' – middle aged Gypsy male, south-west England, interviewed by Greenfields for a GTAA) has been demonstrated to impact negatively on both social relations and employment opportunities for a population that has largely valued physical trades and skills over academic qualifications – a preference which, in an era of declining manual labour and increased demand for a regulated, accredited, IT literate labour force, limits employment opportunities significantly for many members of their community.

As discussed in great detail in Cemlyn *et al.* (2009) and texts considered within that review, Gypsies and Travellers are, for a variety of reasons, associated with nomadism, cultural mistrust of education and gender segregation as well as a tradition of early school leaving, educational disadvantage, and high levels of illiteracy (which are consistently reported across the populations including young adults and teenagers). As one interviewee cited in Greenfields and Lowe (2013) pointed out, young women tend still to 'marry young [and leave school very early] . . . they are not expected to be literate . . . it is not seen as a requirement or a necessity'. In a highly gendered society, young men too (Cemlyn *et al.*, 2009; Greenfields, 2008) tend to report a desire to follow their fathers into traditional family trades such as tree-lopping, market trading and tarmac laying – work which has come to replace field labour for adaptive individuals or households who still seek to practise (and strongly stress a preference for) family-based self-employment.

One recent study into employment practices within Gypsy and Traveller communities (Ryder and Greenfields, 2010) identified various forms of economic activity practised by a sample of 95 respondents (and their household members). First, there were those engaged in the 'traditional Traveller economy', that is, earning a living in traditional Gypsy/Traveller work practices distinguished by some or all of the following characteristics: self-employment often within close family and kin networks, in-family training, non-separation of work/home place, sharing of labour and tools, entrepreneurialism, and so forth. Such work included trading at markets, landscape gardening, dealing in scrap metal and cultural trades/arts such as being a semi-professional musician. Second, there was 'employment in mainstream sectors' (service industries, professional practices such as teaching, and office work), and third (at the time the study was undertaken a major growth industry) 'community development'/intra-ethnic community work.

Among interviewees engaged in the Traveller economy, one quarter had received no or virtually no formal education, while nearly two thirds had received some education (mainly at primary school level). The overwhelming majority of respondents had no formal qualifications despite frequently being highly skilled. Only six interviewees working within the Traveller economy had gained any vocational qualifications (e.g., City and Guilds certificates in practical skills), and none had academic qualifications.

It was noteworthy that Gypsy and Irish Traveller women were far more likely than men to move away from the Traveller economy into waged labour, with only a quarter of all female interviewees below the age of 30 engaged in traditional Traveller economy practices. Housed Gypsy and Traveller women (particularly if unmarried or divorced) were most likely to be involved in 'mainstream' employment practices, engaging with colleagues in settings that transcended expectations or performances of ethnicity. One woman (an estate agent in a small town in a rural area) interviewed for Smith and Greenfields's (2012) exploration of employment practices among housed Gypsies and Travellers stressed that, while not actively disguising who she was, she would not openly reveal her ethnic identity to either colleagues or clients: 'I sell them houses. They don't know who I am. I'm just a nice lady who finds them a home.'

One particularly striking finding was that the decline in the Traveller economy had in recent decades led to a dramatic reduction in 'traditional' manual kin-based labour, to the extent that only 40 per cent of the sample (compared to over 80 per cent of their parents' generation) worked in traditional trades (see above). While individuals engaged in such work consisted mainly of networks of male kin, such as brothers, fathers and sons, or brothers-in-law, in a number of cases female relatives were also actively engaged in working in such family businesses, either directly in administration duties, such as dealing with booking clients and keeping books/paperwork if they were more literate than their husbands, or, where market-trading was involved, working alongside their male relatives selling such items as three piece suites or carpets.

The retention of attenuated traditional economic practices (e.g., manual kin-based employment working with intra-ethnic networks) was found to correlate closely to place of residence, with most of such respondents (76 per cent of those employed in the Traveller economy) living on Gypsy caravan sites. The majority of these sites consisted of privately owned single-family residences, which allowed access to a pool of kin-based labour and the use of closely bonded capital to provide intelligence about employment opportunities. Clearly, access to accommodation on sites, with linked homespace–working areas and close kin networks (in essence a traditional model of residence such as would have been found prior to large-scale sedentarisation) facilitates engagement with the Traveller Economy. Conversely, individuals resident in housing, whose social and community networks had frequently been disrupted (Greenfields and Smith, 2011), and who did not have the skills or literacy to enter into adaptive forms of employment, were found to be in steep economic decline, with high rates of unemployment (see Smith and Greenfields, 2012). Shortages of Gypsy and Traveller sites, therefore, had a clear correlation to decline in economic well-being and increased rates of unemployment among Gypsies and Travellers (see Cemlyn *et al.*, 2009, for a discussion of high levels of unemployment among members of the communities).

While Smith and Greenfields (2012), Greenfields (2008) and Ryder and Greenfields (2010) all found that young women in particular were more likely to seek employment (or education) outside of traditional Traveller economies (albeit with a relatively high percentage of women engaged in poorly paid and low skilled service industry roles such as cleaning), in terms of economic status and employment opportunities all the above studies suggested that a polarisation was occurring within the communities, with many Gypsies and Travellers experiencing high rates of long-term unemployment, poverty and multiple forms of disadvantage, while better qualified or more adaptive individuals (particularly those with access to traditional networks and forms of accommodation that enable them to retain traditional employment practices) were sustaining a relatively high standard of living.

Ryder and Greenfields (2010) in their targeted study of employed/professional Gypsies and Travellers found that approximately 60 per cent of the interviewees in waged employment (as distinct from self-employed respondents) were female; and of those women who had made a successful transition to mainstream fields of work, a significant number were working in the *at that time* (prior to fiscal austerity and significant cuts in public funding) growth industries of community development, arts and culture, enabling them to retain links to their community and exercise their cultural capital without outraging proprieties through engaging in work that transcended ethnic boundaries. As one woman stated, 'working with your own community is alright – but if you were working in a pub or outside – your husband wouldn't allow it'. For a number of these women, volunteering in a community project aimed at their own population was a major step into paid employment, boosting their confidence and allowing them to develop bridging capital and transferable skills that then enabled them to apply for work in other community settings (e.g., ethnic minority education achievement service support staff; community outreach officers in multi-ethnic settings).

In contrast, male respondents (other than a small elite of highly qualified individuals who overwhelmingly reported 'hiding' their identity and ethnicity from their colleagues in settings such as education, local government or other professional contexts) were repeatedly found, in all of the employment studies cited above, to have a reportedly lower level of engagement with non-Gypsy/Traveller communities than would appear to have been the case within their parents' generation. To some extent this was an artefact of lower levels of employment engagement for a substantial minority of the population, as GTAA evidence consistently finds unemployment among Gypsy/Traveller men at levels of 40–50 per cent, complicated by high rates of ill health and premature morbidity associated with genetic predispositions to certain conditions (e.g., chronic arthritis/cardio-vascular disease) and with injuries received working in manual trades (see Cemlyn *et al.*, 2009).

While GTAA evidence from a number of rural locations found that self-employed business men (e.g., landscape gardeners, plastic fascia installers, electricians, builders, etc.) were engaged in delivering services to mainstream/*gorja* neighbours or clients, a theme which was repeatedly emphasised (as indeed it also was by a number of women who worked in offices or settings where Gypsy/Traveller ethnicity was regarded as potentially stigmatising – see further Cemlyn *et al.*, 2009) was the need to 'pass' or 'disguise' their ethnicity. One man in a rural area of southern central England indicated that:

> I'm the boss – I employ people and pay wages for a number of people round here. First I'd employ a Traveller, but then a *gorjer* if they're alright – some of the lads – *gorjer* boys – I've known their fathers because their fathers worked along of my father and me when I was younger. So that's alright – we're straight. But I'd not tell or say to the people who phone up – see the advert and want the work doing – they don't know Travellers, [they] believe the stereotypes we're all thieving and lying. *So they don't know and won't be told by people round here* [emphasis added] that we're Travelling men. We just go in quote and do the work well – nice and simple. And no complications.

Typically, men working in the self-employed traditional Traveller economy would also refer to techniques that emphasised and supported their separation from surrounding rural populations:

- 'use a care-of address so they don't know we're on a site';
- 'mobile phone number – they can't tell where we are then';
- 'wouldn't tell them I'm a Traveller – once they know that – the work would dry up'.

In contrast, while women in 'professions' or working in offices/shops were more likely to disguise their ethnicity from colleagues than were those employed in service industries, there was evidence from several GTAAs and focus groups/interviews for the studies considered above that Gypsy and Traveller women (perhaps because they were regarded as unthreatening as a result of their gender) felt more comfortable in revealing their ethnicity to co-workers than did men:

- 'several [other] Travelling women I'm working with';
- 'actually working at the hairdresser is good – my boss likes it 'cos all my cousins and aunties come in to get their hair done';
- 'oh they knows I live on the site but that's alright because we're local and I'm reliable and he knows I will clean it lovely and don't mind doing the extra hours when needed – as long as he pays me'.

There is thus evidence to suggest that men working in the Traveller economy (and also people in the role of a 'professional', which one may posit is thus perceived as an oppositional category to an ethnic identity as a Gypsy or Traveller) are (or believe themselves to be) largely constrained in their social relations with surrounding populations, identifying a belief that close contact with gorjers/country people who are not familiar with Gypsies and Travellers will have negative repercussions on their economic and social well-being.

Challenging stereotypes and inter-ethnic contacts

The duration of relationships, as well as the context in which social relations first occur, appears to be a mediating variable that impacts on whether or how Gypsies and Travellers relate socially to those of other communities. Smith and Greenfields (2012) found that, of the housed interviewees in the four study areas in which they worked, most respondents aged 35 and over had experience of farm work and recalled travelling with their families for such employment when younger. Consequently, focus groups and interviews revealed a strong sense of nostalgia for field work and the sense of community engendered by such side-by-side working with other rural residents. The decline in agricultural employment and resultant reduction of social contact with non-Gypsy labour was identified by several respondents:

> Everyone used to be on farms, whether they be Traveller or *gorjer*, we were all on farms and we all worked together. But nowadays that's not

> there, that's gone. And because that's gone, I think that is the reason attitudes towards us have got worse.
>
> (Female, south-east England)

> We've growed up around here – seen a lot of changes – but we're local for generations – but nowadays most of the people they're not from round here – moved out here ten years ago or so when the housing went up – not got the memories, don't know how it works – drive to the supermarkets, don't use the local pub – go somewhere fancy, don't stop and say hello – because we've not had the same experience – and they'd not think that is X and I knows his brother and his dad and his brother-in-law so he's alright he's from round here – they'd be thinking X is a dirty Gypo if they knew what we was.
>
> (Male, south-west England)

When considering the nature of inter-ethnic connections and contacts in rural contexts, identification with both place and shared tradition stand out strongly. One man living in housing in a semi-rural area interviewed by Smith and Greenfields (2013) broke away from the stereotyping of [non-Gypsy] communities which characterised some interviews, observing that 'I've known quite a few people round here anyway. All my life – and there's good and bad in all. I've had a few rows with gorgers and that [but] some are good some are bad.'

The social and geographical proximity of community members (regardless of whether or not residents lived on sites or in housing) would appear therefore to be key to the *quality* of relationships in rural settings. When coupled with a tendency for Gypsies and Travellers to settle in localities close to former stopping places, which retain continuity of association between travelling people and certain areas (see above for a discussion of localities that explicitly refer to Gypsies and Travellers in their names), this can sometimes achieve great significance in terms of the dynamics of a local neighbourhood. Thus for example, some years ago when interviewing local residents (both Gypsy and non-Gypsy) to assist in preparing a planning appeal in relation to a private site, the author of this chapter was struck both by the insistence by a number of local *gorja* residents that the site residents were 'local':

- 'got their people buried in the churchyard – you go look at the graves';
- 'known they all my life – and their parents afore – where they going to be if not there – that's always had Gypsies on it';

and simultaneously, by the outrage expressed that the lead agency campaigning against the site and challenging the right of the land owners to apply for a licence was the American Airforce, who wished to keep all locals some distance away from their base. So strong was local feeling that a petition was organised and supported by the local paper in support of the families, who were deemed to be both authentic and 'our people' in opposition to international incomers.

While this is perhaps an extreme example, a number of studies and interviews undertaken for Smith and Greenfields (2013) found that clear demarcations were drawn between 'local' people (both Gypsy/Traveller and *gorjer* with whom many interviewees had a long and close relationship marked by both conflict *and* cooperation) and outsiders (see Greenfields, Chapter 6 in Clark and Greenfields, 2006, which explores community relations, family and identity).

One woman in a south-east focus group (in a formerly rural but now peri-urban/London overspill area where close 'mixing' had taken place for generations, associated with hop picking and agricultural work, which ultimately had led to the settlement of large numbers of Gypsies into housing) reported that:

> I live with mostly Travellers up the same road as me but I live with gorgers as well. I get on quite well with them actually. 'Cos I've been brought up with them I've known them all my life. Most of them live up my road anyway.

Another respondent in the south-west for example, cited a common pattern among the sample: 'born a few roads away, went to school local, married away – the next estate – then we come back when we got a chance. We're local people.'

While a woman in another study area reported:

> didn't want to be in a house but there were no places [on the official site]. I said if it had to be a house the only place I'd go was on [local estate] it's full of Travellers and I had loads of family on my mum's side there. I knew a lot of the gorgers from school so it weren't like I'd be around strangers.

In several localities studied by Greenfields and Smith there was a clear consensus among respondents that the major source of organised local prejudice against Gypsies and Travellers was regarded as having a clear class dimension, with organised opposition against new sites or unauthorised encampments being very rarely identified as driven by 'locals' (where any conflict is more likely to be of an individualised and personal nature), but more commonly as arising from the influx of 'middle class yuppies – don't know why they have to sell up from Lonnon [*sic*] and come down here', moving out from the cities in search of rural peace and quiet and the idyllic colour supplement lifestyle so beloved of wealthy incomers:

> You've got Londoners moving in and all our locals all the original old locals that we grew up with, me dad grew up with, me aunties and everyone else their children have never had that chance to grow up [together]. All they've grown up with is these Londoners coming in and

> everyone else from up-country and the cities saying how bad we are. How do they know? They've never lived with us.

In conclusion, this chapter commenced with a reference to a picture book 'Midsomer Murders' England – non-ethnicised, eccentric (if – in fiction – murder-prone), where close-knit networks of villagers co-reside, know each other's business and generally exist in tight webs of communication and connection. It was posited that Gypsies and Travellers would be forever 'outsiders' in the performative and imaginary context of modern rural England (as viewed by those who have forgotten or never known their narrative of belonging), perceived as having no loyalty and no right to utilise the land that 'belongs' to others, namely the white (wealthy) rural majority.

However, as demonstrated above, there is a long and deep history of local identity and associated 'belonging' in the context of the countryside, with Gypsies and Travellers frequently being the 'invisible' weft in the weave of local life, solidly grounded in the 'imagined community' (Anderson, 1991). This grounding is threatened by some incomers' dreams of a classed, non-ethnicised, geographically exclusionary rural idyll. However, Gypsies and Travellers retain significant social capital, connections which may potentially – albeit not without difficulty – be re-activated to challenge and contest these incomers' narratives of place and space, and restore Gypsy and Traveller populations to their central place in English social life.

Notes

1 *Gorger* is the Romani word for someone who is not of Romany Gypsy origins. The equivalent term used by Irish Travellers is country person (or countryman/woman) regardless of whether the person spoken of is an urban dweller.

2 These are the languages used, respectively, by many members of the Irish Traveller and Romany Gypsy communities for conversing among themselves, often admixed in the same sentence with the use of English.

3 GTAAs arose as a result of considerable policy interest within the New Labour governments of 1997–2010 in the causes of and solutions to the widespread discord between Gypsies/Travellers and mainstream society over site provision, as well as substantial anecdotal evidence from registered social landlords that significant numbers of housing placements of Gypsies and Travellers broke down fairly rapidly. Accordingly an amendment to the Housing Act 2004 required that every local authority with housing duties should seek to ascertain the preferences of members of the above communities in relation to accommodation type (see Cemlyn *et al.*, 2009, for an extensive discussion of findings, methodologies and policy approaches to site and accommodation provision for Gypsies and Travellers). Greenfields (and subsequently David Smith of Greenwich University, with Greenfields as co-researcher on a series of linked studies listed in the bibliography) was co-author with Robert Home of the first GTAA undertaken in the UK ('The Cambridge Project') (see Cemlyn *et al.*, 2009). In addition, Greenfields later worked on a series of GTAAs in rural areas as well as follow up depth qualitative studies, culminating in the major research with David Smith into the experiences of housed Gypsies and Travellers (Smith and Greenfields, 2013).

Quotations in this chapter have been drawn from a number of sources – for example, various GTAAs on which the author has worked; Smith and Greenfields (2013); and Gypsy/Traveller health needs assessments in rural areas (Greenfields with Lowe 2013).

References

Anderson, B. (1991) *Imagined Communities: Reflections on the Origin and Spread of Nationalism*. London: Verso.

Agyeman, J. and Spooner, R. (1997) 'Ethnicity and the rural environment', in P. Cloke and J. Little (eds), *Contested Countryside Cultures: Otherness, Marginalisation and Rurality*. Routledge: London: 197–217.

Bailey, D. (2011) 'Vulnerable adult migrants in East Anglia', in M. Greenfields, A. Fanning and R. Dalrymple (eds), *Working with Adults at Risk of Harm*. Buckingham, UK: Oxford University Press: 231–50.

Belton, B. (2005) *Gypsy and Traveller Ethnicity: The Social Generation of an Ethnic Phenomenon*. London: Routledge.

Cemlyn S., Greenfields M., Burnett, S., Matthews, Z. and Whitwell, C. (2009) Review of Inequalities Experienced by Gypsy and Traveller Communities. London: Equalities and Human Rights Commission

Clark, C. and Greenfields, M. (eds) (2006) *Here to Stay: The Gypsies and Travellers of Britain*. Hatfield, UK: University of Hertfordshire Press.

Easton, M. (2011) 'Midsomer Murders producer suspended over race row'. *BBC News*, 15 March 2011. Available at: www.bbc.co.uk/news/uk-12741847 (accessed 10 April 2013).

Erfani-Ghettani, R. (2012) Localism, Populism and the Fight against Sites. London: Institute of Race Relations. Available at: www.irr.org.uk/news/localism-populism-and-the-fight-against-sites (accessed 27 March 2013).

Fraser, A. (1995) *The Gypsies*. Oxford: Blackwell.

Greenfields, M. (2008) *A Good Job for a Traveller? Exploring Gypsy and Travellers' Perceptions of Health and Social Care Careers: Barriers and Solutions to Recruitment Training and Retention of Social Care Students*. High Wycombe: Bucks New University/Aim Higher South East.

Greenfields, M. (2010) 'Romany roots: Gypsies and Travellers in Britain, sustaining belonging and identity over 600 years of nomadising', in L. DePretto, G. Macri and C. Wong (eds), *Diasporas: Revisiting and Discovering*. Oxford: Inter-Disciplinary Press: 245–65.

Greenfields, M. with Lowe, L. (2013) The North Somerset and BANES Gypsy/Traveller/Showman/Boater/Roma Health Needs Assessments. High Wycombe: IDRICS.

Greenfields, M. and Smith, D. (2010) 'Housed Gypsy Travellers, social segregation and the reconstruction of communities', *Housing Studies* 25(3), May: 397–412.

Greenfields, M. and Smith D. (2011) 'A question of identity: The social exclusion of housed Gypsies and Travellers', *Research, Policy and Planning* 28(3): 65–78

Halfacree, K. (1996) 'Out of place in the country: Travellers and the rural idyll', *Antipode* 28(1): 42–72.

Holloway, S. (2005) 'Articulating otherness? White rural residents talk about Gypsy-Travellers', *Transactions of the Institute of British Geographers* 30: 351–67.

Holloway, S. (2003) 'Outsiders in rural society? Constructions of rurality and nature – Society relations in the racialisation of English Gypsy-Travellers, 1869–1934', *Environment and Planning D: Society and Space* 21(6): 695–715.

Kenrick, D. (2004) *Gypsies: From the Ganges to the Thames*. Hatfield, UK: University of Hertfordshire Press.

Kenrick, D. and Clark, C. (1999) *Moving On: The Gypsies and Travellers of Britain*. Hatfield, UK: University of Hertfordshire Press.

McKinley, R. (2011) *Gypsy Girl. A Life on the Road: A Journey to Freedom*. London: Hodder & Stoughton.

Markova, E. and Black, R. (2007) East European Immigration and Community Cohesion. York, UK: Joseph Rowntree Foundation/University of Sussex Centre for Migration Research

Mayall, D. (1988) *Gypsy-Travellers in Nineteenth-Century Society*. Cambridge: Cambridge University Press.

Mayall, D. (1995) *English Gypsies and State Policies: Interface Collection*. Hatfield, UK: University of Hertfordshire Press.

Morris, R. (2000) 'Gypsies, Travellers and the media: Press regulation and racism in the UK', *Communications Law* 5(6): 213–19. Available at: www.media-diversity.org/en/additional-files/documents/Z%20Current%20MDI%20Resources/Gypsies,%20Travellers%20and%20the%20media%20-20press%20regulation%20and%20racism%20in%20the%20UK.pdf (accessed 7 April 2013).

Powell, R. (2007) 'Civilising offensives and ambivalence: The case of British Gypsies', *People, Place and Policy Online* 1(3): 112–23.

Richardson, J. (2006) *The Gypsy Debate: Can Discourse Control?* Exeter, UK: Imprint Academic.

Ryder, A. and Greenfields, M. (2010) *Roads to Success: Routes to Economic and Social Inclusion for Gypsies and Travellers*. London, ITMB.

Richardson, J. and Smith-Bendall, M. (2012) 'Accommodation needs and planning issues', in J. Richardson and A. Ryder (eds), *Gypsies and Travellers Empowerment and Inclusion in British Society*. Bristol, UK: Policy Press: 21–42.

Samuel, R. (1973) 'Comers and goers', in H. G. Dyos and M. Wolff (eds), *The Victorian City: Images and Realities*, vol. 1. London: Routledge: 123–60.

Sibley, D (1997), 'Endangering the sacred: Nomads, youth cultures and the English countryside', in P. Cloke and J. Little (eds), *Contested Countryside Cultures. Otherness, Marginalisation and Rurality*. Routledge: London: 218–52.

Simmel, G. (1971) 'The stranger', in D. Levine (ed.), *Georg Simmel: On Individuality and Social Forms*, Chicago, IL: University of Chicago Press: 143–9.

Smith, D. and Greenfields, M. (2013) *Gypsies and Travellers in Housing: The Decline of Nomadism*. Bristol, UK: Policy Press

White, Anne (2011) 'The mobility of polish families in the west of England: Translocalism and attitudes to return', *Studia Migracyjne-Przegląd Polonijny* 37(1): 11–32.

Williams, C. (2007) Revisiting the rural/race debates: A view from the Welsh countryside, *Ethnic and Racial Studies* 30(5): 741–65.

Part IV

Consumed rurality

16 Capitalising on rurality

Tourism micro-businesses in rural tourism destinations

Claire Haven-Tang and Eleri Jones

Introduction

The backbone of the tourism industry, whether urban or rural, comprises a plethora of private-sector businesses that are dominated by micro-businesses employing less than ten people and straddling several different standard industrial classifications. In Wales, micro-businesses (0–9 employees) account for 94 per cent of the total number of enterprises in Wales with the highest proportion located in rural local authority areas, such as Ceredigion, Carmarthenshire, Gwynedd, Isle of Anglesey, Monmouthshire, Pembrokeshire and Powys (Welsh Government, 2011a). Micro-businesses dominate the wholesale, retail, transport, hotels, food and communication sector (which incorporates tourism-related businesses) in terms of the total number of enterprises and employment accounting for 92 per cent of employment in these sectors (Welsh Government, 2011a). These figures illustrate the critical importance of micro-businesses to the economic sustainability of the Welsh tourism industry, particularly in rural destinations.

Rural destinations face significant transformation (Roberts and Hall, 2004); as 'traditional views of farming and the rural landscape are not consistent with the realities of agriculture today' (Thorbeck, 2012: 57). Urry and Larsen (2011) suggest modern agriculture, together with tourist inclinations for alternative and purportedly 'authentic' experiences, is changing traditional rural life and escalating rural tourism destination consumption. Tourists have always been attracted to certain kinds of rural destinations (Edgell and Harbaugh, 1993; Alexander and McKenna, 1998; George and Reid, 2005; Sharpley, 2007; Lane, 2009), and Howie (2004) defines rurality from a tourism perspective to include not just the characteristics of the places themselves but also the cultural meaning attached to them. This suggests that coherence between an internally understood and externally communicated rural identity is particularly important for rural business strategies and tourism policies so as to avoid simplistic assumptions about the meaning of rurality in a touristic context (Giles *et al.*, 2013).

To support and maintain rural economies, tourism has been adopted as a development strategy in many rural destinations and is often seen as a way of resolving many problems facing rural communities (Wilson *et al.*, 2001; George and Reid, 2005; Nylander and Hall, 2005; Williams and Ferguson, 2005; Garrod *et al.*, 2006; Huang, 2006; Mair, 2006; George, Mair and Reid, 2009; Lane, 2009; Haven-Tang and Jones, 2012; Melsen, 2012). This approach is encapsulated by Page and Getz (1997:18):

> With changes in the economic structures of rural areas, as agricultural employment declined in the post-war period, rural planning has adopted a more positive strategy towards rural tourism as a form of employment generation to off-set out-migration and a declining population base, and to sustain thresholds for service provision.

The significance of tourism to the rural economy was crystallised following the 2001 Foot and Mouth Disease (FMD) outbreak in the UK, when tourism was shown to be more important to the rural economy than agriculture (Sharpley and Craven, 2001; Scott *et al.*, 2004; Sharpley and Vass, 2006; Lane, 2009) with 'economic losses to tourism estimated at four times the loss to agriculture' (Sinclair, 2004, cited in Cochrane, 2009: 69). In addition, the FMD outbreak raised the profile of the tourism industry in terms of government support and rural development strategies (Cochrane, 2009). Consequently, rural tourism is pivotal in relation to: job creation; farm diversification; developing local food and drink supply networks; reducing leakage through promoting linkages; destination resource stewardship and community cohesion. Tourism also has the capacity to positively contribute to rural communities and synchronise other economic sectors, for example, transport and food production.

The European Commission (2007: 18) suggest that stakeholders take an integrated and holistic approach to destination development and define a tourism destination as:

> An area of visitor appeal which includes accommodation, attractions, and support services. It may be defined by physical, thematic, or administrative boundaries and it embraces a set of distinctive images and qualities that give it a brand identity. Destinations should be places with which tourism stakeholders have a natural affinity and within which it is practicable for them to work together.

Embedded within this definition is the principle that tourism destinations can only function successfully if they prove consequential to relevant stakeholders (e.g., tourism businesses, local authorities, local communities, tourists) and have a distinct identity that accords with local perceptions (Giles *et al.*, 2013). However, the composition and scope of the tourism industry emphasises fragmentation within destinations, as some businesses, e.g. pubs and golf clubs, may not see themselves as part of the tourism industry. Thus, despite tourism destinations being perceived by tourists as a coordinated set of places to stay and visit, the reality is that tourism destinations may be uncoordinated with incoherent images and therefore be less competitive in domestic and international markets than is desirable.

Howie (2003: 1) emphasises destination complexity in terms of the lack of 'a single owner or manager of a destination, and so . . . there is less chance of a coherent set of goals and objectives'. This situation is often exacerbated in rural tourism destinations because of their characteristics – the combination of natural and human landscapes within a working landscape, together with sparse and scattered communities, geographical isolation and low population density compared to urban areas (Richardson, 2000; Thorbeck, 2012).

In Wales, in order to promote economic growth and sustainable jobs, the Programme for Government (Welsh Government, 2011b) identifies several key actions to support the economy, businesses and rural communities, including: diversifying and strengthening the rural economy through the development of innovative products and tourism activities; identifying niche markets; investing in quality tourism businesses to ensure Wales has a high-quality tourism offer; and taking a holistic approach to promoting Wales as a tourism destination. This chapter discusses the opportunities offered by rural tourism critiquing the generic challenges for tourism micro-businesses and the additional challenges for micro-businesses within rural tourism destinations, such as Wales. Rurality presents various challenges, such as marketing, product differentiation, destination branding, information and connectivity, and exploitation of the tourism value chain. Specific business examples from Monmouthshire – a rural county in Wales, where tourism is a significant economic contributor – £163 million in 2011 (GTS (UK) Ltd/Monmouthshire County Council, 2012) – helps to develop insights and enhance understandings of rurality and tourism micro-businesses.

Rural tourism

The repositioning of the rural economy from an 'agricultural orientation to a service orientation' (Cochrane, 2009: 65) with tourism as a key player and 'an attractive object of the tourist gaze' (Urry and Larsen, 2011: 108) has been considerable, spurred on by the growth in niche tourism markets (e.g., fishing tourism, walking tourism, equine tourism, cycling tourism, food tourism, adventure tourism), short breaks and staycations (Fox, 2009; Sharma, 2009; Alexander *et al.*, 2011). However, consuming the rural environment for leisure purposes is not a recent trend and existed before the Industrial Revolution (Howie, 2003; Beeton, 2006; Urry and Larsen, 2011), albeit as an activity for the more affluent sectors of society until the mid-twentieth century (George *et al.*, 2009).

The transformation of the Olympic Stadium into an English rural idyll at the beginning of the London 2012 Opening Ceremony emphasised that 'the rural idyll remains an important image and motivator to today's rural tourists' (Beeton, 2006: 145) with rural tourists attracted by what Garrod *et al.* (2004, cited in Garrod *et al.*, 2006: 119) termed 'countryside capital' for example, landscape, wildlife, geology, agricultural buildings, rural settlements, historic features, distinctive local customs, water features, woods. Mair (2006) outlines a range of aspects that make tourism an attractive development opportunity for rural communities, including destination topography, which determines the type of activities that might be suitable, the socio-economic history and how this is aligned with regional and national economies, and the increased external demand for rural tourism activities and cultural experiences.

Page and Getz (1997) accentuate that tourism in rural destinations may not always be a panacea for rural economic diversification and regeneration because of the characteristics of tourism, for example, seasonality, low pay, low skills and economic leakage. Indeed, the essence of rurality in a destination may even be threatened by the commercial and urbanising influence of tourism (Lane, 2005; Inkson and Minnaert, 2012). Similarly, Cresswell, while accepting the image and heritage of the rural idyll, reminds us that the rural image can be vulnerable, for example following 'Mad Cow Disease, Foot and Mouth and the increasing visibility of rural poverty' (2004: 113). Nevertheless, George *et al.* (2009: 9) assert that 'rural is constructed, perceptually at least, as a contrast to the urban . . . However false these assumptions may or may not be, in tourism development, this perception is a key factor'. This assertion underpins the definition, classification and structure of rural tourism systems.

Challenges for rural tourism micro-businesses

Tourism micro-businesses have very different approaches to setting and maintaining quality standards, which are critical for business and destination-level competitiveness. Many micro-businesses adopt short-term approaches to business planning and are disinterested in growth as a business strategy or in contributing to destination development and the overall destination proposition. The 'implications of this, not only for the individual SME but also for the image of the destination, are profound' (Jones *et al.*, 2004a: 78). Furthermore, many tourism micro-businesses have difficulties in asserting their own identity and recognising the role they play in the bigger picture of destination development.

There are 'few handicaps to entering the industry but some operators are poorly prepared and therefore businesses are underperforming' (Wales Tourist Board, 2000: 40) and Beeton (2006: 152) refers to 'false expectations and naivety' of people who retire to run a tourism business. This ease of entry to the tourism industry for new operators often results in weak endemic business models, perpetuated by an 'anyone can do it' mentality. Skills gaps exist among some owner–managers who often lack the knowledge and skills to manage their business and/or their staff. This has major implications for human resource functions and 'poor retention rates are often the result of poor management abilities' (Haven and Jones, 2004: 25), with operators accepting labour turnover and recruitment difficulties as part of the industry, rather than recognising the extra pressure these difficulties create for existing staff coupled with an inability to operate at full capacity. Naturally, this impacts on product development, business performance and investment in training and development (Haven and Jones, 2004).

There are reports that some tourism operators still 'compete on price rather than on value' (Wales Tourist Board, 2000: 64), ignoring other aspects of customer perceptions of quality. Ultimately, this reduces competitiveness, restricts profitability and limits opportunities for re-investment at an individual business level, consequently impacting upon the destination. Such approaches, coupled with a lack of embeddedness, do little to promote linkages within rural tourism destinations. Sourcing non-local produce on the basis of cost creates leakage in the local economy – the Danish bacon effect, whereby food products are selected on price rather than quality and provenance. To achieve the full potential of the tourism value chain (Mitchell and Ashley, 2010) in the destination and benefit local supply chains, imports need to be minimised and local supply chains promoted. Weak business models and underdeveloped management infrastructures and quality systems obstruct the creation of 'joined-up' destinations that have a coherent marketing image (Jones and Haven, 2004).

Individually, tourism micro-businesses have very different business strategies – some are well managed and effectively exploit their resources for business growth, others are 'lifestyle' businesses and seriously lack business and management skills. Beaver *et al.* (1998) highlight disparities among tourism micro-businesses in relation to the aims and objectives of individual businesses, which are not always consistent with commercial objectives, for example, business growth and profit maximisation or their extent of engagement with public-sector interventions to aid destination development: 'The entrepreneurial metaphor can suggest more homogeneity than is the case' (Beaver *et al.*, 1998: 165). Beaver *et al.* (1998: 166) identify self-employment and control as important motives for entrepreneurship and offer a taxonomy of entrepreneurial types: the 'entrepreneurial venture' describing firms dedicated to growth that embrace emergent opportunities; the 'lifestyle enterprise' providing economic survival and desired lifestyles for owner–managers; the 'family enterprise' providing family members with homes and jobs; the 'female enterprise' for women entrepreneurs. Beeton (2006: 152) asserts that small family businesses are primarily motivated to enter the tourism industry, by exploiting the assets of their location and existing business, in an effort to diversify and 'move away from a mono-economic base'. While this approach might add diversity to the destination, it can often compound a lack of coherence within the wider destination, as individual micro-businesses do their own thing, regardless of any wider destination strategy.

Di Domenico's (2005) study of lifestyle entrepreneurs in Scotland strengthens the belief that the personal motivations of lifestyle entrepreneurs are not necessarily aligned with rational economic decision-making. Her study found that lifestyle entrepreneurs do not measure business success in terms of growth criteria but desire profit, financial success and other non-economic goals, such as quality of life, independently of growth. Entrepreneurs needed a specific 'way of life' influenced by their particular circumstances with business needs deemed less important than negative impacts on quality of life. This supports another study by Hall and Rusher (2005: 150) who argued that for lifestyle businesses, owner–manager's lifestyle goals are congruent with business goals as 'lifestyle is a strategic business objective'. Nevertheless, Di Domenico (2005) cited examples of downsizing, supporting the argument that lifestyle entrepreneurs lack commitment to business growth.

Particular challenges relate to inputting business support to tourism micro-businesses that are not interested in growth as a business strategy or in contributing to destination development (Tinsley and Lynch, 2001; Paniagua, 2002). 'The decision to enter the industry is often motivated by non-commercial reasons; quality of life and a desire to be one's own boss are more important considerations' (Wales Tourist Board, 2000: 40), a view supported by Bosworth and Willett (2011) who found that entrepreneurs in Cornwall were motivated by lifestyle rather than commercial objectives. Additionally, operational difficulties for micro-businesses, for example, employee issues and bureaucratic red tape, are barriers to expansion; with some operators deliberately downsizing to run employee-free businesses (Haven and Jones, 2004). This fragmentation and lack of coherence has significant implications for destination development, in terms of coordinating the consequential elements for destination stakeholders and harnessing a distinct destination identity. More sophisticated understandings of micro-business heterogeneity must be reflected in public policy designed to encourage tourism micro-businesses to participate in destination development.

Tinsley and Lynch (2001) emphasised the dynamic role of micro-business networks in destination development, but recognised that destination development is usually expressed in terms of physical infrastructure developments rather than individual businesses or destination network behaviour. Gunn's (1993: 68) assertion that 'service businesses gain from clustering' is not always appreciated by the businesses themselves, and many neither communicate nor cooperate with each other or public-sector support agencies. Lynch (2000: 99) comments on the 'fortress mentality' of micro-businesses and their resistance to external interventions. At destination-level, the culture of self-reliance can be a barrier to accessing support and sharing good practice with other businesses (Wales Tourist Board, 2000).

Does rurality exacerbate these challenges?

While all tourism micro-businesses face challenges, rural micro-businesses face further complexities that can exacerbate their negative characteristics. George *et al.* (2009: 8) assert that rural landscapes and their associated communities are distinctively different in terms of lifestyle and culture and are 'a polar opposite' to the notion of urban; hence attractive to tourist markets. Conversely, for tourism micro-businesses, rurality presents a number of challenges, such as marketing; product differentiation; destination branding; information and connectivity; and exploitation of the tourism value chain within the destination. Jones *et al.* (2004b) identified clear differences between rural and urban SMEs; while location does not impact upon core competencies, it does influence specific actions. For example, rural tourism micro-businesses need to be better informed about their customers and markets – they cannot depend on transitory custom unlike their urban counterparts. Other differences include communication, partnerships and networks and strategic approaches to the workforce (Jones *et al.*, 2004b).

The nature of rural tourism destinations and the distinct lack of differentiation between destinations and products is a challenge – many have similar assets in terms of landscape, culture and heritage, so it is difficult to create a strong sense of identity with implications for destination branding. In addition, rural destination topography makes rural tourism micro-businesses geographically dispersed and fairly isolated, which reduces destination visibility and profile. Dispersion and isolation often negatively impact on the development of a coherent destination proposition and the overall destination brand. Furthermore, there is a tendency for some businesses to see themselves as 'the destination', which further complicates the coherence of the destination proposition, particularly when defining destination core resources and attractors, that is, the pull factors. Rurality and the physical structure of the surrounding environment mean that transport and technology infrastructures are under-developed, so that inaccessibility and lack of connectivity exacerbate problems of dispersion and isolation.

Inkson and Minnaert (2012) cite the inability of rural tourism micro-businesses to meet tourist expectations and consistently deliver quality experiences as a challenge for destinations that rely on the private sector to attract tourists and deliver the experience. Some rural tourism micro-businesses find it difficult to define service quality and understand the link between service quality and destination competitiveness; hence fail to recognise the role they play in overall destination development and tourist experience and the implications this has for the tourism value chain within the destination. Accordingly, rural tourism destinations probably need effective destination partnerships more than anywhere else to ensure that the benefits of tourism are distributed throughout the rural environment through linkages rather than leakages and to coordinate the small-scale private sector. As suggested by the European Commission (2007), a successful tourism destination should embrace an integrated approach towards the diverse components of the tourism system. The role of destination management organisations (DMOs) is vital to provide leadership, coordination and coherence for destination stakeholders (Ritchie and Crouch, 2003). DMOs can adopt a more localised remit than tourist boards; therefore, they can facilitate and coordinate a bottom-up approach to destination development. Interventions by DMOs and related business support services seek to promote integration and quality standards through the development of destination-level approaches to benchmarking, training and marketing to enhance destination image and its appropriate projection, maximising the potential of tourism as a vehicle for economic development in rural destinations.

How rural tourism microbusinesses can capitalise on rurality

Ritchie and Crouch (2003) advocate the development of competitive advantage, in terms of the effective longitudinal utilisation of destination resources, arguing that a resource-rich destination may be less competitive than a resource-weak – but effectively utilised – destination. However, to ensure competitive advantage for a destination, stakeholders must share a common destination vision and appreciation of how to effectively utilise destination resources (Ritchie and Crouch, 2003) to differentiate both the destination and its component products. Garrod *et al.* (2006: 126) argue the importance of dependence and embeddedness:

> While rural tourism has long been understood as an important force in the countryside, there has been little understanding of its crucial linkages to and dependence on the countryside capital assets that are its fundamental resource . . . a better understanding of this dependence is vital if tourism is to continue to make a positive contribution to sustainable rural development. If the tourism industry and its stakeholders neglect this resource base then the quality of the tourism experience is bound to decline and so will the rural tourism industry.

As a stereotypical rural tourism destination, faced with an economically unsustainable agricultural industry, Monmouthshire is a good example of how rural tourism micro-businesses can capitalise on rurality to the benefit of the business, tourists and wider rural community. Monmouthshire is one of ten unitary authorities in south-east Wales, located on the Wales–England border. In 2011, tourism generated just over £163 million for Monmouthshire, compared to £157 million in 2010 (GTS (UK) Ltd/Monmouthshire County Council, 2012). Adventa is Monmouthshire's LEADER+ rural development programme, responsible for the Axis 4 activity of Monmouthshire County Council's (MCC) Rural Development Programme and, together with the tourism department of MCC, acts as a DMO for Monmouthshire. Axis 4 funding instigates high-quality and innovative rural development projects (Adventa, 2011; Welsh European Funding Office, 2011) that add value to local products, facilitate the way in which local producers distribute and market products and emphasise cross-sector cooperation and networking.

Therefore, Adventa has a multi-faceted role within Monmouthshire and, in order to fulfil their remit, Adventa is organised around a number of strands – food, tourism, festivals and events and arts and crafts – with lead officers for each strand. Many Adventa-led projects attempt to encourage and support business opportunities and strengthen the local rural economy through cross-sector activities that encourage cooperation and collaboration. They facilitate the way in which local producers distribute and promote products to ensure that local businesses benefit from the value added when goods are marketed as traditional 'Monmouthshire' products. They coordinate farm–processor–retailer linkages, thus enhancing the local food and drink supply chain, and they identify alternative methods of promoting Monmouthshire's portfolio of natural, recreational and cultural resources; as well as new and sustainable markets for tourism and food products. The Adventa-led development of local food supply networks, for example, strengthens the local food value chain, benefits local communities, preserves local foodscapes through positive perceptions of local food and illustrates the integral role of food producers in sustainable and competitive destination development. This coordinated approach creates opportunities for wider benefits and should ensure that rural tourism businesses receive a coherent support package aligned to the development of Monmouthshire as a rural tourism destination (Haven-Tang and Jones, 2012).

Adventa led the development of the *Made in Monmouthshire* (www.madeinmonmouthshire.com) brand that supports rural economic development and adds value by showcasing the creativity and skills of local makers and producers through the promotion of high quality art, crafts and produce. The brand links non-tourism businesses to tourism businesses and vice versa, thereby enhancing linkages, strengthening the local rural economy and raising the quality of the tourism offered and tourist experiences.

At a destination-level, problems of connectivity across rural Monmouthshire are being incrementally addressed. The launch of *Monmouthpedia* – the first Wikipedia project to cover a whole town – has been a catalyst for MCC to install free wireless Internet (Wi-Fi) throughout Monmouth to facilitate the project and address connectivity issues in the town (http://en.wikipedia.org/wiki/Monmouthpedia). *Monmouthpedia* is a specific bottom-up approach to addressing connectivity issues through the installation of free Wi-Fi, as the rural nature of the area had previously been a barrier in terms of connectivity. *Monmouthpedia* uses QR (Quick Response) codes to mark points of interest, which are scanned and read through smartphones, taking tourists directly to a Wikipedia article in one of 22 languages. Addressing information and connectivity problems enables the provision of additional interpretation using QR codes and augmented reality. Thus, Adventa and MCC facilitate initiatives at destination-level to promote tourism opportunities in Monmouthshire and enable rural tourism micro-businesses to capitalise on their rurality. However, the installation of Wi-Fi supports not just destination development in terms of tourist interpretation and experiences, but also enhances quality of life and connectivity for the local rural community.

Marketing and customer information is often a problem for rural tourism micro-businesses (Jones *et al.*, 2004b); however, through the *Made in Monmouthshire* brand, some Monmouthshire businesses have opened Facebook shops that have revolutionised their business, generated new markets, provided customer information and allowed them to stay personally connected with their customer base – regardless of geographical location. *The Fabulous Fish Company* (www.facebook.com/fabulousfish) is reputedly the first in the world to sell ambient food (fresh produce) through Facebook and enables exploitation of the tourism value chain through cross-promotion of other Monmouthshire makers and producers.

Differentiation in terms of the core product and consistent delivery of quality experiences (Inkson and Minnaert, 2012) are also challenges for rural tourism micro-businesses; however, there are several micro-businesses in Monmouthshire that differentiate their products on the basis of quality and accepted industry standards. Beacon Parks Boats (www.beaconparkboats.com), for example, operate a fleet of luxury narrowboats on the Monmouthshire and Brecon Canal, which are graded as five-star by Visit Britain. This product differentiation is distinctive, developed in alignment with recognised accommodation accreditation schemes, and attracts new markets in luxury narrowboat tourists. Similarly, Ancre Hill Vineyard (www.ancrehillestates.co.uk) produces award-winning wines using biodynamic principles and practices – one of only two vineyards in the UK to do so. They also promote local cheese producers and artisan bakers through their 'Welsh cheese platter' lunches. Their approach, and the highly-regarded wine awards, puts them on national and international platforms in terms of product and place promotion; while sourcing local produce provides traceability, economic benefits for the destination by exploiting the tourism value chain within the destination, and reduces food miles. These business examples illustrate the importance of rurally focused DMOs, e.g., Adventa, in facilitating rural tourism opportunities upon which micro-businesses can capitalise.

Conclusions

In this chapter we have argued that rural tourism micro-businesses can capitalise on rurality, challenging stereotypical assumptions about size and being rurally located. While any tourism micro-business has the opportunity to capitalise on tourism regardless of their location, rurality should not matter but it does, mainly because of the complexities of rural tourism micro-businesses compared to their urban counterparts. However, rural tourism micro-businesses, including family enterprises, need robust strategic plans that reflect business marketing and development and that link with local rural communities – who form part of the rural tourism experience (Beeton, 2006), as well as other destination stakeholders. Furthermore, Garrod *et al.* (2006) advocate the use of local rural tourism projects as a way of encouraging rural tourism micro-businesses to develop destination ownership, which can enhance connections between the positive economic impacts of rural tourism and stewardship of destination countryside capital.

A destination's success is predicated on the quality of the overall tourist experience of all the destination components; yet individual components are the responsibility of individual operators. The requisite coordination and collaboration to ensure dependable quality standards is often best achieved through DMOs (Ritchie and Crouch, 2003; Dredge, 2006), particularly in rural destinations (Haven-Tang and Jones, 2012). While this chapter reflects the wider application of the DMO approach, it also demonstrates how rurality distinguishes rural tourism from urban tourism, and how rurally based DMOs encounter additional challenges in their attempts to coordinate the consequential elements for destination stakeholders and harness a distinct destination identity. Monmouthshire's distinct destination identity is based upon the award-winning, high-quality food and drink offered within the county, which gives Monmouthshire competitive advantage and is, in part, a consequence of being a rural location. Monmouthshire is the only county in Wales to be awarded the title of Top Food Tourism Destination, so the new marketing campaign is designed to promote Monmouthshire as the Food Capital of Wales and is underpinned by a food and drink themed marketing strategy and a food tourism consortium that demonstrates a partnership approach.

Rural DMOs need to create and maintain effective and sustainable symmetry between advocating rurality as a pull factor for tourists; while recognising that the very thing that attracts tourists creates challenges for micro-businesses in rural tourism destinations. Rural-based DMOs, such as Adventa, with local membership and a sound understanding of the challenges facing rural tourism micro-businesses, have a very different focus to that of larger, urban-based DMOs, which tend to be more focused on external promotion. DMO approaches that meet the needs of local rural communities as well as tourists tend to have greater measures of success (George *et al.*, 2009) as activities that fulfil community interests often appeal to wider tourist markets and are more sustainable than tourist-only activities and initiatives. In Monmouthshire, this is evidenced by the installation of free Wi-Fi, which has provided connectivity and enabled the development of *Monmouthpedia* – a vehicle for civic pride and local history – but also serves an important interpretation role in relation to the tourist experience within the destination. This approach, coupled with increased destination ownership, should help to facilitate collaboration in the development of rural tourism destinations and ensure that rural tourism micro-businesses capitalise on their rurality.

References

Adventa (2011) Adventa – Funding [online]. Available from: www.adventa.org.uk/content.php?nID=16&lID=1 (accessed 26 May 2011).

Alexander, A. C., Lee, K. H. and Kim, D. H. (2011) Determinants of Visitor's Overnight Stay in Local Food Festivals: An Exploration of Staycation Concept and Its Relation to the Origin of Visitors [online]. Available from: http://scholarworks.umass.edu/cgi/viewcontent.cgi?article=1083&context=gradconf_hospitality (accessed 1 July 2012).

Alexander, N. and McKenna, A. (1998) Rural tourism in the heart of England, *International Journal of Contemporary Hospitality Management* 10 (5): 203–7.

Beaver, G., Lashley, C. and Stewart, J. (1998) Management development, in R. Thomas (ed.), *The Management of Small Tourism and Hospitality Firms*, London: Cassell: 156–73.

Beeton, S. (2006) *Community Development through Tourism*. Collingwood, Australia: Landlinks Press.

Bosworth, G. and Willett, J. (2011) Embeddedness or escapism? Rural perceptions and economic development in Cornwall and Northumberland, *Sociologica Ruralis* 51(2): 195–214.

Cochrane, J. (2009) Changing landscapes and rural tourism, in R. Thomas (ed.), *Managing Regional Tourism: A case study of Yorkshire, England*. Ilkley, UK: Great Northern Books: 65–77.

Cresswell, T. (2004) *Place: A Short Introduction*. Oxford: Blackwell.

Di Domenico, M. (2005) Producing hospitality, consuming lifestyles: Lifestyle entrepreneurship in urban Scotland, in E. Jones and C. Haven-Tang (eds), *Tourism SMEs, Service Quality and Destination Competitiveness*. Wallingford, UK: CABI: 109–22.

Dredge, D. (2006) Policy networks and the local organisation of tourism, *Tourism Management* 27 (2): 269–80.

Edgell, D. L. Sr. and Harbaugh, L. (1993) Tourism development: An economic stimulus in the heart of America, *Business America* 114 (2): 17–18.

European Commission (2007) Action for More Sustainable European Tourism: Report of the Tourism Sustainability Group [online]. Available from: http://ec.europa.eu/enterprise/newsroom/cf/_getdocument.cfm?doc_id=237 (accessed 15 October 2012).

Fox, S. (2009) *Vacation or Staycation?* [online]. Available from: www.neumann.edu/academics/divisions/business/journal/review09/fox.pdf (accessed 1 July 2012).

Garrod, B., Wornell, R. and Youell, R. (2006) Re-conceptualising rural resources as countryside capital: The case of rural tourism, *Journal of Rural Studies* 22 (1): 117–28.

George, E. W. and Reid, D.G (2005) The power of tourism: A metamorphosis of community culture, *Journal of Tourism and Cultural Change*, 3(2): 88–107.

George, E. W., Mair, H. and Reid, D. G. (2009) *Rural Tourism Development: Localism and Cultural Change*. Bristol, UK: Channel View.

Giles, E., Bosworth, G. and Willett, J. (2013) The role of local perceptions in the marketing of rural areas, *Journal of Destination Marketing and Management*, 2(1): 4–13.

GTS (UK) Ltd/Monmouthshire County Council (2012) STEAM Report 2011 [online]. Available from: www.monmouthshire.gov.uk/fileadmin/mcc/downloads/visit_monmouthshire/MomRepRR11.pdf (accessed 22 November 2012).

Gunn, C. A. (1993) *Tourism Planning Basics, Concepts, Cases*. London: Taylor & Francis.

Hall, C. M. and Rusher, K. (2005) Business goals in the small-scale accommodation sector in New Zealand, in E. Jones and C. Haven-Tang (eds.), *Tourism SMEs, Service Quality and Destination Competitiveness*. Wallingford: CABI: 143–54.

Haven, C. and Jones, E. (2004) An Assessment of the Labour Market and Skills Needs of the Tourism and Related Sectors in Wales. Cardiff: Tourism Training Forum for Wales.

Haven-Tang, C. and Jones, E. (2012) Local leadership for rural tourism development: A case study of Adventa, Monmouthshire, UK, *Tourism Management Perspectives* 4: 28–35.

Howie, F. (2003) *Managing the Tourist Destination*. London: Continuum.

Huang, L. (2006) Rural tourism revitalization of the leisure farm industry by implementing an e-commerce strategy, *Journal of Vacation Marketing* 12(3): 232–45.

Inkson, C. and Minnaert, L. (2012) *Tourism Management: An introduction*. London: Sage.

Jones, E. and Haven, C. (2004) Joined-up Tourism: Coordinating Public-sector Interventions to Develop Tourism-SMEs in South-east Wales (Paper Number 0142). Retrieved from Proceedings of Tourism State of the Art II Conference (The Scottish Hotel School, University of Strathclyde, CD-ROM, June 2004 release).

Jones, E., Botterill, D., Lynch, P. and Thomas, R. (2004a) United Kingdom, in A. Morrison and R. Thomas (eds), *SMEs in Tourism: An International Review*. Arnhem: ATLAS: 73–80.

Jones, P., Lockwood, A. and Bowen, A. (2004b) UK hospitality and tourism SMEs: Differentiation by size, location and owner style, *Tourism and Hospitality Planning and Development*, 1(1): 7–11.

Lane, B. (2005) Sustainable rural tourism strategies: A tool for development and conservation, *RIAT Interamerican Journal of Environment and Tourism* 1(1): 12–18.

Lane, B. (2009) Rural tourism: An overview, in T. Jamal and M. Robinson (eds), *The Sage Handbook of Tourism Studies*. London: Sage: 354–70.

Lynch, P. A. (2000) Networking in the homestay sector, *The Service Industries Journal* 20(3): 95–116.

Mair, H. (2006) Global restructuring and local responses: Investigating rural tourism policy in two Canadian communities, *Current Issues in Tourism* 9(1): 1–45.

Melsen, L. (2012) Rural tourism, in P. Robinson (ed.), *Tourism: The Key Concepts*. Abingdon, UK: Routledge: 173–5.

Mitchell, J. and Ashley, C. (2010) *Tourism and Poverty Reduction: Pathways to Prosperity*. London: Earthscan.

Nylander, M. and Hall, D. (2005) Rural tourism policy: European perspectives, in D. Hall, I. Kirkpatrick and M. Mitchell (eds), *Rural Tourism and Sustainable Business*. Clevedon, UK: Channel View: 17–40.

Page, S. and Getz, D., (1997) *The Business of Rural Tourism: International Perspectives*. London: International Thomson Business Press.

Paniagua, A. (2002) Urban–rural migration, tourism entrepreneurs and rural restructuring in Spain, *Tourism Geographies* 4(4): 349–71.

Richardson, J. (2000) *Partnerships in Communities: Reweaving the Fabric of Rural America*. Washington DC: Island Press.

Ritchie, B. R. and Crouch, G. I. (2003) *The Competitive Destination: A Sustainable Tourism Perspective*. Wallingford, UK: CABI.

Roberts, L. and Hall, D (2004) Consuming the countryside: Marketing for 'rural tourism', *Journal of Vacation Marketing*, 10(3): 253–63.

Scott, A., Christie, M. and Midmore, P. (2004) Impact of the 2001 foot-and-mouth disease outbreak in Britain: Implications for rural studies, *Journal of Rural Studies* 20(1): 1–14.

Sharma, S. (2009) *The Great American Staycation and the Risk of Stillness* [online]. Available from: www.journal.media-culture.org.au/index.php/mcjournal/article/view/122 (accessed 1 July 2012).

Sharpley, R. (2007) Flagship attractions and sustainable rural tourism development: The case of the Alnwick Garden, England, *Journal of Sustainable Tourism* 15(2): 125–43.

Sharpley, R. and Craven, B. (2001) The 2001 foot and mouth crisis: Rural economy and tourism policy implications: A comment, *Current Issues in Tourism* 4(6): 527–37.

Sharpley, R. and Vass, A. (2006) Tourism, farming and diversification: An attitudinal study, *Tourism Management* 27(5): 1040–52.

Thorbeck, D. (2012) *Rural Design: A New Design Discipline*. New York: Routledge.

Tinsley, R. and Lynch, P. (2001) Small tourism business networks and destination development, *International Journal of Hospitality Management* 20 (4): 367–78.

Urry, J. and Larsen, J. (2011) *The Tourist Gaze 3.0*. London: Sage.

Wales Tourist Board (2000) *Achieving Our Potential: A Tourism Strategy for Wales*. Cardiff: Wales Tourist Board.

Welsh Government (2011a) Size Analysis of Welsh Business, 2011 [online]. Available from: http://wales.gov.uk/docs/statistics/2011/111027sdr1982011en.pdf (accessed 15 March 2012).

Welsh Government (2011b) Programme for Government [online]. Available from: http://wales.gov.uk/docs/strategies/110929fullen.pdf (accessed 15 March 2012).

Williams, C. and Ferguson, M. (2005) Recovering from crisis: Strategic alternatives for leisure and tourism providers based within a rural economy, *International Journal of Public Sector Management* 18(4): 350–66.

Wilson, S., Fesenmaier, D. R., Fesenmaier, J. and van Es, J. C. (2001) Factors for success in rural tourism development, *Journal of Travel Research* 40(2): 132–8.

17 Ageing in rural communities

From idyll to exclusion?

Wesley Key

Introduction

This chapter explores changing conceptions of rurality as people move from middle-age into later life. It examines the meaning of 'rural' for older people living in British rural settlements, and the extent to which rural is seen less as an 'idyll,' and more as a contributory factor to social exclusion, when people reach their seventies and eighties. The chapter is informed by findings from a qualitative study of the social exclusion of people aged 75-and-over living within rural areas of mid-Lincolnshire (Key, 2005), a sparsely populated arable farming area in eastern England. The chapter suggests that it is in sparsely populated settlements that older rural residents are at greatest risk of exclusion from social relations and service provision. Such settlements may be the most likely places to have the 'idyllic' qualities (open green space, peace and quiet) that attract people to move to them earlier in the life course, but they typically lack the in situ service provision and support networks that older people require when their personal mobility declines.

Substantial changes to the socio-economic fabric of rural Britain have occurred since the mid-twentieth century, including the decline of facilities and sites of social contact such as shops, churches, post offices and public houses (see Markham, this volume). The erosion of rural employment options, shops, community meeting places and face-to-face interaction between neighbours has run parallel to the ageing of rural populations and the out-migration of young adults to employment and affordable housing opportunities in urban areas (Milbourne and Hughes, 2005). Mobile, affluent commuters and retirees have been attracted by cleaner, greener rural landscapes and the slower pace of rural life, and, by 2006, the median age in rural England (44.4 years) was older than in urban England (38.5 years, Commission for Rural Communities, 2010). Rural populations are ageing faster than those of urban areas, and this trend is particularly pronounced among people aged 85-and-over: from 2009–29, population increase among the over-85s has been projected to be 114 per cent in rural areas, compared to 86 per cent in urban areas (Oxford Consultants for Social Inclusion, 2009). The changing composition of rural communities has also been influenced by planning restrictions on the building of new housing (e.g., in green belt areas), and by the limited construction of the 'affordable' new homes within many of England's small towns, villages and hamlets that are required to meet local housing needs (Taylor, 2008).

The in-migration of people in middle and early old age has been a significant contributory factor to the ageing of rural Britain (Hardill and Dwyer, 2011), and fewer rural communities consist of inter-generational kin networks than in the twentieth century. Within England, during 2001–2008, the 45–64 age group showed a net movement from urban and commuter areas to more sparsely populated rural areas (Commission for Rural Communities, 2010), suggesting that this is a stage in life when people are most likely to be able to afford to outbid other groups for rural housing stock. Older people 'ageing in place' within rural communities can become increasingly surrounded by better-off households with different perceptions of rurality (Countryside Agency, 2000), and the out-migration of younger relatives may intensify older people's perceptions of exclusion.

Across England, population growth from 2001–2008 was faster in rural than in urban areas, and faster in less sparse villages and small towns than in sparse areas (Commission for Rural Communities, 2010). The older age profile of rural areas is due to a larger proportion of people aged 60-plus and a smaller proportion of people aged 16–29. Sparse rural areas show the oldest population distributions, while people aged 30–59 tend to predominate in commuter areas in southern England and around the northern conurbations, and people aged 16–29 are most likely to live in cities. By 2007, rural England had nearly 400,000 fewer 15–29 year-olds than twenty years before – 'a rural demographic which is older and ageing faster than urban areas' (Commission for Rural Communities, 2007), and, over the first quarter of the twenty-first century, the number of people aged 65-and-over in rural areas of England will increase by more than that for England as a whole (ONS, 2004). Such demographic patterns mirror those seen across Greece, Italy and Canada (Eurostat, 2009; Statistics Canada, 2009), where old-age dependency ratios – the number of people aged 65-and-over relative to the number of people aged 15–64 – are higher in rural than in urban areas, as many young adults have left rural communities to find a wider choice of paid employment opportunities. However, the risk of exclusion from service provision and social relations appears greater for older people in rural areas of England than in many other European nations, due to southern European cultures retaining more positive attitudes to intergenerational mixing.

Rural areas of England are experiencing the effects of ageing sooner than other parts of the country (Lowe and Speakman, 2006), with population ageing placing pressures upon public service providers (DEFRA, 2004) such as General Practice surgeries. Twenty-two per cent of people in sparsely populated rural areas are aged 65-plus, compared with 15 per cent in urban areas (DEFRA, 2004), and the most rural districts have received significant net inflows of older, professional and managerial people, alongside the out-migration of younger workers (Buller *et al.*, 2003; Commission for Rural

Communities, 2008). The long-term sustainability of remote rural settlements as communities where people can access employment, affordable housing and services has therefore been questioned, and the impact of intra-regional retirement migration has placed particular pressure upon coastal areas such as south-west England (ONS, 2003).

The rural idyll and the gentrification of rural Britain

Throughout much of nineteenth century Victorian England, there was an assumption that 'community' was a rural phenomenon (Davidoff *et al.*, 1977), and the term community was often preceded by the adjective 'organic', linking agriculture with mutual cooperation for the social good. The organic community epitomised the stable social hierarchy that the Victorian upper and middle classes wished to preserve (Davidoff *et al.*, 1977), and this view of rural community life became an English literary convention, alongside the notion of the rural idyll, from the nineteenth century. This has meant that, for many people who grew up in twentieth century Britain, the adjective 'rural' has undertones of beauty, order and peacefulness. However, the idealization of the rural social order, stemming from the nature poetry of the eighteenth century, where rural life was depicted in terms of harmony and happy poverty, left a legacy of misunderstanding of rural needs that has affected rural service provision (such as healthcare – British Medical Association, 2005) into the twenty-first century.

As Britain became increasingly urbanized, the notion of the organic rural community became susceptible to the nostalgia for a half-remembered past (Davidoff *et al.*, 1977). Such nostalgia involved instilling the notion of community with an emotional power, and idealized notions of rural communities as places of cross-class neighbourhood relations may have been imbued within the mind-sets of people who grew up in rural Britain between the two World Wars. Members of this generation are now aged 75-plus, and many are now 'ageing in place' within the communities that they grew up in, yet can now feel excluded from, and it is the idyll of a tight-knit community life that can be harder to maintain past the age of 75. Organic communities of mutual dependency between landowners and their agricultural labourers have been superseded by the dispersal of commuter families, long-term older residents and dwindling numbers of farming families and land-based workers.

The broader notion of the 'rural idyll' has influenced the denial of the existence of rural deprivation by British policy-makers and rural dwellers, and the spatial dimensions of rural disadvantage – the dispersal of poorer people across rural landscapes, their presence within socially mixed communities, and the limited provision of welfare services, act to reduce the physical, social and political visibility of rural deprivation (Milbourne, 2004). The 'rural idyll' encapsulates assumptions about rural lifestyles being healthy, problem-free and based around close-knit communities (Cloke and Milbourne, 1992), and this idyllic paradigm has led many rural residents to accept low levels of service provision as a natural part of rural life (Cloke *et al.*, 1994). The notion of the rural idyll has led to 'many people finding it difficult to believe that social exclusion exists in picturesque surroundings' (Countryside Agency, 2000: 5), and such assumptions can influence rural older people to downplay the extent that they are excluded from accessing service provision and social relations. Furthermore, the imagery of the rural idyll identifies rural places as green spaces with low crime rates, but such cultural imagery has not included symbols of poverty and hardship (Cloke *et al.*, 1994), and 'to admit the existence of poverty in rural areas is to challenge one of the most pervasive images of our social heritage' (Bradley *et al.*, 1986: 25). This is especially true for people growing older within rural communities where they have spent their whole lives, drawing on social norms of self-sufficiency and reluctance to seek assistance from statutory service providers.

The imagery of the rural idyll has also contributed to the gentrification of much of rural Britain (see Phillips, 2005). Many high-income people in their forties and fifties have moved from urban to rural areas, further ageing the populations of rural communities, and such people are also likely to 'age in place' themselves in due course. The parallel re-location of younger adults away from rural housing markets that they have been priced out of is placing pressures on the sustainability of the rural service infrastructure, with rising car ownership levels meaning that services such as general stores are less likely to be able to survive in remote rural areas. To 'age in place' in remote areas of rural Britain has increasingly come to mean dependence upon transport to population centres (e.g., market towns) where shops and financial and medical services remain viable. It is therefore likely that 'rural' becomes less of an idyll as people move from mid-life to later life, and the chapter now details why this is so.

Over recent decades, gentrification research (such as Phillips, 2005) has belatedly acknowledged the gentrification of rural areas of Britain (Stockdale, 2010), a by-product of which has been the aforementioned pushing out from rural areas of young adults on low incomes unable to afford local housing. Since the 1980s, rural Britain has become more likely to house well-educated, professional migrants, and consequences of this urban-to-rural migration include rising rural house prices and an increased commuter population who may contribute little to day-to-day socio-economic life in their home neighbourhoods. This period has seen rising numbers of affluent middle-aged migrants purchase detached rural homes or renovation projects, often displacing lower-income households from their areas of origin. It is this displacement of lower-income groups that distinguishes rural gentrification from processes of counter-urbanisation (Stockdale, 2010), and the impact of this out-migration of displaced younger relatives upon older rural people 'ageing in place' can be considerable. The gentrification of much of rural Britain in the late twentieth and early twenty-first centuries by service-sector professionals has led to the evolution of new rural businesses (often tourism or IT based), parallel to the decline of traditional forms of rural employment such as agricultural labouring. However, the new rural businesses (set up by incomers attracted by the rural idyll) may provide few long-term employment opportunities for young adults who have grown up in countryside communities.

The transition from the 'Third Age' to the 'Fourth Age' within rural Britain

During the late twentieth century, the growth of early retirement led gerontologists to talk of a 'Third Age' between work (the 'Second Age') and the 'Fourth Age' of physical and mental decline (Phillipson, 1998; Gilleard and Higgs, 2002, 2005). In the Third Age (age 55–74), paid employment usually ceases, children reach adulthood, and health and mobility remain sufficient to pursue an active retirement, often in an 'idyllic' rural environment of green space and tranquillity. By contrast, the Fourth Age (age 75-or-over) usually brings a loss of independence and increasing reliance upon other people to meet transport and personal care needs. People in the Third Age tend to have higher incomes and broader friendship networks than people aged 75-plus, along with higher levels of household car ownership, while research from Scotland and the USA shows that Third Age people living in rural areas are more likely than Fourth Age people to engage in community events, volunteering and social entrepreneurship (Scottish Executive, 2000; Bosworth and Glasgow, 2012).

Fourth Age rural residents are more likely than younger rural dwellers to experience exclusion from access to services and to social relations, and less likely to experience rural lifestyles as idyllic, particularly if they live in sparsely populated areas with poor service provision. People in the Fourth Age may have to relocate from sparse rural communities to less sparse areas if declining health and mobility bring exclusion from services and social relations at a time of increased need for accessible healthcare and other welfare provision from agencies, relatives and friends. People in the Fourth Age are more vulnerable to multi-faceted disadvantage than younger pensioners (Patsios, 2000), and they have poorer access to public, private and voluntary services, largely because they are less likely to drive or to be able to use public transport.

'Push' factors from sparse rural communities in later life

The re-location of people aged 75-and-over from sparsely populated rural communities is usually due to one or more of the following factors:

- loss of household car access (e.g. due to widowhood or ill health);
- poor alternative transport options: taxi, community transport and regular bus services are typically unsustainable in sparse communities;
- falling numbers of rural services: there was a 23 per cent fall in the number of rural post offices across England from 2000–2010, alongside

a 15.3 per cent fall in the number of bank and building society outlets (Commission for Rural Communities, 2010: 27);

- the onset of health and personal mobility difficulties;
- the out-migration, decline in health, or death, of neighbours, friends and relatives who have provided transport, practical support and social contact;
- housing that is unsuited to declining personal mobility (e.g., if stairs are no longer manageable).

All of these 'push' factors from sparse rural communities are most apparent when people are aged 75-and-over (Key, 2005).

The main advantages to the over-75s of moving from sparse rural to less sparse communities are:

- more neighbours located within walking distance;
- broader choice of services (general stores, post offices, banks, other shops) and sites of social activity (e.g. village halls, churches): access to these facilities is less likely to be transport dependant;
- better public transport provision to urban centres;
- broader choice of housing options suitable for 'ageing in place' (e.g., bungalows in 'sheltered' housing schemes).

The social exclusion of rural older people

Rural dwelling and older age are both associated with a higher risk of social exclusion (Shergold and Parkhurst, 2012), and the chapter now explains how exclusion from access to social networks and service provision can affect Fourth Age residents of rural Britain.

Social networks

The social networks of rural dwellers aged 75-plus can include co-resident and other relatives, neighbours, and friends living in other settlements. Beyond the age of 75, there is a decline in the significance of friendships in older people's lives (Johnson and Barer, 1997), as access to social networks and informal social relations is heavily linked to access to transport, which declines in later life. People aged 75-plus are also at higher risk of exclusion from face-to-face and telephone-based social contacts than people aged 60–74 (Scottish Executive, 2000).

For people aged 75-plus, children are increasingly important providers of emotional and practical support (Johnson and Barer, 1997). The longer that a rural older person has lived in their home neighbourhood, the more likely they are to have frequent contact with relatives and to have relatives living nearby (Wenger and Burholt, 2001). Frequent contact with proximate relatives may help to sustain older rural residents' idyllic perceptions of rural living as they age in place, and support from relatives can limit rural older people's exclusion from service provision and broader social relations.

From their study of older people living in rural Wales, Wenger and Burholt (2001) suggested that relationships with nieces and nephews become centrally important in the absence of proximate children. Within rural Lincolnshire, Key (2005) found evidence of similar patterns, with godchildren, cousins and neighbours also providing assistance with household chores and collection of shopping and benefits for people aged 75-plus who were without children living nearby. Childless people living alone had occasional contact with siblings, nieces and cousins, but typically relied upon proximate friends to provide support that would otherwise be given by adult children.

Transport and disability are more common factors than low income in preventing older people from maintaining social networks (Patsios, 2000). Where transport and disability are not constraints, rural older women appear to have more proactive approaches to maintaining friendship networks than rural older men (Key, 2005), with older women being more likely to telephone friends, to visit their friends' homes, and to attend local social events, than older men. The impact of retirement from work can be worst for older men, who, if they live alone, may be more likely than lone older women to need, and to receive, daily support from adult children with personal care and food preparation, but such gender differences in support needs may lessen in future generations where older men will be more likely to undertake domestic chores for themselves. However, a projected rise in childlessness among older people in Britain, coupled with rising economic activity rates for middle-aged women (Pickard *et al.*, 2007), may lead to future generations of rural over-75s being at increased risk of exclusion from service provision and social relations, as the support available from younger family members could be reduced.

Mid- or later-life migrants to rural areas can draw on both proximate and long-distance friendship networks, but the friendship networks of rural people 'ageing in place' are largely centred within their home neighbourhoods, and primarily involve long-term bonds with other pensioners ageing in place in the communities in which they have spent most, or all, of their lives (Key, 2005). The Key study of rural Lincolnshire also identified the highly privatized nature of older people's lives, with contact between older neighbours most often made by chance (e.g., in a shop, or in the street) or in each other's homes, rather than at large-scale social events.

The migration, illness or death of friends, and the ill health and restricted transport options of older people themselves, can localize friendship networks, and, within rural Lincolnshire, popular sites of social engagement were parish church events and neighbourhood older people's club meetings (Key, 2005). Despite the high rates of population ageing within rural Britain, older people's clubs are attended by limited numbers of Third Age and Fourth Age people, and the long-term future of some clubs is in doubt. People attracted in middle-age to rural lifestyles by perceptions of strong, close-knit communities may subsequently make limited contributions to rural community life, having little contact with older neighbours if they commute to work and to weekend leisure activities. Putnam's discussion of social capital within the USA around the notion of 'Bowling Alone' (Putnam, 1995) is increasingly relevant to rural older people at risk of exclusion from social networks as they reach the Fourth Age of life, with limited social exchange evident between the indigenous and incomer sectors of rural communities (Gibbins, 1984; Key, 2005). Furthermore, participation in neighbourhood and other social activities in later life can vary due to disability, car access, family support networks, caring responsibilities, income, and individual preferences.

Research conducted in rural Canada suggests that communities which provide high levels of support to older adults typically have small populations, long distances from service centres, and high percentages of older and widowed people and inhabitants with over five years' residence (Eales *et al.*, 2006). Members of such communities are likely to be more familiar with one another's circumstances and thus more aware of people who require assistance, with much of the support for rural over-65s coming from other rural residents aged 65-and-over. This implies a need for more purpose-built housing developments for older people across sparse and less sparse areas of rural England, enabling Fourth Age people to remain living near to their Third Age friends and relatives (who provide them with social contact and practical assistance) when larger housing units become unsustainable for them.

Access to service provision

The other key dimension of rural social exclusion in later life is difficulty with accessing basic services (Key, 2012). Across Britain, the populations of rural areas are older than those of urban areas, and there are greater concentrations of older people in large villages and small towns than in remote hamlets (Wenger, 2001a), as service provision is more extensive in these more densely populated areas. The erosion of much of the service infrastructure of rural Britain (bus services and businesses such as shops and post offices; public amenities like village halls and churches) has impacted Fourth Age rural residents more significantly than younger age groups, due to lower levels of car use among Fourth Age households. Such institutional disengagement (Scharf *et al.*, 2000) across rural Britain differs markedly from perceptions of rural settlements as idyllic communities with multiple service outlets and social group meeting places that help to foster strong bonds between neighbours within such communities. Within England, few service outlets are located within rural areas: just 11.1 per cent of cash-points, 20.1 per cent of convenience stores, and 11.9 per cent of pharmacies (Commission for Rural Communities, 2011). Access to banks, supermarkets and general practice surgeries is poorer from rural than from urban areas (Commission for Rural Communities, 2010), largely due to the higher per capita costs of service provision in sparsely populated areas (Craig and Manthorpe, 2000).

Exclusion from basic services stems from a lack of access to adequate public and private transport (Kenyon *et al.*, 2003). Access to public and private service provision is a key indicator of social exclusion in later life, and analysis of the English Longitudinal Study of Ageing developed seven dimensions of social exclusion relating to older people, of which only access to basic services was more prevalent in rural than in urban areas (ODPM, 2006). Access to services is highly car dependant for people living in rural communities, with lift-giving networks helping to sustain older people's rural living and to combat mobility-related exclusion, particularly among the oldest old (Shergold and Parkhurst, 2012).

For rural Fourth Age Britons, use of a household car, or that of a relative or friend, is typically seen as a more reliable means of accessing service centres (and tackling social exclusion) than buses, taxi services or community transport provision, all of which can be infrequent or non-existent, particularly within remote rural areas. Health problems and disabilities can force rural Fourth Age people to scale down, or cease, driving activities and their use of public transport, but a lack of alternative transport can force some people to continue driving in spite of physical and/or mental deterioration, in order to sustain access to service provision. Forty-four per cent of people aged 75–79 have a physical disability or health problem that makes it difficult to use public transport, rising to 72 per cent of people aged 85-plus (DTLR, 2001), with health and physical capability reducing the further people move beyond the age of 75 (Falkingham *et al.*, 2010). The 80-and-over age group are likely to be less able to make use of active travel modes (Shergold and Parkhurst, 2012), such as walking to a bus-stop or to visit neighbours.

Limited awareness of demand-responsive transport services (such as 'Call Connect' in Lincolnshire) can mean that rural older people with the greatest need for flexible transport provision fail to utilise schemes designed to help them. Better targeting of demand-responsive transport to Fourth Age rural dwellers could help to preserve their access to services and social relations, but policy options are restricted by the network limitations of traditional public transport in low density rural areas and the fiscal constraints facing demand-responsive services (Shergold and Parkhurst, 2012).

The loss of household car access can bring increased dependence upon proximate relatives and friends, and a contraction of social networks located beyond people's home villages. However, older people are often reluctant to 'burden' relatives and friends for car-lift favours that they are unable to reciprocate (Gilhooly *et al.*, 2003), aiming to preserve self-perceptions of independent rural living for as long as possible. Such a self-reliance ethos is especially strong among older people living in rural areas (Heenan, 2006) who have been socialized from a young age into providing for themselves and their families, with minimal use of state service provision. Where Fourth Age rural dwellers do receive assistance, proximate relatives (usually adult children or daughters-in-law) tend to provide transport for shopping and collection of pension monies, or they deliver the shopping and pension payments to older housebound people directly.

Single pensioners are more likely than dual-pensioner households to have difficulty accessing services (Patsios, 2000), partly due to lower levels of car ownership. Most single pensioners are women, as they live longer than men, meaning that women are more likely to live alone in the Fourth Age. In 2006–7, in settlements of less than 10,000 people, 50 per cent of women aged 70-and-over held a full car driving licence, compared to 80 per cent of men (Cabinet Office/DEFRA 2009), and, although the numbers of older women drivers are rising (Transport Statistics, 2010), the current generation of rural 'Fourth Age' women are more likely than rural 'Fourth Age' men to have difficulty accessing service provision from rural communities. Age appears to be a stronger indicator than gender in determining exclusion from basic services, with people aged 75-plus having the greatest difficulty accessing general practice surgeries, hospitals, shops and post offices from rural communities (Ruston, 2002). This is principally due to the age-related decline in household car access: 51.2 per cent of over-75s lived in car-owning households in England and Wales in 2001, compared to 74.8 per cent of over-50s (ONS, 2003). Furthermore, with lower concentrations of service outlets in rural areas, older people living in such areas experience more difficulty with accessing services than older people living in urban communities (Scottish Executive, 2000; Scharf and Bartlam, 2006), despite car ownership rates being higher in rural than in urban areas (Commission for Rural Communities, 2010).

Convenient access to transport (and service provision located elsewhere) can be lost if people's health deteriorates as they move from the Third Age to the Fourth Age. The impact of reduced access to transport is greatest when people have passed the age of 75, due to older age groups' greater need to access primary care services (General Practice surgeries, hospitals) and younger age groups' higher levels of digital literacy that enable greater use to be made of online financial, shopping and medical services that reduce the need to travel from home. Older people affected by ill health and low income are worst affected by the loss of local services (Scharf *et al.*, 2002), while the loss of home visits from mobile services (e.g. hairdressers, podiatrists) can trigger a need for an older person to move to a less remote community where such mobile service rounds remain economically viable.

Aside from being less likely than younger people to hold a driving licence, own a car or use public transport, Fourth Age people are more likely to distinguish between 'essential' (e.g. medical appointments) and 'discretionary' travel (Davey, 2004), typically focusing their car use on the former, and reducing, or giving up, the latter. Current generations of rural over-75s have to travel to access most public and private service provision, with few services directly accessible to them via home deliveries, unlike the delivery rounds by butchers, bakers and grocers to past generations of rural older people, or the online service provision (e.g., internet food shopping orders) that may reduce the transport dependency of future Fourth Age rural dwellers. Rural service cutbacks and a reduction in (or removal of) accessible transport and/or practical support and companionship from friends and relatives can leave Fourth Age rural dwellers excluded from service provision and social relations, and force them to leave what may no longer be a 'rural idyll' to relocate to less sparse areas with better service provision. Within rural Lincolnshire, Key (2005) quotes a woman aged over eighty detailing how 'the fisherman brings our tablets from the butcher's as they're dispensed from there rather than the surgery five miles away.' Flexible adaptations of this kind are needed to cut the distances that rural older people, and those who are assisting them to age in place, have to travel to access healthcare and other essential service provision.

Conclusion

This chapter has considered how perceptions of rural settlements as 'idyllic' places in which to live can attract affluent middle-aged and newly retired people to sparsely populated communities. It has examined how sparse rural areas can attract professionals and recent retirees with high disposable incomes, and how this gentrification can displace young adults who have grown up in these communities. Furthermore, this in-migration of people in their forties, fifties and sixties, coupled with the aforementioned net out-migration of people aged 15–29, is ageing rural communities in the longer-term, which will place greater demands upon service providers that existing patterns of provision may be unable to meet. For example, fewer rural primary schools may be needed, but demand for sheltered housing schemes within rural areas may increase as rural populations age (Bevan *et al.*, 2006).

It has been shown that people living in sparse rural communities with limited in situ service provision are at high risk of experiencing exclusion from access to service provision and to social networks when they reach the Fourth Age (age 75-and-over), as members of older age groups are most likely to have difficulties with accessing transport and with using IT. While the isolation of sparse and peripheral rural settlements can attract people in mid-life who are car-drivers and in search of peace and privacy, the same isolation (from other people and from services) can exclude people as they 'age in place' within these sparse, and peripheral, rural communities. Loss of a household car, and a parallel increase in dependence upon kin and friendship support, are the clearest symbols of the switch from an 'idyllised' understanding of rural living to experiencing exclusion from service provision and from social relations, and such a switch typically occurs when people reach the Fourth Age of their lives.

The research of Key (2005) indicated that the following can help Fourth Age rural dwellers to prolong an idyllised lifestyle:

- support from proximate adult children with car transport lifts, low-level practical tasks (food shopping and preparation, gardening, house-cleaning) and day-to-day companionship;
- similar assistance from long-term, typically Third Age, neighbours and relatives alongside, or in place of, proximate next-of-kin;
- utilising surviving local services (e.g., post offices, general stores) to reduce the need to travel to services elsewhere and to depend on other people for transport provision;

- participation in organized social activities which can provide social contact and help to counteract the apparent diminution of informal ties between rural neighbours of different generations; and
- an income high enough to meet transport and disability-related costs and to maintain involvement in social activities (e.g., by claiming full benefit entitlements, take-up of which may be lower for rural, than for urban, older people).

The first three of these points are particularly significant to housebound people who may have few opportunities to travel to engage in face-to-face interaction or discretionary spending. If support networks break down, or local service outlets close, this can precipitate the switch from perceiving rural living as 'idyllic' to experiencing social exclusion, which can require the older person to move to a more densely populated area with easier access to service provision. Rurality can exacerbate age-related decline in quality of life (Philip *et al.*, 2003), and there is evidence that health outcomes for rural patients are poor compared with patients in urban areas (British Medical Association, 2005) – the further patients live from specialist cancer centres, the poorer their survival chances. Exclusion from service provision and social relations are not issues that solely affect rural residents or people aged 75-plus, but its impact appears to be greatest upon people aged 75-plus who live in sparse rural communities with few proximate dwellings or services.

High levels of self-reliance among rural older Britons may preserve their perceptions of residence in a rural area as 'idyllic' beyond the increasingly difficult, and dependant, reality of their daily lives. Many rural older people downplay the impact that the causes (e.g., low income, lack of transport) and consequences (e.g., social isolation, loneliness, poor access to services) of exclusion can have on their lives, preferring to extend their independent rural living for as long as possible, through the use of complex coping strategies (Cloke *et al.*, 1994) and reduced expectations about their quality of life. Reluctance to 'trouble' relatives and friends can prevent assistance being sought unless it is seen as a necessity (e.g., medical appointments) – trips to friends may be dispensable in the absence of car transport, with negative effects on health and well-being. Furthermore, rural Britons 'ageing in place' often have little social contact beyond proximate relatives, neighbours and healthcare appointments, and they may be increasingly excluded from the gentrified communities in which they have spent their lives, but from which their children and grandchildren are now being priced out of. Middle-aged and Third Age people on higher incomes are more likely than lower-income groups to be able to choose to live in rural areas, whereas those ageing in place have been tied to rural lifestyles by past local employment and have been more likely than older rural in-migrants to have proximate children (Wenger, 2001b).

Within England, rural districts will see the largest future increases in the numbers of residents aged 75-and-over (Champion and Shepherd, 2006), and this age group is most likely to have difficulty accessing basic services, partly due to the high cost and limited availability of private and public transport (Murakami *et al.*, 2008). Low-income Fourth Age rural households are at the highest risk of exclusion from services and social relations, and future rural population ageing will increase demand for health and social care provision in the areas from which such provision is hardest to access. With low-wage care workers finding it difficult to afford to live within the rural areas where their skills are most needed, it is unclear how effectively the needs of growing numbers of Fourth Age rural residents can be met in future.

Compared to the Fourth Age rural residents of the early twenty-first century, future generations are likely to have better car access (especially women), enhanced digital literacy, wider travel horizons, higher disposable incomes, and higher expectations of service providers. However, across Britain, and many other developed nations, they are set to face a scarcity of services in remote areas and to live increasingly far from their adult children, with more reliance upon car transport and IT to replace the neighbourhood-based, face-to-face forms of social contact and service provision consistent with the mythology of the 'rural idyll'. Although many better-off middle-aged people and recent retirees continue to migrate from urban areas to sparse or less sparse rural communities, their often 'idyllised' notions of rurality differ from the reality of mobility deprivation that forces many Fourth Age residents of sparse rural communities to relocate back to less sparse service centres (when they can no longer drive) to retain independent, 'idyllic,' rural lives. A growing proportion of the older old may become increasingly excluded relative to the younger old, with people aged 80-plus being three times as likely as people in their sixties to be 'prevented' from participating in activities due to lack of transport (Shergold and Parkhurst, 2012). Ultimately, ageing in place may become a less widespread phenomenon across much of rural Britain for people in the Fourth Age of life, due to the inaccessibility of essential service provision and the impact of social and spatial isolation.

References

Bevan, M., Croucher, K. and Rhodes, D. (2006) The Housing and Support Needs of Older People in Rural Areas. London: Commission for Rural Communities/ The Housing Corporation.

Bosworth, G. and Glasgow, N. (2012) 'Entrepreneurial behaviour among rural in-migrants', in M. Shucksmith, D. L. Brown, S. Shortall, J. Vergunst and M. E. Warner (eds), *Rural Transformations and Rural Policies in the US and UK*. Abingdon, UK: Routledge.

Bradley, T., Lowe, P. and Wright, S. (1986) *Deprivation and Welfare in Rural Areas*. Norwich, UK: Geo Books.

British Medical Association (2005) Healthcare in a Rural Setting. London: British Medical Association Board of Science.

Buller, H., Morris, C. and Wright, E. (2003) The Demography of Rural Areas: A Literature Review. London: DEFRA

Cabinet Office/DEFRA (2009) Working Together for Older People in Rural Areas. Available at: http://webarchive.nationalarchives.gov.uk/+/www.cabinetoffice.gov.uk/media/226170/working-together-older-people-rural-areas-july09.pdf (accessed 4 March 2011).

Champion, A. and Shepherd, J. (2006) 'Demographic change in rural England', in P. Lowe and L. Speakman (eds), *The Ageing Countryside: The Growing Older Population of Rural England*. London: Age Concern: 29–50

Cloke, P. and Milbourne, P. (1992) Deprivation and lifestyles in rural Wales: 2, Rurality and the cultural dimension, *Journal of Rural Studies* 8: 360–74.

Cloke, P., Milbourne, P., and Thomas, C. (eds) (1994) Lifestyles in Rural England, Rural Development Commission. Rural Research Report 18.

Commission for Rural Communities (2007) State of the Countryside 2007. Available at: http://webarchive.nationalarchives.gov.uk/20110215111010/http://ruralcommunities.gov.uk/files/socr2007-fullreport.pdf (accessed 11 June 2013).

Commission for Rural Communities (2008) State of the Countryside 2008. Available at: http://webarchive.nationalarchives.gov.uk/20110215111010/http://ruralcommunities.gov.uk/files/The%20State%20of%20the%20Countryside2.pdf (accessed 11 June 2013).

Commission for Rural Communities (2010) State of the Countryside 2010. Available at: www.defra.gov.uk/crc/documents/state-of-the-countryside-report/sotc2010/ (accessed 11 June 2013).

Commission for Rural Communities (2011) 2011 Rural Services data series for England. Available at: http://webarchive.nationalarchives.gov.uk/20110303145243/http://ruralcommunities.gov.uk/category/data-statistics/ruralservicesdataseries/ (accessed 11 June 2013).

Countryside Agency (2000) Not Seen, Not Heard? Social Exclusion in Rural Areas. Wetherby: Countryside Agency.

Craig, G. and Manthorpe, J. (2000) *Social Care in Rural Areas: Developing an Agenda for Research, Policy and Practice*. York, UK: Joseph Rowntree Foundation.

Davey, J. A. (2004) Coping Without a Car: Executive Summary. Wellington: New Zealand Institute for Research on Ageing.

Davidoff, L., L'Esperance, J. and Newby, H. (1977) 'Landscape with figures: Home and community in English society', in J. Mitchell and A. Oakley (eds), *The Rights and Wrongs of Women*. Harmondsworth, UK: Penguin.

DEFRA (Department of the Environment, Food and Rural Affairs) (2004) The Government's Rural Strategy. London: The Stationery Office.

DTLR (Department of Transport, Local Government and the Regions) (2001) Focus on Personal Travel. London: The Stationery Office.

Eales, J., Keating, N., Rozanova, J., Bardick, A., Swindle, J., Bowles, R., Keefe, J. and Dobbs, B. (2006) Caring Contexts of Rural Seniors – A Case Study of Diversity among Older Adults in Rural Communities, Phase 3 Technical Report. Edmonton, Canada: University of Alberta.

Eurostat (2009) Regions of Europe, Data from September 2009, Eurostat, European Commission. Available at: http://epp.eurostat.ec.europa.eu/statistics_explained/index.php/Regions_of_Europe (20 August 2012).

Falkingham, J., Evandrou, M., McGowan, T., Bell, D. and Bowes, A. (2010) Demographic Issues, Projections and Trends: Older People with High Support Needs in the UK. ESRC Centre for Population Change.Available at: http://eprints.soton.ac.uk/338999/1/JRF_report_Falkingham_2010.pdf (1 September 2011).

Gibbins, R. (1984) 'Incomes of the elderly in rural Norfolk', in G. Clark, J. Groenendijk and F. Thissen (eds), *The Changing Countryside*. Norwich, UK: Geo Books, 137–44.

Gilhooly, M., Hamilton, K., O'Neill, M., Gow, J., Webster, N. and Pike, F. (2003) Transport and Ageing: Extending Quality of Life via Public and Private Transport, Research Findings 16. Sheffield, UK: ESRC Growing Older Programme.

Gilleard, C. and Higgs, P. (2002) 'The third age: Class, cohort or generation?' *Ageing and Society* 22(3): 369–82.

Gilleard, C. and Higgs, P. (2005) *Contexts of Ageing*. Cambridge: Polity Press.

Hardill, I. and Dwyer, P. (2011) 'Delivering public services in the mixed economy of welfare: Perspectives from the voluntary and community sector in rural England', *Journal of Social Policy*, 40(1): 157–72.

Heenan, D. (2006) 'The factors influencing access to health and social care in the farming communities of County Down, Northern Ireland', *Ageing and Society* 26(3): 373–91.

Johnson, C. L. and Barer, B. M. (1997) *Life Beyond 85 Years: The Aura of Survivorship*. New York: Springer.

Kenyon, S., Rafferty, J. and Lyons, G. (2003) 'Social exclusion and transport in the UK: A role for virtual accessibility in the alleviation of mobility-related social exclusion?' *Journal of Social Policy*, 32(3): 317–38.

Key, W. (2005) The social exclusion of older people in rural areas: A case study of mid Lincolnshire. Unpublished Ph.D. thesis. University of Lincoln.

Key, W. (2012) 'Ageing and social exclusion in rural areas,' *Sociology Review* 21(4): 16–19.

Lowe, P. and Speakman, L. (eds) (2006) *The Ageing Countryside: The Growing Older Population of Rural England*. London: Age Concern.

Milbourne, P. (2004) *Rural Poverty: Marginalisation and Exclusion in Britain and the United States*. London: Routledge.

Milbourne, P. and Hughes, R. (2005) Poverty and Social Exclusion in Rural Wales, Cardiff, Wales Rural Observatory, Research Report 6.

Murakami, E., Atterton, J. and Gilroy, R. (2008) Planning for the Ageing Countryside in Britain and Japan: City-Regions and the Mobility of Older Populations. Newcastle, Centre for Rural Economy, University of Newcastle.

ODPM (Office of the Deputy Prime Minister) (2006) The Social Exclusion of Older People: Evidence from the First Wave of the English Longitudinal Study or Ageing Final Report. London: Office of the Deputy Prime Minister.

ONS (Office for National Statistics) (2003) Census 2001: National Report for England and Wales. London: The Stationery Office.

ONS (Office for National Statistics) (2004) Sub-National Population Projections for England. London: Office for National Statistics.

Oxford Consultants for Social Inclusion (2009) Mapping the Level of Need: Assessing the Social Exclusion of Older People in Rural Areas: Report for Cabinet Office, Social Exclusion Task Force. Brighton, UK.

Patsios, D. (2000) Poverty and Social Exclusion amongst the Elderly, Poverty and Social Exclusion Survey of Britain. Working Paper no. 20. Bristol, UK: Townsend Centre for International Poverty Research.

Philip, L., Gilbert, A., Mauthner, N. and Phimister, E. (2003) Scoping Study of Older People in Rural Scotland. Edinburgh: Scottish Executive Central Research Unit.

Phillips, M. (2005) 'Differential productions of rural gentrification: Illustrations from North and South Norfolk,' *Geoforum* 36: 477–94.

Phillipson, C. (1998) *Reconstructing Old Age: New Agendas in Social Theory and Social Practice*. London: Sage.

Pickard, L., Wittenberg, R., Comas-Herrera, A., King, D. and Malley, J. (2007) 'Care by spouses, care by children: Projections of informal care for older people in England to 2031,' *Social Policy and Society* 6(3): 353–66.

Putnam, R. D. (1995) 'Bowling alone: America's declining social capital,' *Journal of Democracy* 6(1): 65–78.

Ruston, D. (2002) Difficulty in Accessing Key Services. London: Office for National Statistics.

Scharf, T. and Bartlam, B. (2006) Rural Disadvantage: Quality of Life and Disadvantage amongst Older People – A Pilot Study. London: Commission for Rural Communities.

Scharf, T., Phillipson, C., Kingston, P. and Smith, A. (2000) Social Exclusion and Older People: Towards a Conceptual Framework. Keele University School of Social Relations, Working Paper no. 6.

Scharf, T., Phillipson, C., Kingston, P. and Smith, A. (2002) *Growing Older in Socially Deprived Areas: Social Exclusion in Later Life*. London: Help the Aged.

Scottish Executive (2000) Scottish Household Survey 2000. Edinburgh: The Scottish Executive.

Shergold, I. and Parkhurst, G. (2012) 'Transport-related social exclusion amongst older people in rural Southwest England and Wales,' *Journal of Rural Studies* 28(4): 412–21.

Statistics Canada (2009) 2006 Census: Portrait of the Canadian Population in 2006, by Age and Sex: Sub-provincial Population Dynamics. Available at: www12.statcan.ca/census-recensement/2006/as-sa/97-551/p17-eng.cfm (accessed 11 June 2013).

Stockdale, A. (2010) 'The diverse geographies of rural gentrification in Scotland', *Journal of Rural Studies* 26(1): 31–40.

Taylor, M. (2008) Living Working Countryside: The Taylor Review of Rural Economy and Affordable Housing. London: Department for Communities and Local Government.

Transport Statistics (2010) Transport Statistics Great Britain, 36th edition. Available at: http://webarchive.nationalarchives.gov.uk/20110218142807/dft.gov.uk/pgr/statistics/datatablespublications/tsgb/ (accessed 19 August 2012).

Wenger, G. C. (2001a) 'Myths and realities of ageing in rural Britain', *Ageing and Society* 21(1): 117–30.

Wenger, G. C. (2001b) 'Introduction: Intergenerational relationships in rural areas', *Ageing and Society* 21(5): 537–45.

Wenger, G. C. and Burholt, V. (2001) 'Differences over time in older people's relationships with children, grandchildren, nieces and nephews in rural North Wales', *Ageing and Society* 21(5): 567–90.

18 The rural public house

Cultural icon or social hub?

Claire Markham

The public house, or as it is known to many 'the pub', has been a feature of the English landscape for hundreds of years. It can be summed up as 'a place where you can buy a drink and drink it without the obligation to do anything else, such as buying a meal' (Gorham, 1950: 16). Although it has unequivocally undergone some change in terms of its appearance, what it retails and the custom it attracts, it continues to play an important role within society. The focus of this chapter is on the social and cultural roles of the public house in rural localities. It starts with a brief contextualisation of the decline in number of rural public houses before proceeding to focus on how and why this establishment remains socially and culturally important. Additionally, the economic role of the pub cannot be overlooked, as, in reality, this role is interwoven with the social and cultural roles. The chapter will draw principally upon interview data conducted as part of an ongoing grounded theory doctoral study (Markham, forthcoming) to emphasise the importance of rural public houses. To complement the findings, examples and comparisons from existing public house and rural sustainability literature will be utilised.

In England, the public house can be described as being an iconic yet taken for granted institution (Markham, forthcoming). For many, it is viewed as being firmly embedded in England's heritage: it is 'just there' and always will be. This view, however, is naive and erroneous. In fact, there has been a decline in the number of public houses since the early 1970s (Hutt, 1973; Jennings, 2007), and this decline has accelerated in the last few years. In 2010 it was estimated by the British Beer and Pub Association (2010) that 39 public houses closed every week, equating to 2,028 annually. In rural areas it has been approximated by the Campaign for Real Ale (CAMRA) that the current closure rates stands at four per week (2012). Although the reasons for the decline are complex, numerous and interrelated (Muir, 2009), it is possible to distinguish three types of factors, each with sub-factors. First, changes in the capitalist economy; under this rubric fall the factors of supermarket competition and public house company (PUBCO) behaviour. Second, changes in the behaviour of landlords and the ever-evolving ways consumers use their disposable income and leisure time. Third, changes in government legislation and policies, namely the drink drive laws, licensing laws, the smoking ban and taxation of alcohol. Although the decline is taking place country-wide in both urban and rural localities, it is more significant in rural areas. In contrast to rural public houses, urban public houses often experience reinvention into chain public houses, theme bars, luxury restaurants or hybrid clubs (Chatterton and Hollands, 2002). This is not to say that rural public houses have not undergone change, far from it. Nevertheless, in a large proportion of cases, when a rural public house closes it is never re-opened (Lost Pubs Project, 2013). This holds implications not only for village imagery but also for 'locals' and 'communities'.

The rural public house – a cultural icon?

The rural public house can be described as being unique and synonymous with perceived English identity. 'When you have lost your inns, drown your empty selves, for you will have lost the last of England' (Hilaire Belloc, 1943, cited in Hutt, 1973: 7). The association between the public house and England is one that has central importance to the perceived survival of villages as places of social activity, with a thriving community defined as an assemblage or assemblages of people who either reside in or have an attachment to, as well as recognition of, a specific 'rural' location (see Markham, forthcoming). For some village residents, particularly older people, the public house and its sign offer reassurance that their village is still a 'real' village with a beating component. 'When villages lose their public house it's a shame, it makes the village feel gloomy and unoccupied of life' (village resident, 2011).[1] To some extent this is understandable if the public house is the only service remaining in a village. When a village loses its final service, communal or commercial, it essentially becomes a collection of dwellings that could be described as a location rather than a place. Although a community may survive, its strength and spirit often decline. There becomes a void: where once there were public buildings and spaces where communication exchanges and meetings could freely occur, there are now only private properties. From a cultural perspective, the implication is that these villages become perceived, spoken about and portrayed, particularly by the British media, as lacking the fundamental features needed to be branded a village. The consequence of this is that they can get labelled as no longer being a 'proper' village (Hill, 2008).

The constitution of a 'proper village' is contestable, as there are no universal or even England-wide criteria. However, many hold expectations as to how villages should look aesthetically and how their inhabitants should function in terms of attitudes and behaviours. Aesthetically, one of the most widely held ideas is that villages should have a functioning public house, which cosmetically has an open fireplace, wood-grained furniture, beer pumps and an atmosphere that is warm, friendly and inviting (Markham, forthcoming). Other preconceived attributes relating to the public house include the retailing of real ale and the presence of locals of all generations mingling and socialising with one another. These conceptions are not new: although based on the then London public houses, Orwell's (1946) newspaper article, detailing his conception of the 'perfect' public house, encompassed all of the aforementioned qualities. That said, as time has elapsed, another idea has come into play, the all day serving of home cooked 'traditional' food. Reflecting on this gives us the opportunity to see the rural public house as a being a blend of conservatism with hints of modernisation but lending itself overall as the antithesis of the 'McDonaldisation' of the large chain and theme public houses (Muir, 2009). When a village no longer has a public house with the aforementioned qualities it can become viewed as being under threat from globalisation and commercial interests. 'A village can't really be called a village when it don't have things like a traditional public house with real ale on tap and an open fire or services like the Post Office, it's just dead, nothing more; nothing less' (village resident, 2010).

The counter argument to this idea is that it is not villages *per se* that are under threat from the decline in the number of amenities such as the public house, but instead society's image of them (Hands, n.d., cited in Hill, 2008). For decades many individuals, particularly those who reside in towns and cities, have been influenced by sources such as the paintings of John Constable and the writings of authors like Jane Austen, which have depicted villages as being places that are serene, surrounded by areas of green, with a close knit community served by a local grocery store, public house, school and church (Newby, 1979). These images, it can be argued, conceal the reality of living in many rural villages. Since the beginning of the twentieth century there has been a steep decline in the number of villages that house amenities such as a school, chapel, hall, shop, public house and green (Buckton, 2005). The portrayals, therefore, although partly accurate at their time of dissemination, continue to project an imagined village experience, which feeds into the 'rural idyll'. The rural idyll has to a degree been imposed onto the rural by media sources and as a result can be described as a concept that seeks to re-present rurality in a certain way rather than describe a rural locality or a lived rural experience. Villages rarely live up to the media representations of the 'rural', however, and those moving to them in search of this idyll often find that their expectations are not met. 'I don't regret moving to [the village] but it's not the social haven I anticipated . . . I'm just glad it's retained its pubs . . . otherwise I think I would have regretted coming here' (village resident, 2010). Further analysis (Markham, forthcoming) has shown that migrants to the countryside often want to keep the representations of the rural idyll alive, even though the lived rural experience often does not match them. The existence of a rural public house can be seen to perform a role in keeping the 'rural idyll' concept alive. It is, therefore, part of the 'idyll' and as a result how it should look and the role it should perform is often part of the imagined rather than the lived experience.

Other commentators, such as Faulks (2008) and Kingsnorth (2008), see the public house as a unique and integral part of England's history and identity. For these authors public houses and their signs are a connection to the past and, when they are lost, so too is our link to the past. Initial findings from the research upon which this chapter is based suggest that some village residents hold similar views to those advocated by Faulks (2008) and Kingsnorth (2008). For example, a number of interview respondents argued that, wherever you are in England, the sight of a rural public house and its signage evokes comfort and reassurance. A high proportion felt that the public house, and more importantly its sign, transported them back to their past as well as their present village of residence. The public house name and sign are usually one of the first things we notice about a rural public house, and according to one village resident (2012) they subconsciously shout the message, 'Come in, everybody is welcome'. This may arise because there is an expected appearance that publicans then try to recreate in order to benefit from people's positive images. People might also expect similar social interactions to occur in public houses in different villages and that these would be similar to the conversations among previous generations in those public houses. However, we must acknowledge that social divisions can be created and reinforced within the rural public house as the lived experiences may not always match the idyllic perceptions (see Markham, forthcoming; and see below).

The rural public house – a social hub?

'Public houses once had an important socialising influence, particularly among the working classes. They were the only places, apart from churches, where teenagers and pensioners rubbed along together' (Wilby, 2008). This statement implies that public houses no longer perform an important socialising role; it can be argued, however, that the social value of the pub has increased, although the form of that value has changed. Historically, the public house in general, and the rural public house in particular, was a place where generations of mainly working-class men congregated to unwind from work before going home (Brandwood *et al.*, 2004; Buckton, 2005; Pratten, 2007a). As one Lincolnshire village resident recalled (2010): 'when I was growing up it was only men who went to public houses; they would go there to socialise with work colleagues and friends of all ages.' It can be proposed that the rural public house was a social centre for men and that, alongside the local shop and Post Office, it formed one of the main social hubs of the village. In general, before 1980 women did not frequent the rural public house. Unless accompanied by their partner for Sunday lunch, it was deemed an inappropriate environment for them (Titchmarsh, 2010). Now, however, it is perfectly acceptable for men, women, couples and families to visit public houses any day of the week, any time during opening hours.

It can be proposed, therefore, that the rural public house remains one of the main social hubs of many villages. It provides a place where individuals can meet (pre-planned or by chance), have a chat, enhance knowledge and generally have a good time. By doing this the rural public house, like other rural services, such as the village shop and Post Office, helps to create, expand and strengthen social networks. Research by The Social Issues Research

Centre (SIRC, 2008) and Muir (2009) draws explicit attention to the fact that rural public houses matter when it comes to social networking. The rural public house provides an atmosphere that is conducive to social interaction and communication. It is an informal establishment where individuals are able to come and go as they please and interact on different levels, ranging from simple greetings through to in-depth social and conversational engagement with others (Muir, 2009). This lends itself well to the creation, expansion and strengthening of social networks. As several Lincolnshire village inhabitants remarked, 'public houses provide people of all generations a place to meet one another' (village resident, 2010). The rural public house is 'a good place to meet up with old friends and a good place to meet new people from different walks of life' (village resident, 2010). Sentiments such as these have been commonly expressed by interview respondents, not only from my own investigation but also from other studies:

> I walk into the public house and I nearly always get introduced to people I've never met before . . . I wouldn't necessarily be associating with them outside of the public house but I'd always say hello to them and ask them how they've been getting on and things and then I'd probably settle down with the group that I almost certainly always see in the public house everyday . . . so it's kind of a mixture really.
>
> (Interview respondent, cited in SIRC, 2008: 21)

The idea, suggested by one Lincolnshire village resident (2010), that the rural public house can play a significant role in sustaining community networks, is one which warrants some discussion. An opinion poll conducted as part of Muir's (2009) investigation yielded the notion that many individuals perceive the community public house as being the primary social establishment for encouraging positive relations among individuals from differing backgrounds. On one level the rural public house may aid community networks. It is open to all, and its atmosphere is one that invites and encourages conversation among users. However, it is questionable as to what extent this occurs, for two reasons. First, some people visit the rural public house for personal space and time and thus do not want to engage with other users, be it their neighbours or strangers. As SIRC (2008) acknowledges, on occasions people elect to visit less familiar rural public houses over their own local on the basis that they can be anonymous. Second, while the rural public house is open to all, not everyone frequents it; some groups are more prevalent than others. For example, despite an increase in female patrons there is still a gender disparity; in general male patrons outnumber their female counterparts (Muir, 2009). As a consequence of these two factors, it can be proposed that the role the rural public house plays in maintaining community networks is limited. While it can undeniably facilitate social integration between different walks of life, it cannot make it happen – that requires a variety of factors including individual willingness to engage with others.

Although early findings from the research upon which this chapter is based echo many of the sentiments disseminated by SIRC (2008) and Muir (2009) regarding the positive role the rural public house plays in the creation, expansion and strengthening of social networks, there have been some anomalies. While many acknowledge that the rural public house can add significant substance to social networks, some village residents have remarked that the rural public house and its atmosphere can have negative consequences for social and personal networks. 'I personally think [public houses] can have a negative influence, they are places where gossip can be spread and that can cause damage to individuals and their personal relationships . . . ultimately helping to erode the community bond that exists in many villages' (village resident, 2010). Such a statement cannot simply be disregarded; it is possible that on occasions social networks can be impeded as a result of visiting a rural public house. Alcohol consumption, particularly if excessive, can affect people in differing ways ranging from getting merry through to becoming subdued or even aggressive (see Institute of Alcohol Studies, 2007). This, combined with the 'easy come, easy go' public house atmosphere, can lead to words being spoken and interpreted in a variety of ways, the upshot being that tensions between patrons can occur, possibly resulting in breakdowns of personal and social relationships. As one village resident commented (2010), you can make friends in rural public houses but you can also lose them, especially if you get 'smashed', lose your inhibitions and say things you do not mean. This highlights that it is not the rural public house *per se* that can impede social networks but rather a combination of atmospheric and individual attributions.

When a rural public house ceases to trade, the ramifications can be fairly described as immense. There can be an impact on individual village residents, the local community, the local economy and the imagery of the village. In some respects it is difficult to separate out these impacts as they are often interrelated; however, to allow the reader an insight into these impacts a limited attempt will be made. When a rural public house closes so too does the social gathering point it provides. When this is lost those who rely on this place and space for their social interaction and networking may experience a decline in their quality of life. It has been documented by the Commission for Rural Communities (2007) that certain groups living in rural communities, for example those over 75 (see Key, this volume), frequently experience isolation and loneliness. It can be proposed that the closure of vital rural services compounds this. 'Some people rely on village services such as the public house to keep their social lives alive; when they shut, those people can withdraw from village life and become isolated' (village resident, 2010). This has implications because, if individuals withdraw from village life, they run the risk of further loneliness and possible social exclusion. For example, if an individual declines or shows no willingness to embrace offers by others to frequent either other village public houses or community social events, then slowly these offers by others could be withdrawn, thus leaving the individual on their own, alienated from the rest of society. It is not only individuals that can suffer when a village public house closes – so too can the community it serves. As services become fewer, communities have fewer places where they can discuss matters and organise events. If there is no gathering point for community members to mingle and chat, potentially there will be an attenuation of the community. The lack of a physical space may mean that communication between members becomes at best sporadic. As Scruton (2006) notes, when important social institutions cease to exist, communities can experience isolation and members can become alienated from one another. The potential upshot of this is that a breakdown in community spirit can take place, leading to a disjointed or divided community. This does not always happen. Occasionally, the cessation of village services can bring the community closer together and strengthen the bonds between residents. For example, when The George and Dragon in the village of Hudswell, North Yorkshire, closed, the village community pulled together to create a cooperative in a bid to save what many villagers saw as a vital service for their personal and community well-being. The result was a successful reopening of the village public house, with many village residents holding a stake in the establishment (Wainwright, 2011). This is not a common occurrence but is becoming a more visible feature throughout rural England (see Cabras, this volume).

When any rural enterprise ceases to trade there are repercussions not only for those involved in the enterprise but for the community as a whole. This is because of the ways in which rural enterprises are intertwined within rural communities. Thus, when one rural enterprise ceases it can have a knock on effect on the survival of other enterprises (Burgess, n.d., cited in Hill, 2008). This is especially the case if one rural enterprise makes use of other rural enterprises for goods provision. For example, if the rural public house gets its food provisions from local sources but then ceases to trade, the sources from which it acquires its goods will lose custom, potentially resulting in produce providers becoming commercially unviable and unsustainable in the long term. The implication of this for communities is that they lose yet another local service, and therefore another place of congregation. 'When villages lose their social meeting places communities die . . . [the village] becomes sleepy and the life is sucked out of its community' (village resident, 2010). There are two separate points relating to 'loss' that can be identified here. One, the loss of a rural enterprise could be a social loss because of the social functions it performs. Two, the loss of a rural enterprise results in the decline of other rural enterprises that depend on it, and hence a loss to the community as a whole.

Although there is a physical aspect to the 'rural idyll' there is another element, which Kraak and Kenway (2002, cited in Valentine *et al.*, 2008) term the moral component. This relates specifically to rural communities. Representations of rural communities are ones of close togetherness where all generations are socially integrated with one another in a friendly 'everyone is everyone's neighbour' scenario, and the village pub is seen to aid this

(Woods, 2011). Such representations are out-dated and to some degree have always been an embellishment of the truth.

> Unlike today the village was more lively, there were always things to do for us kids . . . my street was cliquey – everyone seemed to know everyone's business. It was stifling but at least it meant I never got lonely . . . it's not like that anymore – there are so many comings and goings you never get chance to know your neighbours. Even if they stay, many aren't sociable.
>
> (Village resident, 2010)

> Villagers have always mingled, especially in and outside the services but in the 90 years I've lived here it's never been like on Heartbeat or Emmerdale, they're so false.
>
> (Village resident, 2011)

As times have changed so too have villages and their communities. In contrast to previous decades a high percentage of those who live in rural localities work and socialise in or around other, particularly urban, localities. This, combined with greater personal mobility, has led a number of residents to have other commitments and responsibilities outside of the village. Consequently, while these residents may embrace their local services and community, they simply do not want to or cannot afford the same level of commitment that previous generations had.

Sustainability of the village community

Over the last few decades the rural public house, like many other rural enterprises, has diversified, either to remain economically viable, or to retain a communal hub within the village in the long term. There have been different levels and types of diversification. The public houses that have been principally concerned with profit margins have tended to focus solely on the diversification of retailing good quality, locally sourced food (Pratten, 2007b). By contrast, those that have taken a key interest in helping to keep their local community sustainable have taken more novel approaches including the housing of another rural service, namely the rural Post Office and/or village shop. There are many villages where this has taken place, with early examples including The Craven Heifer Hotel in Stainforth, North Yorkshire, and the White Hart Inn, Blythburgh, Southwold, Suffolk (Countryside Agency, 2001). In both of these places the reaction among village residents has been positive with clear benefits to the local community including the keeping open of vital services and the ongoing provision of a focal point where individuals can congregate and community meetings can take place (Countryside Agency, 2001). Although in these instances the housing of one service in another has been warmly embraced, some Lincolnshire village residents have concerns about the changing ethos associated with this. The early findings from this research suggest that, while many village residents would go along with the idea, they do not like it and would prefer services to remain separate from one another. As one Lincolnshire resident (2010) expressed:

> Public houses should stick to what they are good at, selling alcohol and food . . . Post Offices in rural public houses is wrong. Village services should, as far as is possible, remain separate. That said if it keeps services open and gives people a place to meet it could be a worthwhile venture.

Findings also suggest that while residents do see social and community value in the housing of one service in another they also believe that it lessens the value of individual services and is detrimental to the image and status of a village.

> I think one service in another is problematic, whilst it does maintain the services and provides communities with a meeting place it devalues the worth of the services and the village as a whole. Ultimately the services lose their identity and the village loses its character and its charm.
>
> (Village resident, 2011)

This suggests there is ambivalence among some residents: on one hand they dislike change but on the other they recognise that change may be needed for the village to survive.

To conclude, while there has been a decline in the number of rural public houses there has been little to no decline in their cultural and social importance. They continue to be a cultural icon and a social lifeline for some residents. They provide communities with a focal gathering point where they can mingle, have a chat and generally discuss community matters. In doing this they can help to create, expand and strengthen social and community-based networks among those residents that use rural public houses and want to engage with fellow customers. Such attributes can be seen in recreational centres in rural settlements across many parts of the world, although the historically specific significance of the English public house extends beyond this.

When rural public houses cease trading there can be immense implications for village residents and rural communities. There is a loss of a social gathering place, which can lead to some experiencing a decline in their overall quality of life, with increased isolation and possible social exclusion. To combat the negative social effects of such closure some rural public houses have offered and embraced the idea of delivering other services such as the Post Office. This idea is one that has in some instances been received warmly and in others with some trepidation. The main concern voiced by some village residents is that this change devalues the services and the image of the village. For many decades it has been the 'norm' for villages to have separate services, except for the Post Office, which has often been situated in the village store. Thus when one service is relocated in another there occurs not only a geographical change to the village but, more importantly, a cultural change for its residents and society as a whole. This is sometimes hard to accept and is reinforced by representations of the rural and 'rural idyll' that often do not reflect the reality of rural life. It could be argued that the pub itself is an icon or that it contains a set of icons (e.g., pub sign and internal paraphernalia), all of which have a place within the rural idyll. Likewise it could be argued that it is the social function of the pub that expresses the idyllic community of the village. Either way, the pub forms part of England's history and heritage and continues to play a role, be it experienced or imagined, in the lives of many.

Note

1 All the interviews took place between 2010 and 2011. Data was collected from a variety of Lincolnshire villages. For full list see Markham (forthcoming).

References

British Beer and Pub Association (2010) Pubs Still Closing but at a Slower Rate. Available at: www.beerandpub.com/news/pubs-still-closing-but-at-slower-rate (accessed 28 February 2013).

Brandwood, G., Davison, A. and Slaughter, M. (2004) *Licensed to Sell*. London: English Heritage.

Buckton, H. (2005) *Yesterday's Country Village*. Newton Abbot, UK: David & Charles.

CAMRA (2012) CAMRA Releases New National Pub Closure Research. Available at: www.camra.org.uk/article.php?group_id=6095 (accessed 28 February 2013).

Chatterton, P. and Hollands, R. (2002) 'Theorising urban playscapes: Producing, regulating and consuming youthful nightlife city spaces', *Urban Studies* 39(1): 95–116.

Commission for Rural Communities (2007) The Economic Significance of Post Offices Combined with a Village Shop. London: CRC.

Countryside Agency (2001) The Public House is the Hub: A Good Practice Guide. Wetherby, UK: Countryside Agency Publications.

Faulks, S. (2008) 'Reading the Signs', in B. Bryson (ed.), *Icons of England*. London: Think Books: 145–8.

Gorham, M. (1950) 'The Public house and the People', in M. Gorham and H. McG. Dunnett (eds), *Inside the Public House*. London: Architectural Press: 15–43.

Hill, A. (2008) How Our Villages are Fighting to Stay Alive. Available at: www.guardian.co.uk/uk/2008/sep/14/ruralaffairs.britishidentity (accessed 10 October 2008).

Hutt, C. (1973) *The Death of the English Public House*. London: Arrow Books.

Institute of Alcohol Studies (2007) Medical and Social Consequences of Binge Drinking. St Ives, UK: Institute of Alcohol Studies.

Jennings, P. (2007) *The Local: A History of the English Public House*. Stroud, UK: Tempus Publishing.

Lost Pubs Project (2013) The Lost Pubs Project. Available at: www.closedpubs.co.uk (accessed 16 March 2013).

Kingsnorth, P. (2008) *Real England: The Battle Against the Bland*. London: Portobello Books.

Markham, C. (forthcoming) *The Rural Public House*. Ph.D. study, University of Lincoln.

Muir, R. (2009) *Public Houses and Places: The Social Value of Community Public Houses*. London: IPPR.

Newby, H. (1979) *Green and Pleasant Land: Social Change in Rural England*. Worcester, UK: Billing & Sons.

Orwell, G. (1946) 'The Moon Under the Water', *The Evening Standard*, 9 February.

Pratten, J. D. (2007a) 'The development of the modern UK public house – Part Two: Signs of change to the UK public house 1959–1989', *International Journal of Contemporary Hospitality Management* 19(6): 513–19.

Pratten, J. D. (2007b) 'The development of the modern UK public house – Part Three: The emergence of the modern public house 1989–2005', *International Journal of Contemporary Hospitality Management* 19(7): 612–18.

Scruton, R. (2006) 'Closing time', *New Statesman*, 28 August.

SIRC (2008) The Enduring Appeal of the Local. Oxford: The Social Issues Research Centre.

Titchmarsh, A. (2010) *When I Was a Nipper: The Way We Were in Disappearing Britain*. London: BBC Books.

Valentine, G., Holloway, S., Knell, C. and Jayne, M. (2008) 'Drinking places: Young people and cultures of alcohol consumption in rural environments', *Journal of Rural Studies* 24(1): 28–40.

Wainwright, M. (2011) *The English Village, History and Traditions*. London: Michael O'Mara Books.

Wilby, P (2008) More Important Than Post Offices. Available at: www.newstatesman.com/society/2008/07/public houses-beer-drink-brewers (accessed 10 October 2008).

Woods, M. (2011) *Rural*. London: Routledge.

19 Conclusion

Interrogating rural coherence

Peter Somerville, Keith Halfacree and Gary Bosworth

The chapters in this book have covered a wide range of topics, from a variety of perspectives and involving many different disciplines. This chimes well with contemporary rural scholarship, whereby many different approaches to the rural have been identified (see Woods, 2011). In this book, however, rurality has been interpreted variously as: *material* – a territory constituted largely by economic activity; *represented* – a mainly cultural artefact, in particular the rural idyll, but also culturally prescribed or sanctioned practices such as those associated with animals, music and 'nature'; *contested* – a distinct realm of collective action and political conflict, e.g. around 'development', social class, ethnicity and biodiversity; and *consumed* – a specific type of attractor for human beings such as tourists, pleasure-seekers, older people and those seeking greater closeness to 'nature' and improved well-being. In short, rurality comes across overall as *relational*; that is, its existence always relates to a specific domain. This chapter assesses the apparent relativity expressed by these different interpretations, partly in the context of the rural studies literature. Its aim is to establish the extent to which we can ultimately conclude that rurality can have any generally accepted meaning across the different domains. Or, perhaps this relationality of the rural – and we may also note here the presence of numerous quasi-synonymous expressions: country, arcadian, rustic, bucolic, pastoral, and so on – is instead indicative of what Laclau called an *empty signifier* (Laclau and Mouffe, 1985), that is, a privileged element that gathers up a range of distinct elements and binds them together into a discursive formation, but only by emptying it of its content.

An obvious starting point for a theoretical discussion of rurality is to propose the idea that rurality is spatial. If 'rural' is to be distinguished from 'urban' at all, one possibility is that it refers to a different kind of space (see the Introduction to this volume). This raises the question, however, of what is meant by 'space' and, further, of what kind of space 'rural' is. Almost immediately, a problem arises, in that it is usually assumed that 'space' has structure, but there seems to be no general agreement about its exact form (and this lack of agreement is reflected in the chapters in this book). Therefore, to investigate this structure, we begin with Halfacree's (2006, 2007) argument that space in general, and rural space in particular, may be interrogated in terms of the extent to which it demonstrates 'structured coherence'. This is defined (drawing on Harvey, 1985; Cloke and Goodwin, 1992) as a social formation in which economy, state and civil society mesh together in a relatively stable fashion. If such a structured coherence can be consistently identified, across the different domains of the rural, then it may be concluded that a coherent rural exists.

Following Massey (2005), however, such a prospect is less immediately forthcoming. For her, space is not a static and closed container, and forms of structured coherence do not exist *in* space; rather, space is constituted *through* its relations (Massey, 2005: 107), so structured coherences are always likely to be transitory. As Marxian terminology has long depicted, space is continually (re)created by labour, the action of human on non-human; it is 'produced' (Smith, 1984). Further, the relations that constitute space have increasingly been seen to involve many different kinds of entities, human and non-human (Jones and Cloke, 2002; Jones, 2003; Castree, 2005), and numerous kinds of performance (Thrift, 1996). It is the routine repetition of complexly multifaceted performances by these multifaceted entities in everyday practices that produces relatively stable but always provisional and never complete forms of structured coherence. In short, space – and anything one may label 'rural space' – is an (ever-changing) pattern of performed complexly populated relationships. Rural coherence thus becomes an inherently relational challenge and, as with 'regulation' within regulation theory more comprehensively (Goodwin, 2006: 312), any coherence that becomes apparent is better seen as remaining 'liquid' (Bauman, 2000) than as expressing a relatively solid state.

The previous discussion does not tell us, however, how we can characterise the range of coherences that space may demonstrate. In order to do this, Halfacree (2006, 2007), building on Lefebvre (1991), first characterises specifically *rural* space as composed of the triad of: rural localities, relatively distinct spatial practices; formal representations of the rural, particularly related to dominant forms of commodification; and everyday lives of the rural, often individually and subjectively distinctive. Second, when examined together at a particular point in space–time, this totality expresses one of three forms of rural coherence (Halfacree, 2006: 52):

1. *Congruent and unified*, whereby '[a]ll elements of rural space cohere in a relatively smooth, consistent manner. Formal representations of the rural are unified, overwhelming and hegemonic';
2. *Contradictory and disjointed*, with 'tension and contradiction between or within the elements . . . but an overall coherence . . . best appreciated at a more meta-level'; and
3. *Chaotic and incoherent*, with 'fundamental contradictions between or within the elements of rural space'.

Of these three forms, it is only the first that expresses a full structured coherence. As a goal to be attained beyond the local and the very temporary, it is also suggested to be extremely challenging. This is illustrated by Halfacree (2006, 2007) in terms of the (arguably) fatally compromised post-1945 efforts to produce a *productivist countryside* that would unify the rural under the hegemony of a particular discourse of primary production (Murdoch and Ward, 1997). Consequently, within today's potential forms of what may be labelled *post-productivism* (such as *super-productivism*, *consuming idylls*, and *radical ruralities*; Halfacree, 2006) – all of which are represented in different chapters in this book as discussed below – there seems to be a stronger recognition that rural coherence is at best contradictory and disjointed, united through the motif of 'diversity', if not one of spatial chaos and incoherence, speaking of conflict and irresolution.

Consolidating, what is presented above is a framework for making sense of the rural and of rural change that sees rurality as produced by the relationships between the three elements of the triad, which in turn provides the basis for a resulting (in)coherence. Returning to rural productivism, it can be seen as a *project* to create and maintain (or perform or practise) a unified and congruent coherence by the close relationship between capitalist industrial agriculture (practices), the post-war planning and agricultural subsidy system (underpinned by representations), and local landed and farming elites (expressing everyday lives). Moreover, this sounds very similar to the regulationist concept of an accumulation regime, demonstrating that much of Halfacree's argument seems to fit well within the broader conceptual approach of regulation theory.

Regulation theory seeks to problematise the 'regularization or normalization . . . of the economy in its broadest sense' (Goodwin, 2006: 304) or, as Jessop (1997: 288) more fully expresses it within Goodwin's chapter, it 'aims to study the changing combinations of economic *and extra-economic* institutions and practices which help to secure, if only temporarily and always in specific economic spaces, a certain stability and predictability in accumulation'. It has an important pedigree within rural studies, in particular Jessop's strategic relational approach (for a review and rural application of the approach, see Pemberton and Goodwin, 2010). There is, however, a problem with this approach, which was identified originally by Clarke (1991). For Jessop (2002), the state acts strategically, in order to resolve the contradictions of capitalist accumulation, whereas Clarke (1991: 51) argues that the state itself is an expression of those contradictions. Similarly to Jessop, Pemberton and Goodwin (2010: 276) see the state as an internally connected set of institutions rather than as a contradictory unity. Their approach does not tell us where political strategies come from or how they work: indeed, they do not recognise that the 'strategies' they do identify are themselves internally contradictory (e.g., in their example of Ceredigion, the council's 'strategy' both conserves and undermines 'traditional' social relations of class and culture).

Acknowledging this theoretical weakness, however, provokes scepticism about whether the project of rural productivism could have ever succeeded. Instead, although productivism presented some features of unity and congruence, one can argue that it inevitably remained at heart incoherent, being riven by internal contradictions rooted in the capitalist contradiction between value and use-value, or, in other words, between capital itself as self-expanding value (with its cycles of growth and accumulation, most clearly expressed in the abstract terms of flows of money) and 'community', in the sense of the concrete labour, raw materials (including land) and other resources that are exploited and expended in the production process, which itself produces all that we use and consume. Indeed, one may suggest that these contradictions are precisely what drive its (contested) transformations into post-productivist projects (see Moore's chapter in particular).

The relations that constitute space, including rural space, can therefore be seen as predominantly relations of contradiction, at least in capitalist societies. This means that structured coherence, for example as expressed by rural productivism, can only be somewhat superficial, and that lying behind it is always a *dynamic* of exploitation and struggle. If this argument is correct, then it serves to emphasise further the importance of the category 'contested rurality' and of 'produced' space (Smith, 1984), both noted above. From a regulationist perspective, contestation arises from conflicts focused primarily on capital growth and the impacts of that growth. However, it can also occur in conflicts of other kinds. Taking the example of productivism again, one can foreground how what is commonly called 'industrial agriculture' or 'agribusiness' is definitely and predominantly an example of capitalist working, based on the mass exploitation of land and labour to produce agricultural commodities (goods and services for profit). As with all capitalist enterprise, therefore, the primary contradiction expressed here is between, on the one hand, the capitalists, who own the land and means of production, and, on the other, the workers, who hire out their labour to the capitalists in return for wages. Rural capitalism is therefore not really distinguishable from capitalism generally. In addition, however, a contestation may be seen between such capitalist agriculture and the agency/agencies of 'nature' (see discussion on nature and the 'agrarian question': Henderson, 1998; see also Smith, 1996). It can also clash with farmers' own values, which frequently include non-capitalist expressions (Wynne-Jones, forthcoming). A further significant area of contention exists between agrarian capitalism and other forms of capitalism that seek to commodify and profit from the rural (Cloke, 1992; Marsden, 1999), notably through packaging it for various forms of market-based consumption (tourism, leisure, residence).

Recognition of both this latter heterogeneity of (capitalist and non-capitalist) forces and the similarity across spatial categories acknowledged earlier turns discussion to the question of what, if anything, is therefore distinctively 'rural'. If the countryside is just as much a capitalist space as the city is (albeit itself internally contested), dominated by the same kinds of social relations and struggles, then the distinctiveness of rural space must, in short, be of a less categorical kind (Hoggart, 1990). Such a relegation in status must not be assumed *always* to be relevant for every aspect of a particular person's or place's everyday life – see Gibson-Graham's (1996, 2006) critique of the ideologically assumed predominance of capitalism within all aspects of daily life. Certainly, however, trying conclusively to *define* rurality materially runs the risk of perpetuating a 'chaotic conception' (Sayer, 1984) of space that is most unlikely to ground a robust rural structured coherence.

Furthermore, in considering the possible components principally engaged in the construction of a (rural) structured coherence, it is not necessary to restrict oneself to Halfacree's triad. Other components are also possible: for example, the 'hubs' described by Frisvoll (2012: 449–50), which are material (relating to property, its location, usufruct, money and means of violence), immaterial (referring to juridical relations and the informal rules and norms that guide people's actions) and personal (for example, people's careers and/or career plans and family, their dispositions, temperaments, affinities, beliefs, values and aspirations). On top of this added complexity – emphasising just how existentially challenging it will be to attain even relatively fleeting structured coherence – we may also recognise capitalism as 'a society of *non-correspondence*, in which things do not fit together functionally' (Holloway, 2002: 187, our emphasis). We can further note, through this less totalising lens, how both production and consumption need not be entirely capitalist in practice, representation and/or experience (Gibson-Graham, 1996, 2006; Halfacree, 2010).

From all of this discussion, then, we suggest that rurality can be seen as potentially supporting kinds of (often fleeting and possibly ephemeral) structured coherences that are much less completely grounded in the material than is usually understood. The extent to which coherence does or does not exist in the case of any given place is, in fact, an empirical question, and can be answered in different ways, depending, for example, on the nature of the components concerned and the relations between those components. Furthermore, from the variety of answers to this question we can then return to an interrogation of the meaning of rurality itself – that is, what is it that these places have in common that make them cohere – by virtue of which they can all be called 'rural' (whether this be material, represented or whatever)? An attempt is made to answer this question at the end of this chapter.

Turning now to the chapters in this book, it becomes apparent that a variety of types and degrees of (rural) structured coherence are being suggested. Some chapters seem to imply that there is no structured coherence, some suggest that there is, while in other cases it is not clear whether there is or not – or, if there is, whether it can reasonably be called 'rural'. Overall, the existence of structured coherence is rarely made explicit in any chapter, as this was not their remit. However, it may be worthwhile to attempt to clarify what each chapter has to say about the issue and then to draw conclusions from this concerning the diversity of interpretations of rurality today.

Let us start with *material* rurality (the focus of chapters by Siwale, Cabras, Gray and Herron *et al.*). In Siwale's chapter, the meaning of rurality is seen as varying from one country to another, though commonly associated with agriculture and low population density. In countries in sub-Saharan Africa, the legacy of colonialism has meant that rurality is imagined primarily as 'spaces of exploitation and extraction', which supply raw materials and cheap labour for urban areas, leaving rural areas impoverished in the extreme. Most people living in these areas rely on subsistence farming, but this seems a misnomer given that many are failing to subsist at all. If there had existed any structured rural coherence before the arrival of the colonial powers, it seems clear that a lasting effect of colonial rule has been to destroy that coherence and to subjugate the rural population completely to the demands of urban administration and global capitalist markets. Siwale's account starkly reveals the lack of structured coherence in Zambian rural areas due to its annihilation by the forces of global capital actively assisted by postcolonial national urban elites.

Cabras's chapter, focusing specifically on cooperative enterprises in Britain, argues that, compared with urban cooperatives, rural cooperatives tend to be more socially cohesive and more firmly based in local communities. It appears that rural cooperatives can play an important role in ensuring the economic sustainability of villages, giving them a certain degree of structured coherence focused, for example, on a key community service such as a public house or village shop. Basically, the cooperative works to bring together a variety of key economic and social relations so as to achieve a self-organised way of going on. The village's structured coherence then derives from the combination of the cooperative's social inclusiveness and economic viability. It attains 'power' from the strength of the network that is created (Murdoch, 2000). Establishing cooperatives, however, is difficult and, once established, they can be difficult to maintain: economically, they are vulnerable to more ruthlessly profit-maximising competition; and socially, many rural communities are deeply divided. Here, therefore, rural structured coherence can be a distinctly fragile material achievement, which needs ongoing public support (both inside and outside the community) in order to survive. It is not clear, however, whether this form of structured coherence is specifically rural, as it may be possible to identify community facilities in urban areas, such as schools or hospitals, around which collective action and campaigns could focus in a similar way, at least in principle.

The third chapter on material rurality, by Gray, is very different again. This chapter adopts a rigorous economic approach to rurality. Here the rural is understood as 'a territorial unit of analysis below the level of the nation', identified as areas with the lowest population density and lowest concentrations of economic activity. Gray sees rural areas as specialising in industries such as food production, which need larger tracts of land and which produce goods with lower income elasticity (this view resonates with Siwale's argument that rural areas are systemically disadvantaged relatively to urban areas). After reviewing relevant economic theories, Gray argues that interrogating the coherence of material rurality must take account of the relationship between employment and housing markets, and this leads him to conclude (largely because of the effects of commuting) that 'the city-region or the functional urban region provides a better unit of analysis than the rural or urban as separate entities' (p. 47). In particular, while accepting in principle the spatial distinction between 'core' and 'periphery', he argues that: 'It is the non-commutable rural where the term "peripheral" is more appropriate: the commutable and the non-commutable rural have distinct characteristics that put them in separate territorial groupings' (p. 47). This means that there is no structured coherence to the rural in general but there may be coherence to the more peripheral or more remote 'non-commutable rural' (the 'really' rural, if you like) and also to the combined urban and commutable rural (reflecting relatively integrated labour and housing markets). This is an important finding, which no doubt will be contested by other scholars, but it raises the question of whether there is anything distinctive about the 'commutable rural' (which should, perhaps, be seen as *liminal* – see, for example, Lawrence, 2003) and, if so, what that might be.

Finally on material rurality, and radically different again, the chapter by Herron, Jackson and Johnson focuses on how people in rural areas in England organise and change their own communities through long periods of historical time. It highlights in particular the enduring relevance of the concept of a parish, and understands rural structured coherence in terms of a dynamic interaction between parishes of governance (both secular and ecclesiastical) and parishes of place (based on shared attachments, allegiances and related forms of collective action). The parish is conceived fundamentally as a 'lived' territory, both actual and imagined, with boundaries that are recognised and continually reproduced by its inhabitants – a clear site of structured spatial coherence. Here the emphasis is not so much on the economic dimension of coherence as on the everyday political dimension. As the authors explain, however, this is a peculiarly 'parochial' politics, practised by a tiny population living in a small geographical area and typically some distance removed from mainstream political concerns (although these can and do surface from time to time) and centres of major political decision-making. Thus, although parishes can seem remarkably stable and long lasting, they can also seem relatively powerless in the face of wider and more systemic social change. Their parochialism can even echo Siwale's conclusions about the political irrelevance of rural areas in contemporary Africa.

Moving on to *represented* rurality (the focus of chapters by Walker, Parry, Hall, Hildyard and Grau), we again find an extraordinary variety of interpretations of rural structured coherence. Most of these (Walker, Parry, Hildyard) evoke and criticise concepts of the rural idyll (which involves an *imagined* coherence) (for useful historical and critical, respectively, accounts of idyllic rurality, see Short, 2006, and Bell, 2006). Walker harks back to a long history of pastoralism, in which the countryside is constructed as a picturesque landscape, 'innocent, unpolluted and uncorrupted', 'a place of refuge and escape from the demands of city life'. He points out that this is largely a fiction, which city-dwellers have attempted to impose on the countryside (hence imagined, not just imaginary). In imposing this, however, they have tended to produce a coherence of their own – a landscape of 'follies, lakes and leafy arbours' (p. 92). Later, the Romantic movement favoured wilder and less civilised landscapes but still saw the rural as an 'other', to be contemplated and acted upon. As with the material rural, the representation of the rural is firmly subordinated to the concerns and agendas of people from urban areas. It is questionable, however, whether any idealist reshaping of the countryside can ever produce a structured coherence, as the image comes into continual conflict with the materiality of everyday rural living. In his historical study of Lincoln, Walker shows one particular focus of this conflict, where the citizens of Lincoln acted to expel from the city features of rural activity that contradicted their perception of the rural idyll. Essentially, their representation of rurality led them to free themselves from what they saw as rural contamination. The lawlessness and disorder of the cattle market and horse fair were to be replaced by more 'civilised' and urbane activities. This reveals once again the predominance of urban concerns over rural ones, but here the project involved a (successful) reshaping of the city, as part of a long history of attrition against rural practices, driving them out to the periphery, rather than any attempt to change the countryside itself. Whatever coherence the rural might have, this analysis suggests that it would be strongly determined by urban forces.

Parry's chapter adopts an ecocritical approach to understanding represented rurality in the form of English literary landscapes, as revealed through a number of twentieth century novels. Here rurality is conceived explicitly as involving both human and non-human components, and represented as 'an intermediate zone between urbanness as dense human land occupation, and wilderness as an absence of human occupation in a land' (p. 110). This is a very different interpretation of the rural, in that it contrasts rurality not only with 'urbanness' (as argued or assumed in almost all the other chapters in this book) but also with 'wilderness'. Rurality is therefore placed at a point on a continuum, with wholly human at one end and wholly non-human at the other. Such a position could be criticised on the grounds that nothing in this world is either wholly human or wholly non-human, leading one to conclude that just about everything is more or less rural. However, we must remember that Parry is focusing on a representation here, rather than on the totality of rural space, and is not concerned to provide a definitive locating of rurality in the scheme of things but rather a critique of the (English) rural idyll *both* as a tamed landscape (as in the pastoral tradition described by Walker) *and* as an untamed wilderness (as envisaged within the Romantic movement). Through such critique, Parry seeks to find the 'meta-context' or 'sub-landscape' that lies 'below the flat, idealised image of the rural landscape' (p. 109). She shows how different characters tend to subvert the rural idyll while at the same time finding themselves unable to escape from it (a metaphor, perhaps, for humanity as a whole), and that 'nature' and 'landscape' themselves are complex, hybrid forms, in which activity and imagination, materiality and representation, are inextricably intertwined with one another. Parry interprets much of the narrative in these novels as allegorical, and ultimately this seems to form the basis of whatever structured coherence can be identified – that is, the narrative structure of a rural allegory (of humanity's relationship with nature). In Parry's own words: 'what is revealed is an enmeshing of matter, discourse and symbol in which representation, interpretation and originary material are locked together in a dynamic embrace' (p. 119).

Hall's chapter argues that, at least in Britain, livestock grazing functions as an important representation of rurality: 'Without grazing livestock, the characteristic British patchworks of fields, their boundaries, and traditional farm buildings would be threatened and land unfit for crops would be taken over by scrubland or forestry' (p. 123). Here, therefore, rurality is identified with a type of landscape that is produced by interaction between humans and animals, demonstrating clearly the links between representation, practice and everyday life. Like Parry, therefore, Hall sees the rural as intermediate between the exclusively human (without animals) and 'scrubland' (without humans or domesticated animals). Though perhaps not definitive of rurality as such, livestock grazing seems to be a major ingredient in its representation, creating a distinctive and coherent culturally significant landscape, which does not fit easily into either a productivist or post-productivist framework. This point is taken up further in relation to Moore's chapter (see below).

Hildyard's chapter covers similar historical ground to Walker's on the pastoral and Romantic representations of rurality, and also in linking these representations to the changing class relations in English society, particularly the effects of industrialisation and urbanisation. Unlike Walker, however, Hildyard identifies, in the later nineteenth century, 'a shift from a more genteel, distanced and purely contemplative view of the rural to what could be called a hands on engagement with farming life' (p. 135), and the main focus of his chapter is on a number of key 'farm texts', which he uses to illustrate this practical rediscovery (or possibly reinvention) of the rural. Like Parry, he adopts an ecocritical perspective, identifying the contradictions between represented and material rurality within these texts. In the text by Henry Williamson, for example, the rural idyll is to be constructed, not just imagined, but the activity of construction itself (particularly relying on the latest technology) tends to conflict with the vision of how rurality should be (in some sense 'natural', untainted by technology). In contrast, in the text by Adrian Bell, a more pastoral meaning is attached to rurality, with the author immersing himself in that pastorality, so that it is the urban rather than the rural that becomes 'othered' in this representation. In both texts, however, 'the meaning of rurality nearly always carries with it the promise of self-actualisation' (p. 142). The concept of the rural idyll therefore becomes more entrenched in our culture as a result of such 'back to the land' (Halfacree,

2001) projects involving the material creation of heterotopias. These projects have potential to become what Halfacree (2006, 2007) has called 'radical ruralities', but it is not clear how this potential is to be realised. In all of these narratives, it is difficult to find any material coherence or even consistency but only a degree of coherence of represented rurality, for example, in the representation of farming life and rural landscape. Beyond or underneath this representation, which itself is often at odds with material rural change, contradictions abound.

Like Hall's chapter, the chapter by Grau focuses on a very specific representation, namely the brass band. Unlike Hall, however, Grau's representation does not seem characteristically rural. Her contribution is to show that, as a cultural representation, the phenomenon of the brass band is not tied to any particular (rural or urban) locality but nevertheless has long-term historical endurance within a given locality (in this case, Horncastle). There are signs of structured coherence at national and local levels, but the coherence is formed in different ways at these different levels (nationally, through organised competitions and the Brass Band Movement, and locally through features such as overlapping membership networks). Although going some way towards countering the urban bias in our understanding of the brass band, Grau finds little evidence of a specifically *rural* structured coherence, either in its representation or in its material organisation. In the terms of Halfacree (2006, 2007), this seems to be an illustration of 'effaced rurality', which Grau seeks to recover or restore, at least in an historical, even spectral, sense.

The conflicts between material and represented rurality, which recur in many of the chapters in the first two sections, are explicitly addressed in the third section of the book, on *contested* rurality (the chapters by Moore, Bestwick, Somerville, Nurse and Greenfields). Moore's chapter is specifically a case study of the conflict over a proposal to establish a 'mega-dairy' at Nocton in Lincolnshire. This was a classic struggle between the forces of 'agri-business', concerned to maximise the profits from dairy farming, and those adhering to the dominant idyllic view that 'cows belong in fields' – a view strongly supported in media and popular imagery that perhaps emerges from the historical and cultural significance of livestock grazing as discussed in Hall's chapter. Moore's cultural studies approach complements Hall's ecological approach, with represented rurality being understood in terms of a specific form of relationship between humans and (farm) animals. Moore then shows vividly how this latter representation is incompatible with the transition in material rurality from productivism to what Halfacree (2006, 2007) has called 'super-productivism'. She points to new ways of conceiving the human–non-human relationship that go beyond the traditional view and could help to end, if not resolve, this conflict. She further exposes a certain lack of coherence in the (super-)productivist project, in that its own representations of dairy farming contradict the materiality of that farming. Overall, therefore, her chapter suggests an absence of rural structured coherence, either material or representational, except perhaps as regards the continuing (and, of course, contested) 'hegemony' of livestock grazing in the English rural landscape.

Bestwick's chapter focuses on the fox and the grey squirrel in order to illustrate the conflict between urban and rural attitudes, as well as between social classes, over how humans should behave towards such animals. Fox hunting has been claimed by the Countryside Alliance to be integral to English/British rural life and therefore to national identity: 'country' as distinct from 'town' is equated with 'country' as meaning 'nation'. This claim to speak on behalf of the country as a whole, however, is contested primarily by city-dwellers, who see fox hunting as cruel. On the other hand, Bestwick points to the growth of anti-fox attitudes in urban areas as urban foxes appear to get more numerous and perhaps more daring, and lose their exotic and romantic appeal. In contrast, although displaying a similar divide between rural antis and urban pros, attitudes towards the squirrel have been more complex, with red squirrels being transformed from vermin into English national icon, and grey squirrels being actively encouraged in urban areas while being ruthlessly exterminated in rural areas. The strength of contestation in the case of these two species (the fox and the grey squirrel) is especially pronounced because of the way that materiality and representation are both involved – materiality, in terms of the threat that foxes pose to livestock and the damage that squirrels do to crops, and representation, in terms of what could be called the iconography of these particular animals (e.g., the cunning Reynard and loveable Squirrel Nutkin). Although dominant attitudes differ between town and country, there is no particular coherence in either case; rather, in both types of area, attitudes are contradictory and often confused. In her conclusion, Bestwick draws from Smout (1983) to suggest that this may be a conflict between 'use' (a utilitarian approach based on a judgement of how useful or harmful a particular animal is for humans) and 'delight' (a more aesthetic approach based on the intrinsic value of the animal itself). The incoherence in this case, therefore, seems to be a moral or ethical one.

The structured coherence identified in Somerville's chapter relates primarily to social class. In particular, he describes a historically enduring pattern of landowner dominance of rural social relations – 'an uninterrupted and unchallenged hegemony'. He argues that the alleged shift from productivism to post-productivism has not altered this basic fact of English (and indeed British) country life. Although differing in a number of respects, agri-business and the 'new' gentry have a common interest in excluding the 'lower' classes from the countryside. As part of this overall coherence, policy (in particular on planning) has 'largely focused on the "protection" of the countryside, understood in terms of restrictions on non-agricultural development, in order to make it safe for producer-driven agriculture and consumer-driven gentrification' (p. 191). However, Somerville's chapter also suggests the possibility of considerable spatial variation in the form of this structured coherence, in particular between so-called 'growth' and 'non-growth' areas. Although key class relations are being continually reproduced and renewed while staying basically the same, the spatial expression of these relations, particularly in non-growth areas, has changed significantly (mainly due to gentrification). The countryside may therefore have become more spatially divided, with 'new gentry' exclusively occupying small villages and hamlets while larger villages grow to be more like urban areas. Such increased spatial differentiation is perfectly compatible with a general structured coherence, but it does raise the question of how far this process can go before the developing areas cease to be 'rural' in any meaningful sense of the word. Referring back to Gray's chapter, however, this is not a difference between the commutable and non-commutable rural because a large proportion of the new gentry are indeed commuters while many non-commutable rural areas are not gentrified. So it is a spatial division *within* the rural that reflects the class division *of* the rural. Commuters living in the countryside may be tied into urban labour and housing markets, but many of them are powerful consumers of the rural.

Nurse's chapter, like Hall's, suggests that rural structured coherence is a matter of distinctive practices relating to the non-human, such as animals, plants and the 'natural environment', particularly the classically rural activities of hunting, shooting and fishing. Nurse describes another peculiarity of rural areas, however, namely the deep involvement of NGOs in the policing of rural crime, particularly wildlife crime. Although such involvement is distinctive of rural areas, related to perceptions of such crime as being characteristically 'rural', Nurse criticises it on a number of grounds, not least because it results in partial, inconsistent, uncoordinated and often ineffective policing. In this case, therefore, the assumption of a definitive interpretation of rurality appears to be associated with an incoherent approach to the policing of rural areas, and consequently Nurse argues for a redefinition of rural crime (to include *all* crime that occurs in rural areas) as a step towards achieving fairer and more effective rural policing. The identification of rural structured coherence with specific human–non-human relationships remains, but it is also recognised that the policing of rural areas involves a much wider spectrum of activities than just the policing of these relationships – it is not just about the policing of rural crime. The rationale for treating rural areas differently for policing purposes is thus refuted by this chapter.

For Greenfields, rural structured coherence is understood largely in terms of community cohesion. She records how Gypsies and Travellers, along with other nomadic peoples, were for centuries more or less integrated into the rural English economy, although always recognised, both by themselves and by others, as culturally different. After World War II, however, the rural economy changed (with the ascendancy of the productivist project), such that Gypsies and Travellers were less likely to mix with non-Gypsies or to be seen by them as an integral part of rural life. A nomadic way of life became increasingly difficult to follow, particularly when the economic changes were accompanied and supported by a policy of 'enforced sedentarism'. A former, pre-industrial, possibly pre-capitalist structured coherence was therefore undermined and gradually destroyed by a project for a new capitalist structured coherence that had no place for longstanding rural 'traditions'. Greenfields shows how this has led to divisions not only between Gypsies/Travellers and non-Gypsies (or *gorjas*) but also within Gypsy and Traveller communities themselves, as some members have managed to get by and even to thrive while many others (particularly males) have been unable to cope and have ended up in long-term unemployment. Greenfields lays bare the classed and racialised exclusionary character of the rural idyll in all its destructive force and argues strongly that it should be contested and resisted if any socially just rural structured coherence is to be achieved. The incomers to rural areas who have, either wittingly or unwittingly, caused the destruction of Gypsy and Traveller communities are primarily the landowning elites (and their fellow-travellers) discussed in Somerville's chapter.

The final section of the book, on *consumed* rurality, focuses on the ways in which rurality is consumed, for example, by tourists (Haven-Tang and Jones), older people (Key) and pub-goers (Markham). In each case, as in other chapters in the book, tensions are revealed, within the consumer experience, between the materiality of the rurality that is consumed and the representation of that rurality to the consumer. Haven-Tang and Jones's chapter, for example, emphasises the importance of tourist destinations having a clear and coherent identity in order to secure a competitive advantage in tourism markets. They argue that each rural area can develop its own brand of rurality that highlights its distinctive qualities in relation to specifically rural activities such as food production and rural arts and crafts. This argument seems to suggest that the representation of a rural area, so long as it is matched by the right quality of consumption, can outweigh the material drawbacks of that area. It is not clear, however, why a consumed rurality has to demonstrate overall coherence in order to be a successful tourist attraction. The need for coherence seems to arise not from the consumers' point of view but from that of the tourist industry itself, whose marketing and business strategies have to reflect a certain coherence around the identity of any space in order for the industry to function collectively, with businesses working for rather than against one another.

As the population of rural areas is ageing at a significantly faster rate than in urban areas, due to the in-migration of older people and the out-migration of younger people, the situation of older people in rural areas becomes an increasingly important focus for research. As in other chapters in this book (particularly Somerville, in relation to the motivation for rural gentrification), Key's chapter reflects on the meaning of the rural idyll and its power to influence both people's choices about where to live and their perceptions of where they do live. The tension between material and represented rurality is most clearly noted in the changes experienced by rural older people as they approach their late 70s. At this age, they change from being reasonably healthy and mobile, with effective networks of family and friends, to becoming frailer, no longer fit to drive a car, increasingly living alone and isolated from many essential services. Consequently, their lives are transformed from idyllic (an idyll that they have either inhabited for many years or to which they chose to move) to socially excluded. Interestingly, it is the population of the more sparsely populated small villages and hamlets, which are the idyllic attractors for the 'new gentry' (Somerville), that are most dependent on car ownership and least well provided for in terms of basic services. Overall, Key's chapter on rural older people provides no evidence of structured coherence but only a set of stories of transient personal experiences, whose only common underlying theme seems to be one of inexorable and inevitable bodily and mental decline into death and oblivion. This is a bleak message to convey, so it seems only fair to point out that it stems from a rather parochial perspective (see the chapter by Herron *et al.*), which is strangely abstracted from any links with an actual parish or any other definitive social structure or social purpose. In this perspective, 'social exclusion' becomes little more than a cypher for personal isolation, and it is implied that this isolation is entirely the result of either individual choices or the ageing process, and therefore nothing to do with how we, as a society, have decided our affairs should be organised.

The focus of Markham's chapter, on rural public houses, is very different. As is well known, the English pub is a well-established institution in both urban and rural areas. Markham, however, argues that the rural pub is both of special iconic significance in the history and culture of England and is also integral to the life of many village communities. The power of the rural pub lies, at least partly, in its capacity to combine material, represented and consumed rurality under one roof – that is, an enterprise that evokes the English rural idyll while also satisfying a wide range of human desires (e.g., for conviviality as well as drink, food and entertainment). Markham shows, however, that actual rural pubs do not always live up to this promise, with problems of social divisions (not only between social classes, but between men and women and between drinkers and non-drinkers), and play only a limited role in maintaining social networks. While being proposed by some commentators as a possible source of structured coherence, therefore, it seems doubtful whether many pubs are sufficiently equipped for such a role. In certain villages, however, as also detailed by Cabras earlier in this book, the pub has been seen as vital to the survival of the village itself, and, where a village pub has been threatened with closure, the community has joined together to save it and run it as a cooperative. It seems that a pub in a small community can function as a link to a number of other enterprises and services, so that the closure of the pub can result in the decline of the community. This suggests, therefore, that in some smaller villages the pub may well act as a facilitator of structured coherence – economic, social and cultural.

The chapters can be reviewed as a whole by grouping them into their respective sections. On material rurality, the chapters by Cabras and Herron *et al.* both point to the existence of *locally* structured rural coherences in England. In Cabras's case, however, the cooperatives he identifies as sources of coherence seem fragile and perhaps unlikely to endure, whereas Herron *et al.* show that the parishes they focus on as sources of coherence are remarkably long-lasting (with well-marked and relatively solid boundaries). This suggests that at least some structured coherences rooted more in the economic (as in Cabras's examples) may be more fleeting than those that are rooted more in the political and cultural (as in Herron *et al.*'s examples), although the distinction between economy and politics/culture is by no means clear-cut here. The other two chapters (by Siwale and Gray) do not identify any specific forms of local structured coherence but all four chapters seem to agree that, whatever local rural coherence there might be, it must be relatively powerless in the face of national and global economic and political forces – hence the characteristically 'parochial' politics in countrysides as different from each other as Zambia and the UK. This political weakness is so great that both Siwale and Gray do not identify any specifically *rural* structured coherence at all; even in the more upbeat assessment by Cabras, it is not clear what is distinctively rural about the structured coherence focused on cooperatives, and in Herron *et al.* it is not clear why parishes have not been or could not be developed on a similar basis in urban areas. Overall the chapters serve to remind us of the importance of *territory* in defining material rurality, but the relationships or flows (Massey, 2005) that constitute that territory seem almost unimaginably variable and yet also peculiarly vulnerable, precarious and little understood (or misunderstood). Moreover, local coherences, where they exist at all, seem to coincide with wider non-local incoherence.

The chapters on represented rurality all (with the possible exception of Grau) focus either on the rural idyll or on rural icons such as livestock grazing and the farm. Structured coherence is imagined rather than material, and typically contrasts with and contradicts material rurality (as also in the group of chapters on contested rurality). Rurality is understood largely, though not entirely (again, Grau's chapter is the exception), in terms of a relationship between humans and animals within a certain kind of landscape. The character of this landscape varies (e.g., pastoral, romantic, performed) according to the *projects* of those who are engaged with it. All of these projects appear to involve an attempt to establish structured coherence by redefining the relationship between represented and material rurality. Walker and Hildyard, for example, see pastoralism and Romanticism as projects by (mainly) wealthy landowners to (re)create rural landscape as spectacle, to be enjoyed for its beauty and charm – what Halfacree (2006, 2007) has called a 'consuming idyll'. More generally, the countryside comes to be viewed, and thence materially shaped, as a place for leisure pursuits – for example, grouse moors, golf courses, and the whole paraphernalia of the tourist industry. Whatever coherence is achieved by these projects, however, is even more fragile than those considered under material rurality, not least because its intended coherence frequently conflicts with the spatial practices expressed by the latter. Indeed, this has been recognised by some of the protagonists themselves, e.g. in the use of the word 'folly'. Thus, if represented rurality has any coherence of its own, Parry suggests that it must lie in the narrative structure of an allegory that points to the existence of a complex interpenetration of domains of something that is 'other' than urban or wild. It is certainly not a representation that achieves the domination suggested by Lefebvre (1991).

The term 'contested rurality' of course suggests either a lack of coherence or a contradictory and disjointed coherence. Moore and Bestwick both suggest that there is no coherence at all. In Moore's case, the project of super-productivism is fundamentally incompatible with the rural idyll, and Bestwick argues that not only do rural and urban attitudes conflict, but within both urban and rural areas there is deep confusion and division of opinion concerning humanity's relationships with animals and the place of animals within the town as well as the countryside. Somerville and Greenfields, however, argue that rurality today displays a contradictory and disjointed coherence. For Somerville, although radical changes have occurred in rural English life over the centuries, landowner hegemony has remained remarkably resilient, and it is this that continues to provide a degree of coherence. Greenfields appears to concur with this view, finding that, although a more congruent and unified coherence may have existed in pre-capitalist times, the ascendancy of the productivist project has created new forms of contestation and conflict (basically, between landowners and landless), and this conflict has only been exacerbated by more recent developments. Nurse also suggests that a disjointed form of rural coherence exists but this focuses specifically on human relationships with farm and wild animals, plants and the non-human environment. He argues for a policing project that will achieve a more congruent and unified coherence but this will not be a specifically rural coherence. Furthermore, and as something of an elephant in the room up to now, some of the argument in these chapters suggests that specifically rural structured coherence may not actually be desirable as it is likely to consolidate and normalise inequalities. Instead, new projects may be needed to address inequalities, divisions and ethical and political conflicts that cut across distinctions between urban and rural.

Of the chapters on consumed rurality, only Markham's identifies a clear focus for structured coherence, namely the rural public house. Like Cabras and Herron *et al.*, this is a very local (or parochial) focus. Haven-Tang and Jones propose a project for coherence, around the identity of a particular space (a tourist destination), while Key does not appear to find any coherence at all (although this should not be taken to imply that there is no coherence here). These chapters suggest a need for caution and further reflection on the potential of 'consumption' to provide a new underpinning for rural life – a potential that is strongly implied in some academic and policy discourses.

Overall, in summary, the contributions to this book reveal a huge variety of interpretations of rurality, which we have grouped, for convenience, under the headings of material, represented, contested and consumed. Both within and across these domains, structured coherence, where it exists at all, is indeed shown to be always only fluid and transitory, produced by the repetition of performances of rurality. Projects to achieve any kind of 'permanent' coherence never really succeed, though it seems that some projects, such as productivism and some more recent local projects to perform the rural idyll, have been more successful than others. Rurality, in short, is always in an unfinished state of becoming. Moreover, all forms of structured coherence involve exclusion as well as inclusion, and this is what gives rise to categorical social inequalities, for example, of gender, class, age, race, sexuality, and so on (all of which of course have material, imagined and performed aspects). This book has tended to focus on the categories of class and, to a lesser extent, age, but nothing is implied by that with regard to the relative significance of different categories. Clearly, though, the fragility and liquidity of structured coherence generally will tend to be reflected in a similar looseness, vagueness and ambiguity of these categories. The rural studies literature contains many examples of attempts to highlight, but also to question, the 'othering' of those who do not appear to fit into particular rural social formations or projects or idylls. The paradox of community, in other words, as both inclusive and exclusive, reveals itself once again.

In conclusion, we return to the question of what, if anything, is the core meaning of 'rural', common to all the interpretations of rural that have been explored in this book. Being unable to define it convincingly *a priori* in material terms, we suggest that its 'essence' may be taken from a reading of the predominant structured coherences expressed. Our tentative and contestable conclusion is that rurality is more than an empty signifier, not least with respect to the critical fissures opened above, but also because of its common meaning, which has to do with the relations between human and specific kinds of non-human entities (which actor network theory calls 'actants'), whether this be within a social formation (material rurality) or a project (involving represented rurality). What is *distinctive* about the rural is that its structured coherences and, from these, its distinctive spatiality, foreground 'nature'. This may be expressed by the involvement of animals directly in a labour process (e.g., for producing raw materials from the land, as in livestock grazing), or by humans working directly on the land for a living (as in arable farming), or by interactions between humans and a wider 'natural environment' that contains a diversity of non-human species ('wildlife'). However, the boundaries of the rural are immensely permeable, as Massey's (2005) insights would lead us to expect. The commutable rural, for example, can be described as 'rurban', given its more or less complete interpenetration of urban and rural, ensured by the daily mobility from rural to urban of most of its inhabitants. Even the non-commutable rural can be penetrated as a result of the attractions it may offer for urban tourists and counterurbanisers, while at the same time its young people may be attracted in the opposite direction in search of work, wider opportunities and the 'bright lights' of the city. Ultimately, therefore, while the rural may be more than an empty signifier, it is not a distinct 'produced' (Lefebvre, 1991) space or type of space but is constituted by the same relations as those that make urban space. And capitalist social formations and capitalist (and anti-capitalist) projects are not specifically urban or rural but cut right across all urban/rural distinctions. While recognising that production and consumption relations exist beyond the grasp of capital (Gibson-Graham, 2006; Halfacree, 2010), we thus reiterate the conclusion that both the urban and the rural as we know them today have been largely *created* by capitalism (and perhaps by modernity more generally, as illustrated most vividly in Walker's chapter) and need to be understood, first, in this way. The rural's ongoing (re)production into rural futures is equally being forged under this banner, albeit always adapted, battered and modified both internally and externally, through contradictions within capitalism and through its conflict with extra-capitalist forces, respectively. In short, the production of the rural is far from dead, and within this ongoing process the struggle to attain at least a degree of coherence (whether desirable or not) will itself carry on.

References

Bauman, Z. (2000) *Liquid Modernity*. Cambridge: Polity.

Bell, D. (2006) 'Variations on the rural idyll', in P. Cloke, T. Marsden and P. Mooney (eds), *Handbook of Rural Studies*. London: Sage: 149–60.

Castree, N. (2005) *Nature*. London: Routledge.

Clarke, S. (1991) 'The state debate', in S. Clarke (ed.) *The State Debate*. Basingstoke, UK: Macmillan: 1–61.

Cloke, P. (1992) '"The countryside": Development, conservation and an increasingly marketable commodity', in P. Cloke (ed.), *Policy and Change in Thatcher's Britain*. Oxford: Pergamon: 269–95.

Cloke, P. and Goodwin, M. (1992) 'Conceptualizing countryside change: From post-Fordism to rural structured coherence', *Transactions of the Institute of British Geographers* 17(3): 321–36.

Frisvoll, S. (2012) 'Power in the production of spaces transformed by rural tourism', *Journal of Rural Studies* 28: 447–57.

Gibson-Graham, J. K. (1996) *The End of Capitalism (as We Know It): A Feminist Critique of Political Economy*. Cambridge, MA: Blackwell.

Gibson-Graham, J. K. (2006) *A Postcapitalist Politics*. Minneapolis, MN: University of Minnesota Press.

Goodwin, M. (2006) 'Regulating rurality? Rural studies and the regulation approach', in P. Cloke, T. Marsden and P. Mooney (eds), *Handbook of Rural Studies*. London: Sage: 304–16.

Halfacree, K. (2001) 'Going "back to the land again": Extending the scope of counterurbanisation', *Espace, Populations, Sociétés* 1–2: 161–70.

Halfacree, K. (2006) 'Rural space: Constructing a three-fold architecture', in P. Cloke, T. Marsden and P. Mooney (eds), *Handbook of Rural Studies*. London: Sage: 44–62.

Halfacree, K. (2007) 'Trial by space for a "radical rural": Introducing alternative localities, representations and lives', *Journal of Rural Studies* 23: 125–41.

Halfacree, K. (2010) 'Reading rural consumption practices for difference: Bolt-holes, castles and life-rafts', *Culture Unbound* 2: 241–63.

Harvey, D. (1985) *The Urbanization of Capital*. Oxford: Blackwell.

Henderson, G. (1998) 'Nature and fictitious capital: The historical geography of an agrarian question', *Antipode* 30: 73–118.

Hoggart, K. (1990) 'Let's do away with the rural', *Journal of Rural Studies* 6: 245–57.
Holloway, J. (2002) *Change the World Without Taking Power*. London: Pluto.
Jessop, B. (1997) 'Survey article: The regulation approach', *Journal of Political Philosophy* 5: 287–326
Jessop, B. (2002) *The Future of the Capitalist State*. Cambridge: Polity Press.
Jones, O. (2003) '"The restraint of beasts": Rurality, animality, actor-network theory and dwelling', in P. Cloke (ed.), *Country Visions*. Harlow, UK: Pearson: 283–307.
Jones, O. and Cloke, P. (2002) *Tree Cultures: The Place of Trees and Trees in their Place*. Oxford: Berg.
Laclau, E. and Mouffe, C. (1985/2001) *Hegemony and Socialist Strategy: Towards a Radical Democratic Politics*. London: Verso.
Lawrence, M. (2003) 'The view from Cobb Gate: Falling into liminal geography', in Cloke, P. (ed.), *Country Visions*. Harlow, UK: Pearson, 93–115.
Lefebvre, H. (1991) [1974] *The Production of Space*. Oxford: Blackwell.
Marsden, T. (1999) 'Rural futures: The consumption countryside and its regulation', *Sociologia Ruralis* 39: 501–20.
Massey, D. (2005) *For Space*. London: Sage.
Murdoch, J. (2000) 'Networks: A new paradigm of rural development?', *Journal of Rural Studies* 16: 407–19.
Murdoch, J. and Ward, N. (1997) 'Governmentality and territoriality: The statistical manufacture of Britain's "national farm",' *Political Geography* 16: 307–24.
Pemberton, S. and Goodwin, M. (2010) 'Rethinking the changing structures of rural local government: State power, rural politics and local political strategies?', *Journal of Rural Studies* 26: 272–83.
Sayer, A. (1984) *Method in Social Science: A Realist Approach*. London: Routledge.
Short, B. (2006) 'Idyllic ruralities', in P. Cloke, T. Marsden and P. Mooney (eds), *Handbook of Rural Studies*. London: Sage: 133–48.
Smith, N. (1984) *Uneven Development: Nature, Capital and the Production of Space*. Oxford: Basil Blackwell.
Smith, N. (1996) 'The production of nature', in G. Robertson, M. Mash, L. Tickner, J. Bird, B. Curtis and T. Putnam (eds), *Future Natural: Nature, Science, Culture*. London: Routledge.
Smout T. C. (1983) *Nature Contested: Environmental History in Scotland and Northern England since 1600*. Edinburgh: Edinburgh University Press.
Thrift, N. (1996) *Spatial Formations*. London: Sage.
Woods, M. (2011) *Rural*. London: Routledge.
Wynne-Jones, S. (forthcoming) '"Reading for difference" with payments for ecosystem services in Wales', *Critical Policy Studies*.

Index